HISTORICAL CONSCIOUSNESS

Also by John Lukacs

THE GREAT POWERS AND EASTERN EUROPE

A HISTORY OF THE COLD WAR

DECLINE AND RISE OF EUROPE

(*Editor and Translator*)

THE EUROPEAN REVOLUTION AND CORRESPONDENCE WITH GOBINEAU

by Alexis de Tocqueville

John Lukacs

HISTORICAL CONSCIOUSNESS

or the remembered past

HARPER & ROW, PUBLISHERS

New York, Evanston, and London

1817

FIRST EDITION

LIBRARY OF CONGRESS CATALOG CARD NUMBER: 67-28809

G-S

MEMORIAE PATRIS
DOCTORIS PAULUS L.
EQUES ORDINIS F. J. I.
VIR ERUDITISSIMUS
EXSORS CONSOLATIONE FIDE CHRISTIANA
VITA SAEPE INFELIX
AMOREM LIBRORUM ARTISQUE
INCULCAVERAT
FILIO IN AETERNAM GRATO

CONTENTS

vii

HISTORICAL CONSCIOUSNESS

I

❦

OUR HISTORICAL CONDITION

or the evolution of historical thinking

(1) "Historical thinking has entered our very blood"

For some time I have been interested in the changing fortunes of the adjective *old-fashioned*. I find it significant that this adjective has by now shed all of its pejorative associations. For example, the Oxford English Dictionary shows that a century ago *old-fashioned* had a wide currency in the sense of a child "having the ways of a grown-up person; hence, precocious, knowing." Dickens would have Miss Blimber say of the little Paul Dombey that he was "an old-fashioned boy," in a spirit of disapproval.[1] This usage seems to have disappeared completely. It is significant that even the present principal definition in the O.E.D.—"1. Antiquated in form or character" —seems to be now slightly out-of-date, since *antiquated* connotes something that is fragile and corroded and largely useless whereas I believe that *old-fashioned* has come around to mean less and less something that is outdated and unfashionable and more and more something that is solid and useful and durable. More and more, I think, *old-fashioned* appeals not merely to our intellect but also to our senses. I believe, for instance, that the appeal of a term such as "modern comfort" has been diminishing recently, while at the same time the appeal of "old-fashioned comfort" may have risen; that

---

[1] Miss Blimber to Paul: "This analysis, you see, Dombey, is going to be sent home to your respected parent. It will naturally be very painful to him to find that you are singular in your character and conduct. It is naturally painful to us; for we can't like you, you know, Dombey, as well as we could wish."

under no circumstance is *old-fashioned* any longer the antonym of *modern* in the sense of being the pejorative contrast to the approbatory term; indeed, that perhaps the opposite has been happening, since *modern* sounds, *modern* sights, *modern* tastes have lost many of their intimations of airiness and freshness which they maintained only a generation ago, whereas the sensual as well as the intellectual associations gathering around *old-fashioned* have become more agreeable to us. (Who today in the United States would prefer a restaurant advertising "modern food" to another advertising "old-fashioned cooking"?)

Similar developments are detectable in the recent evolution of many European languages. For the changing fortunes of words illustrate the changing fortunes of sentiments. Through this simple example I wished to cast light not so much upon the now sometimes rapidly decaying appeal of modernism as upon the slower and more hesitant rise among us of a sentiment toward the past which is relatively unique and relatively new: not merely is our past different from past pasts; our thinking about the past may be different from past thinkings about the past.

At this point I must set certain limits to these generalizations. I spoke of "our" past, and of attitudes that seem to prevail "among us." By this I include the peoples who are still the more or less direct descendants of what may be called European civilization. I do not know enough—I doubt whether our specialists know enough—of the inclinations of the peoples of Asia or Africa to essay such a tentative statement about deep-seated matters going on within their consciousness. From what I know I tend to believe that these relatively new evidences of what I shall henceforth call historical consciousness are among the few phenomena which are not yet typical of the otherwise rapidly developing world civilization; that historical thinking is still something particularly "European" or "Western." I put "European" and "Western" within quotation marks: they are neither equivalent nor accurate; still they must serve for a shorthand notation.

In any event, many of us now think of the past as something substantial and even as something real—even though we may not be quite conscious of this condition of our thinking. This tendency is probably involved not only with the decay of modernism but also with that of futurism. There are very many examples of this; perhaps one, chosen at random, will suffice: *Nineteen Eighty-Four*. This famous utopian novel by an English Socialist is not unusual among modern utopian novels in the sense that its view of the future is stark and horrible; what is unusual is Orwell's view of the past rather than of the future. This, indeed, is the profoundest difference between *Nineteen Eighty-Four*, published in 1949, and Huxley's *Brave New World* which, published in 1932, still had many of the marks of the futuristic twenties. In *Nineteen Eighty-Four* Winston Smith, the protagonist, moved by his deepest convictions, offers a toast in the small circle of his conspirators "to the past." Like the recent fortunes of *old-fashioned*, this attitude in *Nineteen Eighty-Four* is a symptom.

A symptom of what? I do not think that Winston Smith's sudden and moving toast to the past is attributable simply to nostalgia. "Nostalgia" means the painful, sentimental, nearly hopeless evocation of something; pain is one of the two components of the Greek word: *nostos*+*algos*, *nostalgia*, like *neuralgia*.[2] But not only is Winston Smith's reverence directed at a past that he himself could not have known (he was born in 1945); his evocation of the past issues not from a source of emotional pain but, to the contrary, it fills him momentarily with a superb kind of exaltation, yes, even of pleasure. Consider, today, Dante's classic lines on nostalgia: *Nessun maggior dolore* ("Nothing is as painful") *che ricordarsi al tempo felice nella miseria* ("as the remembrance of happy times during misery"). But is this really so? Often—not only now, approaching middle age, but in my early youth during the war in Europe and after—I thought that Dante was wrong, that even in the dreariest and worst of situations (or, perhaps, especially in such situations) the remembrance, indeed, the contemplation, of past scenes of happiness have been sources of pleasure rather than of pain for me. Indeed, I believe that certain evocations of the sense of the past may, on occasion, amount to the exquisite sensation of experiencing something uniquely *real*; as a matter of fact, I believe that this sensation is something akin to the sudden recognition, in the midst of great wretchedness, of something that is *beautiful*. And I do not think that these are merely the singular reactions of a historian, of a person endowed with singular humors and with a singular temperament: I believe that they cor-

---

[2] Note the ahistorical characteristics of the original Greek term *nostalgia*, meaning the dolorous missing of the home: it suggests, thus, distance in space rather than in time.

respond to the recognizable experiences of millions in the twentieth century, at least in the Western world, to the effect that our evolving attitudes to the past are not merely the attitudes of nostalgia; that these are our historical reactions to our historical situation, a situation which is different from Dante's.[3]

In any event, amid the present flood of unprecedented cultural anarchy, we, in the West, are now experiencing a broad recurrence of historical interest. In the United States, for example, there exists now a widespread popular interest in history, probably for the first time in the American national experience: the sales and the contents of books, magazines, articles, television programs attest to this.[4] I need not illustrate this in detail: consider only the Civil War "fad" of the 1950's or the First World War "fad" of the early 1960's or the publishing success of "documentary" reconstructions of certain brief episodes (Days, Battles, Tragedies) of the past by enterprising journalists. The same phenomenon exists in Europe. Literature on all kinds of levels is involved in it, of course; so is popular entertainment, including television; I shall not analyze it at this point where all I wish to say is that these are superficial symptoms of an evolution whose sources are more profound. Of course this evolution coexists (and often within the mind of the same person) with an older and vaster development which, in the name of Science and of Progress, liquifies traditions and promotes a kind of mass rootlessness now on all levels of education*; in America as well as in Europe we face now massive manifestations of the twentieth-century kind of conformism that might as well be called "presentism." Yet I believe that of these two countervailing developments the slow evolution of a

[3] An Italian 650 years after Dante: ". . . for me, no less than for her, the memory of things was much more important than the possession of them. . . . How well she understood me! The way I longed for the present to become the past *at once*, so that I could love it and gaze fondly at it any time; it was just exactly the way she felt. It was *our* vice, this: looking backwards as we went ahead. . . ." Giorgio Bassani, *The Garden of the Finzi-Continis.*

[4] The success of more-or-less popular historical magazines (*American Heritage, Horizon, History, History Today, Historia, Miroir de l'histoire, Historama, L'Histoire pour tous*), while remarkable in itself (in France alone their monthly sales amount to more than 600,000), is only a superficial symptom: we ought to consider these figures together with the rising proportion of historical books in what is still called the "nonfiction" field.

* This symbol indicates a relevant note to be found in the *Certain Notes* section (pages 325–359) which may be read separately.

historical consciousness is more significant than the evolution of what some people, perhaps too facilely, have called "post-historic man"—even in the mass-democratic societies of the West; even in the Far West; even in California; even in the university of Berkeley.* I strongly feel that even if a great physical catastrophe would smite our civilization, destroying most of its institutions, this novel attitude to the past, this new thirst for a kind of historical knowledge would survive, indeed, that it would exist in acute forms.

In short, we may be to some extent ahead of José Ortega y Gasset's pessimism in *The Revolt of the Masses* (a pessimism that Ortega himself later transcended) when, around 1930, he proclaimed his angry impatience with the democratic mass-man who lives only for the present, whose mind is wholly unhistorical, who is no longer influenced by the past. More relevant for us is Johan Huizinga's phrase, around the same time. "Historical thinking," he then wrote, "has entered our very blood." Note that this was not a statement by a facile optimist but by a patrician historian who, more than most of his professional contemporaries, was deeply worried about the decline of historical judgment in our mass-democratic age. Still he wished to state the existence of an already embedded, and at least for some time ineradicable, condition of our thinking.

Let me sum up this condition in these words: I believe that the most important developments in our civilization during the last three or four centuries include not only the applications of the scientific method but also the growth of a historical consciousness; and that while we may have exaggerated the importance of the former we have not yet understood sufficiently the implications of the latter.

(2) History as a form of thought. Its definition?

How does this historical consciousness affect our thinking? Let me attempt to give a simple initial answer: *history, for us, has become a form of thought.*

This means that historical thinking may be applied—indeed, that we often apply it, consciously or otherwise—to every kind of human experience. We can describe and, consequently, understand a person, a nation, any kind of human society, virtually any kind of human endeavor, not only through their material or spiritual, their physical or psychic characteristics but through their history. The character of a person will best appear not so much from information of his physical or psychic properties as from what we know of the history of his life; the same is true of a character of a nation. The history of a problem, of an idea, of a concept, of a theory may reveal its evolving diagnosis. There is no field of human action that may not be approached, studied, described, and understood through its history.

In the nineteenth century it became evident that literature, art, philosophy might be studied profitably through their histories. In the twentieth century some of our best physicists have suggested that the clearest explanation of the new concepts of physics may be that of the history of their development. It is even conceivable that chemistry, biology, perhaps even medicine could be taught and learned "historically." (Terms such as "case histories" suggest how historical thinking has now penetrated our language through a not always conscious process.) Instead of proceeding, for example, from organic to inorganic chemistry, one could begin with, say, the Greeks: What did they find out about chemical substances and processes? What were their chemical theories? What is still valid in their discoveries? Where did they go wrong? What did the Romans add to this body of knowledge? Where did *they* go wrong? and so on. I am not saying that this would be always the most propitious approach: what I am saying is that, potentially at least, the history of chemistry is chemistry itself.

Inevitably this brings us to certain relationships of history and science. For it is at this point that we must recognize, for the first time, that history as a form of thought is "larger" than science: because, as we have seen, science can be studied historically, because human science is nothing more than the sum total of its history, because the history of science is nothing more than the history of its human practitioners. In the last chapter of this book I shall have to return to certain implications of this condition. Here it will be sufficient to recognize that it is science which is part of history and not the reverse, and that this is not a complicated philosophical proposition but a common-sense recognition to the effect that human science is part and parcel of the history of mankind, since "nature is earlier than man—but man is earlier than natural science"—the felicitous formulation by the German physicist V. von Weizsaecker (*circa* 1949).*

As a form of thought, therefore, history is "more" than science. But in a different sense, our knowledge of history is "less" than our knowledge of *a* science: history is not a science in the modern sense of the word.[5] Historical information is incomplete: while science and scientific knowledge are the same things, such a complete identity between the past and our knowledge of the past does not exist. Moreover, historical, unlike scientific, information is often inaccurate and not measurable. But, then, the very purpose of historical knowledge is not so much accuracy as a certain kind of understanding: historical knowledge is the knowledge of human beings about other human beings, and this is different from the knowledge which human beings possess of their environment. Of course there are sciences, such as anthropology, sociology, medicine, which involve the study by human beings of other human beings. But these, too, are unlike history (this is, for example, why history should not be considered as a "social science")—because history, unlike these, does not and cannot borrow its methods from the natural sciences. Behind the condition of the unpredictability of history lie many "causes," one of them being that historical causalities are quite different from the categories of scientific causality. At this point it may be sufficient to state a truism: while science, including the so-called social sciences, deals principally (though not exclusively) with what is typical and with what is routine, history deals primarily (though not exclusively) with what is unique and with what is exceptional. ("Exceptions to the rule," said Proust, "are the magic of existence.") As a form of thought, history is a pragmatic but unsystematic knowledge of humans about other humans.

[5] By *science* I mean of course its current English sense, which has become inseparable from physical science. "In modern use," says the O.E.D., "science" means "natural and physical science." (The same meaning holds for "scientists," a word "deliberately made by Whewell, as there was no common word till then to describe students of different kinds of science." Logan Pearsall Smith, *The English Language*.) This means that *science* is somewhat narrower than the Italian *scienza* or the French *science*, and considerably narrower than the German *Wissenschaft*. But these mutations of meanings are not only national; they are historical. A century ago *science* had a broader meaning in English, too: like *Wissenschaft*, it suggested knowledge as well as science. (Before 1903 *science* in Oxford was applicable even to philosophy, a usage that the O.E.D. now marks as obsolete.) Thus during the last one hundred years, while the applications of the scientific method have widely spread, the intrinsic meaning of *science* has narrowed—the opposite development of *history*, whose meaning as well as whose applications have been broadening.

It is because of this unsystematic character of historical life that history cannot be easily defined. Or perhaps it should not be defined at all. When it comes to definitions let me fall back on the pragmatic wisdom of English genius. ("Definitions," said Dr. Johnson, "are tricks for pedants"—an opinion upon which Dickens would expatiate with gusto in *Hard Times*.) Certainly, as not only unphilosophical Englishmen but spokesmen for Latin clarity, such as Salvador de Madariaga, remarked, things such as *atmosphere, beauty, rhythm* exist: we know and feel clearly what they are, even though it is bothersome and difficult and perhaps even senseless to "define" them. So it is with history. In an article entitled "A Definition of a Concept of History" Huizinga in 1936 showed how stiff and pompous and senseless were two current definitions of history, two tapeworm-sentences, by the German historical methodologists Bauer and Bernheim.[6] ("What does Herodotus tell us; why does he tell us?" Huizinga asked. "Neither of the two definitions can answer this.") Interned during the German occupation of his fatherland, Huizinga did not live to see the even more ludicrous attempt at definitions produced by Professor Sidney Hook whom a committee of American historians had commissioned in his capacity as a philosopher in 1942–1946 for the purpose of producing Historical Definitions—these, together with other staggeringly obtuse matters, were then published in a Thing entitled *Bulletin 54 of the Social Science Research Council.*

Huizinga, in his article, came up with a definition: "History is the spiritual form in which a culture is taking account of its past."*

With all respect to Huizinga, this is a statement rather than a definition. Unlike most definitions, it is strong and clear; it is suggestive rather than accurate; it leaves a taste in our mouths, as does Droysen's century-old phrase (1868): "History is Humanity's

---

[6] "History is the science which seeks to describe and with sympathetic insight to explain the phenomena of life, so far as it concerns changes brought about by the relation of men to different social entities, selecting them with an eye to their effect on subsequent epochs or with regard to their typical characteristics and concentrating chiefly on those changes which are temporally and spatially irreproducible." (Bauer) "The science of history is the science which investigates and narrates in causal connexion the facts of the development of mankind in their activities (individual as well as typical and collective) as social beings." (Bernheim)

knowledge of itself, its certainty about itself. It is not 'the light and the truth,' but a search thereof, a sermon thereupon, a consecration thereto. It is like John the Baptist, 'not the Light but sent to bear witness of that Light,'" a superb poetic statement by a younger contemporary of the Schopenhauer who proposed that history was meaningless and "unworthy of a science." (But, then, History has a Muse.) For our purposes, however, I shall rest satisfied with a simpler statement: *History is the remembered past.*[7]

(3) What history was: from historical existence to historical consciousness

We shall see, in a moment, that this simple statement—*history is the remembered past*—is something more than a truism; indeed, that it represents, in an unorthodox and perhaps even revolutionary sense, a departure from the tenets accepted by many professional historians. But before we address ourselves to the problem of what history now *is*, we should attempt to survey quickly what in the past it *was*. Evidently this order of approach accords with history being a form of thought: the history of a problem may be the principal approach to its diagnosis. Let me, therefore, embark on a short (though perhaps not unoriginal) survey of the history of history—or, rather, of the history of historical thinking. How did historical thinking "enter our very blood"? or, to paraphrase Huizinga, our very minds? Or, again, if I follow my preferred statement: how did the remembered past become history? and how did history become the remembered past?

Someone may object at this point that this equation of history with the remembered past is so broad as to be useless. I acknowledge that it is broad; I deny that it is useless. For history the remembered past is not quite the same as history being memory. All living beings have a kind of unconscious memory; but the remembering of the past is something uniquely human, because it is conscious as

---

[7] Two similar statements: V. H. Galbraith: "History, I suppose, is the Past—so far as we know it." (*Why We Study History,* Historical Association Publications No. 131, London, 1944.) H.-I. Marrou: "L'histoire est la connaissance du passé humain." (*De la connaissance historique,* Paris, 1954, the most lucid book written on the nature of history and of historical study in the last thirty years, perhaps even in the entire twentieth century.)

well as unconscious, because it involves cognition together with re-cognition, because it involves thinking, and because human thinking always involves some kind of construction; I am interested in the evolution of this construction, and in the operations of human memory only inasmuch as they are influenced by this construction— not the reverse.

Let me begin with a simple statement sounding like primitive "historicism."[8] Human existence is historical existence. Here, too, we meet one of the distinctions of history when compared to other kinds of human knowledge about humans: life existed before biology, society existed before sociology, the psyche before psychology, man (anthropos) before anthropology (and God before theology); but in the broadest sense of the term "historical existence" such a thing as a *wholly* "pre-historic" man did not exist—for the term *pre-history*[9] refers to the absence of orderly written records, and my very point is that we must go beyond this nineteenth-century category of "scientific" historiography: if history is the remembered past, then historical existence refers to more than to the existence of documents.

We exist in a material, in a spiritual, and in a historical sense: the historical condition of human existence is universal, true of the very beginning of mankind ever since Adam and Eve, and not something new: but *what is relatively new is our consciousness of this condition.*

We know that the direct ancestor of our word *history* is the Greek *historia* which may be translated as "research" or "inquiry"; we are aware that a certain kind of historical curiosity is manifest in the early examples of Greek historianship, that the way in which Thucydides and Herodotus thought of history and wrote history is close to our mentalities, that their whys and hows are substantially akin to our whys and hows. I do not think that it would be an exaggerated generalization to say not only that the Greeks perfected first the art of history but that the aspiration and the achievement of a Thucydides mark a decisive cultural jump from historical existence to historical thinking. And this kind of thinking is inseparable from a certain realistic view of human nature. Not only does there

---

[8] About the uselessness of this term "historicism" see below, p. 19.

[9] O.E.D.: Prehistory (1871): "The account of events or conditions prior to written or recorded history."

exist a very close relationship between this kind of thinking and a certain ethic of *rhetoric*: an important and profound relationship exists, too, between the traditions of historical and of philosophical and of artistic *realism*, between the realistic purpose of representation by a Pheidias and by a Thucydides, for example. This may seem to be a reactionary statement in our times, when intellectual capacity is so often regarded as if it were the capacity of increasing abstraction—nevertheless I believe it to be true. The "inquiry" or "research" meaning of *historia* reflects, as Canon Alan Richardson put it, the existence of "the kind of intellectual exercise which the Greeks practised and the Hebrews did not"*—or, in other words, it reflects a striving for truth even more than for justice.

But, then, the "cultural jump" of Thucydides and Herodotus, in a very important sense, led to no further progress. As a modern English classical scholar (Cornford) suggested in a salutary manner, even Thucydides was not yet aware of the historicity of his thinking; as another (Finley) said, the Greek Age of Enlightenment, unlike the European Enlightenment twenty-two hundred years later, was not followed by a widespread extension of historical thinking: "of all the lines of enquiry which the Greeks initiated, history was the most abortive." It was not completely abortive—whence probably the more realistic historicity of the New Testament compared to the Old, or the literary achievements of certain Roman historical writers. Historical thinking in various degrees, the practice of various kinds of realistic historiography are characteristic of the ancestors of our civilization; they are detectable in its Greek, Roman, Jewish, Christian, early European antecedents. After Thucydides and Herodotus, Xenophon, Polybius, Cicero, Caesar, Livy, Tacitus, Plutarch, Suetonius, Sallust, the Evangelists, Josephus, Lactantius, Eusebius, St. Augustine, St. Jerome, Ammianus Marcellinus, Symmachus, Cassiodorus, Gregory I, Bede, Isidore of Seville, Gregory of Tours, Einhard, Joannes Antiochenos, Anna Comnena, John of Salisbury, Otto of Freising, Saxo Grammaticus, Agobard of Lyons, Abelard, Joinville, Villehardouin, Froissart . . . historical writers, they are our ancestors. And yet they are different from us. The medieval mind was quite ahistorical. The study of history did not figure in the seven Liberal Arts of the Middle Ages, neither in *trivium* nor in *quadrivium*. And the mentality of the Renaissance too, contrary to general belief, was not very historical either: certainly it was not historical in the way in which our mentality is accustomed to the past. The meaning of historical development, of a constant continuity with the past, was alien to the Renaissance mind. It is true that the Renaissance (like the French but unlike the Russian Revolution) was promoted by an intellectual cult of antiquity; that it came in with a—somewhat primitive and naïve—exaltation of the classical past;[10] that the modern concept of *history* (like the political concept of *Europe,* and the social concept of the *bourgeois*[11]) grew with the Renaissance. But the origins of the real development of historical consciousness, a new way of historical thinking involving our awareness of this kind of thinking, the quickening steps before the next cultural jump—these were not Renaissance events but a relatively recent development,[12] beginning with the seventeenth century.

History as "a formal record" appears in English around 1482, according to the Oxford English Dictionary; as "a career worthy of record" it appears in 1654; between these two dates we may detect the opening up of a new dimension of consciousness. The word *historian* appears in English around 1500; by 1531 it means something different from mere "annalist" and "compiler." Who was the first modern historian? Flavio Biondo, Lorenzo Valla, Pérez de Guzmán, Leonardo Bruni, Villani, Machiavelli, Guicciardini, Commynes, Vasari, St. Thomas More . . . ? But this is beside the point. I am concerned with something that is deeper and more important, in the long run, about something that was beginning to happen, here and there, in western Europe during the sixteenth, and which did not develop until the seventeenth, century. It is not enough to mark the beginning of this mental, and spiritual, revolution by the birth dates of certain historical writers or by the publication dates of certain historical works. Because of the subtle, though widespread, nature of this development I must illustrate it through the appearance of a

---

10 Giordano Bruno: *"i veri antichi (cioè i saggi) siamo noi"*—we are the true classical figures. But, as Federico Chabod pointed out in regard to this passage, the concepts of progress and of development were completely unknown to this kind of mentality, *"completamente sconosciuti alla mentalità del Rinascimento."*

11 Re "Europe" see Denis Hay, *The Idea of Europe,* Edinburgh, 1957, *passim,* and John Lukacs, *Decline and Rise of Europe,* New York, 1965, chapters iv-v; re "bourgeois" see below, pp. 45–47; 182–183; 331–332.

12 *Development:* 1756–. (O.E.D.)

spate of historical words in English—sure symptoms that certain new ideas and feelings had risen to the surface of consciousness. The distinctions *ancient* and *modern*, the innovations *retrograde* and *progressive*, appear around 1600; Francis Bacon seems to have lent the modern meaning to *progress* in time (as distinct from its earlier meaning in space, "a royal progress"). The very term of the *Middle Ages*, this concept of a long dark trough of time between Ancient and Modern, was a historical concept, the product of a new kind of consciousness which during the Middle Ages had not existed, when the sense of time, too, had been different, and when people had not thought in terms of earthly progress.*

Primitive, a sixteenth-century adjective applied to the early Church, was, according to Logan Pearsall Smith, "probably the first word in which our modern historical sense finds expression." And then, as the seventeenth century progresses, we find the sudden, and at times tumultuous, appearance of two sets of new words, one scientific (for example: *acid, astringency, cohesion, elasticity, electric, equilibrium, fluid, gas, pressure, static, temperature, tension, volatile*), the other historical (for example: *antiquated, century, contemporary, decade, epoch, historic, out-of-date, primeval*). In western Europe and in England the seventeenth century marks the emergence not only of the modern scientific but also of the modern historical outlook.

Let me repeat: it is regrettable that of these two intellectual revolutions we have tended to exaggerate the implications of the first, while we have paid little attention to the second. Of course the new kind of historical and the new kind of scientific thinking were often combined, as Bacon's case suggests. But modern historical thinking may have been developing before modern scientific thinking; and what is more important, the former involved a more profound change in the forms of European consciousness than had the latter.

For the rising of historical consciousness was involved intimately with another contemporary change in the European mind: with the development of something that we might call personal understanding, or self-awareness, or self-consciousness. The new historical *outlook* was (and it still is) inseparable from what I might call a new *in-look*. Montaigne and, in a deeper vein, Pascal are the two outstanding testimonial witnesses of this development. This emergence of a personal self-consciousness is marked, symptomatically, by the appearance of yet another spate of words and of word-formations, involving the prefix *self: self-love, self-confidence, self-command, selfhood, self-esteem, self-knowledge, self-pity.* . . . Toward the end of the seventeenth and during the early eighteenth century, *disposition, character, ego, egoism, conscience, eccentric, melancholy, apathy, agitation, embarrassment, sensible, sentimental, self-conscious* appear in English for the first time in their modern sense. I suggested that the first "jump," the one from historical existence to historical thinking during the Greek Age of Enlightenment, occurred together with a certain kind of jump toward a realistic recognition of human nature; and I venture to say that something like this seems to have happened again, three centuries ago, when our awareness of our historical dimension developed together with our self-awareness.* Since this is a brief survey of the development of our present historical consciousness and not a psychological history of the European mind, I cannot illustrate this development in the seventeenth century in greater detail; in this book I am principally interested in the present conditions of our modern historical consciousness, and not in its origins; I shall only say that the history of this development of a historical consciousness transcends the history of professional historical knowledge.[13]

At the same time this increase in the dimension of human awareness, this decisive jump involving the personalization of knowledge was to be complemented by the increasing impersonalization of reality through what were to be called The Laws of Nature. During the last three hundred years, while we have attempted to deepen our understanding of human nature on the one hand, on the other hand we displaced the human being from the center of the universe . . . of our universe. After three hundred years this paradoxical intellectual movement helped to bring about the interregnal condition of the Western mind in our times, a condition to which I shall return later in this chapter; here I shall only say that the least we

---

[13] This is one of the reasons why I chose some of my illustrations of the preceding exposition from historians of language rather than from historians of historiography: from the suggestive books by Logan Pearsall Smith and Owen Barfield and not from the otherwise so valuable works of Friedrich Meinecke (*Die Entstehung des Historismus*), Paul Hazard (*La crise de la conscience européenne; The European Mind*), or F. Smith Fussner (*The Historical Revolution*).

can do is to recognize that such a contradiction has indeed come to exist, and that this has affected our entire culture, including the development of historical scholarship during the last three hundred years.

One last look backward before I turn to this development. Let us keep in mind that historical consciousness (like the remembered past) is in itself a historical phenomenon, and not only a psychological one (like memory). In the seventeenth century it rose to the surface during the passing of a historical epoch and the crystallization of another. For every historical development is inseparable ultimately from its recognition. The Middle Ages did not pass suddenly: while the Modern Age may have begun earlier, the Middle Ages also lasted longer than we have been accustomed to think. And of course the very term and the concept of *Middle* Ages meant a middle phase in the history of humanity between the ancient period and a new, third, modern, and what was somewhat naïvely presumed, endless age of universal history. The term and the concept of "Middle Ages" has a history of its own: it was first proposed by the German Cardinal Nicolaus Cusanus as early as in the middle of the fifteenth century, it appeared in pieces of French heraldic literature and in the chronicle of Flavio Biondo toward the end of the fifteenth century, Calvin himself employed it during the sixteenth century, and in the end the definition was printed categorically in the texts of two second-rate historians, Hornius and Cellarius, in the 1680's; that was that.

The 1680's are full of turning-points in the history of European civilization. The Turks are turned back from the portals of central Europe, the Russians reach the borders of the Chinese empire, the English make their constitutional revolution, the long series of wars between England and France that will lead to the rise of the United States of America is beginning. Paul Hazard called this decade the beginning of the crisis of European consciousness and the emergence of the European mind. In 1681 there appears Mabillon's *De Re Diplomatica* which, as such different historians as Dom David Knowles and Marc Bloch suggested, is probably the first example of modern historical scholarship. Later in the decade Cellarius' history text, with its three-epochal division, appears within the year of Newton's *Principia,* of the great fixed system of the physical universe of which it has been said that it reduced God to the role of a constitutional monarch who reigns but who does not rule: a telling metaphor, also because of its historical coincidence with the "glorious revolution," that is, with the triumph of monarchical constitutionalism in England. Thus in the 1680's our still-present concept of "modern" history and the synthesis of our "classical" physics—indeed, of our modern concept of the universe—appear at the same time. Less than three hundred years later we are beginning—but only beginning—to outgrow them, together, again.

(4) What history has become: the last three hundred years

During the last three hundred years the development of historical thinking was not predictable. I think it probable that during these centuries the growth of historical awareness may have been unbroken in the *subconsciousness* of successive European (and later American) generations—but I am not a charlatan, I cannot deal with the history of the subconscious: I can but attempt to trace the conscious development of historical thinking.

Ambiguous, for instance, was the historical consciousness of the Enlightenment. During the eighteenth century, history in western Europe (principally in France, England, Scotland) flourished as literature. The cultivated public read Voltaire's histories avidly. "*L'histoire,*" Voltaire himself wrote, "*est la partie des belles-lettres qui a le plus des partisans dans tous les pays.*" "History is the most popular species of writing," Gibbon said. "I believe," Hume wrote around the middle of the century, "this to be the historical age and this the historical nation." This kind of interest in the historical form of narrative suggests the growth of a European mentality which was getting accustomed to history as a form of thought: but it still failed to recognize that it *was* a form of thought. For much of the thinking of the Enlightenment, like that of the Renaissance, was still considerably ahistorical. Voltaire proclaimed that Newton was the greatest human being since Christ; Hume made statements sounding like the scientism of Buckle or Comte a century later: "The same motives always produce the same actions, the same events follow from the same causes." Together with a widespread interest in narrative historical writing there existed a lack of history-mindedness during the eighteenth century which is attested, for instance, by the usual common-sense testimony of Dr. Johnson. "We must consider how very little history there is," he told Boswell, "I mean real authentic history. That certain kings reigned and certain battles were fought we can depend upon as true; but all the colouring, all the philosophy of history is conjecture."

This intellectual shortcoming of the Enlightenment was not, however, a uniform condition. For example, Vico in Naples, in what was then a rich, brackish tributary of the mainstream of European civilization, stated early in the eighteenth century in his *Scienza Nuova* that history is man's knowledge of man; and, as Paul Hazard wrote two centuries later, the course of European culture would have been different if people in the eighteenth century had read Vico instead of Voltaire. But, then, they hadn't. Moreover, already at the end of the seventeenth century there emerged, especially in France, a group of scholar-priests who, for the first time in history, applied critical or, as some people might say, modern scientific, methods to their dealings with medieval documents and other source materials. These so-called Erudites or Antiquaries were truly the first modern academic historians: among them Mabillon and Tillemont stood out. Yet it is not only that by the middle of the eighteenth century the Erudites' influence faded; it is also that their admirable handling of documents was not sufficiently evocative; they were, still, in the exact sense of the word, *antiquaries;* their methods, as G. N. Clark put it, were not enough "to bring the Middle Ages back to life."[14]

That achievement was the intellectual consequence of romanticism—of the deep-going reaction to the eighteenth century, the impact of which reaction was evident far beyond the confines of literature and of art. It may be said that between 1770 and 1840 there occurred a sudden and precipitous deepening of the European

[14] G. N. Clark, *The Seventeenth Century*, London, 1929. The Antiquaries "loved the past for its own sake," writes Richardson, "not for the sake of the present; and to this extent, despite the immense debt which is owed to them, they were something less than historians in the full contemporary [sense]. . . . The notion that there could be an existential encounter with the past, compelling men to make a decision concerning the present, or bringing them to a new self-understanding, was utterly foreign to the Age of Reason. . . ."

There is one exception to this. It is the early recognition of the existential utility of history for the study of foreign relations. George I established the Regius Professorship of Modern History in Oxford in 1724, for the sake of training young diplomatists, probably emulating Torcy's "Academy of Politics" in France (1712).

consciousness: a deepening of the in-look, the deepening sense of nationality, the deepening of historical thinking were part and parcel of this phenomenon. Now the historical manner of writing was complemented by a historical, rather than epical, kind of imagination which millions had come to share: and it may not be farfetched to see in this development a correspondence with the development of historical literature from narration to description. Scott's historical and Balzac's historical-social novels exemplified this evolution of the European historical consciousness: their influence (especially Scott's influence on the professional historians of his time) has been attested often.

Since about the middle of the nineteenth century the rapid extension of compulsory education in the Western world disseminated all kinds of historical information among millions of people—especially when history, as a separate subject, was beginning to be taught, for the first time, on almost all levels of schooling (this, too, happened only after about 1860, much more recently than we are inclined to think). The rapid extension of literacy brought all kinds of historical literature to millions of previously unaffected readers; and toward the end of the century these practices spread to southern and eastern Europe and to the Americas. This extension of historical education and this dissemination of historical literature were immensely widespread and protean in their manifestations; and despite their often superficial nature, they had, in the long run, a definite impact on the minds of millions of the same people who at the same time were relinquishing many of their old and durable traditions, habits, and habitations.

It is only about 150 years ago that the historical approach became a form of thought, that some people recognized that it is possible to study everything (including history) through its historical development. Meinecke, the principal German historian of this process, called it "the greatest spiritual revolution which Western thought has undergone" in modern times; and that Huizinga in 1936 could say that "historical thinking has entered our very blood" is mainly (though not exclusively) the result of this revolution. Yet during the last 100 or 120 years two complementary intellectual developments have compromised as well as retarded a fuller recognition of what the historical form of thought may mean for our evolving consciousness in the Western world.

First, the historical form of thought became confused in many minds with the deterministic concept of progress[15]: hence, for example, the unhistorical character of philosophies such as Marxism and Darwinism—even though they, too, were unwitting by-products of the historical form of thought. Second, the emerging scientific concept of history, in spite of its undeniable merits, retarded the issue. During the nineteenth century the idea of history as science replaced gradually the previous practice of history as literature.[16] This was, to some extent, the consequence of the way in which Germanic thinking was beginning to replace France's pre-eminence in the cultural history of Europe during the beginning of the romantic revolution. Already around 1770 a German "scientific" school of historianship, around Schlözer in Göttingen, proposed the definite formation of a professional discipline: Schlözer insisted that history was something more than the memorization of the past, that it was "philosophy, perpetually connecting results with causes." Thus emerged the modern professional concept of historianship. I need not describe its many achievements. They include a most creditable, and possibly enduring, accumulation of historical information, involving records of many kinds, extending gradually over more and more portions of time (the past) and more and more portions of space (other continents and other civilizations); it improved and to some extent refined the methods and the standards of historical study; most important, it exposed the minds of millions of people to history in classrooms, and through print. Yet the professional concept of history as science fell short precisely because it underestimated the extent and the nature of its concerns: while it stressed, at times rigidly, the scientific character of historical study, believing that through scientific methods and professional training an objective and indisputable record of the past could be constructed,

---

[15] This is, in reality, what Professor Karl Popper calls "historicism"—a term so broad as to be useless.

[16] Not of history as "art"—because the modern debating question as to whether history is "art" or "science" would not have made much sense in the eighteenth century. It is true that the eighteenth century treated, by and large, history as "art"—but the spirit of that century did not yet comprehend that kind of contradiction between art and science which is so obvious to us. Veronica Wedgwood's recent phrase, "History is an art, like the other sciences," for us is a felicitous paradoxical epigram; for the eighteenth century this was a truism.

it failed to recognize the profounder implications of the historical form of thought. And even though now, in the twentieth century, it is no longer fashionable to assert that history is A Science, this originally nineteenth-century tendency continues to haunt, to influence, to impress, to dominate professional historiography—and, indirectly, popular opinions regarding historianship.

There are, of course, many singular exceptions to these necessary generalizations. The most important among them was the reaction against historical "scientism": a reaction which was, again, wholly involved in a general philosophical and ideological reaction, on the European continent, against the nineteenth-century materialistic and positivistic trends of thought. (The span of this—by no means romantic—reaction, 1874–1941, the history of which still remains to be written, curiously repeated nearly exactly the time span of the romantic reaction, 1770–1840, against the eighteenth-century mentality a century earlier.) The beginning of this reaction may be marked by an essay by Nietzsche on "The Use and Abuse of History" in 1874 and by Dilthey's *Ueber das Studium der Geschichte* in 1875, in the middle of the Germanies, at that time the very center of Europe. The end of this phase may be marked, I think, by a political and world-historical event: by the decisive intervention of the United States in the Second European World War in 1941, which meant the coming military defeat and the political bankruptcy of the nation (Germany) and of the philosophies (ideological nationalism) which incarnated some of the vulgarized and extreme principles of this originally widespread and culturally respectable reaction against the materialist, positivist, determinist mentalities of the nineteenth century. It is, I believe, the cultural consequence of the indisputable emergence of the United States and of the Soviet Union as the principal world powers (and, to some extent, the sociological consequence of the spreading of mass democracy after 1945) that after the Second World War even in Europe "neo-positivist" practices grew again within historical scholarship, and that powerful attempts are still being made in order to apply the methods of the so-called social sciences to the study of history. Yet beneath the present proliferation of professional historianship it is easy to detect a deep sense of uneasiness, including symptoms of chaos not unsimilar to those now affecting the arts. This crisis in historical thinking has lead to ever-increasing theorizings about history and about the nature of historical knowledge itself; there are now professional historians who have made these theorizings their speciality in their academic careers.[17]

Thus historians, in the second half of the twentieth century, speak of a "crisis" because of their very uncertainty of what really constitutes history. Since the human mind usually advances through its asking of serious new questions this would be in itself a salutary development, were it not that it is compromised by deadening habits and vested intellectual interests. For instance, even those professional historians who by now refuse the categorical assumption of history being A Science still tend to write and teach as if human history were largely determined. Also, even those professional intellectuals who by now tend to react against the dominations of neo-positivism feel somehow compelled to express themselves in a language which is abstract, reflecting not only the intellectual temptation of substituting vocabulary for thought but also the inroads on their mentality of their colleagues' prestige in the natural sciences. It is true that specialized jargon has made—as yet—fewer inroads in the territories of professional historiography than in the field of political science: but disturbing symptoms of its appearance crop up here and there, not least in the "specialized field" of historical theoretics.

Still I believe that these holdovers of what are now antiquated habits of thought, these gigantic vested interests of the intellect do not compare in importance to the widespread development of historical consciousness all over the Western world, on nearly all levels of society and in the most unexpected places and ways: to the event that we have been developing a new attitude to the past, and especially to the remembered past. As Jules Romains made his hero Jallez speak in his monumental novel of the early twentieth century, *Men of Good Will: "La grande découverte de l'homme moderne, c'est la présence de l'historie"*—modern man's greatest discovery is the (omni) presence of history. It may be too optimistic to expect people to swallow in one gulp,[18] and consequently digest, G. M. Young's strong statement, written down in 1950, at the

---

[17] A symptom of this development, among others, is *History and Theory*, an American-edited international periodical devoted to these subjects.

[18] Samuel Butler, *Notebooks:* "Diffuseness sometimes helps, when the subject is hard; words that may be strictly speaking unnecessary still may make things easier for the reader by giving him more time to master the thought while his eye is running over the verbiage. So a little water may prevent a strong drink from burning throat and stomach."

chronological turning-point of this century, burning as it is with light and hope: "I often feel that we are standing just before the dawn of a Second Renaissance which will need history in order to understand the world with which it will have to deal, just as the First Renaissance had to go to the Classics to find the right way of saying all the new things that had to be said." Let me reverse the famous Neapolitan saying: *È ben vero, se non è ancora trovato.* We have novel attitudes to the past: we regard it as an asset, not a burden. Perhaps this is what distinguishes our mentality not only from the First Renaissance but from that of the sometimes schizophrenic mentality of the last romantic reaction: for attitudes such as Goethe's and Hegel's (!), when they, 150 years ago, expressed a nostalgic hope for unhistorical America as they bewailed the "useless historical burdens" of Europe,* are hardly conceivably today.

To sum up, therefore: the evolution of historical consciousness ever since its first definite emergence about three centuries ago may have developed through the following phases:

Eighteenth century: History as *literature; the narrated* past.

Nineteenth century: History as *science; the recorded* past.

Twentieth century: a dual development: on the surface, history as *a social science; the ascertained* past. But, in a deeper and wider sense: history as *a form of thought; the remembered* past. I am concerned with the implications of the latter.

(5) *History a Western form of thought*

I am writing, evidently, about the deepening of a certain form of thought. And deepening, at least in one sense, means narrowing, converging, concentrating: going deeper into things about which one more or less knows something. In this book this restricts my scope to "Western" history. Thus the very direction of my intellectual enterprise seems to move against the grain of contemporary intellectualism which so often stresses the principal necessity of the widening, rather than of the deepening, of our knowledge of the world. Now, it is true that the historical and the technical development of the world has brought different continents and races and civilizations closer together; that we cannot ignore the present and the past of other cultures; that the human race is more interdependent than at any time before; that we have begun to experience the first symptoms of a world civilization—or, to use another, less fortunate term, we are "entering the age of universal history." Western civilization has now spread all over the world; neither the scientific method nor the professional study of history are any longer European and American intellectual monopolies. Yet historical consciousness is still something specifically "Western."

"Western civilization," "European tradition"—these are not definite or accurate or closed categories. Still the historical form of thought seems to have been the evolving product of our civilization, involved as it has been with a specific kind of realism and with a particular tradition of rhetoric and with a certain conception of human nature. Let me repeat that all human existence is historical existence, that historical thinking is potentially inherent in all human nature, and that some kind of a historical sense may be found among all human societies, including the most primitive ones: but the development of these capacities depends on their recognition: the actual consciousness of these qualities differ.

Outside the West the memory of the past is marked by a kind of historical insufficiency. Archaeology or ethnography is needed for the reconstruction of even relatively recent developments; and even when written records exist, as in certain Asian countries, their quality is defective: they are chronicles stuffed with legends and interspersed by long anecdotes.[19] In the words of the Orientalist William Haas, the East, in historical knowledge, "has produced little comparable to the achievements of the West. . . . Only in Western civilization could genuine history have arisen and grown as it did." The reliable histories of the otherwise highly articulate peoples of India, China, Persia, Japan have been written by Westerners (such as Murdoch, Curzon, Boxer, De la Vallée Poussin, Elphinstone, Buller, Sansom, Basil Hall Chamberlain). "If we had to depend solely on Japanese sources," the latter wrote about an eventful phase of Japan's history, "we would know next to nothing"; as late

19 William Haas: "Not even Szu Ma Chien, who is considered the greatest Chinese historiographer, transcends this general model." The character of *historian* in early Chinese "represented a hand holding a receptacle used to contain tallies in archery contests." (Barzun-Graff, *The Modern Researcher*—an American introductory text for beginning historians which, for once, does not cringe from saying that "Western culture may be said to be the historical culture par excellence," and that almost nothing like ancient histories exist in Indian or Chinese literature.)

as in 1950 C. R. Boxer added that this was exactly as true as when it had been written before the turn of the century.*

It is rather evident that this inadequacy of historianship outside the West has involved not merely a deficiency of a method but differences of mentality:* not only insufficiencies of "records" but distinct differences in which different cultures have remembered their past. And this is one of the reasons of the relative importance of Western history even on the scale of world history. Even now a person in the West may disregard most of Oriental history with little consequent loss to his proper understanding of the processes of history, while the converse is not so: no intelligent Oriental can afford to remain ignorant of Western, and specifically of European, history. And this is true not because the West has ruled the East longer than the East ruled the West; it is true because historical thinking has been a Western, though relatively recent, achievement; and because the history of the West has been exceptionally "paradigmatic"—that is, full of potentially instructive examples. History in the West has been less repetitious than elsewhere; exceptions have broken through the surface of routine more often. The historical pattern of other civilizations is more repetitive and more uniform, corresponding to some extent with the frequent element of religious fatalism which, in turn, is involved with the insufficient maturity of their historical thinking. It is thus that, by and large, similar conditions have repeatedly tended toward similar results in the "mythic and mysterious" East rather than in the "systematic and rational" West. (Still, uniformity and repetitiveness do not necessarily mean predictability. In the East history may have "repeated" itself more often than in the West: but this does not mean that what was happening in the East was more predictable, except perhaps in a negative sense: for in history, unlike in science, it is more reasonable to predict what is *not* going to happen than what is going to happen.)

If people who do not know history are perhaps not *condemned*— as Santayana put it with poetic sternness—they are certainly *prone* to repeat it; as Burckhardt wrote, "the shackling of custom by symbols, etc., can only be loosed by knowledge of the past."

This insufficiency of knowledge of the past is not, of course, a matter of retention, of quantity; it really involves an insufficiency of historical thinking—which, in turn, is the consequence of different forms of consciousness.[20] The mind gives form to feelings—to physical and spiritual feelings.* While it is absurd and wrong to speak of different peoples having different souls, it is legitimate to speak of different forms of consciousness. Certainly a Christian may not speak of an Oriental soul that is different in nature from his: but we may speak of the different characteristics of Western and of Oriental minds. And different minds are formed not only by different perspectives, not only by different habits of recognition but also by different habits of expression: this is what I meant earlier when I referred to the Greek ethic of rhetoric. It seems, for example, that the Greek and European tradition of realism has been something unique in the history of the world, not only because of its production of certain forms of realistic representation in art but also because—at least until very recently—in our civilization abstract thought and poetic expression have served the purpose of conveying a deeper sense of reality: whereas the abstractness of many Oriental languages conveys not so much expressions of ideas as a kind of imagery which may be on occasion beautiful but which is quite divorced from reality. For different expressions, different languages, and different habits of speech are at the same time consequences as well as causes of different habits of thought and even of different habits of truth.*

[20] E. H. Carr in *What Is History?* (1961): "One reason why history rarely repeats itself among historically conscious people is that the *dramatis personae* are aware at the second performance of the *dénouement* of the first, and their action is affected by that knowledge." This is very true: but Carr's illustration of this argument is wrong. "The Bolsheviks," he wrote, "knew that the French revolution had ended in a Napoleon, and feared that their own revolution might end in the same way. They therefore mistrusted Trotsky, who among their leaders looked most like a Napoleon, and trusted Stalin, who looked least like a Napoleon." This is nonsense: for Trotsky's principal handicap was something entirely different. It was not that he looked Napoleonic: it was that he was Jewish: his assumption of Lenin's mantle would have made the Bolshevik regime unpopular and extremely vulnerable: and this was something that the Bolshevik leaders, including the Jewish ones among them, knew. It was not historical consciousness, it was the uncomfortable deadweight of popular and racial inclinations which influenced the revolutionary bosses of Russia: for the Russian Revolution was less historically conscious than had been the French Revolution: the actions of a Stalin, for example (and I am not overlooking his Georgian origins), were influenced by Russian cultural and national traits much more than Robespierre's had been influenced by French history and by French national characteristics. The most important thing about the Russians after 1917 is not that they have become Marxists but that they have remained very Russian indeed.

"We can neither define what we mean by truth, nor be in doubt to our meaning," Samuel Butler wrote. "And this I suppose must be due to the antiquity of the instinct that on the whole directs us toward truth." This instinct is universally human: but its recognition, its consciousness are particularly Western. "Western man" (whatever that might mean) is not superior to other human beings, but certain Western traditions of truth and of justice are superior to the standards of other civilizations, which is why I should expect better justice before an English jury than before an Oriental court. But the applications of these standards are not restricted to ourselves: for it is not only the principle of free will but also the teaching of charity (which is nearly inseparable from understanding) which distinguished the universality of Christianity above and beyond the older concepts of tribal and patriotic religions. Thus when the Marxist Dr. Pannikar, a leading Hindu intellectual and historian, admits that the new Asian nationalisms came from a rediscovery of native cultures "to which European scholarship had also materially contributed," this is an understatement: it would be more correct to say that European scholarship had not only contributed but to a large measure created that "rediscovery." And why? Because the European historians were exceptionally accurate pedants? No: because they had inherited a tradition which, with all of its faults, had been exceptionally generous.

There exist, after all, practical consequences of the Western idea of truth. Consider, for example, this relationship between the existence (and not merely the preservation) of certain records and of a certain sense of history. We need not go to Asia in order to illustrate this condition. At least during the thirty years of Stalin's regime, Russia closed herself off from the rest of Europe: and it is because of the then barbaric conditions of her political history that it will be very difficult to reconstruct accurately and reliably certain phases of Stalin's rule, but not only because there may be few documents extant. It is quite likely that even if the minutes of Politburo meetings were to be found and published someday, they will tell us little: for it is not only that a civilized society will keep records, it is that only a civilized society will have such records in which evidences of critical intelligence are reflected.* And the sources of this kind of critical intelligence are not merely those of a "scientific" attitude. Russia under Stalin, again, illustrates how the advancement of the physical sciences and of their applications in an increasingly industrialized and technological society can coexist with a relapse into barbaric patterns of behavior, rhetoric, and thought. Some of the sources of this relapse may be detectible in certain Byzantine and non-Western traditions of Russia. Even the writings of Tolstoy and of Dostoevsky reveal at times, in a flash, the very divergent tendencies of Western and Eastern Christian traditions.* "History," said Tolstoy to Gusev, "would be an excellent thing if it only were true." "If anyone could prove to me that Christ is outside the truth," Dostoevsky wrote in one of his letters, "and if the truth really did exclude Christ, I should prefer to stay with Christ and not with the truth." This is exactly what a Western Christian cannot do: he cannot separate Christ from the truth; and in this very Dostoevskian statement there gleams a fideistic, a near-Buddhist* tendency which, notwithstanding its Christian fervor, departs from the entire Western tradition—it is a renunciation of our aspirations, and of our concept of historical truth. I shall have to return to these inevitable relationships of Western historical consciousness and Western Christianity later in this book: here it may be sufficient to say that Christianity, as indeed Judaism, is rooted in history; its claims, at least in part, are historical, whereas the claims of most Oriental religions are mythological; and it is this emphasis on the historical Christ which is *historically** sensed in the consciousness of Western peoples while it is underplayed in the Eastern Christian folkish-religious traditions. "The conflict between religiosity and rationality in Europe developed relatively late," as Otto Brunner put it, "and even in the Church, in its constitution, in its concepts of its rights, in its scholastic philosophy there have been peculiarly European and rational tendencies that are missing in other places." A fundamental factor in this kind of Western rationalism was the prevalence of historical thinking.

Unless we understand this condition, and unless our Asian brethren understand that the progress of civilization (which, by now, is a progress of a kind of "Westernization") is *not* merely the dissemination of tools and of skills, there is, I believe, enormous chaos ahead of all of us—the symptoms of which, already apparent here and there, are the usual ones of a blind and unwitting relapse into intellectual primitivism. This is the primitivism of those who do not see that determinism and fatalism are far from being antitheses, that the most "advanced" and "exciting" American social philosophers of a Computer Civilization proceed from assumptions regarding human nature that are fundamentally akin to the assumptions of the most primitive and barbaric Oriental religions: for scientism and fideism— these opposites of idealism and of realism—a kind of belief in mechanical abstractions and a kind of belief in certain dogmas, are not at all such opposite inclinations as they may seem at first sight. The antitheses are, rather, abstract thinking vs. historical thinking, materialism vs. idealism, systematic vs. existential forms of consciousness, unquestioning vs. rational belief, mechanical vs. realistic concepts of human functions. Again it is later in this book that I must return to this strange modern convergence of scientism with fideism which is unfortunately so characteristic of the present intellectual climate in the West, and perhaps especially in the United States. All I want to say here is that the sources of cultural decay as well as of cultural immaturity are attitudes which are unhistorical rather than unscientific, and that it is our responsibility to impress our Oriental colleagues with this conviction.

When, for example, Dr. Bambang Utomo, an excellent man who courageously criticizes nationalism, sentimentalism, Marxism, deplores above everything else the "unscientific" nature of Indonesian historiography, it is obvious that the concept of History As A Science has taken a strong hold upon his mind. Most of the modern Asian intellectuals are agnostics; they are right when they criticize the superstitions and the myths of their earlier "histories"; of course the dissemination of the scientific method has had beneficial effects in the East—and yet the necessary corrective for unhistorical habits of thought (and of rhetoric) is something more (and also something else) than the emulation of the scientific method. True, in the traditional chronicles of Asian peoples invasions were natural disasters, the acts of demons, while people were on occasion saved through the wile of some prince, by his magical know-how; as Dwight Macdonald, an otherwise sympathetic observer of the London conference on Asian history in 1957 wrote, history in Asia "was magic, cosmology, poetry, legend, ritual, anything except an accurate account of what happened"—but we should, perhaps, write "truthful description" instead of "accurate account": for the problem is not so much a problem of method as of consciousness, not so much of

accuracy as of different concepts of truth, and, of course, not of a
new kind of magical know-how.* We, in the West, have produced
some of the greatest liars in the history of the world: but at least
we know that we lie when we lie. Our peculiarly Western "preoccupation" (note the literal sense of *pre-occupation*) with reality is,
at its best, not vulgar but truthful: a mental tendency toward particular fragments of truth, nourished by a particular germination of
critical intelligence.

It is the propagation of this kind of critical intelligence of which
the now multiplying professional historians of the Orient are in
greatest need. And this involves not only an intelligent skepticism
before the newest methods and gimmicks of Western "social science"
but the recognition, too, that they cannot accept uncritically the
historical terminology of the West. There are all kinds of historical
realities, *bourgeois, feudal, nation,* for instance, which are European
rather than universal phenomena; but now Asian historians have
taken them up, applying them to the histories of their own countries
which they, too, divide into "Classical," "Medieval," "Reformation"
periods. This is senseless, for many reasons, one of these being that
while these historical movements have, by and large, involved most
of Europe, Asia, in the words of one of its most eminent historians,
Dr. Alishtabana, "is living in thirty different centuries at the same
time." In any event, "Asia," as a category, is a simplified Western
notion; unlike Europe, it has remained a geographical term; it is
not a cultural or political or national or religious or racial unit of
any kind; peoples and cultures as close to each other as Persia and
India or India and China have had surprisingly little influence on
each other: the ignorance of Persians of Indian, or of Indians of
Chinese, history has remained very great. Even "India" or "Indonesia" have been, until recently, vague concepts: consider only
the multiplicity of their languages. This is changing now. But what
has been happening in most instances in Asia and in Africa is not the
formation of new nations but of new states—while the Asian *lingua
franca* is American-English.

There is, conversely, "a serious danger," as Christopher Dawson,
certainly not a narrow nationalist, recently wrote, "that the relative
widening of the historical perspective to include the non-European
civilizations may be accompanied by an absolute decline in the
quality and standard of general European history." In many parts

of the West there exists now a flaccid tendency of sorts, a spineless and insubstantial affection of historical "universalism." Many (though surely not all) of those American professors buzzing about nowadays in India or Japan on Ford or Fulbright grants do not really have much of a deep human interest in the East: they have, rather, chosen the Orient as a Field because of their inadequate interest in the historical traditions of the West. Yet our greatest historical thinkers were not universalists: they were convinced of the uniqueness of the Western heritage, including that of Christianity. Burckhardt and Tocqueville had not esteemed Islam and Buddhism very highly; profoundly aware as he was of the paradigmatic character of European history, Burckhardt showed little interest in the Orient, Egypt, Babylonia; yet, as his biographer Werner Kaegi rightly put it, Burckhardt did have "a full and unbroken consciousness of the unity of the history of mankind." The same is true of Tocqueville, the answer to this seeming paradox being that "historical universalism," like "toleration," is not necessarily the mark of a superior mind. Toleration and generosity, like indifference and high-mindedness, are quite different things: it is easier to profess abstract virtues than to practice real ones; it is easier to be humanitarian than human; it is easier to propagate a superficial appreciation of faraway peoples than to be racked with pain and concern in attempting to understand one's own.

From "know thyself" to "know thy history," from the Greeks to the great western European patrician thinkers of the near past flows the stream of our self-consciousness: unique, as it is historical;* historical rather than scientific. Even though Herbert Butterfield was right when he said that "the publication of Newton's *Principia* in 1687 is a turning-point in history for peoples to whom the Renaissance and the Reformation can hardly mean anything at all—people amongst whom the Battle of Waterloo would hardly be calculated to produce an echo," his hierarchy of respective events may be correct for Asia but not for Europe and America—and, consequently, not for the general history of the world. Yet there are now influential people in the West who think and act as if the discovery of the spinning jenny or Newton's date of publication were *the* principal events of importance *in our own* history. They are wrong for many reasons: and this, among other things, is what this book is about.

(6) History the remembered past

Does this imply that certain persons or certain peoples "do not have history" or that they are constitutionally incapable of history-mindedness? No: what I have tried to suggest is merely that at least in one "field," in the development of historical consciousness European civilization is still ahead of the rest of the world, since historical thinking represents the beginning of an awareness of the limitations of the scientific method, whereas the rest of the world has only recently begun to abandon some of its habits from a "prescientific" era for the things and the categories of scientific civilization. We shall see later that one of the marks of "post-scientific" thinking is the recognition that Descartes's division of the universe into "subjects" and "objects" no longer makes sense. This necessarily involves a novel, and often painful, reconsideration of the kind of "scientific objectivity" which has implied the necessary separation of the observer from the thing observed: "post-scientific" thinking must proceed from the very opposite of that order, from personal "participation," meaning the recognition of our involvement with the universe.[21] This understanding of the inevitability of personal (personal, rather than "individual," or "subjective") character of our knowledge means not much more than a new, chastened, and deepening, version of the ancient *know thyself* through the recognition that *know thyself* must also mean *know thy history*. The relevance of this to the foregoing subchapter lies in the condition that the kind of history which we are apt to understand best may be our own; that the particular understanding which we possess of the history of human beings involves a kind of knowledge which, contrary to the spirit of the natural sciences, is different not only in degree but in kind of the knowledge we have of other living beings; and that our potential understanding of people whose level of consciousness is to some extent similar to ours will be potentially (though not necessarily) deeper than our understanding of people who are more remote from us. What this means is not so much that our

[21] See Chapter VI, pp. 267–272. Ortega already in 1914 (*Meditations on Quixote*): "Man reaches his full capacity when he acquires complete consciousness of his circumstances. Through them he communicates with the universe."

study of the history of Europeans and of Americans of the last three hundred years is *of especial value;* it merely means that in dealing with this kind of contemporary history we are potentially capable of drawing upon a kind *of particular understanding* of which we are largely (though not completely) deprived when we confront ancient Egypt or the modern Congo.

This is not, of course, a reactionary argument for narrow-minded-ness: it is reactionary only in the sense of reacting against the kind of modern broad-mindedness which is so broad as to be flat: and it is arguing not for the narrowing but for the deepening of our histori-cal concerns. Indeed, having only now said that a kind of widening of interests might lead to shallowness, I must now turn to the corol-lary argument: that, in another sense, our present concept of pro-fessional history is not wide enough.

By saying this I am not merely referring to the now standard arguments in favor of the necessary "broadening" of the historical discipline: that history must cease to be the chronicle of presidents, princes, premiers, politics, and battles and that it must include the story of "the common man," of "the masses," of "the crowd"; that political history must be complemented by the research and the study of economic and social and cultural factors. All of these things are obvious. But they are not the consequences of the advancement of science; they are the consequences of developing democracy. Whenever modern statistical information must be considered by the modern historian the true reason for this is not to be found in the superior veracity of the scientific method but in the condition of democracy: we have to deal with more and more people in their capacity of active historical agents; at best in the twentieth century we have to deal with the history of peoples and of nations, and not only with the history of governments and of states. Here, however, my main point is not that history is something else (and something more) than a social science; it is that a preoccupation with the social-scientific approach in itself may have obscured a profounder impli-cation of that very democratization of the historical process: and this is the spreading of the historical form of thought, with its corollary of history being the remembered past for millions of people.

Now, by keeping in mind that history is the remembered—and not merely the recorded—past, what the modern historian ought to consider are not merely increasing varieties of records (social statistics, pictures, films, oral-history tapes, computer-processed information, etc.). *That* is rather obvious, too. Those historians who, in the second half of the twentieth century, argue with knitted brows that what this means are New Tools, New Disciplines, and so on, in posing as daring reformers in their profession are merely doing what other pedants have always done when they (to paraphrase Wilde) pursue the obvious with the enthusiasm of short-sighted detectives. The slow and gradual evolution of mankind toward some kind of democracy and some kind of unity in itself compels us to abandon the restricted bourgeois and patrician view of history as the history of influential minorities, of *certain* people and of *certain* sources, indeed, the nineteenth-century view of history as a matter of "documents": we must recognize that history encompasses potentially *all* of the past, and that it includes *all* kinds of records of the past. And what historians ought to consider are not only increasing varieties of records but a deepening consciousness of the functions of human memory; that different kinds of records are reflections of different kinds of memory—and this is what I mean when I, too, restate something that may sound obvious: that the remembered past is a much larger category than the recorded past, and that this is especially important in the democratic age in which we live.

These functions of remembering involve understanding beyond accuracy, a preoccupation with problems rather than with periods, an exploration in depth rather than in width, a constant rethinking of the past, involving qualities rather than capacities of memory. History is incomplete, fragmentary, inaccurate because it is the remembered past: we do not remember all of the past: our memory is limited, and oddly selective (among other things, we often remember what we want to remember). But while memory may be inaccurate, it does not exist in the abstract; my memory is *my* memory; it is inaccurate not only because of the mechanical limitations of the brain's capacity; it is inaccurate, too, because it is personal. The intrusion of this personal factor is the reason why historical knowledge is different from mathematical concepts of knowledge and from the still broadly accepted "classical" concepts of the physical sciences; and a fleeting attempt at introspection ought to reveal to any sensitive person how an encounter with a historical truth touches our mind and our senses quite differently from an encounter with a scientific truth.

There is, then, a reverse side to this. If, on the one hand, historical knowledge is inseparable from personal knowledge, on the other hand personal knowledge is, to a large extent, historical knowledge —"past-knowledge"—of *some* kind. Let me bypass the profounder implications of this condition (that, for instance, every kind of human cognition is, to some extent, a recognition)—let me only say here that "past-knowledge" involves quality even more than it involves quantity. The latter decreases as our life goes on: we may remember acutely hundreds of details of an incident that happened to us yesterday; one, five, ten years later we will have forgotten many, if not most, of these details. But this decrease in the quantity of our knowledge of a particular past does not necessarily mean a decrease in the quality of our understanding of it: after ten years we might recollect that particular incident more remotely but more justly, less acutely but more clearly, with fewer details but with more understanding. The operations of our memory do not improve, while our comprehension of the past may improve. (And if by "function" we mean purpose rather than mechanical operations it may be even said that, in many ways, the function of our memory may improve as life goes on, even though, mechanically speaking, the quantitative peak in the retentive capacity of our memory occurs relatively early in life.)

How, then, is this possible? How does this eventual improvement in our understanding of the past come about? In part because of our own accumulating experiences; in part because we, in the meantime, may have learned different and newly revealed things about a particular incident from others—other participants, observers, reporters, historians. For historical thinking is the constant, the frequent *rethinking* of the past. The important historian, unlike the important scientist or the inventor, is not necessarily the person who for the first time discovers or, rather, "covers" a portion of the "field" up to then "unresearched." ("We have good standard professional biographies of every President except for Millard Fillmore. *You* must do Fillmore.") The great historian is the one who retells the same portion of the past for the twentieth or fiftieth time perhaps: but when he does this he draws attention to it and sheds light on it from new perspectives which issue, in turn, perhaps not so much from new quantities of material as from new qualities of evidence; and in so doing he deepens our understanding perhaps even more than he extends our information. . . .

It is thus that the study of history involves problems rather than periods—of ever recurrent human problems incarnated by ever different human beings. It is thus that, in a sense, all history is contemporary history too. And it is thus that the meaning of *the remembered past* involves the complexities of what *remembering* is together with the complexities of what is *the past*. The functions of human remembering—what and how and why some things are remembered—are fantastically complex, because our memory is personal and because we are historical beings. But the past, too, is something that cannot be stowed away into a simple, definite, closed category. It is not as completely irrevocable as it may seem. Death and the past are not the same. Death is irrevocable; the past is not. And, if death and the past are not the same, life and the present are not the same either. The present is an abstract illusion, the elusive and slightly sickening sensation of past and future meeting in our minds; but life, unlike the present, is not an illusion at all: it is a reality. Thus, in a sense, it is life and the past that belong together; and, in another sense, it is death and the present: for death is not the freezing of the past, it is the freezing of the present.

We shall see, in the last chapter of this book, that these are not recondite poetic statements but that some of the recognitions of modern physics militate for a serious rethinking of the three categories of past, present, future. All I am arguing at this point is that the existential consciousness which we in the West in the twentieth century possess has probably a larger element of "past-knowledge" inherent in it than we are accustomed to think. All of us are conscious of this condition *to some extent:* this is why for example, most good writing in our times is historical, as in Homer's time it was legendary-epical. Writing is an account of one's consciousness; this consciousness always has a historical element within it. This was true of Homer as well as of Shakespeare and of Proust as well as of Macaulay: but, I repeat, what is relatively new in our situation is the sometimes dim but always pervasive consciousness of this condition, whereby Balzac was already more of a historian than was Voltaire, or Proust than Shakespeare.

Thus it is that historiography and the development of professional historianship are only part and parcel of the broader development of the historical form of thought; that this book which I am now writing is about history in the broadest sense of the term. But isn't this category too broad? Am I not a historian rather than a novelist? Yes: primarily; but not exclusively. As a matter of fact, literature and history, after a century of divergence, may be now coming together again, though probably not from the direction in which most people concerned with their divergence think: now when so much of professional history becomes less and less literary, great literature may become more and more historical.[22] We are, all, historians now. This condition is reflected in the abortive progress of the word "historiography." During the last two hundred years, even as the notion of professional historianship grew, the term "historiography" did not catch on; it failed to eradicate the sense that history is something more than a professional discipline or an enclosed "field" of research; "historiography" and "historiographer" (unlike, say, "sociology" and "sociologist") did not take root in most Western languages because of the latent awareness of peoples that *historiography* cannot be anything very definite or different from *history*— or indeed, from *story*.*

Still our problem is not so much that history has become too serious a thing to be left to professional historians (even though this is often true); it is, rather, that the concept of "professional history" is narrow. There are not many serious historians who would contest this point.

And yet the meaning of the present proliferation of historical interest, on all levels, sometimes escapes them, too. For example Professor J. H. Plumb, in his Prospectus (1965) of a new and ambitious *The History of Human Society,* to be published by Alfred A. Knopf, having first criticized the cancerous proliferation of professional specialization during the last one hundred years, writes: "But the gap between professional knowledge and history for the masses gets steadily wider; professional history becomes more accurate, more profound, whilst public history remains tentative and shallow." This juxtaposition is mistaken. The standards of what Professor Plumb calls "public history" have improved actually during the last fifty years, probably because of the increasing appetite of great numbers of people for this kind of literature —in itself, as we have seen, a symptom of the development of a

---

[22] See below, Chapter III, pp. 114–127.

historical consciousness. The "gap" between the best kind of "public history" and the best kind of "professional history" may be smaller now than perhaps at any time since the eighteenth century—because of the skill and the dedication of certain "nonprofessional" historians, *amateurs* of history in the best sense of that term. On the other hand, whenever the "gap" is wide nowadays this happens not so much because the historical vulgarizers have become much more vulgar (though some of them have) as because many professional specialists have become narrow and abstract, so that the *worst* kind of "professional history" is now again readable only with difficulty and as remote from the general reader as were the works of certain German antiquaries in the eighteenth century.

There is, then, a more important question: Are the two categories of "public" and "professional" history reasonable at all? Here I see eye to eye with Professor Plumb: we shouldn't be reconciled to their separate existence. Only, let me take another step to ask: Do they *really* have a separate kind of existence? Is there really a difference in kind between "public" and "professional" history? I do not think so: there being no difference between a fact and a historical fact, between a source and a historical source, between a document and a historical document, between a word and a historical word. Of course we need professional historians: but is there something in the method of the professional historian that definitely distinguishes him from other practitioners of his craft, in the sense in which a physician's method and training in medicine makes him distinct from the apothecary's?[23] Certainly in the "field" of modern and contemporary history there isn't. I can impart the "method" of historical research to a group of intelligent students in about twenty minutes. The rest is experience: experience in reading quantities of history, experience in understanding their differing qualities, experience in knowing something of the world and of the varieties of human motives, experience in writing, experience in how to quickly wade through haystacks of print as one is attracted by the magnetism of certain needles, experience of what to look for and of what to disregard. As

[23] Nowadays, when thousands of poets are striving for doctorates in literature, we must keep reminding ourselves that there is something absurd and ridiculous about this business. To have a doctorate in history is, of course, neither absurd nor ridiculous. What *is* absurd and ridiculous is the idea that a historian cannot be a historian unless he has a Ph.D. in History: exactly as absurd as to say that every poet ought to have a Ph.D. in Poetry.

Burckhardt said, *bisogna saper leggere*—one must know how to read. That is about all. It requires lots of time and a certain kind of maturity. It is because of the time at his disposal, which is consequent to his academic occupation, that the professional historian is somewhat ahead of the amateur: he is (or, rather, he ought to be) acquainted with most of the written material which is pertinent to his subject. That in virtue of his academic background he knows better than the amateur what to *do* with this material is yet to be demonstrated.

In a democratic society the professional historian certainly ought to have a strong sense of responsibility for "the public"—which is just what is becoming rare nowadays when so many professionals write mostly to impress other professionals. But beyond this evident statement of the historian's responsibility there is yet another argument against the strictly professional concept of historical studies. This is that the professional historian who compiles details or writes monographs mostly (which, in practice, means only) for other professional historians performs a service which is hardly worth while at all—while even the most specialized paper by a professional scientist may have ultimately an important public and pragmatic function. The reason for this condition is that the professional historian must write—indeed, he does write—in everyday language. Thus even the most recondite research paper or monograph is potentially open to the public. If he thinks that he doesn't write for the public he is profoundly mistaken. He uses public language. There is no other language for him.

That this condition is fraught with great cultural responsibilities should be obvious. I am sometimes surprised how seldom historians are conscious of this blessed responsibility of their profession: of the circumstance that history does not, as yet, have a professional language, a jargon, of its own. (At times I suspect that certain historians are hankering for one.) The notion of history being one of the "humanities" may have a venerable, fuddy-duddy, antiquated sound to many people in our era of the "social sciences;" and yet history was readmitted to the academic humanities only relatively recently.[24] This, however, is not the point. What a developing

---

[24] Richardson: "There is a story that when A. F. Pollard [1869–1948] once prophesied that there would come a day when there would be many professors of History in the University of London, those who heard him laughed disdainfully."

recognition of the historical form of thought means is not merely a return to an older humanism but an advance toward a new one, which differs from the humanism of the First Renaissance precisely in the sense that whereas the first humanism was classical, the second one is historical.

Of course it is not enough to say this. In the third quarter of the twentieth century the conditions of our civilization are really too forbidding for me, in my capacity of a history teacher and history writer, to simply say "I Am a New Humanist" and leave it at that. I, too, am affected by the critical problems of our historical condition and of our thinking; and it is, too, my consciousness of these conditions that led me to certain philosophical recognitions. This is not a unique experience. During the last fifty years a growing number of historical thinkers have addressed themselves to philosophical problems of history; and recently we have acquired a group of specialists on these subjects, something that I consider to be another awkward consequence of specialization. But what I am concerned with is not a philosophy of history but historical philosophy; I am attempting to deal not so much with the knowledgeability of history as with the historicity of knowledge. *What Is History?* is the title of a recent (1961) book by E. H. Carr, dealing with some of these subjects, and while his emphasis should read: what is *history?*, what *is* history is what interests me.

(7) Our interregnal condition

To sum up, therefore: the appetites of all kinds of people for all kinds of history have been increasing at the same time when the aspirations of professional historians have become more specialized. My view of the future of professional historianship is obscure. At least in the near future its development will be probably inseparable from the general development of meritocracies, meaning professional aristocracies composed by intellectuals and technocrats, in new and short-lived status societies where distinctions of formal education will replace the earlier distinctions of wealth and of birth. I have a profound distaste for this prospect: but, fortunately, it is not with this that I am principally concerned. My interest rests with the broader issue, with the growth of historical consciousness beyond the confines of professional historiography. My view of this broader issue is clearer: that the appetites of all kinds of people for all kinds of history will grow, of this I am almost sure.

What are the sources of this phenomenon? I said earlier that I do not think that they are simply attributable to nostalgia. Nor do I think that what we are facing is merely another recurrent wave of interest in historical literature, of the kind which happened in western Europe in the 1750's or in the 1820's. I believe that *this* is something different. It is an appetite for a particular kind of realism. It is fed by the half-conscious feeling that the historical form of reconstruction is one of the few things nowadays that can give people a particular mental connection with reality. This, I believe, is the principal reason behind the success and the very genesis of the new and twentieth-century genre of "documentary" accounts of past episodes. Whatever the enduring value of books such as *The Longest Day* or *The Last Hundred Days* or *Is Paris Burning?* they are unquestionably a kind of historical writing which is different from the historical novels as well as from the popular histories of the last century; they are different, too, from the historical novels and the popular histories following the First World War. Considering, thus, the evolution of popular historical literature, isn't it arguable that the tendency is that of less and less sentimentalism, and more and more "documentary" realism? Aware as I am of the limitations of the "documentary" genre, I nonetheless welcome its existence, for it means that the desideratum implicit in Ranke's famous phrase *wie es eigentlich gewesen,* "as it really happened," which more than a century ago was meant to sum up the intellectual interests of professional historians, has now filtered down to large masses of people: it is they who are interested in readable but also reliable reconstructions of what "really" happened.

This phenomenon is part and parcel of our historical situation in the Western world. It reflects the growing disillusionment with whatever is called "modern"; it reflects, too, the beginning of disinterest in whatever is called "scientific." Whereas during the nineteenth century scientific thinking seemed to bring us into contact with things and matters and perspectives that were tangible, commonsensical, *real,* in our times more and more people find that "scientific" has often come to mean something that is not only impersonal but also abstract and unreal. We are still far from a situation when these sentiments shall be so widespread and popular that we shall witness their expressions in all kinds of actions: how much longer the present trends of technological development will continue in the West I do not know: what I know is that we are at the threshold of something new: that we may be outgrowing the scientific view of reality. One of the clearest evidences of this assertion lies latent in some of the discoveries of modern physics. These have been, up to now, hardly considered by historians at all. I shall devote most of the last chapter of this book to them. There, too, I shall have to say something of the tremendous obstacles heaped together by vested interests and held together by ingrained habits of thought which obstruct and delay the process whereby new and fundamental recognitions of realities filter down to more and more people. I beg my readers' leave for this postponement of the common-sense illustrations of these evolving historical conditions to the last chapter, which is where they belong. Here I am concerned with our historical situation only inasmuch as it involves our thinking.

What is unique in the twentieth century is that we *think* that we live in an intellectually revolutionary age—when, so far as ideas go, this is not really so: during our democratic interregnum, all superficial impressions and the extraordinary rapidity of external communications notwithstanding, the movement of ideas has been remarkably slow. "Our minds are lazier than our bodies": La Roche-foucauld's maxim is at least as true in the twentieth century as when it was written, three centuries ago. Only this laziness no longer means a tranquil acceptance of stagnation but, rather, of current routines—routine categories and routine directions—of thought. For, with few exceptions, we have been moving on by the momentum of nineteenth-century ideas of "progress"—which is why the movement of ideas has become so slow; which is why "progressive" is *the* most unexceptionable adjective and "reactionary" *the* most universally condemned one, on both sides of the Iron Curtain. Yet many of our experiences in the twentieth century should have shown us that many of our "progressives" have been doing not much more than projecting the continuation of accepted categories of thought, whereas those who have "reacted," in various ways, against the scientific-progressive-mechanical views of human nature and of the universe have often demonstrated a better kind of insight into our tendencies and problems. Even now the engineer who forecasts the ten-lane superhighway or skiing trips to the moon or poetry written by a computer is being called by many people A Daring Mind, An Innovator, A Progressive—even though it is obvious that in more and more instances of living experience more superhighways and more teaching machines and increased mechanization *do not really work:* or, at least, they do not work at all in the ways in which we have been told they would work.

But this is beginning to be recognized by millions of people; in an uneasy fashion they are beginning to *feel* the increasing sense-lessness of "progressive" futurism. How rusty, how corroded our dreams of the future have already become! Here is an instructive example: leaf through old magazines in a library, looking for those —until recently—frequent features of theirs, those pictorial articles entitled "How We Shall Live Twenty (or Thirty, of Fifty) Years from Now," joint efforts of sub-editors and the staff artists, usually presided over by some respected scientist from some Franklin Institute. There was a significant change in their performance sometime around the last world war. Most of the futuristic articles, with their inventive drawings, were reasonably prophetic before the thirties: they showed features that have actually come into being. Like the science fiction of the nineteenth century, beginning with the Verne and the Robida school, these articles used to show airplanes, dirigibles, submarines, helicopters, skyscrapers, cities brilliantly lit by night, transatlantic journeys in hours, houses scientifically heated and cooled, women wearing pants (the few things in which these projections have usually gone wrong were universal disarmament, and the railroad over or under the Bering Sea). It is instructive to compare the reasonably accurate record of these earlier, childish, imaginative projections with the more earnest, "scientific," and pretentious magazine articles composed during the last thirty years ("How the U. S. Family Will Live after the War"; "Our Future Cities"; "U.S.A. 1965") which are usually very wide of the mark. They portray housewives who have hardly any chores left, no traffic jams, the family helicopter in addition to dream cars, a vast panorama of leisure, electronic (this pseudo-word having replaced the more prosaic "electric" in America around 1935) machines doing most of the work, bright-colored, resplendent, hygienic cities serving generations of free, informal, progressive, science-minded people. But most of this did not happen; and many people sense that it is no longer bound to happen in this way. (Perhaps this is the reason why, at least in the United States, the number of these kinds of magazine articles has been diminishing in recent years; probably this is the reason why the futuristic and "progressive" features of

world's fairs, from Chicago in 1893 to New York in 1939, seem to
have appealed to all kinds of people, whereas the New York World's
Fair of 1964–1965 was, in this respect, too, a flop.) The magazine
writers, together with the daring minds and the exciting people, have
been wrong: because of the laziness of their minds, because of the
captivity of their intelligent imagination by routine and outworn
categories, because they have been predicting and projecting merely
the continuation of what has been going on. . . .

On the highest level of creative intelligence the progressive ideology was dying out as early as the 1890's. Two generations and two
world wars later certain doubts about the automatic and beneficial
march of Progress began to appear, here and there, in the hearts and
minds of millions of people. After 1945 people knew that perhaps
for the first time in history it has become possible by scientific
methods to destroy the larger portion of mankind and perhaps even
all life on earth. Thus, for the first time in the modern period of history, a growing number of people in the West have felt some kind
of wish to limit the progress of technology, at least in some fields.
At the same time the reaction against the earlier, optimistic concepts
of human nature which had followed the First World War in Europe
spread to the United States, too, in the form of a deep-seated psychic
uneasiness. The principal intellectual element in this uneasiness has
been the new recognition that even the materialist certitudes were
crumbling. It is only natural that people should be confused when
their accepted institutions and truths, their categories of thought and
concepts of life, show cracks in their foundations. ("Sea-sickness,"
Samuel Butler wrote, "is the moral pain at seeing our converts escape
us.") There is an immense fragmentation of knowledge; the power
of concentration weakens, sometimes fatally; there is feverish activity but without purpose, efficiency becoming fret and fuss, running in
circles; private anarchy and public over-organization abound. Once
large and inspiring words—Liberty, Freedom, Democracy, Justice—
are losing their meanings; the meanings of other terms change, it
appears that about more and more things the Opposite of Everything may be true, that the existing state of affairs might be best
expressed through paradoxes, that satire even illuminates less and
less, since serious Facts are often more absurd and ridiculous than
their exaggerated Fiction could be. These are the marks of an interregnum.

At the time when this is written a recognition of some of these matters has become popular in the United States. This is in itself an important development, this—temporary or permanent?—abandoning of the typically American creed of rhetorical optimism. Whether this marks the maturation of the American mind or a prolonged lapse into destructive despair I cannot tell. But I believe that the self-appointed diagnosticians and analysts of this phenomenon now err rather on the side of facile pessimism than of optimism. I am thinking of the now gradually crystallizing national character of the American people; and I am thinking of what is even more important, of the condition that the present climate of disillusionment involves no longer only the categories of Religion and of Morality but also the myths of Science and of Progress; and I, for one, consider this to be a potentially salutary phenomenon. I do not only disagree with Lord Snow about the existence of Two Cultures (one culture is enough); I see a promising portent in the condition that many intelligent people nowadays are not very much interested in science; that some of them nourish an inner skepticism toward "scientific" claims (even though they are seldom brave enough to admit this); and I find it quite heartening that millions of people show signs of having already become bored—yes, bored—with the otherwise impressive achievements of men whirled around the earth in "space." All of these things, to my mind, may mark another phase of our "internalization," meaning a further deepening of our self-consciousness. For self-consciousness and self-knowledge are marks of the historical evolution of the Western mind in the twentieth century: man turning inward rather than outward, the recognition that he is facing himself, alone.

This existential condition provides the key to the few really meaningful intellectual developments of the century: to the recognition that all philosophy is, really, epistemology now; that science can no longer be separated from the scientists whose statements are, really, statements about our statements of knowledge; and that the questions of history are concerned, really, with the conditions of our historical knowledge.

(8) History the new humanism?

We have entered the interregnum. The end of the Middle Ages came together with the development of communications: of external as well as of internal communications. What we are facing now, toward the end of the Modern Age, is the very opposite development: the breakdown of internal communications, a development that in many places, and on many levels of life, has already begun. We can fly across continents in hours, telephone phrases and televise images from one end of the world to another in a matter of minutes: but at the same time the very contact of personal understanding between people and people, among artists, scholars, writers, and readers, between neighbors, friends, and lovers, and sometimes even within families, is becoming confused, meaningless, weak, often breaking down.

I think that this is a temporary phenomenon. In any event, many symptoms of widespread intellectual confusion had occurred during the last great interregnum, three to five centuries ago. But history does not repeat itself. One distinct feature of our interregnum is that through excessive applications of scientific methods we may destroy ourselves. Another distinct feature of our interregnum is the condition that we may, historically thinking, recognize its existence. We know, *to some extent,* what is happening to our civilization— and this is something that our ancestors at the time of the Renaissance or at the end of the ancient world did not know. There are great potential dangers latent in this intellectual condition: for the notion of inevitability furthers the very progress of something that seems inevitable. Even more than the passing of the Middle Ages, the passing of the Modern Age has been inseparable from the idea of its passing. On the other hand we *may*—I am not saying that we *will*—confront our interregnum through our better understanding of ourselves: through the actual recognitions and the potential realism of our historical consciousness. The now present coexistence of widespread historical thinking with widespread intellectual confusion is unique: for, while intellectual confusion is characteristic of every great interregnum, historical thinking may be our principal heritage from the last three or four centuries, from "the Modern Age," "the bourgeois age," "the last age of reason," whatever we may wish to call it.

And here we may recognize another distinct condition of our evolving historical consciousness. I believe that now, in the second half of the twentieth century, our attitudes toward the bourgeois past are undergoing a subtle but significant shift, something unique in the history of historical thinking. Five hundred years ago the Renaissance generations turned sharply against the Middle Ages: the humanists rediscovered not Aquinas and not even Abelard but Seneca and Plato, not Notre Dame but the Pantheon. But we, literally sick and tired as we are of the present cultural chaos, are not inclined to jump *two* steps back, over the Modern Age to the Middle Ages. Four hundred years ago Montaigne wrote: "We know the Roman Capitol before we know the Louvre, and the Tiber before the Seine." This is not so now; the opposite is true for most of us; we know Napoleon better than we know Julius Caesar.

For long centuries after the Renaissance had turned against the Middle Ages *medieval* had a pejorative meaning, and *gothic* was nearly synonymous with *vandal* and *barbarian*. Centuries had to pass until *gothic* received a new meaning, losing much of its pejorative sense: this happened at the time when new historical recognitions of medieval institutions, aesthetics, and art developed anew. Something similar may be happening to the word *bourgeois*, which is losing some of its pejorative sense now, a little more than a century after 1848.* We react to certain Victorian matters differently from our fathers forty years ago; and, unlike our forefathers four hundred years ago, we do not reject the epoch immediately preceding ours as gothic or barbaric; we are inspired as we encounter the great common sense of a Dr. Johnson, the beautiful verities of a Corot. Thus Proust, that very bourgeois Hamlet of the pen, with all of his aristocratic aspirations, rediscovered not Byzantium but Vermeer. Thus we experience subtle intellectual delights of recognition in reading Trollope. Thus, forty years after the mechanical revolutions of modern art and the vulgarity of modern furniture burst forth from the bohemias and the factories, sensitive people hanker after the luminous realities of Hobbema or of Robert Adam —*after the durability of their goods*, in the broadest sense of the term.

There are many reasons for this tendency, one of them being that the reaction against the bourgeois epoch, in Europe especially after the First World War and in America especially after the Second World War, was often so violent that it has become repellent. But a deeper reason is our widespread historical consciousness. We understand the Modern Age better than the people of the Renaissance understood the Middle Ages; we find the Modern Age more interesting because we know more about it; and it is also because we know more about it that we find it more interesting.

Three hundred years ago, as the modern idea of *progress* and the modern idea of *history* were crystallizing in their minds, some of our ancestors in western Europe developed a new view of the future, together with a new view of the past. During the centuries which followed, the progressive development of our vision of the future outraced the development of our vision of the past—until very recently we have become more skeptical of this kind of vision of the future, so that that Other Thing, our view of the past, may be catching up. We must recognize this condition, the *historical* evolution of our concepts of science and of progress: for if we are so stupid as to tackle the idea of progress and the meaning of science without considering the history of scientific thought and the history of the idea of progress, we shall soon find that we are face to face with the same kind of childish perspective as were the biologists of the eighteenth century who, as Owen Barfield put it in *Poetic Diction,* "attempted to tackle the variety of natural species as though there were no such thing as evolution."

Three hundred years ago our modern concept of history and the first synthesis of our scientific concept of the world were completed about the same time when the separation of historical and of religious and scientific thinking had begun. Three hundred years later we may be coming around to terminate this separation. We are outgrowing some of our standard intellectual "problems," at least in the West, where the conflict between science and religion has become outdated; and it is at least possible that history and religion, and history and science, may be brought together, but on a higher level. It is, for example, historical thinking that provides us with the best explanation of the chaotic development of scientific thinking during its last phase; and it is not impossible that as we struggle through a tremendous jungle of dying concepts and half-truths, many convergent paths in science, history, religion may emerge before us: there are certain discernible symptoms that point in these directions.

Meanwhile we must struggle along, conscious of the interregnal condition in many minds, one of the symptoms of which is the coexistence of two contradictory sets of beliefs in many heads. Leaving aside the interesting question whether it is not Doubletalk which results in Doublethink even more than Doublethink leads to Double-talk, we may recall some of the features of the intellectual history of the last interregnum, including the kind of Early Doublethink that existed in the minds of some of the greatest thinkers between 1450 and 1700: for it was not merely a kind of politic lip-service to the established Powers that made Descartes pay homage to God in his prefaces or that made Kepler appeal to the Trinity. Those theologians of the University of Paris who, sometime in the fifteenth century, were reputed to have obtained, for the first time, the permission to measure the weight of the soul (they weighed a criminal before and after his execution and came up with a figure, of course): was this the moment when the Middle Ages ended? was it the beginning of the Modern Age? was this the last step in the degeneration of medieval theology? was it the primitive beginning of the scientific method? I think it was all of these things—just as it is useless to argue whether the Kinseyites and the cybernetists represent the last phase in the degeneration of the modern scientific method or the beginnings of a new kind of Far Western Buddhism. If civilization survives at all, our great-great-grandchildren will laugh at those American scientists who in the 1950's made scientific studies of the placebo and ended up by themselves believing that certain categories of non-drugs have stronger medicinal qualities than have others. When that day comes, Science will have regained some of its earlier, more spacious, and more reasonable sense of human Knowledge. Until that time we shall have to face the condition that science is the kind of sacred cow which theology was five hundred years ago, and it is history which is closest to a new humanism.

Near the end of the Middle Ages dogmatism was sliding toward scientism; near the end of the Modern Age scientism is sliding into dogmatism. Does this mean that the historians will now be the new humanists, just as during the Renaissance some of the humanists were the first new historians? Yes and no. Historical consciousness may be the most precious heritage of the passing age, historical thinking may be the principal asset of Western civilization: but it is not enough to say this: historical thinking has been disorganized and weak and, what is most important, insufficiently conscious of itself, even among its professional practitioners; and historical consciousness, too, may be employed to deceive and poison the passions of peoples. Meanwhile the professionalized study of history, too, is deeply affected by the intellectual crisis of our interregnum. It must now consider not only the inherent dangers of specialization, the condition that its own specialists tend to know more and more about less and less; it must consider, too, a quite novel condition: the existence of great masses of people who tend to know less and less about more and more.

It is therefore especially in recent history that certain concepts and techniques of professional historiography that were developed during the last two centuries are no longer adequate. "A new science of politics," Tocqueville wrote more than a century ago, "is indispensable for a new world." (No matter how indispensable, it has not been forthcoming.) I now dare to add that new concepts of history are indispensable for us when, through the universal development of democracy, there is a change in the texture of history, involving a change in the very structure of events, implying, in consequence, changes in the requirements of historical description.

II

᯽

HISTORY IN THE DEMOCRATIC AGE

or the new texture of history

(1) Tocqueville on democratic historianship

The "new world," to which a "new science of politics" was to be indispensable, to Tocqueville did not merely mean the United States: it meant the world of democracy. Contrary to the general impression, his principal subject even in *Democracy in America* was democracy rather than America: he himself felt it necessary to point this out, especially in the second volume, which appeared five years after the first: indeed, the precise title, *De la démocratie en Amérique,* suggests it. In this second volume we find one of Tocqueville's few general observations on historianship, a short chapter entitled "Some Characteristics of Historians in Democratic Times." Even though we have recently witnessed a revival of Tocqueville's reputation, as well as a boom in studies of historical theory, these few pages have been neglected. This is a pity: for the forty-eight short sentences (fifteen short paragraphs in the Reeve-Bowen translation) of this brief chapter are certainly worth reading and rereading over and over again. They are so concise and succinct that I hesitate to sum them up here: still, I must do so because Tocqueville's propositions will serve very well for the starting point of this chapter.

In line with his usual method of rhetoric Tocqueville sets up a juxtaposition between "aristocratic ages" and "democratic ages," and he states his main thesis at the beginning. Historians who write in aristocratic ages (note that he writes *in*, not *of*: he takes it for granted that the historian's person and his circumstances are decisive) "are inclined to refer all events to the particular will and character of certain individuals; and they are apt to attribute the most important revolutions to slight accidents. They trace out the smallest causes with sagacity, and often leave the greatest causes unperceived." Historians who live in democratic times" exhibit precisely the opposite characteristics"; they do not deal much with individuals: instead, "they assign great general causes to all petty incidents." This is easily explainable. In aristocratic ages "a very small number of prominent actors . . . occupy the front of the stage, arrest attention and fix it on themselves," which gives historians an exaggerated impression of their importance, at the cost of neglecting the lives of the multitudes. The opposite impression is given by historians of democratic ages, when the influence of certain individuals becomes obscured, as "society would seem to progress by itself through the free and willing cooperation of all the people who compose it."

Up to this point these are the sweeping generalizations of a magisterial mind. But there is more to this short Tocqueville chapter, in the second half of which he launches into what, to him, is the heart of the matter. The danger is not only that historians of democratic ages will emphasize what is general, at the cost of neglecting what is exceptional: latent in this condition there is another, more dangerous, tendency: the emphasis on "general causes" obscures and weakens the principle of human free will. "A cause sufficiently extensive to affect millions of men at the same time . . . easily seems as if it were irresistible." For historians of democratic ages, therefore, "it is not enough to show what events have occurred; they wish to show that events could not have occurred otherwise." Now Tocqueville rises to his conclusions which, as so often with him, are really moral exhortations: he warns against "this doctrine of necessity, which is so attractive to those who write history in democratic ages," for its general acceptance by the public will lead to moral apathy, paralyzing the functions of personal judgment and of free will.

Thus Tocqueville who, unlike his conservative contemporaries, detected in democratic individualism less of a tendency toward anarchy and disorder than toward apathy and conformity, foresaw the natural penchant of the democratic mentality for deterministic philosophies. This chapter reflects not only his great clairvoyance: it suggests elements of his historical philosophy, which has not received the attention it deserves. The reasons for this relative neglect are numerous, one of them being that only recently has this uncategorizable thinker become recognized, here and there, as a historian and not only as an aristocratic sociologist or a political thinker. Yet within the large and scattered body of Tocqueville's writings (very much including his letters) there lie the elements of an exceptionally coherent and vital historical philosophy: indeed, I believe that among the four premier historical thinkers of the nineteenth century the quality of Tocqueville's vision outranks Ranke's and Acton's and perhaps even Burckhardt's. The reason why I am making such a statement here is not an excursion from the main corpus of this book in order to pay homage to a thinker whom I have for long admired: it is, rather, that Tocqueville is very relevant to its theme, dealing as it does with history in the democratic age. Whereas Ranke laid down many of the canons of modern historical research, Tocqueville attempted to penetrate beneath the surface of political history to the opinions and sentiments of peoples; whereas Acton regarded history as the story of liberty, Tocqueville saw modern history as the history of evolving democracy; and, though he was not a professional historian, his insight into the new problems of history in democratic ages was profounder than either Ranke's or Acton's. It is significant that while Acton did not go much beyond seeing in Tocqueville an exceptionally intelligent political thinker, regarding him as a conservative liberal, the man who went further and did not hesitate to put Tocqueville among the three greatest political philosophers of all times, ranking with Aristotle and Machiavelli, was Wilhelm Dilthey, whose work, as we have seen above, in 1875 marked the beginning of the historical reaction against the deterministic philosophies of the nineteenth century and who was one of the first philosophical architects of the modern idea of consciousness. I, then, believe that Tocqueville's importance as a historical and social and political thinker transcends even Machiavelli's: Tocqueville, in my opinion, is *the* premier thinker of the now evolving democratic age, whose insights will remain as meaningful for ourselves and for our descendants as were Aristotle's philosophical categories for two thousand years of aristocratic societies.

"I have always said," Tocqueville wrote to Gobineau in 1857, shortly before he died, "that it is more difficult to stabilize and to maintain liberty in our new democratic societies than in certain aristocratic societies of the past. But I shall never dare to think it impossible. And I pray to God lest He inspire me with the idea that one might as well despair of trying." In the above-mentioned chapter, twenty years earlier, he wrote that the causes of historical action "are infinitely more various, more concealed, more complex, less powerful, and consequently less easy to trace, in periods of equality than in ages of aristocracy, when the task of the historian is simply to detach from the mass of general events the particular influence of one man or of a few men."[1] This is of central interest to us. For Tocqueville realized not only that the task of safeguarding essential freedoms will present new and particular difficulties in democratic societies: he realized, too, that the task of their *historical description* will become especially difficult. And thus from these general statements of this premier philosopher of democracy to some of these specific problems of democratic historianship I now must turn.

(2) Far too much in print

The main problem of democratic history is the overwhelming quantity of its materials. Whereas the historian dealing with earlier times customarily faces a scarcity of documents, any writer who is serious in trying to reconstruct the history of anything during the last century and a half is plagued by a proliferation of documents of all sorts. This is the result of the abundant production of paper and of the technical development of reproductive printing of numerous kinds, ranging from carbon paper to electrotype. Like almost all of the features of the so-called Industrial Revolution these are causes only in a shallow sense of "cause," for they are, too, consequences of the development of democracy, with its vast increase in the numbers of people who read or, rather, who are supposed to read. The twentieth century suffers from an inflation of words: and printed paper multiplies in what seems to be a geometrical ratio of progression. Our manufacturers of printed stuff are always on the safe

---

[1] He continued: ". . . M. de Lafayette says somewhere in his *Memoirs* that the exaggerated proposition of general causes affords surprising consolations to mediocre statesmen. I will add that the effects are no less consolatory to mediocre historians: it can always furnish a few powerful reasons to extricate them from the most difficult part of their work, and it indulges the indolence or incapacity of their minds while it confers upon them the honors of deep thinking."

side: whereas in the Middle Ages and even in the early Modern Age there were seldom enough copies of anything worthwhile to go around, what we have to face is the tremendous wastage of copies of everything, from the remaindered best seller through the Sunday paper to the extra smudged carbon.*

In any event, the fantastic and overwhelming proliferation of typed and printed[2] material may suggest that the successor of the aristocrat is not the democrat but the bureaucrat. This is not a mere witticism. In the United States, for example, by 1956, more people were employed in administration than in industrial and agricultural production combined. This is a new phenomenon in the history of mankind: I believe that it is pregnant with enormous consequences, and that these will include radical and painful readjustments of historianship. The National Archives in Washington are said to contain many more millions of cubic feet of "material" relating to World War II than to all of the previous history of the Republic from 1789 to 1940. In the average American public or college library four-fifths of the books and periodicals date from the last thirty years. The very number of libraries multiplies alarmingly: it has become recently an American national custom for former Presidents or for their descendants to sponsor the erection of entire libraries the contents of which would consist primarily, if not exclusively, of the "materials" relating to the few years of their national administration. In addition to the standard kind of "documents," the contemporary historian must consider an entire array of new "sources": magazines, films, photographs, phonographic recordings, oral-history tapes, teletypes, etc. These developments are self-consciously applauded by historical associations. I, for one, cannot share in these pompous and circumstantial expressions of joy: at times I am tempted to wish that there were a long-term moratorium, forbidding the erection of presidential, indeed, perhaps of *all* new libraries. My reason for this impious desire is simple: the quantity of historical "material" has already become unmanageable.

Evidently, therefore, the openness of the archives is not such an

---

[2] But not handwritten. It is at least possible that the economy of style practiced in the eighteenth century was in some measure due to the physical effort of writing; surely the weakening of this practice is to some extent connected with the diffuseness of expression which is characteristic of the twentieth century. Another consequence of technological civilization is the barbaric deterioration of handwriting.

unquestionable boom for the democratic historian as people think. Since secrecy is particularly distasteful for democratic ideals (though perhaps not for the democratic temperament), modern governments, on all levels, pride themselves on the openness of their archives "to all qualified researchers," indeed, practically to all citizens. In the United States the official archives of the government are open after seventeen years, in West Germany all of what remained of the archives of the Reich before its collapse in 1945 are open, in Britain the rule of closure is fifty years which, according to A. J. P. Taylor, is "much too long." Perhaps. I said that the availability of all of these documents makes the historian's task unreasonably difficult. Others, no doubt, would say "challenging." Yet there must be *some* degree of reasonableness in the relationship between the difficulties and the challenge: the labors of Sisyphus were admittedly difficult, but it would take a strong Calvinist temperament to see them as "challenging." Few historians possess such a temperament nowadays, even though they may not be willing to admit it.

Yet admit it they must. They must come to terms with a condition which may be unprecedented in the history of history. This is that in an increasing number of instances it is no longer possible for a historian to be acquainted with all of the printed material which is reasonably pertinent to his subject. This historiographical turning-point may have occurred sometime in the first half of the twentieth century, in the United States a little earlier than in western Europe. Woodrow Wilson may have been the first President of the United States whose historical biography, principally because of the enormous volume of things printed, said, written, and recorded about him throughout the world during his lifetime, would present problems of documentation which are different not only in degree but perhaps also in kind from the problems which historians of previous Presidents had to face, since in dealing with such a mass of material the principal prerequisite is the intelligent understanding of how to disregard most of it without ignoring it altogether, since no Wilsonian bibliography can be anything but "selective." One of the principal requirements of professional historianship has been the more-or-less complete bibliography which the historian has been expected to append to his text, partly in order to assist future scholars, partly in order to prove his acquaintance with virtually all of the historical material relating to his subject. We may have to resign ourselves to a novel condition: all of us are necessarily historians now, and all of our bibliographies are necessarily selective.

Is this an admission of defeat? I do not think so. In reality, no historian has ever read *everything* that was pertinent to his subject, no matter how minuscule that subject may have been. There exist many excellent monographs that have come close to this ideal: their authors, however, would be first to admit that "complete" documentation is a chimera, an impossible desideratum. It is barely possible that a historian, dealing with a very much restricted subject, might have read every available document in certain archives, together with every historical book and every historical article which were relevant to it, and which were in print before his own work was completed. Yet even this imaginary possibility is contingent upon our acceptance of the traditional, but increasingly questionable, distinction between documents and historical documents, between histories and professional histories, between articles and historical articles (that is, articles printed in professional historical journals)—something that, again, implies that there is a distinction between facts and historical facts, and between words and historical words. If any of these distinctions ever made any sense, in this democratic age they certainly don't: when it is high time that we recognize how every record is a historical record, how every source is a historical source, potentially at least. And it is from this kind of recognition—which carries within itself the germs of the knowledge that all historical reconstruction is necessarily partial and incomplete—that a chastened and a more realistic view of the democratic historian's task may emerge.

Yet not to admit defeat means not to counsel complacency. There are many symptoms which suggest that the dangers of professional intellectualism are now the opposite from what people had thought: instead of pedantry, sloppiness; instead of the narrow burrowing of the parochial bookworm, the sleazy superficiality of the professional intellectual. Tocqueville's conservative contemporaries used to rail against the bookish pedants of the coming democracy, against the epoch of the specialist who would replace the more spacious epoch marked by the chivalry of the mind. But Tocqueville saw further: he foresaw that the successful professional intellectuals would be the prime idea-mongers. There still exist cultured people who think that our civilization is endangered by the propagation of barbarian specialists, of men unconcerned with anything beyond the tight confines of their intellectual interests, of intellectuals who know more and more about less and less. Yet the very type of the specialist bookworm is already passé: his image is a nineteenth-century one, out of a very bourgeois civilization: indeed, by now there is something old-fashioned and endearing about *ces vieux messieurs avec leurs fiches* —elderly gentlemen with their file cards. For there are at least two things to say for the genuine, even if narrow, specialist: first, that he is obsessed with his particular intellectual interest which is something more than a means of his personal or professional ambition; second, that anyone who seriously devotes himself to the study of one subject soon becomes aware of the limitations of his own knowledge. The single-mindedness, the unworldly devotion of the historian-specialist is, I am afraid, quite out of keeping with the spirit of the second half of the twentieth century, when professional intellectuals abound and when even professional historianship has become a lucrative occupation, attracting many people whose principal ability consists in their exemplification of those general ideas that are currently respectable in professional and intellectual circles.

To be a first-rate specialist nowadays requires a lifetime of application, reading, and perhaps even a dash of genius. I am, of course, speaking of first-rate specialists, not of self-appointed ones who may establish their reputation in an ephemeral manner. The latter condition has now become possible, since the tide of secondary works is so overwhelming that few people can keep up with the literature in their "field." (I have been saddened to find recently how often widely respected authors are ignorant of important works published about their subject, sometimes even within the same country.)

The difficulty of keeping up with the literature is, then, compounded by the condition that this proliferation of historical materials occurs in many countries simultaneously. The historian whose attention is already hopelessly torn by the publications pouring forth from the presses within his own country and his own language (the once quiet and agreeable task of opening his morning mail has become a disagreeable and guilt-ridden chore, as he must dispose of dozens of lists and announcements of books, many of which he feels he cannot afford to ignore) must keep track of many foreign publications, too. All this is in line with the increasing recognition of historiographical as well as of historical interdependence: meaning, first, that an American historian may read with profit an article by an Englishman in a German journal about certain events in Austrian history; second, that those particular events had been closely connected with developments in other countries at the time of their occurrence. . . .

An endless story, this unfolding of interdependence! As the democratic aspect of world history unfolds, it is not only "horizontal," involving various nations at the same time, but also "vertical," involving the fabric of an entire society. That it is in the very nature of democratic history that the traditional concern with government is no longer enough; that political history must be complemented by social history, with economic statistics, with data concerning public opinion; that history is no longer only the history of those who govern but of those who are governed, not only of minorities but of majorities, not only of political and cultural events but of social tendencies, categories of ideas, habits, fashions, fads current among millions of people—all of this sounds obvious to the dull point of a platitude. And yet it is a relatively recent development. As A. J. P. Taylor put it about one of the oldest democracies of the world, it was only during the First World War that "the history of the English state and of the English people merged for the first time." I have now tried to sketch what this means: new quantities of materials. How about their quality? We face the usual characteristics of inflation: the more there is of something, the less it is worth. Like all laws, however, the Law of Inflation is full of economic holes and of historical exceptions. We must take a closer look at the quality of democratic documents.

(3) Mutation in the quality of materials

Things are less durable than they used to be. (For one thing, the paper used for books and for correspondence is of a poorer and less durable quality than in the past.) But the deteriorating quality of our contemporary historical materials is, of course, an intrinsic condition: it involves the decay of the personal factor in its recorded expressions. Consider the example of a "primary source," say, a letter by a political personage. Until recently every letter, by no matter how important a personage, was either personally written, personally dictated, or at least personally signed. This is no longer so. Not only are the letters of political or social eminences, with few exceptions, composed by anonymous assistants or secretaries:[3] frequently they are not even signed by their alleged writers, since there exist ingenious holograph machines imitating inked signatures complete with dots and with blotches. Much of this is true of state papers, memoranda, speeches, and entire books, which are nowadays often the results of anonymous technical collaborators almost in their entirety. It is this sort of thing which involves a difference not merely in style but in content, and not merely in degree but in kind between, say, the memoirs of a Churchill and of an Eisenhower—as well as in much of the "primary material," that is, the papers left by their respective authors.

This deterioration in the authenticity of records is, of course, the inevitable result of technology and of bureaucracy. Contrary to what people may think, technology has made the work of the historian in trying to reconstruct the past more, not less, difficult. The telephoned (or the radioed) conversation or instruction remains nearly always unrecorded for posterity (one of the reasons why it will be more difficult to write about President Lyndon B. Johnson than about the "complex" and "secretive" Charles de Gaulle). Secrecy, together with impersonality, characterizes our age, in spite of its vaunted openness. In spite of our documentary mania there are reasons to believe that records of important decisions, of secret sources of information, of police operations are systematically suppressed and destroyed by democratic governments as much (if not more) as by totalitarian dictatorships. Whereas some of the clandestine connections and the secret intelligence of certain ministers of the seventeenth and eighteenth centuries have been recovered by historians, this is the kind of information which, I am afraid to say, will not survive the—probably transitory—period of open archives. It is a mistake to believe that secrecy was a phenomenon peculiar to aristocratic societies. It is instructive, for example, that research in the history of slavery in Brazil is difficult because the first republican government of that country in 1889 had the archives of slavery

---

[3] It is telling how the original meaning of these two terms has become reversed: assistants have become more important than personal secretaries, since it is they who may know the secrets while secretaries merely assist in routine and menial bureaucratic tasks.

burned in what Gilberto Freyre called "a republican auto-da-fé."
It is doubtful whether the archives of the FBI or the CIA will be
ever fully available to historians. The history of the twentieth century has its own Blank Spots. Consider, for example, the death of
these important personages in the 1940's: the Hungarian Vice-
Regent Stephen Horthy in 1942, Admiral Darlan in the same year,
King Boris III of Bulgaria in 1943, the Polish Premier General Sikor-
ski in the same year, Jan Masaryk in 1948, the Bulgarian Communist Dimitrov in 1949: probably two and perhaps as many as five
of them were murdered by intelligence technicians. What is new is
not the fact of possible assassination but the condition that in vast
bureaucracies secret deeds can be managed through subordinates,
through engineers and technicians of murder rather than by a tight
gang of criminal conspirators. That bureaucracy and technology expedited the horrors of the Third Reich is—or, rather, ought to be—
obvious.

The problem, thus, is the more complex one of impersonality
rather than that of old-fashioned secrecy. This is the case of the
ghostwritten book or of the committee memorandum, reducing the intrinsic value of the record: for the less personal the document, the
less historical it is. "Living movements," said Newman, "do not come
out of committees." Lenin said the same thing: "If we take our huge
bureaucratic machine, that huge pile, we must ask: 'Who is directing
whom?' The leading comrades take shelter behind committees. Nobody knows what is going on, who is responsible; everything is
mixed up. . . ." This applies to America as well as to Russia: go and
find the origins of Politburo decisions, go and find the origins of
things such as the Eisenhower Doctrine. It is consequent to the
democratic character of our societies that the number of "important"
people and of their "policy-making" organizations multiplies. The
result is a fantastic amount of duplication in the "sources" which the
painstaking historian may not afford to neglect since there might be
at least one golden needle of vital information in every bureaucratic
haystack. This is not only true of democratic states: the history of
National Socialist Germany shows how even in such a centralized
totalitarian Führer-state important policy-making agencies prolif-
erated, and that they often acted rather independently from each
other. The contemporary diplomatic historian, for example, must
look at the papers of various, and often ephemeral, semi-diplomatic

agencies, committees, missions, *ad hoc* groups, since the records of the foreign offices, with all of their inflated paperwork, no longer suffice. George Kennan dealt with this condition in his *Russia Leaves the War,* even though he was reconstructing the strands of the relatively thin fabric of Russian-American relations in 1917–1918. In *The Decision to Intervene* he returned to "the problem that is bound to beset diplomatic historians in increasing measure . . . the huge number and complexity of contacts between the bloated governmental bureaucracies and the stupendous volume of the written record to which they have given rise. In these circumstances it becomes simply unfeasible to attempt to permit the sources to tell their story. The historian has no choice but to simplify, to generalize and to ask the reader to lean on his judgment."

Such an admission, by a thoughtful historian, is not altogether different from Samuel Butler's aphorism: "The test of a good critic is whether he knows when and how to believe on insufficient evidence." Let me repeat: the insufficiency of the democratic evidence exists not only because of its inflated quantity but because of certain inherent weaknesses in its quality: for the impersonality is implicit not only in the anonymity of authorship but also in the often lifeless language of the heaps of papers left behind these complex institutions. Historians of democratic ages, therefore, face problems of authenticity that involve not only the writings but the very opinions of men, problems that are not only textual and technical but personal and moral. The kind of "hermeneutical" knowledge of which Dilthey spoke, meaning the capacity of a kind of profound insight into the nature and character of a document, is required of contemporary historians more than ever before. (This is, at any rate, something quite different from the "Content Analysis" whereof the computerizers and the cybernetists nowadays prattle.) Anyone who knows anything about life in totalitarian countries should know how not only personal opinions and feelings but significant oppositionist propositions may be concealed behind the verbiage of the official public language. And not only in totalitarian countries: for impersonality is perhaps only a consequence of the complexity which is characteristic of the democratic personality, all of the rhetoric to the contrary notwithstanding. "Man is born free," Rousseau wrote, "and everywhere he is in chains." This is all wrong: man is born in a state in which he is utterly dependent on others; he gains his freedom and independence as he grows up; and often it is this very condition of free choice and independence, with its inevitable consequence of personal responsibility, that he cannot bear. Hence the secretive nature of democratic rhetoric, which conceals at least as much as it reveals. Anyone who has lived in a democratic nation ought to know how, despite the seemingly (but only seemingly) unbridled vocabulary and informal grammar of democratic rhetoric, the communication of persons in such societies is governed by hidden and complex conventions. There have always been, of course, gaps between what people said and what they thought. But now it seems that there is a difference not only between what they say and what they think but also between what they think and what they believe—or, rather, between what they think they think and what they really think. "Now I'm going to tell you what I really think" —isn't this a typically American expression?

It would be very wrong to assume that aristocratic statesmanship abounded in frankness: the contrary is true. Our problem, however, is not so much the increase of outright lying but that of doubletalk. There are many reasons to believe that, together with the increasing complexity of modern life, and with the increase in the frequency and the quantity of external communications, the thinking processes of modern man have become more complex: that, contrary to what Freud and Jung proposed, it is not so much the cultivation of a *persona* as the perfection of a kind of public rhetoric which has become the principal skill in democratic ages—just as, contrary to what was current during the Victorian Age, it is not so much hypocrisy as it is insensitivity to untruth which among us abounds. The principal misconception of the older democratic social philosophies was that "simple people are simple." In reality, they are more complex than great men. Since this is not a treatise in social psychology I cannot elaborate this matter further, save to sum up how this condition relates to the historical record: and this is that when people are complex their expressions tend to be complex—which, then, is inherent in the documentary residue they leave behind. And it is in this sense that the historian dealing with Wilson has a more difficult task than in dealing with Napoleon; that the diplomacy of a Dulles presents problems which are more complex than those of a Talleyrand; that, in many ways, Churchill was not really "complicated" when compared to the "simple" Chamberlain; that it is easier to reconstruct certain thoughts of Theodore Roosevelt than those of Dwight Eisenhower.

It is this mutation in the quality of historical materials, even more than their cancerous multiplication, which suggests that we reconsider the hitherto sacred professional canon established by Ranke and B. G. Niebuhr about the indispensable nature of "primary" documents. "When Ranke began to write," G. P. Gooch said, "historians of high repute believed memoirs and chronicles to be primary authorities. When he laid down his pen, every scholar with a reputation to make or to lose had learned to content himself with nothing less than the papers and correspondence of the actors themselves and those in immediate contact with the events they describe." True: but since then new questions have arisen. Are some of these actors really in immediate contact with the events they describe? Are their notes and correspondence really their own? Are these, then, really "primary" sources? There may be reasons to reconsider the standard historiographical distinctions between manuscripts and printed materials, between primary and secondary sources. Heeren's old categorical differentiation of the former (*Quellen*) from the latter (*Hilfsmittel*) makes less and less sense for us; so does the professional mania of French academic historians for *documents inédits* —unpublished documents[4]—now, when our historiographical requirements are affected together with the very meaning of *wie es eigentlich gewesen.*

(4) Mutation in the texture of history itself

What does all this mean? Documents are, after all, the residues of life, the remnants of its expressions. Their mutation reflects the muta-

---

[4] On the other hand, the contemporary historian does have a new kind of "primary" source: the testimony of the "man-in-the-street" who witnessed certain events. This kind of *témoignages inédits* may be of great value for the history of this democratic age when it is indeed important to reconstruct what people thought and how they felt on certain critical occasions and in certain conditions. But these *par excellence* democratic "sources" must be handled with great caution. It is by no means sure that just because someone witnessed certain events his memory and his reconstruction of those events are reliable. Moreover, it is just this kind of testimony which it may be impossible to verify. The historian who deals with this kind of evidence must be, therefore, a man of exceptional probity, psychological introspection, and judgment: for all that he can do is rely on his judgment while the reader, in turn, must rely on his own.

tions of the processes of historical life. The change in the character of documents means that the texture of history has changed—something that is likely to happen even before historians catch up with its many implications.

This is perhaps most evident in the history of the United States. No great nation in the world has a more fully "documented" or "documentable" past, with documents and statistics covering the entire span of its constituted history. And yet a great history of the United States still remains to be written. The reasons for this condition are the very difficulties of democratic history. It is a condition of which thoughtful Americans themselves have been aware: "To write well and worthily of American things," Henry James wrote in 1871, early in his career, "one needs even more than elsewhere to be a *master.*"

What James may not have known was that his desideratum was (and still is) even more applicable to historians than to novelists. A few years after 1871 the German concept of professionalized and scientific historical research was taken up by some of the principal American universities; American historianship was coming of age; these practices spread quickly across the land. Yet, in spite of its many merits and eventual achievements, the methods of this kind of history may have been *especially* unsuited for the comprehension and the description of the main currents of the history of the American democracy. For one thing, these methods were particularly applicable to the study of the relations of predemocratic political societies. This was true of most of European history during the nineteenth century; the texture was still predominantly political: it was the history of states rather than of peoples. Three competent historical biographies—of Napoleon, Metternich, Bismarck—would furnish a substantial introduction to the hundred years 1795–1895 in Europe: three biographies—of Jefferson, Jackson, Lincoln—would not provide anything comparable for American history. Then, from Lincoln to Theodore Roosevelt, the history of the United States is largely devoid of great statesmen: yet at the same time the development of American industrial democracy, the peopling of the West, the immigration of masses of people are enormous, near-epic stories: social rather than political events, comprising profound changes in the national composition of the American people, mutations in national characteristics, habits, manners, morals, institutions, modes of thought and of speech during the fifty years after the Civil War. In dealing with the general history of such a period the emphasis must not lie with political events, including the dreary catalogue of party quarrels, verbose laws, second-rate figures, with their droning and often monotonous sequence largely determined by the mechanical framework of quadrennial elections, with their often artificially generated "issues."

American historians have been aware, of course, of the needs for a new kind of history which would serve a democratic civilization. From time to time claims were made and plans were laid for a New History, a scientific, democratic history of people rather than of governments or of upper classes. Yet, in spite of the heat and the public response generated around many of these attempts, they did not prove to be very durable. The principal reason for this lies within the American penchant for whatever is "scientific": for even those historians who became aware of the limitations of the older kind of history could not overcome that basic article of faith in "science"—an intellectual faith, with its hidden Anglo-American roots in Puritanism. In other words, while American historians, in one way or another, were aware of the new texture of history, they have not taken the other step in considering what these changes might mean for the structure of events. One of the effects of this condition is the recurrent tendency toward a kind of economic determinism, shared by Marxists and non-Marxists alike, leading, among other things, to a confusion of economic factors with social ones. But even when American historians, chastened by experience and by controversy, had been able to rise above the temptation of seemingly profound but, in reality, shallow economic interpretations—as, for instance, in dealing with the origins of the Civil War—the scientific chimera shone for many of them as brightly as before. This was of little help in dealing with American history, with its many elements hidden beneath the political and the legal superstructure of events, with its motive factors swaddled within the peculiar traditions of American rhetoric. Consider the antecedent political events of the Civil War, wrapped as they were within layers and layers of legal arguments (for the law is often a peculiarly American substitute for philosophy); there is a lofty trickiness in the Lincoln-Douglas debates which is very American; and the fundamental problems were, of course, much deeper than the legal, constitutional, political arguments. There is something puritanical and naïve in the expressions of those American historians (including

Southerners; e.g. Professor Avery Craven as late as 1942: scholars are returning to the study of the Civil War "as scientists and not as partisans") who for the last one hundred years have been professing to believe that the Truth about the Civil War would inevitably come forth once historians approach it with the pure mind and technical know-how of the scientist. It was through his study of American historians' interpretations of the Civil War during an entire century that Professor Thomas J. Pressly, a thoughtful American historian, reached his own conclusion—not without reluctance[5]—that historians may not be "as much agreed as they sometimes think they are in describing the 'facts' of an historical situation, and thus I favor a revision in present concepts and methods of historical research."

I shall say something about the historian and his "facts" in the next chapter. At this point I am dealing with the mutation of the texture of history in democratic ages, a kind of *Strukturwandel*, which many historians did not sufficiently comprehend, perhaps because of rather than despite their professional training. Let me say, however, that this condition has existed because of the deadening hand of certain now antiquated historiographical and philosophical concepts, and not because the professional training of American historians has been particularly inadequate. For example, native Americans who have devoted their lifetime to studying certain matters in the history of Europe, men of a long and venerable list, from Prescott to Mattingly, have not only proven themselves to be masters of their craft but they were very often better at it than were American historians dealing with the history of their native country, from Bancroft to Hofstadter. This is a curious phenomenon, quite different from the European experience, where many of the best scholars have been primarily attracted to the past of their own province, region, country, nation.

The United States has had great students of her society: not yet a great historian. There are certain American social novels—*Roderick Hudson, The Age of Innocence, Washington Square, The Great Gatsby*—which are, in a sense, historical "sources," more than mere background materials: for, beyond their respective literary merits,

---

[5] Introduction to the new paperback edition of his *Americans Interpret Their Civil War* (New York, 1965). Written in March, 1962, this phrase did not figure in the original Introduction, written in 1952.

they uniquely illuminate certain historical realities of American society. They deal with social tendencies and not with politics (Henry Adams's political novel *Democracy* is an interesting curiosity but rather a failure); and in the history of American democracy, perhaps until very recently, social developments were generally speaking even more important and more pregnant with consequences than were political events. This may be changing now. On the one hand, the traditions of the descriptive social novel may be disappearing. On the other hand, the historical consciousness of the American people is rapidly growing; and while certain amateur historians are making unexceptionable contributions to historical literature, there is a growing interest among the best professionals in cultural history, in the exceptional, disorderly, rich manifestations of the history of ideas in a democratic society. (William Leuchtenburg's work is an excellent example of this salutary trend.)[6] All of this is significant, since the texture not only of American but, in a sense, of all history is changing; only some of these changes appeared in the history of the United States before they become evident elsewhere in the world.

Does this mean that the history of the world is becoming "Americanized"? I do not think so. The development of social institutions is one thing; that of national cultures another; and the history of peoples is formed by their characters even more than by their institutions. Tocqueville's *Democracy in America* was a classic analysis, not a history: a correspondingly classic and profound history of the American people has not yet been written: for such a history will have to deal not so much with *democracy* in America as with the development of an *American* democracy. The American national character, the formation of which was interrupted by mass immigration beginning more than a century and ending more than forty years ago, is only now crystallizing. This is the particular experience of the United States: but there is a more general factor, too. This is that, all of the superficial experiences and impressions of "internationalism" notwithstanding, the national characteristics of *all* dem-

[6] Especially *The Perils of Prosperity* (Chicago, 1958). The history of the twenties, of course, lends itself especially to this kind of treatment: for that was the last decade when the social and cultural history of the American people was *in almost every way* more meaningful than the doings and the sayings of their politicians.

ocratic societies are crystallizing, because democracy nationalizes even more than it internationalizes, because our modern societies are almost without exception becoming more, and not less, homogeneous. Thus it is not only the influence of democratic institutions on national characteristics, it is, rather, the influence of national characteristics on democratic institutions which becomes *principally* significant now, when American democracy is no longer the only one, when there is an English, a French, a Belgian, a Scandinavian, even a West German democracy—societies whose institutions and laws may show certain similarities and convergences at the same time when their deeper national characteristics, diffused as they have become through most of the component parts of the nation, remain distinct and different.

This continued predominance of historical over sociological, of national and cultural factors over governmental politics, affects the history of what we still—somewhat euphemistically[7]—call "international relations." Not only must "international" history replace the narrower field of diplomatic history; as Professor Richard W. Van Alstyne has demonstrated,[8] the relations of nations were beginning to intertwine with the relations of states as early as two hundred years ago. After 1914, then, these relations of nations become supremely important, since they involve the relations of entire peoples, including the very images which nations form of each other. This is a field which has been hardly touched by historians even now:[9] it is a field which, however, ought to be of especial interest to American historians, since there are many symptoms which indicate that national and cultural, rather than political or ideological, preferences and dislikes (for example, Anglophilia and Anglophobia, Germanophilia and Germanophobia) were deeper factors in the sentiments and opinions of great masses of Americans (and I am not only speaking of Irish-Americans or German-Americans) than

[7] "International" was coined by Bentham. It has been considerably misused since: for, whenever people speak of international relations, international law, etc., they mean the relationship of states, not of nations. See below, Chapter V, pp. 194 ff.

[8] In the Preface of *Empire and independence. The international history of the American revolution*, New York, 1965.

[9] It has been scratched, here and there, by scholars of comparative literature. A superb, profound, and to some extent, pioneer study in this field is the recent work by René Rémond, *Les Etats-Unis devant l'opinion française 1815–1852*, in two volumes (Paris, 1962).

were their attitudes toward monarchy or dictatorship or their preferences for isolationism or internationalism. All of this requires a profound knowledge, by the historian, of the tendencies, and of the culture, of the rhetorical habits and of the thinking processes of his own people. The task of the national historian increases in depth: the traditional documentary reconstructions of surface history no longer suffice: still his principal problem is not how to become a social scientist: it is how to describe the history of a people.

(5) Who are "the people"?

Up to this point I have been mainly concerned with the essentially secondary phenomenon of documents: with the fact that in the democratic period of history there are more and more records, because more and more is being written as it is presumed that more and more is being read.* But the primary concern of democratic history lies with those who read rather than with those who write: the majority not the minority—the people. This is the principal difficulty: how to describe the lives of great masses of people, how to delineate the opinions and the sentiments of the majority— problems of historical reconstruction which exist in spite of (or, as I suggested, to some extent because of) the enormous and growing material deposited in open archives and in all kinds of libraries.

For the image of *the people*—obscured as it is by rhetoric, and obfuscated by statistics—is an elusive phenomenon. We live in an age of democracy, of popular sovereignty, of popular rule: but who *are* the people? Intelligent opponents as well as some of the proponents of modern democracy recognized that of Aristotle's three principal types of government—monarchy, aristocracy, democracy— the last one, government by the people, by the many, is the most difficult. But there is more to this. Rule by "the people" is not only difficult; it is also the most complex; and the most abstract. It is abstract because, while it is possible to find out, and later relatively easy to reconstruct, what a certain ruler wanted, or even what a ruling group wanted,[10] who can say what "the people" wanted— with any reasonable degree of certainty? Many dangers of modern

---

[10] Or, rather, what *they said they wanted*. But when do "the people" really speak? A statement by Napoleon is a statement by Napoleon: a statement by the people is, almost always, a statement made *in the name* of the people— a profound difference.

democracy exist precisely because of this abstractness, because of misconceptions of "the people." But this is not a problem of political theory only. It is a historical problem. Our histories are full of phrases such as "the people wanted," "people demanded," "the people overthrew the government." "The people" overthrew the monarchy in Paris in 1792, in 1830, in 1848, in 1870; in Berlin in 1918; in Rio de Janeiro in 1889; in Cairo in 1952 ... but is this phrase sufficient? Aren't we facing different events, different movements, different passions, different procedures, different *peoples*? I do not only mean Frenchmen, Germans, Brazilians, Egyptians: I mean different concepts of "the people": for the very idea of who "the people" are has changed during the last three or four centuries.*

The history of "the people," *le peuple, il popolo* during the last four hundred years is the development of a generally pejorative term to its present approbatory meaning. It is a story moving through four centuries, from Machiavelli to Mussolini. Machiavelli reaffirmed, in his way, the argument of *vox populi vox dei:* in many important matters the people are more constant than the prince, he wrote. But this was an indirect, a negative defense of the people: Machiavelli used it only to illustrate the dangers of wholly unlimited arbitrary rule. In the sixteenth century even the most forceful opponents of absolutism disdained, feared, rejected "the people." *Vulgus, plebs, populus* were nearly synonymous terms.* By the end of the century certain distinctions were beginning to form. A little later *populus* and *popularis* gained some respect, especially among certain Neapolitan writers. After the defeat of the first attempts at popular tyranny in France, Naples, England the populist argument faded: by the middle of the seventeenth century the more bourgeois idea of contractual government rose instead. As Isaac D'Israeli wrote in his *Amenities of Literature*:

> The history of the English "people," considered in their political capacity, cannot be held to be of ancient date. . . . [Henry VIII] was sufficiently enlightened in the great national revolution he mediated to desire to gain over the multitude on his side. . . . When Elizabeth ascended the throne, there was yet no recognized "public" in the commonwealth; the people were mere fractional and incoherent parts of society. . . . [Toward the end of her reign] there was now "a people," who might be worthy of entering into the views of the statesman; but it was a divided people. . . . But at the very time she was ruling them with

a potent hand, Elizabeth courted the eyes and the hearts of "the people" . . . she was it who first gave the people a theatre . . . she commanded that the awful tomes of Fox's "Acts and Monuments," a book written, as the author has himself expressed it, for "the simple people," should be chained to the desk of every church and common hall. . . . The advancement of general society out of its first exclusive circles became apparent when "the public" themselves were gradually forming a component part of the empire. . . .

Althusius, a radical German Calvinist whose influence on the democratic thinkers of Puritan England was considerable, mentioned "the people" with increasing confidence: yet he hated and feared the *plebs*. In France the Huguenot Hotman extolled the sovereignty of "the people" while he emphatically denied the rule of the majority. Even the English Levelers were apologetic on occasion: "We are for Government and against Popular Confusion," said Walwyn in his defense, "and though Tyranny is excessively bad, yet of the two extremes Confusion is the worst." Marchamont Needham, the extremist radical, insisted that "when we talk of the people, we do not mean the confused and promiscuous mass of men, nor those who have forfeited their rights by delinquency, apostasy or even neutrality." Halifax, the moderate Trimmer, meant by "the people" what we now would call the masses: he did say that *salus populi* was an important principle "but it is not altogether immoveable." The genius of politics, wrote Harrington, is peculiar to gentlemen: "an army may as well consist of soldiers without officers, or of officers without soldiers, as a commonwealth . . . consist of a people without gentry, or of a gentry without a people." The balanced system of order upon which his famous theory of Mixed Government rested had been upset, he thought, earlier in the century when the element of "popularity was running like a bowl down hill."

During the eighteenth century the image of "the people" acquired a sentimental value on occasion: and the same men and women who evoked *le peuple* in French employed the word in a good as well as in a bad sense. Yet we must keep in mind that when Saint-Simon spoke of "toute la France," he meant perhaps 100,000 people, 30,000 families; as W. H. Lewis put it, when Saint-Simon "begins a sentence with *even the common people,* he is talking of what we should call the middle classes." In 1789 the Anjou deputies blamed the riots in Paris on "that part of the people known under the name of populace." In England not even the radical commonwealth's-men used the term always in an approbatory manner: as late as 1770 only the demagogic Gordon and Wilkes spoke of "a party of the people": they, too, insisted, like Hobbes a century earlier, on distinguishing between "the people" and "the multitude" or "the mob" (a word that appeared first in 1688). The American Federalists were at times even more skittish than were Tories in England. ("Glory," said Bolingbroke, "is the only thing worth the ambition of the great, and what the voice of the people only can bestow!" John Adams' marginal comment was sarcastic: "Glory and popularity then are synonymous terms!") The *Federalist No. 10* wrote that the majority may be more dangerous than the minority: "The form of popular government . . . enables it to sacrifice to its ruling passion or interest both the public good and the rights of other citizens." (Note the distinction between "popular" and "public.") Yet George Mason, another Founding Father, said that "notwithstanding the oppression and injustice experienced among us from democracy, the genius of the people is in favor of it, and the genius of the people must be consulted."

But who were "the people"? At the time the issue was far from clear. Nor was it clear later to those historians of the nineteenth century who regarded the democratic revolutions in retrospect.[11] To Barnave in 1790 *le peuple* were those who were neither aristocrats nor bourgeois; Michelet in the 1840's often used *peuple* and *patriotes* interchangeably; what to conservatives or to demophobe liberals such as Taine were the "vile multitude" or the "canaille," to radicals or demophiles such as Michelet or Aulard were *le peuple* or *tout Paris*.* The terms *menu peuple* and *gens sans aveu,* employed by French conservatives during the nineteenth century, suggest by themselves that *le peuple* was no longer a pejorative term.* Slowly "the people" became an approved concept. This corresponded with the developing acceptance of "democracy,"[12] at least in western

---

[11] See below, p. 78. The recent studies of George Rudé about the composition of "crowds" in the French Revolution and in the first half of the nineteenth century are instructive in this respect.

[12] "Democracy," "democrat" became fully acceptable terms in the United States by 1830, in Britain around 1880, in western Europe before 1914. As Diana Spearman wrote in her *Democracy in England:* "In 1867 politicians

Europe and in the English-speaking nations. In 1831 even the radical Brougham defined "the people" as "the middle classes, the wealth and the intelligence of the country, the glory of the British name." In 1845 Disraeli still said to the Tories: "The Whigs invoke the people. Let us appeal to the nation." But by the middle of the century "the people" had become an approbatory term: indeed, so much so that the liberal broad-minded Dickens was vexed no longer with the insufficiency but with the possible falsifications of the term: in *Hard Times* he attacked "the national dustmen," that is, Members of Parliament, for their "abstraction called a People."

Thus it was about one hundred years ago that "the people," in the Western world, were finally recognized to be the principal category of the polity and the principal historical factor. This democratic development had two important consequences.

First, the appeal to "the people" was no longer the monopoly of the Left. Populism and the populist terminology often moved from its originally liberal and "Leftist" connotations in a "Rightist" direction, especially after 1900: in the Latin nations of Europe, for example, this development led from *L'ami du peuple* in 1790 through Proudhon to Mussolini's *Popolo d'Italia* in 1914. (In France it is significant that while *Le Populaire* was still a Socialist daily, the Fascist newspaper founded by Coty in the 1930's bore the title *L'ami du peuple*.) In the Germanies and throughout central and eastern Europe folkish and *völkisch* became Rightist rather than Leftist terms in the twentieth century. In the United States, too, it is at least arguable whether the Populist movement of the 1890's was still a movement of the Left: certainly some of its direct descendants, in the South and in the Midwest, from Bryan to Joseph R. McCarthy, had moved from the Left toward American versions of national socialism. In the history of political ideas we must recognize that the variations of national socialism after World War I were populist rather than reactionary movements, calling forth "the people" against what seemed to have been the an-

---

could still say that they were against the rule of 'mere numbers'; in 1884, although there were still men who were opposed to democracy, they were already considered as slightly eccentric. They were writers, professors, or soldiers. No active politician could any longer be against democracy, although it was not yet necessary to be enthusiastic about it. The Representation of the People Act, 1884, was not opposed by the Conservative party either in the Commons or in the Lords."

tiquated and corrupt systems of liberal capitalism and parliamentary government. And this recognition that "the people" were, more than often (though not always), illiberal rather than liberal, nationalistic rather than internationalist, led to the profound (though usually hidden) alienation of intellectuals from "the people"—a deplorable phenomenon, some of the most extreme consequences of which have occurred in the United States, in the principal democratic nation of the world.

Another consequence of the democratic development after 1850 was the appearance of sociology. The first proponents of this democratic discipline, from Comte onward, thought that the time had come to apply scientific methods to the study of society. Yet sociology was the consequence of great new numbers, not of great new methods—of the development of democracy rather than of science. The description, even more than the scientific study,[13] of majorities, of masses, of peoples became instructive and important. Did this mean—does this still mean—that sociology would eventually replace history, in the sense that while the latter is the study *par excellence* of aristocratic ages, the former is the study *par excellence* of the democratic epoch? This is what certain democratic social thinkers believed during the last one hundred years; and, even though they might neither know or admit this, this is what certain historians now imply as they apply themselves (and their grants) to the propagation of Quantification, Scientific Sampling, Data Processing, Correlational Mathematics, Content Analysis.[14] Yet this is not what has happened. Leaving aside the basic argument which I mentioned in Chapter I, about the essential differences between man's study of nature and man's study of man, that the very complexity of the latter ought to preclude undiscriminating applications to it of methods borrowed from the natural sciences, all I wish to say here is that the convergence of scientific sociology with scientific historiography has either not occurred at all or has led to all kinds of dead ends. What have been converging are historical sociography

[13] In England where the democratic development of society advanced faster than in France, the first thorough descriptions of all kinds of populations, including the working-class and the lower orders of society, by a series of earnest investigators, from Eden to Mayhew, appeared before the term and the practice of sociology became current. These descriptions are still very valuable and telling sources of information: they are sociographies, not sociologies.

[14] But the more motorized the historian the more pedestrian he may become.

and democratic history. During the last one hundred years conscientious historians have found it more and more necessary to practice a kind of sociography, to delineate the profile of an entire society at certain times, while conscientious sociologists have learned that their studies of societies must, by necessity, be historical and not merely statistical, dynamic rather than static, since the meaningful description of a society is at any time inseparable from the study of its development in time, that is, of its past.

What, then, historians and sociologists have had in common has been their growing preoccupation not so much with what "the people" do as with what they say and what they think. This brings us to a prime problem of democratic historiography: to the study of public opinion.

(6) The question of "public opinion"

"Opinion," says Shakespeare's *Henry IV*, "that did help me to the crown." "You may outwit this man or that," La Rochefoucauld wrote, "you cannot outwit all the world." Machiavelli as well as Burke, Napoleon and Metternich, Talleyrand and Tocqueville: dictators, absolutists, conservatives, aristocrats, all spoke of it in the same vein.[15] It is wrong to think that the reign of public opinion is a relatively recent, a democratic phenomenon. "Opinion," wrote Pascal, "is the Queen of the world."[16] In a broad sense this has always been true: the rule of public opinion is no more synonymous

[15] Napoleon: "Public opinion is an invisible power, mysterious and irresistible. Nothing is more mobile, nothing vaguer, nothing stronger. No matter how capricious, it is nonetheless truthful, reasonable and just, far more often than one would think." Metternich: "To despise public opinion is no less dangerous than to despise moral principles." Talleyrand in 1820: "In our time it is not easy to deceive for long. There is someone, who is cleverer than Voltaire, cleverer than Bonaparte, cleverer than any of the Directors, than any Minister in the past or in the future: and that person is everybody." Tocqueville in 1850: "It would, in fact, be a great mistake to think that the Tsar's immense power was only based upon force. It was founded, above all, on the wishes and the ardent sympathies of the Russians. For the principle of the sovereignty of the people lies at the root of all government, whatever may be said to the contrary, and is hidden beneath the least independent institutions."

[16] This once famous phrase is a truncated version of the passage in *Pensée* 82: "Je voudrais de bon coeur voir le livre italien, dont je ne connais que le titre, qui vaut seul bien des livres: *Della opinione regina del mondo.* J'y souscris sans le connaître, sauf le mal, s'il y en a."

with the rule of democracy than is the history of reason synonymous with the history of rationalism. (As Herbert Butterfield wrote about Ranke: "In his *History of the Popes* he repeatedly stresses the importance of public opinion, and says that we must not imagine that it only began to be operative in the nineteenth century.")

There is, however, a narrower and more definite meaning of public opinion which was the particular property of the nineteenth century. Our ancestors in the Western world a century ago distinguished between two admittedly overlapping but still distinct phenomena: between *public opinion* and *popular sentiment*. Even today the generally approbatory sense of the first and the somewhat pejorative implication of the second linger on.[17] There is, after all, a difference between "public" and "popular," and between "opinion" and "sentiment."* This distinction appears clearly in a passage written in 1821 by Blanco White in the English *New Monthly Magazine*. "The mob fury," wrote that radical writer about a horrible riot in Seville, "was blind, headlong, unhesitating, a loud popular cry which every individual is afraid not to swell with his whole might, and which, though it may express *the Feeling* of a great majority, does not deserve the name of public *Opinion* any more than the unanimous acclamations of an auto-da-fé. . . ."

The classic age of public opinion was the nineteenth, not the twentieth, century—more specifically, the first part of the nineteenth century, which was also the last golden age of political thought. Public opinion, then, in western Europe and to some extent even in the United States, meant the opinion of a politically conscious minority. It was after 1770 that the phrase *l'opinion publique* began to replace *l'esprit publique* in France; in 1780 Marie Antoinette, in 1784 Necker remarked the growth of the authority of *l'opinion publique*; in 1787 the notables assembled in the Parliament of Paris wrote this pompous sentence into their remonstrance: "Public opinion is rarely mistaken; it is rare that men receive impressions contrary to truth." Between 1793 and 1800 the term, translated from the French, appeared in Germany through the writings of Schlegel and Wieland. In 1801 Bonaparte instructed his personal librarian

[17] The difference between "public" and "popular" is old; it is embedded in the instincts of most Western languages. It is not an etymological accident that we find it natural in English to speak of the "animal population" but not of the "animal public" of a place. Even today "public" retains some of its patrician, and "popular" its proletarian, tinge. ("Unpopular" is not always pejorative: on occasion it may connote personal, lone-wolf courage.)

to read all the newspapers "carefully and analyze whatever they contain that might influence public opinion, especially as regards religion, philosophy and political ideas. . . ." The cultivation of public opinion ceased to be the monopoly of the Left. As early as 1794 a Royalist agent was sent to Paris "for the purpose of watching and expediting the training of public opinion"; in the 1830's similar "surveys" were made by the Royalist conspirators around the Duchesse de Berry. Napoleon III found it necessary to sound public opinion regularly through his prefects; he made some of his best as well as some his worst diplomatic decisions dependent on these surveys; his great opponent Bismarck was profoundly interested in public opinion, including the possibilities of its manipulation.

Yet all of these soundings involved what was still a minority: the upper and the middle classes. Even in England the proposition of public opinion for the principal factor in politics did not emerge until the 1840's, a decade or so after the first great electoral reform.* "The middle classes—the ordinary majority of educated men," Bagehot wrote in the 1860's, "are in the present day the despotic power in England. 'Public opinion,' now-a-days, is the opinion of the bald-headed men at the back of the omnibus." But soon thereafter the political domination of the middle classes was beginning to fade: and, like their attempts at limiting universal suffrage, the conservative liberals' wish to keep "the public" distinct from "the people" was bound to fail. Among these theorists the Swiss Sismondi's distinction was harshest: the right to vote, he said, ought to be denied to those who are "incapable" of having their own opinions. Yet this was an impossible circumscription: who are those whose opinions are really their own? As early as 1870 Sismondi's compatriot Burckhardt saw the problem more clearly. Public opinion, he said in one of his lectures, was the *Hauptphaenomen* of the modern age; by 1789 people had learned "that opinion makes and changes the world—as the traditional authorities had become too feeble to put obstacles in its ways, and as they themselves had begun trafficking with some of its features. . . . But today," he went on, "the success of the press lies more in the general levelling of views than in its direct function . . . often the press shrieks so loud *because* people no longer listen." Burckhardt saw that the prime of public opinion was passing; and that it was to be henceforth confused with what used to be called popular sentiment.

"Public opinion is strong," Samuel Butler wrote toward the end of the century, "while it is in its prime. In its childhood and old age it is as weak as any other organism." Public opinion, in its classical sense, was in its prime during the early nineteenth century, when it was taken for granted that the public was the more articulate portion of the people; that it was almost always a minority; that public opinion was, simply, opinion made public; and that it was articulate, active, actual, while popular sentiment was potential rather than actual, and its expressions usually depended on the ideas presented to it by public opinion. By the end of the century universal suffrage and, what is perhaps even more important, universal literacy were coming into being; manufacturers, distributors, divinators of publicity were at work, making a living out of what people still called public opinion but the character of which had changed to an extent that to distinguish between public opinion and popular sentiment became increasingly difficult, if not altogether senseless on occasion.

From the foregoing it will be evident that the historian dealing with public opinion in the nineteenth century faces a different phenomenon from the historian who is trying to reconstruct opinion in the twentieth century. To some extent—but only to some extent—the task of the former is less difficult, less complex. Yet those who during the nineteenth century for the first time attempted to describe the history of public opinion have not really succeeded.* The historical reconstruction of public opinion is an immensely complicated task: it calls for a kind of special sensitiveness, together with a kind of dedication where the assiduous and concentrated industry of the specialist must be complemented by the detailed and extensive knowledge of the entire culture of the society and the period which he is investigating. This calls for a new kind of historical epistemology rather than for a new kind of historical technology: implicit in it are new approaches rather than new instruments of research. For one thing, the documents reflecting public opinion, this basic (and often sub-surface) factor of democratic politics and of democratic society, are overwhelmingly not "primary" but "secondary" sources, printed materials of every possible kind. The historian need not bewail the fact that there were no public opinion-polls in the nineteenth century: there are reasons to believe that these would have told him little that is not already in print. But: this printed material is enormous: because of the fast development of universal literacy the 1840's mark possibly the last period in western Europe and in the United States when a more-or-less complete reconstruction of any subject of public opinion could still be made from printed sources: after that time it becomes impossible practically to cope with the entire mass of its materials.

How curious this is! The accurate reconstruction of public opinion becomes impossible at the very time when public opinion emerges as the dominant factor in politics: thereafter the historian must again proceed on the basis of the insufficiency of his evidence. At the same time he must be aware of the inner complexity of the subject: how and why do opinions become public? how do they emerge? how do they die? what is their relationship to their documentary residues, to print? It is namely in the nature of many documents reflecting public opinion that they are unclear residues: the fact that a certain opinion appears in print is at the same time cause and consequence, the reflection and the propagation of a certain matter. The documentary evidence is both residue and germ of public opinion: this condition is as true of its most complex as it is of its most primitive manifestations. The history of public opinion is often inseparable from the history of opinion-making. Yet its developments are predictable only in the sense that public, even more than private, opinion will respond to such matters which it is already disposed to receive: while, at the same time, the rhetorical habits, the cultural characteristics, and what is perhaps most important, the memories of masses of people tend to transform the very substance of the information of which the matter of opinion is partly (but only partly) composed. Thus, notwithstanding the now fashionable ideas propagated by cybernetists and computerizers, the development of opinions is altogether different from the development of "communications" because the causalities of the latter are mechanical and direct, whereas the causalities involving the former are indirect and complex ones. (For example, exchanges of opinions, while by no means necessarily propitious, are altogether different from the increase of communications: it is a great error to believe that the latter *necessarily* provides an increase of understanding between peoples.) Here, again, the statistical methods of inquiry, no matter how sophisticated, are only of limited use for the study of a large historical phenomenon, even for the study of public opinion in the nineteenth century when, to some extent (but only to some extent) the latter was still the "opinion" of the "public."

(7) Majorities, choices, elections, polls

In the twentieth century, then, the historian must face the difficult problem of delineating the mental climate of the majority. This means not only that the earlier distinctions between public opinion and popular sentiment are seldom useful at all: it means the necessary reconsideration of certain phenomena, including such matters as majorities, polls, elections, the press, and publicity.

The very concept of a majority is not merely an arithmetical but a historical phenomenon.[18] During the Middle Ages the unanimity of the community was either taken for granted or the majority meant something like the entirety of articulate public opinion, of the *major et sanior pars.** People denied the existence of divided opinions for a long time. As late as 1641, during the apparent and deep division in the English House of Commons a Dr. Chillingworth was jailed because he had made a reference to the presence of two parties in the House: a dangerous and heretical idea, it was said, for, as a contemporary put it, the House of Commons was comparable to "the seamless robe of Christ." Political parties developed later; and during the nineteenth century it was taken for granted that their arithmetical proportions formed the political profile of the body politic. Yet we have seen that this political majority did not necessarily correspond to the majority of the population.

Now it is obvious that universal suffrage and universal literacy radically affected the structure of societies so that it is no longer possible to divide the "instructed" from the "uninstructed" portions. But this development has not really affected the basic condition that very often the great majority of a population is essentially uninterested, even when its consensus is being evoked in one way or another: that it is frequently a small minority who are strongly pro, another small minority con, while the rest, often comprising the majority, may not have strong opinions at all (even though they

---

[18] Maitland in *Township and Borough,* 1898: "One of the great books that remains to be written is the History of the Majority. Our habit of treating the voice of a majority as equivalent to the voice of an all is so deeply engrained that we hardly think that it has a history."

may be stubbornly inclined to certain prejudices.)* This does not mean that the majority are uninstructed, inarticulate, or stupid. It means that the intensity (and, consequently, the portent) of their opinions on certain issues are not comparable to those of the more committed minorities—suggesting, in turn, that when it comes to sentiments and opinions, differences in degree may be as significant as a difference in kind: considerations of quality intrude, affecting the very essence of the quantitative sampling.

It is significant that the word "poll" is no longer principally associated with elections but with public opinion research. Those historians who nowadays rely on the statistics furnished by opinion-polls are not always aware of the inherent limitations of this kind of information. I do not see, for example, why scholars dealing with the crucial years 1940–1941 in the history of the United States clutter up their pages with figures culled from ephemeral polls that were beginning to proliferate at that time. It is true that the American people were then divided about the role of the United States in the Second World War. Yet the historical reconstruction of the development of an "interventionist" majority, at least until Pearl Harbor, on the basis of opinion-polls, may be quite misleading: for the data of opinion in these polls are one-dimensional, primitive ones. In 1940 a small but influential and important minority of the American people thought that the United States should enter the war on the British side. Another, even smaller, minority did not want to help the British at all. But these were, still, minorities: and consequently all of the opinion-polls recording 65 to 85 percent pro-British or anti-German majorities were fundamentally wrong, since they usually registered primitive responses through artificial evocations of "opinion."[19] For the meaning of a majority is not only something that cannot be reduced to slices of size; it fluctuates: it is, by

[19] American university students were polled in 1940: to the question whether the United States should give all-out aid to Britain, the overwhelming majority said "Yes"; to another question, whether the government should risk warlike action against Germany, the great majority said "No." In 1955: "Are you in favor of American journalists going to Russia to tell us what they see there?" Seventy percent answered "Yes." "Are you in favor of Russian newspapermen coming here under the same conditions?" Sixty-seven percent answered "Yes." Later: "Do you think that Soviet newspapermen should be allowed to come here and go home with all the information they can get?" The "Yes" answers dropped to 35 percent. These are elementary illustrations, of course.

its very nature, elusive. To say that in the mid-thirties not more than 10 percent of the German people were opposed to Hitler may be correct: but this does not mean that at the same time 90 percent were actively in favor of him. Conversely, to say that at another time 20 percent of Germans were active supporters of Hitlerism does not mean that 80 percent were active opponents of the regime. Between these two figures, even if one of them be approximately accurate, there stretches the ocean of human potentiality, separating these reefs of statistics by a large and unmeasurable *non sequitur*.

Thus it is only in a limited sense that opinion-polls are legitimate tools for the contemporary historian: and in no sense are they primary evidence. Recently Professor Karl Deutsch of Harvard University wrote that "the time is perhaps drawing near when a knowledge of public opinion research . . . will be as essential for the modern historian as a knowledge of Latin has long been for the medievalist." This is nonsense. The character, the nature, and the very origins of the "data"[20] provided by opinion-research are not comparable to the character of language, to the information expressed by a person by employing his own choice of words.* Not only are opinion and sentiment not always the same; the history of public opinion differs, too, from the history of ideas on the one hand, and from the history of majorities on the other. So far as their extent goes, we may venture to say that public opinion is usually smaller than the majority which, in turn, is smaller than popular sentiment: but, so far as their articulateness (involving, too, their historical significance) goes, public opinion is often more important than either the majority or than popular sentiment. An undue reliance on the statistics of polls for the historical research of these phenomena is not only of scant help indeed: it may obscure the nature of the phenomena, too.

Statistics of elections, however, are quite another story. There is a great difference between electoral and opinion polls—between ascertaining what people have chosen and what they may have thought. There exist two kinds of mass statistics which are exceptionally valuable to the modern historian: they are statistics of

---

[20] Some historians, emulating social scientists, have recently taken to talk about "raw data." Leaving aside the question whether "data" are ever raw, let us remember that the "data" of opinion-polls are not only cooked: they are precooked.

demography, and of elections. They are valuable because they are the records of irrevocable acts—something that is not true about statistics of opinions and not even of many social or economic statistics. The historical study of electoral results may be meaningful for the modern historian—under certain conditions.* This is a relatively new phenomenon. Liberal democracy, especially in nineteenth-century Europe, rested on certain limitations of suffrage while it allowed a multiplicity of choices. In our age of social democracy, then, universal suffrage is combined with limitations of choice. This is the reason why one field where opinion-polls may be reasonably accurate is that of electoral sampling: a sampling from a field of limited choices, especially in the case of a two- or three-party system. Here during recent decades the techniques of the pollsters registered considerable improvements (after their massive failures in 1936 and in 1948 in the United States, they are now capable of predicting the results of elections with relatively small margins of error). But choosing and thinking are different matters. This is just what most advocates of "opinion-research" tend to overlook. One may ascertain the number of certain limited, and preformulated, choices: one cannot really "measure" opinions and sentiments. It is wrong to coax people in order to elicit preformulated opinions and fictitious choices, just as it is wrong to berate a child with questions that he never asked himself: the more the child is forced to answer prematurely, the less he will know himself what he wants. Subtle and deep influences are at work in this kind of opinion-polling: the very existence of a question may not only influence, it may artificially produce a previously unformed answer or an unformulated opinion—whereby the observation does not only influence the character, it falsifies the essence of the object.

There is, fortunately, still a difference between electoral choice and popularity poll in most places of the world, including the United States. Indeed, one of the safeguards of liberty in modern democracies may lie latent within the condition that the electoral manifestations of the general will are *not* accurate: that electoral choice and popularity polls are not identical. It is by no means certain that this will remain so: the pollsters have already exercised a rather pernicious influence on politics: in the United States political campaigns have recently acquired more and more of the characteristics of popularity polls. It was in the year of the great Reform Bill in

England that in the United States the first great party convention was organized, with the purpose of picking a potential popular winner; and in 1836 William Henry Harrison was the first presidential candidate who decided to "stump" the country in order to make himself popular; he was perhaps the first American who "ran" instead of having "stood" for such an election. This marked a turning-point in the history of American democracy, the turn in the concept of high elective office from delegation to representation. Perhaps it was in 1836 that the transformation of the United States from a constitutional to a democratic republic was completed. Another turning-point may have been 1917, the American entry in World War I, and Wilson's creation of the deplorable Creel Committee on Public Information, the first official American government agency dedicated to large-scale opinion-making: or, perhaps, the 1950's, with the emergence of the pollsters and of the televised electoral campaign, when the measurement and the manufacture of popularity became synchronized and combined operations. Whether 1917 or 1960, these events are not only turning-points in the history of American democracy: they also mark the decline of the function of the press, the history of which has been closely combined with the history of public opinion, at least in the Western world.

(8) About the press

The first newssheets appeared in London in 1641, at the beginning of the English Revolution; the first newspaper on the Continent is said to have appeared in Holland in 1667. At the end of the seventeenth century newspapers were beginning to spread; for the first time they included advertising. Toward the end of the eighteenth century the function of the newspaper began to replace the role of the political pamphlet. But the golden age of the newspaper, as that of public opinion, was the nineteenth century. It became independent,[21] assertive,[22] powerful.[23] This was, of course, consequent to

[21] In 1795 *The Times* newspaper agreed to support the English government in return for a pension of six hundred pounds. By 1815 the Prime Minister complained of the rising independence of the press: "No paper of any character, and consequently an established sale, will accept money from the Government; and indeed their profits are so enormous in all critical times, when their support is the most necessary, that no pecuniary assistance that Government can offer would really be worth their acceptance." Liverpool to Castlereagh, cited by

increasing number of readers and voters. Then the second great electoral reform in Britain nearly doubled the size of the electorate by 1870; by 1900 the same thing had happened in America and in many European countries. Men now lived, Churchill wrote about Balfour, in an "age when almost the only robustly assertive institution in our society was the Press." In 1901 Salisbury said that "the diplomacy of nations is now conducted as much in the letters of special correspondents as in the dispatches of the Foreign Office." After World War I the press had become the inevitable participant of diplomacy; press conferences became regular occasions for the expressions of highest statecraft; and this was true of totalitarian regimes as well as of parliamentary democracies.

Yet the direct influences of the great newspapers had begun to decline. They were now financially competing with the "mass papers" which had been launched by great entrepreneurs after 1880. But Northcliffe, Rothermere, Pulitzer, Hearst, and the central European newspaper magnates were, really, reapers rather than sowers: the appearance of the first cheap mass newspaper was a foregone conclusion: universal education had changed the character of the literate public: by the end of the nineteenth century the time had come to tap these pools of millions of new readers. There were, then, two types of newspapers, the "class" and the "mass" type: for a while it seemed that the former would be addressed to public

---

D. C. Somerwell, *English Thought in the Nineteenth Century* (London, 1929).

[22] Macaulay coined the term "fourth estate" in 1828. Carlyle in 1833: "The stupendous Fourth Estate, whose wide world-embracing influences what eye can take in; in whose boughs are there not already fowls of strange feather lodged?"

[23] Trollope's villain the Reverend Slope "had from his youth onwards been a firm believer in the public press. He had dabbled in it himself ever since he had taken his degree, and regarded it as the great arranger and distributor of all future British terrestrial affairs whatever. . . . He delighted in the idea of wresting power from the hands of his country's magnates, and placing it in a custody which was at any rate nearer to his own reach. Sixty thousand broadsheets dispersing themselves daily among his reading fellow-citizens, formed in his eyes a better depot for supremacy than a throne in Windsor, a cabinet in Downing Street, or even an assembly at Westminster. . . ." Wilde: "In old days men had the rack. Now they have the press. That is an improvement, certainly. But still it is very bad, and wrong, and demoralizing. Somebody— was it Burke?—called journalism the fourth estate. That was true at the time, no doubt. But at the present moment it really is the only estate. It has eaten up the other three. The Lords Temporal say nothing, the Lords Spiritual have nothing to say, and the House of Commons has nothing to say and says it. . . ."

opinion and the latter to popular sentiment: but this distinction of their functions, like the desired distinction of the nineteenth-century liberals of "the public" from "the people," did not stand up for long. After World War I the number of *all* daily newspapers (like the number of political parties) diminished rapidly, from hundreds of newspapers in Paris in 1848 (a temporary frenzy) to forty-seven dailies in 1914 and eleven in 1955; the numbers in London and New York were correspondingly similar. In the end not the "mass" papers but the newsmagazines profited from the decline of classic news-paperdom and from the expanding sphere of readership: and it is at least arguable that the main opinion-making agents are magazines rather than newspapers nowadays.[24]

So much about the development and the devolution of the daily press. This superficial and, for the specialist, surely unsatisfactory sketch has been necessary only inasmuch as it relates to the history of public opinion. For it is not only in their relation to the "mass" papers and the magazines that the "class" papers underwent changes after World War I: while failing to attract new millions of readers, the "class" papers, too, were beginning to allow themselves to be influenced by popular sentiment. "It would be a mistake to suppose that the office regularly followed ministerial suggestions," wrote the historians of *The Times* about the crucial 1930's. "The difference in the pre-1914 attitude of the paper compared with that of pre-1939 had its main root in the increased respect accorded to popular senti-ment." "In order to secure a large circulation," wrote the American sociologist Walter Shepard in 1909, "editors must give their readers what they want, and since people always want to hear their opin-ions, this tends to make the newspaper on the whole a reliable re-flector of public opinion." Historians ought to pause and reflect on the circularity of this argument. It suggests a schizophrenic attitude

---

[24] The few press successes in western Europe after World War II were scored by occasional founders of magazines, imitating American patterns. The maga-zine, not the newspaper, is the typical intellectual vehicle of the twentieth century. The very format of magazines reflects the intellectual conditions of our times: these literary and pictorial supermarkets suggest the schizophrenic char-acter of interest in various ephemeral matters, even while they maintain a pre-tense of propagating more solid values. Like the suburb which was once supposed to have functioned as a bridge between city and country life, the magazine, supposed to serve as the bridge between news and letters, between the world of the newspaper and the world of books, has been devouring both ends.

about public opinion: on the one hand, it presupposes naïvely that people have established opinions before they read the papers; on the other hand it asserts that all they want to hear is their own opinions.[25] Thus we face the paradox that those who profess so great a faith in the reality of public opinion depend on a cynical estimate of it (a condition summed up by a British constitutional lawyer, Professor Keeton: "Just as the extension of the franchise has diminished the significance both of elector and member, so also has the spread of popular education and the universality of the habit of newspaper-reading reduced the significance of public opinion").

The history of the daily press and the history of public opinion are no longer as close as they were a century ago. They still overlap to some extent, of course: but historians must be extremely wary of those dissertations and monographs which attempt to deal with public opinion principally through selected quotes from newspapers. The validity of this kind of documentation ("on the morning of the 19th *The Courier* wrote that . . . The editorial in *The Trumpet* . . . On the other hand, both *The Herald* and *The Post* . . .") is limited. The historian must possess a considerable knowledge and understanding of the "inside" history of newspapers, including their often hidden financial and social connections: a kind of information which is difficult to ascertain. This is one of the reasons why the few examples of "inside" press history are very valuable—the other being that, as the excellent inside historians of *The Times* put it, "journalists who aspire . . . to influence public opinion and public policy are not immune from the verdict of history upon the policy they initiate or support, above all in relation to issues of war and peace."

Through newspapers and recently more and more through magazines, large numbers of people receive opinions which they may adopt as their own: and because of the hardly visible nature of this

[25] Another example of this schizophrenic attitude was recently (1956) expressed by the publisher of the London *Daily Mirror.* In his book, *Publish and Be Damned,* Cudlipp said that "no newspaper can succeed without men in charge who instinctively know what is right, who can assess the temper of public opinion without moving from their desks." Since this newspaper has been one of the most assiduous propagators of opinion-polls, Randolph Churchill justly commented how strange it is "that these brilliant judges of British psychology should have thought it necessary to go through the complicated mechanism of a poll when they can feel instinctively through their pores how the British public feels on each and every occasion."

process, this may be more dangerous in a free than in a totalitarian society. This process involves, namely, the modern wholesale practice of "cooking the news," whereby opinion and information become inextricably confused. In the "class" newspapers of the nineteenth century information and opinion were more conscientiously separated than they are now.* A wholly "objective presentation of the news" does not exist, of course, save in theory. "Information" and "opinion" cannot be altogether separated. But this does not mean that we should resign ourselves to their illegitimate confusion, in the kind of cooking of the news whereby opinion emerges disguised as information. Magazines, radio, movies, television are eminently suited for these practices: but newspapers, too, are far from immune to them nowadays, when even the "straight" news comes from the press-service wires in precooked form. Thus it is hardly an exaggeration to say, as Canon Bernard Iddings Bell said in 1952, that public opinion in modern democracies may be "manageable as truly as in any censor-controlled totalitarian state, perhaps more effectively than in such a state because the reader in this country thinks he is perusing independent journals while, with rare exceptions, he is not. His suspicion of being manipulated is thereby lulled." "In a modern society," W. H. Auden wrote in 1948, "whatever its political form, the great majority prefer opinion to knowledge, and passively allow the former to be imposed on them by a centralized few—I need only mention as an example the influence of the Sunday book supplements of the newspapers upon our public libraries." Auden grasped what may be the essence of the contemporary historical problem of public opinion: the propagation of preferences through the procedures of publicity, procedures which involve new and subtle falsifications of reality peculiar to our age.

(9) Publicity and the production of popularity

The word *publicity*, which originally had meant the quality of something which was public, appeared in its modern sense ("the business of making goods or persons publicly known")[26] only in 1904. To many people publicity is synonymous with advertising. This is an unduly restricted view, since publicity now encompasses a

---

[26] O.E.D. In the United States the term "public relations" is now preferred to "publicity," which is still customary in England: but the two terms are synonymous and I am employing them thus.

much larger sphere than advertising.* It has come to mean the production of popularity: of all kinds of popularity, including the creation of images of majorities.

The contemporary historian must, therefore, consider how certain contemporary practices of publicity may affect the authenticity (as well as the structure) of certain events. Whereas in the past it was fraudulence by secrecy which may have obscured the origin of events, the compromising element now is fraudulence by publicity. During the nineteenth century, for example, lobbies and hired advocates attempted to manipulate legislation secretly but directly: such influences, in the twentieth century, have become not less dangerous as they became more public, precisely because they have been dealing with something that is not tangible: they are attempting to produce impressions of popularity. The volume of a congressman's mail on a certain issue, for instance, may not only have no real relationship to the importance of that issue, it may not have any real relationship to the state of public opinion—whereas the historian dealing with such events in the more remote past may at least assume from the volume of the public reaction that the latter, whatever its merits, was an authentic fact. Thus the problems of authenticity involve not only the documentary residue but the event itself: it is not only the record which may be falsified but the very happening—and this is of particular importance when we consider that what happens is often inseparable from what people think happens. That a report, whether true or false, of an event may be the cause of another, similar, event is not new: what is new is that the report of the effect of a nonexistent event may eventually be one of the causes of the event itself.[27] It is not only that the publicizing of certain acts stimulates more such acts: the report that this person, or product, or idea, is popular may effectively create their popularity. Many political candidates hire their own pollsters nowadays, part of whose function is to publicize statistics proving their client's popularity—in order to induce the latter. This kind of intellectual manufacture involves a peculiarly contemporary kind of untruth which it is not easy to detect: in Andersen's famous story truth triumphed instantly as the little boy cried out that the emperor had no clothes on, but had he cried out "The emperor is not popular!"

[27] Judicious readers of newspapers may recognize the practice whereby an editor or a columnist will thus try to hurry along the happening of some event that he deems to be desirable.

would he have been heard? By repeating that A. is witty or that B. is handsome it is hardly possible to make them witty or handsome if they aren't: but it is possible to make them popular (at least for a while) through publicity, because popularity is not really measurable, because it is, to a large degree, an abstraction.

This intrusion of images of popularity is, then, largely responsible for the erratic speeds with which fads, fashions, opinions, ideas move in our times. On the one hand, the movement of superficial popular preferences—fads, fashions, ephemeral opinions—is fast, because it is ephemeral. In the age of mass democracy it is reasonable to assume that a mass publicity campaign is bound to bring about *some* results: by repeating and repeating a message, *some* people will believe it, and act upon it. Yet this kind of predictable behavior is seldom significant or enduring, since it is akin to the quickness of the conditioned reflex. Much more significant, on the other hand, is the sluggishness with which, all contrary impressions notwithstanding, the more fundamental ideas of public opinion move in a democratic age. Most of the conservative critics of democracy during the nineteenth century feared that popular sovereignty, with its concomitants of universal suffrage, universal literacy, and the abolition of censorship, would lead to unbridled and anarchical conditions where the mercurial temperaments of crowds, exposed to all kinds of demagogues, would fluctuate wildly between extremes. Again Tocqueville was one of the few judicious observers who saw early that this is not what would happen: that opinions crystallize slowly, move slowly, and change especially slowly in democratic societies. He recognized the basic conservatism of democratic peoples when it comes to certain basic ideas, opinions, assumptions— something that is both cause and consequence of their national temperaments,* whence the paradox of the compound of individualism and social conformism in the originally Protestant democracies of the Western world. The problem before the historian of democratic ages, therefore, is not only that the tracing of the pedigree of ideas (and of the origin of certain decisions) is extraordinarily complicated because of the roles that publicity and that impersonal agencies may have played in their propagation: there is the deeper problem of how the adoption of a new idea, or policy, was made contingent on the estimate of its popularity *ab origine*.

Thus democracy, which came in on the wings of a somewhat archaic and naïve exaltation of popular intelligence (this was what its conservative critics had ridiculed and feared), becomes endangered by the very opposite tendency: by its cynical underestimation. John C. Spencer, an American lawyer, impressed Tocqueville in the 1830's when he said that certain "leaders" of public opinion in the United States should be reproached not so much because they flatter the people but because they "do not struggle with enough courage against an opinion believed to be shared by the people." "You can't be a leader," said Governor Meyner of New Jersey in 1957, "unless you know where the people want to go." Is this what some of our thinkers mean by the tyranny of the majority? Probably—and yet the question arises whether we may speak of a tyranny of the majority at all. Is it not, rather, a kind of tyranny exercised by new kinds of minorities *in the name of the people?* It is all very well to say, as Bertrand de Jouvenel said, that *quidquid populo placuit legis habet vigorem*—the will of the people's pleasure —is just as pernicious and despotic as the former principle of absolute monarchy, the will of a prince's pleasure, *quidquid principi placuit legis habet vigorem.* As a matter of principle this is true: only, it is much easier to ascertain what pleased a king than to find out what the people wanted.[28] All we may say is that the people at times do not give active evidence of their displeasure: but in human affairs, to be pleased and not to be displeased are quite different things. It was Burke, the same conservative who said that "politics ought to be adjusted, not to human reasonings, but to human nature: of which reason is but a part, and by no means the greatest part," who also said that the people must "never be regarded as incurable." There is, after all, a vast difference between

[28] On September 30, 1956, an article in the Business section of the *New York Times* described how a large pencil company did its opinion-research on the wood casings of pencils. It distributed identical pencils in green and in the more conventional yellow casings. "The survey," the company said, "found general satisfaction with the yellow ones. As for the green pencils, the leads were 'too brittle,' 'wore down too quickly,' were 'too hard,' or 'too soft,' or 'smudged too much.'" This is the kind of fraudulent evocation of choice that shows up the dangerous cynicism of "experts." Proceeding from the schizophrenic assumption that what the people want is what counts but that the people really do not know what they want, the "experts" conclude that they know what the people want. Thereafter the people want what they are told they want—from which "the people want what they are told" may be a very short step indeed.

politics as the art of the possible and politics as the art of the popular: and we must be concerned with the spreading disillusionment
with democracy now, in the 1960's, when so many American intellectuals talk of the common people as if they were idiots, when
more and more managers and thinkers accept the cynical conclusion
that "the people" (on Madison Avenue they often say "the slobs")
are incurable, that they can neither swallow nor digest the truth.

Many contemporary evils have been attributed to the influence of
public opinion, especially in foreign policy. Yet it is at least questionable whether Munich, Yalta, the war crimes trials, the atom
bomb were, really, due to public opinion. And is it foolish to presume that, had he possessed one in 1588, Philip II would have
dropped an atom bomb on England without much remorse? In the
long run the impact of public opinion may be an ethical influence
. . . of sorts. When Poland was first partitioned, neither Catherine
nor Frederick bothered much about keeping their compact secret;
but even Stalin and Hitler disguised their partition of Poland in
1939 in a kind of cramped language and kept it in a very secret file.
Consider how after 1917, wars were seldom declared openly, how
not only democracies but totalitarian governments have felt compelled to justify their aggressions by attempting to prove that *they*
were about to be attacked; consider the *Kristallnacht* police actions
against the Jews of Germany, ordered by Goebbels in November,
1938, arranged as if it were the people's outburst of spontaneous
indignation. There have been many such examples since that time.

Still the historian will rediscover again and again that past
images of what "the people" thought or wanted must be revised,
and that history tells us little through statistical formulas in this regard. Pieter Geyl, the eminent Dutch historian, asked these questions
in an essay about the American Civil War: "Did the majority of the
Netherlands people will the complete rupture with Philip II and
with the Roman Church? . . . No. Did the majority of the English
people will the overthrow of the monarchy and the execution of
Charles I? . . . No. Did the French people will the Republic and
the execution of Louis XVI? . . . No. Did the majority of the
German people in 1933 want Hitler, did they will war? . . . No."
The very election of 1860, in which Lincoln polled less than 40
percent of the votes, proves that the majority of the American
people had not deliberately willed the Civil War; but Geyl rightly

asks: "Does this prove that the war might therefore have been avoided? Is it not rather one more proof of the general truth that the course of history is not governed by the conscious will of the majority?" Yes: but instead of "conscious will" Professor Geyl should have written "inchoate sentiment": because, unlike inchoate sentiment, public opinion prevails—in the long run.

"There is no argument," George Orwell once wrote, "by which one can defend a poem. It defends itself by surviving, or it is indefensible." Its survival depends on the coagulating consensus of civilized tradition: but this is a long-run consensus, the consensus of public opinion of the ages, formed by the historical thinking of later generations and confirmed by existential experience. For it is in the long run that, somehow, truth may survive—through the decay of untruth.

(10) Contemporary history

I have suggested that the historian of democratic ages must possess what are somewhat extraordinary intellectual and moral capacities and insights in order to detect the real tendencies in the opinions and sentiments of peoples: for, despite the abundance of documentation, these are frequently obscured and hidden. Their description may, to a large extent, depend on personal experience. By this I do not mean that the contemporary historian must double as a kind of walking Gallup poll; I mean, rather, a kind of participant knowledge. The person who, in one way or another, participated in the period which he is describing, who had some kind of a living contact[29] with the people and the events he deals with, has a potentially (but, of course, only potentially) inestimable advantage over other observers. Here we encounter, again, the problem of the categorical ideal of "objectivity": is the separation of the observer from the thing observed the necessary condition of truthful observation?

This inadequacy of detachment used to be the principal argument of professional historians against what we, in English, call "con-

[29] This living contact does not mean full contemporaneity. It may reach back to a generation or two. A close connection with parents, grandparents, a family house, etc., are powerful sources for understanding some things about a past which one has not fully experienced but which is not altogether remote.

temporary" history. "Contemporary history" is a nineteenth-century phrase. In most European languages, until relatively recently, contemporary history, *histoire actuelle*,[30] *Zeitgeschichte* have been synonymous with recent history, current history, the history of our times, suggesting a period in which the observer has himself participated. Naturally the closeness of contemporary history, not to mention the often superficial and biased character of its rendition, may imperil the historian's sense of proportion: this is obvious: yet to many historians it was obvious, too, that they could not abandon this treatment of recent history to journalists or to ephemeral international-relations experts. Still the practice of contemporary history, with few masterful exceptions, was largely spurned by professional historians as something not quite respectable.

After 1945 these attitudes underwent a significant change. In the first place, historians recognized that the term "modern history" somehow did not quite fit the period after 1914, so that the term "contemporary" has now become widely employed for the entire period of the last fifty years or so, which means, too, that many young contemporary historians are no longer contemporaries of the history with which they deal. In the second place, conscientious historians saw that the teaching of contemporary history would not only fill a gap in the now rapidly expanding curriculum of undergraduate college and university studies; they also felt—especially in Germany—that the filling of this gap may constitute an important and instructive civic function.[31] In the third place, it became more and more evident that, somewhat contrary to the tendencies of the public appetite for historical literature in the nineteenth century, in recent times the popular consumption of historical literature was concentrating on more-or-less contemporary subjects, on matters with which most readers have experienced some kind of relationship within their living memories. That this appetite for what I earlier called a certain mental connection with reality may be a symptom of a deepening maturity of historical

---

[30] The French, of course, call *histoire contemporaine* the entire period after 1789. This does not only reflect their historical conservatism: it is also a reflection of the older practice of distinguishing only between ancient and modern history, the latter including the Middle Ages.

[31] "10. If the younger generation is not taught recent history by historians, they will be left exclusively to the influence of press, film, radio, etc." From the *Recommendations to Teachers and Authors of Textbooks* of the 1953 Calw Conference of European history teachers.

consciousness is suggested by some of the studies of the great Swiss child-psychologist Professor Piaget, indicating that while younger children are especially interested in earlier periods of history, "partly because those periods lend themselves to a romantic treatment," one of the reasons for teaching contemporary history ". . . is that most adolescents find it interesting and believe in its utility."[32]

The historian has a duty to his contemporaries. He has "much to answer for," as Veronica Wedgwood wrote in 1942, deploring the antiquarian habits of historians "who failed entirely to understand what was expected of them. They turned their faces away from their audience and towards their subject, turned deliberately from present to past. They began to consider with misguided conscientiousness their duty to the dead. This was nonsense," she wrote, "for no one has a duty to the dead except in relation to the living." Soon after the war G. M. Young in *Last Essays* asked "whether, today, the highest and most necessary duty of the historian be not to infuse into the popular judgment of current events the integrity which the historic judgment pronounces on the past." Perhaps the principal argument for contemporary history is that it springs from the recognition that the principal duties of the historian, perhaps especially in this democratic age, are not only *wissenschaftlich* but always to some extent moral ones: that these tasks involve not merely the addition of historical information about the receding past, but that they involve something that is more important—the *reduction of untruth*.

The reduction of untruth was the principal motive of all of the great historical writers who concerned themselves with contemporary history, beginning with Thucydides as he was more interested in setting the record straight than in bringing it up-to-date.[33] Eighteen

[32] Edouard Bruley and E. H. Dance, editors, *A History of Europe?* (Leyden, 1960).

[33] E.g.: ". . . there are many unfounded ideas current among the rest of the Hellenes even on matters of contemporary history . . . for instance there is the notion that the Lacaedaemonian kings have two votes each, the fact being that they have only one; and that there is a company of Pitane, there being simply no such thing. So little pains do the vulgar take in the investigation of the truth, accepting readily the first story that comes to hand . . . The absence of legendariness in my history will, I fear, detract somewhat from its interest; but if it be judged useful by those inquirers who desire a truthful knowledge of the past as an aid to the interpretation of the future, which in the course of human events must resemble if it does not reflect it, I shall be content."

hundred years later, at the beginning of another great transition in
the Western world,* the Spanish Fernán Pérez de Guzmán made
a remarkably modern assertion of the importance of contemporary
history in his *Generaciones y semblanzas,* the kind of contemporary
history with a moral that has remained something of a speciality
of the Hispanic literary genius, the tradition having been carried
down to our times, represented as it is by writers such as Menendéz
Pidal or Madariaga. Three things, Pérez de Guzmán wrote, are required of good and honest histories: first, the judiciousness of the
historian, together with a high and serious style; second, he should
know how to distinguish authentic and dependable witnesses from
undependable ones; third, he must be free and independent. When
these conditions do not exist the result is "suspicious chronicles"—
coronicas sospechosas—that cause "no little harm." Four hundred
years later, as another phase in the development of European historical consciousness was beginning to unfold, Guizot, one of its
principal witnesses, wrote to Hübner: "Thucydides and Machiavelli
wrote and published contemporary history. Why shouldn't I try
it?" Tocqueville had listened to Guizot's lectures; he shared the
peculiarly modern recognition how, in a way, all history is contemporary history; he would not, as he later wrote, attach "undue
value to those historical curiosities which suffices idle erudite
societies." "In the main it is only the affairs of our time which
interest the public and which interest me also," he said. "As soon
as history approaches our century and our worthy selves," wrote
Burckhardt, "we find everything more 'interesting'; actually, it is
we who are more 'interested.'"

"We are still too close to these events to know many details (this
may seem curious, but it is so)," wrote Tocqueville on the margin of
a sheet of jottings under the heading *Original Concept; General
Approach* which was to serve his, alas, unfinished volume on the
French Revolution and Napoleon. "Details," he went on,

often appear only in posthumous revelations and are frequently ignored
by contemporaries. But what these writers know better than does posterity are the movements of opinion, the popular tendencies of their times,
the vibrations of which they can still sense in their minds and hearts.
The true traits of the principal persons and of their relationships, of the
movements of the masses are often better described by witnesses than
recorded by posterity. These are the necessary details. Those close to

them are better placed to trace the general history, the general causes, the large movements of events, the spiritual currents which men who are further removed may no longer find, since these things cannot be perceived from the memoirs.

Tocqueville the aristocrat and Burckhardt the patrician may have regarded the requirements of historianship in a broader and more democratic sense than had many of its professional practitioners. They understood not only the peculiar validity of contemporary history but its relevance to the structure and to the perception of certain events. They knew that the scientific requirements of objectivity would not guarantee the probity of the historian; that personal participation is far from being an insuperable handicap; that self-knowledge, involving the recognition of one's own historical circumstances and personal interests, is the principal prerequisite; that what he has to confront are not new instruments of research or new methods of documentation but, first of all, himself. Thus Tocqueville and Burckhardt were early testimonial witnesses of that deepening of the personal consciousness of history which is one of the main intellectual developments of *our* democratic epoch— and which must now lead us to a reconsideration of historical "facts," the next step in our inquiry about the structure of events.

III

❦

FACTS AND FICTIONS

or describing the past

(1) A historical reconstruction represents certain realities

Twice in the foregoing chapters I wrote that the now widespread interest in history in the Western world, and particularly in the United States, may exist because to many people a historical reconstruction represents a certain kind of reality. Surely it is difficult to imagine how history could ever be written in the abstract, fantastic, counterrealistic, or nonrepresentational forms with which many artists, including novelists, nowadays grapple. Any slice of the past can be rendered in an account of fantasy: but no one would call that history. This does not mean that the difference between the historian and the writer of fantasy is that between "objective" and "subjective" representation: the historian's and the fantasy artist's mental and imaginative capacities are of the same order, meaning that the thinking processes of both are engaged in a kind of construction wherein the subject matter "received" by their senses is immediately involved. It is only that the historian's subject matter is limited to certain realities of the past which, though powerfully affected by his imagination, cannot be invented in their entirety. History, even in the United States, is no longer bunk (Henry Ford's felicitous statement, *circa* 1925). There are still many people who will not understand how the past could have much meaning for the present: but there are not many people, not even in California, who think that the past is not real. The historian describes things that happened and people who lived; in plain English, he deals with facts. With this sentence most people would agree. For once, however, this plain English statement will not do. The historian does deal with things that happened: but what I am about to argue is that these things are not necessarily facts—indeed, that they may even one day cease to be "facts," without ceasing to have happened.

A minority among my readers may, at this point, suspect what I am about to do: mount an argument against the notion of "hard" or "solid" facts that "speak for themselves." Yes, this is one of the things that I must do: because the majority (or what I hope to be the majority) among my readers, as most English-speaking adults, probably do not question this older idea of historical "facts." On the other hand, those among my readers who have evinced some interest in the philosophy of history may be aware of the condition that the nineteenth-century idea of facts has been occasionally questioned by eminent historians, here and there, during the twentieth century. I shall, however, endeavor to treat this subject somewhat differently from my eminent forerunners, since I am inclined to regard this question of facts not so much as a philosophical but as a historical (and national) problem; and I shall attempt to begin not so much with the facts of history as with the history of facts— in other words, not only with how many facts there are in history but with how much history there is in the word "fact."

(2) A history of "facts"

The word "fact" appears neither in the Old or in the New Testament. "In the beginning was the Word"; and it is the Word that became flesh, *verbum caro factum est,* in what, at least to some of us in the West, is still the central event in the entire history of the universe. *Factum est,* the direct ancestor of our "fact," refers neither to word nor to flesh in this phrase. While "the Word became a fact" might sound dreadfully flat but not altogether absurd to *our* ears, its Latin version, *verbum facto facta est,* would have been absolute nonsense to our ancestors, since *factum est* is the past tense of a verb, not a noun.[1] And when two thousand years after its first

---

[1] Like *datum:* something that is given. Strictly speaking, "data" and "facts" are similar things: yet people nowadays use the former as if it were a more concrete (usually statistical) subdivision of the latter. The reason for this is probably that the weakening of the notion of "solid" facts in millions of minds, in one way or another, may have already begun.

Latin appearance, at the end of the Middle Ages, "fact" first appears as a noun, it still hearkens back to the verb: it still means *factum,* something definitely done, an accomplished feat (as in the Italian *fatto* or the French *fait*). Less than three hundred years ago "a feat" and "a fact" meant the same thing in English, both words having derived from *factum* through the French fait.[2] As late as the early nineteenth century when Jane Austen wrote "gracious in fact, if not in word" she meant deed:[3] a real event, not an ideal category of reality.

The employment of "fact" as a category (indeed, as the principal category) of reality was the product of the nineteenth century. The belief in the solidity of facts was then shared by the romantics as well as by the utilitarians, by historians as well as by scientists. "How impressive," Carlyle wrote, "the smallest historical *fact* may become as contrasted with the grandest *fictitious* event" (his italics). "Sit down before a fact as a little child," T. H. Huxley wrote Charles Kingsley, "and be prepared to give up every preconceived notion . . . or you will learn nothing." After all, facts were infinitely preferable to fictions at a time when the hold of prescientific concepts, survivals from the Middle Ages, were not yet broken everywhere; when these, together with antiquated institutions, still extant here and there, obstructed the progress of the mind. Certain writers were, of course, irritated by the clanking repetitions of the word "fact" and by the thoughtless reverence paid to it, the best known of these instances being Dickens' portrayal in *Hard Times* of Gradgrind the schoolmaster, a veritable idiot for Facts. *Hard Times* is a good example, since its main theme involves the scathing criticism of some of the effects of industrialization. For the nineteenth-century cult of Facts was, like everything else, a historical phenomenon: it was one of the intellectual concomitants of the Industrial Revolution. In the nineteenth century the universe, as well as history, consisted of Facts: there was a place for poetry, religion, art, and rhetoric, but these were the finer things of the mind; the fundamental realities were Facts which the industry of the human race was progressively gathering in all places and on all sides, looking for them in all directions, forward and backward, as when digging up the facts of history.

[2] Larousse: *"fait: action, chose faite . . ."*
[3] "Fact" could also mean "action" in English before 1815.

Now I must say something about the national factor in the history of Facts. My main reason for writing this chapter is that I am writing in English. Were I writing in another language I would treat this problem of Facts in a different and shorter manner: the stature of the problem would diminish because of the different reputation of *their* Facts. When I say this I am not only referring to that pragmatical tradition of English and American philosophy—including popular thinking—which was, until very recently, particularly attuned to the nineteenth-century idea of Facts; I am referring, too, to the condition that these ways of thinking would flourish among peoples whose experiences with industrialization were particularly successful, and among whom it has been taken for granted, by and large, that the advancement of science and the advancement of reason were necessarily synonymous. This, I believe, is the main reason why the English word "fact," unlike most of its European equivalents,[4] has come to mean something like an ideal category of reality—until recently its employment, perhaps especially in the United States, has begun to pass way beyond its original sense, and sometimes even beyond the bounds of reason.

In any event, around 1900 a certain scepticism about the cult of Facts began to appear even in England. "The English," said Wilde, "are always degrading truths into facts. When a truth becomes a fact it loses all its intellectual value." Soon after the turn of the century the young Trevelyan courageously said that "history is only in part a matter of 'fact.'" After World War I Lytton Strachey wrote that history is "not an accumulation of facts but a relation of them." After World War II this decline of the trust in the solidity of facts continued. "We no longer have a high regard for *die historischen Fakten*," read the first sentence of an article by Reinhard Wittram, "Das Faktum und der Mensch," in the February, 1958, *Historische Zeitschrift*; in 1961 E. H. Carr addressed the first of his George Macaulay Trevelyan Lectures, which subsequently were to enjoy a considerable reputation, to "The Historian and His Facts." Carr began his argument by contrasting Acton's first prospectus of *The Cambridge Modern History* in 1896 with Sir George Clark's general introduction to the second *Cambridge Modern History* in 1957, pointing out that the latter revealed a much more chastened and

---

[4] In my native language, for example, "fact" and "deed" are not only synonymous: the same word (*tény*) expresses both.

less certain view of historical facts than the former. Yet, as Carr wittily noted, not even Sir George Clark[5] could quite abandon the nineteenth-century idea of facts, since in an article written in 1952 Clark "himself contrasted the 'hard core of facts' in history with the 'surrounding pulp of disputable interpretation'—forgetting perhaps that the pulpy part of the fruit is more rewarding than the hard core." This is a sophisticated recognition and it comes close to what I am going to say. Still, not even Carr could altogether detach himself from the old idea of Facts: for example, while he was no longer trying to square the circle of historical truth by surrounding it with solid facts, Carr was circling the circle by speaking of two kinds of facts, historical ones and nonhistorical ones, trying to establish "the criterion which distinguishes the facts of history from other facts about the past." But there is no such criterion. The question is not what is a historical fact; our question should be: to what extent is our notion of fact a historical notion? The problem which we face is what is a fact, not merely what is a historical fact; and this problem includes not only professional historianship but the fabric of our civilization, involving as it does human persons and their communications.

In the United States the cult of Facts sometimes went beyond its propagation elsewhere. Some people have written about it amusingly on occasion. In 1900 "Mr. Dooley" gave this excellent American definition of a fanatic: "A man that does what he thinks th' Lord wud do if He knew th' facts iv the case." Americans, wrote Douglas Woodruff in *Plato's American Republic* in 1926, "will often talk as if ideas were less real than facts, instead of more real."[6] In the same year Professor Carl L. Becker delivered a lecture, "What Are His-

---

[5] Nor could his namesake Sir Kenneth Clark, in whose much-admired *The Nude* (1953, 1956) I ran across this passage: ". . . Ary Scheffer, Cabanel, Bouguereau and Henner . . . Each of these artists had its own recipe for success, ranging from the lubricity of Bouguereau to the high-minded sexlessness of Lord Leighton; but all had one characteristic in common; they glossed over the facts." What facts?

[6] "What are these facts?" "They may be anything. Lists of names, and long technical words are accepted as facts. The biggest fact is the Divine Fact, Progress, which they worship." "Might not that be called an idea?" "You might so . . . but I would advise you not to do so, for the Americans dearly love Progress and will not tolerate your insults." "In the long run facts will control," wrote Henry Ford in an article in *Nation's Business* (1920).

torical Facts?", the most telling summary of his relativist view of
history which had been crystallizing in his mind for some time: but
the very condition that Becker shied away from publishing this
paper may have been telling, too:* neither his, nor Charles A.
Beard's later (1933, 1934) unorthodox analysis of facts seemed to
have made much of a dent on the phalanxes of historical industry.
Three decades after the Becker paper Dwight Macdonald could still
speak of "The Triumph of the Fact: an American tragedy;" the obsession with facts, wrote Macdonald, circumscribes American imagination narrowly indeed. My point, however, is a slightly different
one: the trouble is no longer that this obsession is narrow, meticulous,
puritanical: it is, rather, that the concept of what is a Fact has become, on occasion, exaggerated, absurd, unreal. Thus, for example,
American scientists often present future projections under the name
of facts, even though facts ought to mean something that was accomplished in the past. "It is a fact," I read in 1957 in an article by
the scientific director of a Philadelphia planetarium, "that by 1970
we will have put a permanent colony on the moon"; in 1958 the
report of the Findings of the Preparedness Subcommittee of the
United States Senate stated with utmost seriousness: "The facts
which we have been investigating are the facts of the future."

It is because of such absurdities that I have come to dislike the
word "fact"; I have tried to avoid it, in teaching and writing, whenever this is possible; indeed, I have come to prefer the euphonious
word "event" to "fact" whenever I can. Event, at any rate, is the
lovelier word; it compares to Fact as Love does to Sex; it is not dry,
definite, static; it suggests life, flow, movement; whereas "fact" has a
now inevitably scientific tinge, "event," I believe, admirably reflects
the sense of history.[7] Still the argument of this chapter is something
more than an argument for a writer's personal preference. For sometimes I believe that a growing disillusionment with the word "fact,"
that is, with the present and, as we have seen, frequently unreal
usage of the nineteenth-century concept, may be developing in
the minds of millions of Americans, even though they may not yet

[7] "Event" as movement and development: thus it was understood in the
seventeenth century, for example, in an engagingly broad sense: Charles I,
refusing to go up into entangled Scotland, said that he would remain in London
for a time "to see the event of these matters." Disraeli: "Events are wonderful
things. . . ."

relate this to history.[8] This is why I insist that we recognize how things that exist are not necessarily facts: that the difference between something that happened and something that did not happen does not quite correspond to the difference between the two categories of fact and fiction.

(3) "Fictio," or the purposes of historical statements

Let me begin, first, with the most obvious condition. Facts are not independent; no Fact ever stands by itself; a Fact is not separable from other Facts. "We compare, contrast, abstract, generalize, connect, adjust, classify," said Newman, "and we view all our knowledge in the association with which these processes have invested it." "With this one word, *association,* bang goes the simple notion that 'facts are facts,'" commented Seán O'Faoláin a century later, "for facts are thereby only to be called facts when they are isolated in our minds. And are they ever isolated?" They are not: facts are meaningless by themselves: they mean something only in relation to other facts.*

For, in the second place, the value of Facts may depend on their relationships even more than on their accuracy. I do not mean to say that accuracy is unimportant: what I am saying is that often the more "accurate" a Fact the more theoretical it may be. American newspapers are often stuffed with filler items informing us that the average American family consists of 3.2 members or that it consumes 791 quarts of milk a year. The abstractness of such Facts is (or, rather, it should be) obvious. What is not so obvious is that of two statements of fact the more accurate may be the less truthful one. To say that on April 1, 1958, the population of Philadelphia was 2,242,714 is more accurate but less truthful than to say that the population of Philadelphia during the first half of 1958 was between 2,200,000 and 2,250,000, since any definition of who was and who was not a resident of Philadelphia at a static moment is necessarily abstract, leaving a considerable margin of error. Moreover, the meaning of these figures exists only as we relate them to other figures in our minds (how does this

[8] From an item in the *New York Times,* April 19, 1966 ("Merck Told by F.T.C. To Halt Claims For Sucrets Lozenges"): John R. Reilly, writing for the FTC Commissioner: "The skillful advertiser can mislead the consumer without misstating a single fact."

compare to the populations of other cities?) or to direction and movement (is the population rising, or falling?)

The association, therefore—and this is my third point—is profoundly involved with the fact. I say association, not interpretation: because interpretation (the term chosen by Professor Carr) suggests that it is *preceded* by the fact, whereas the association, if it is meaningful at all, is *already* part of the fact itself (when we think of a "fact" we think of something that *is*).[9] At this point we encounter the inadequacy of the Fact-Fiction dichotomy. *Fictio*, deriving from the verb *fingere*, means construction: we have now seen that a fact cannot be separated from its association: that is, from a certain construction of the mind. Because of this construction, not only is *fictio* of a higher order than *factum:* what is more important, every fact is, in a certain sense, a fiction. While it is certainly arguable that what happened is more important than what we think happened, it is hardly arguable that these are separate matters—that, in other words, a fact can be isolated not only from other facts but from our thinking about it. The evidences of this eminently human condition are perhaps more widespread than we are inclined to believe: they are certainly apparent (that is, for those who want to see them) in the Factual Science of Economics;[10] and we shall see in the last chapter of this book how this condition affects physics, that is, the very science of matter itself.

The historian's work is re-lation, involving the *fictio*[11] of events.

[9] We say, for example: "It *is* a fact that Booth killed Lincoln." Fact, indeed, has departed so much from its original verbal ancestry that we no longer relate it in time: we almost always say "it is a fact": we might say, referring to some limited situation, "it was a fact": but "it has been a fact" sounds awkward to us, and "it had been a fact" even rarer. Yet we will say "it is true," "it was true," "it has been true," "it had been true" without such a sense of awkwardness.

[10] See below, Chapter V, p. 216.

[11] Von Below: "A connection among facts cannot be effected without value judgments." Morazé: "Le fait n'est pas une donnée de la nature, il n'est pas une donnée de l'evolution humaine, il est une fabrication d'esprit, de l'esprit de l'historien, de l'esprit qui étudie." Marrou: "Plus que d'établir des 'faits,' il lui importe de les comprendre." Ortega y Gasset: "History is not only seeing, it is thinking what has been seen. And in one sense or another, thinking is always construction." To this I may add that the re-lation of human events to each other may reduce their size but not their meaning. It is thus that historical perception tends toward a microcosmic view of the universe.

Let me now deal with this re-lation rather than pursue deeper the mental processes of the historian (even at the cost of having to postpone, for example, the consideration of how much recognition there is in mental construction). We have now seen that facts are not quite what we used to think they are. Still, no matter how inflated its meaning may be, when we say: this is a "fact," we are making a statement. And this is the fourth, perhaps the most important, point: while, on the one hand, a fact is not separable from its association (or call it construction, recognition, *fictio*), on the other hand, neither is it separable from its expression. Expression is not merely the clothing of the fact, but its very flesh. It is not only that the "hard core"—the fact—is less enjoyable than the "pulpy part of the fruit": the hard core has no seed, it is not hard, and it is not the core. For example, Professor Pieter Geyl is quoted saying that "we could agree about simple facts—the Second World War began in 1939—but such facts were a very small part of history; the rest was made up of judgments of events, situations, and characters, and *they* would be debated till doomsday." But even such a "simple fact" as *the Second World War began in 1939* is not really a simple fact but a statement, an expression, involving a choice of words: and therefore it is not essentially different from a statement such as, say, *Hitler was an evil genius.* There are people who will argue that the Second World War was not really the Second World War but the Second German War, or the First Atomic War, or the European Civil War, or the Sixth, or Seventh, or Eighth Atlantic World War. There are people who might say that the Second World War did not really become a world war until December, 1941. There are others who may argue that, if it was a world war, then it began in Manchuria in September, 1931. This is not mere sophistry: a Chinese historian, for example, might find the statement that the Second World War broke out in 1939 inaccurate or even unjust—unjust, say, if that statement was made in a context slighting the importance of the Chinese part of the war.

For we have to take another, last, step: we must recognize that the expression of a fact is inseparable from its purpose. Even if there is agreement about the same fact—which, as we have seen, is really a statement of a fact—the same statement and the same phrase may be used for different purposes. This ought to be evident:

A

Hitler was a fanatic and a dictator. He wanted to reduce Germany's neighbor states even at the cost of war. After he had conquered Austria and Czechoslovakia, Britain and France offered their alliance to Poland. On September 1, 1939, the German armies broke into Poland, and the Second World War began....

B

By the spring of 1939 Britain and France, supported by certain American circles, decided that Germany should not be allowed to dominate eastern Europe. They offered an alliance to Poland. From then on Poland rejected every German demand. After Germany and Poland went to war on September 1, 1939, Britain and France declared war on Germany; and the Second World War began. . . .

Each of these statements is true. Yet they are true in different ways. Of course, the sophisticated reader will say: the same fact was put in different contexts. Yet it is not enough to say that; the problem is not merely a problem of context; if the fact depends on its statement, and its statement on its context, the context, in turn, depends on its purpose: it is a construction of purpose.

A

Like so often during the previous two decades of almost uninterrupted French triumphs over the armies of Continental Europe, the British were to demonstrate their singular determination in the end. On June 18, 1815, Wellington won the Battle of Waterloo. . . .

B

The rising national spirit of Germany had already become a dominant factor at that time. Wellington won the Battle of Waterloo on June 18, 1815; even there his victory depended on Blücher. . . .

"A" reflects an Anglophile tendency; "B" a Germanophile one. "A" is no more true than "B" than "B" is truer than "A." And yet . . . "A" *could*, suddenly, become "truer" than "B." Suppose that a historian in the middle of Axis Europe stood up and said it in a lecture before a German audience, in the summer of 1940. Or imagine "B," as it is written thus by an English historian, irritated as he was to the point of a noble anger, say, in 1917, in his critical review of a jingo biography of Wellington: wouldn't it be invested by an especial meaning of truthfulness?

We are coming to the end of the argument. Every human statement may be actually true and potentially untrue. "The Anglo-

American-Russian coalition won the Second World War." "The victors of World War II were Soviet Russia and the United States." "China and the colonial peoples turned out to be the real victors of the last world war." Depending on their purpose, each of these contradictory statements may be true. But the relativity of such statements does not mean that there is no truth, just as the inevitable corruptibility of the human flesh does not mean that the human spirit may not reach incorruptibility: it is only that historical truth, as I said earlier, touches our minds and our senses differently (and more deeply) than does scientific truth—since we all are historians by nature while we are scientists only by choice.

I am aware of the uneasiness which may be forming in some of my readers' minds at this point: I seem to have shifted the argument from what is a fact to what is truth: but I could not avoid this; all that I wish to say is that the problem of truth is not necessarily a problem of fact.[12] One evening in 1960, after having worked all day, I drove over the hill to see some friends after supper. My account in my 1960 diary reads: "June went by, closely together with H., in our little country house." "Late on the evening of June 1," someone could write, "Lukacs left his ailing wife alone in a darkened house, and drove off to spend several hours drinking with friends on a well-lit terrace, in an electric atmosphere with pretty women." Absolutely correct. Deeply untrue. I know it to be so. "What is truth?" I cannot answer Pilate's question; but I shall not wash my hands under the laboratory faucet of the specialist; if I cannot answer what truth is, I can at least say what it is not. Apart from all metaphysics, I can but say that the *purpose* of historical truth (like every fact, every truth is to some extent historical) is understanding even more than accuracy, involving the reduction of untruth; and I can say that the *nature* of truth is inseparable from personal knowledge; that it cannot be proven by definitions but that it can be suggested through words.

(4) The historian deals with words

From my window I can see a rock in the garden. Unlike Dr. Johnson, I shall not get up and kick it: but I shall indulge in a little speculation about its existence. "Rock" is an English word,

---

[12] D. H. Lawrence: "Lies are not a question of false fact/but of false feeling and perverted justice."

intelligible only to people who speak, hear, or read English; also, a picture of a rock will be comprehended only by people who have seen or imagined something like it before. Still, doesn't this rock exist apart from our word for it; didn't it exist before our recognition of it? It did exist then, and it does exist now: but it is not necessarily a fact: it became a fact only sometime during the last two hundred years when, for purposes of better human communication, certain people chose to conceive and to express certain realities as facts. This rock (it is a big one) may have been here on earth, perhaps on this very spot, before human beings:[13] but it took human beings to see and think about rocks differently from all other living creatures; they came to call such stones rocks, to make themselves better understood; and much later—at a time when some of them came around to believe that the principal business of man's intellect is to define and to categorize the order of the universe—they thought that it was more realistic to conceive a rock as a fact than to keep it as a "mere" word.

And now, another century or so later, we must recognize the exaggerated applications and the fundamental shortcomings of this belief. We can do this not by reverting to prescientific idealism: my view of the rock is not Bishop Berkeley's (who died in 1753): we can do this because we have lived through the Age of Facts, because we know some of their shortcomings not only through philosophical speculation but also through historical experience. These shortcomings are inherent in any attempt at ignoring words: for that will lead not to an increase of reality but of abstraction. We live in an age where we are taught to believe that H_2O is a more realistic term than water, whereas, to the contrary, it is the more abstract one, for two reasons at least: in the first place, H_2O is a perfectly theoretical formula, since a liquid consisting of nothing but hydrogen and oxygen does not and cannot exist; in the second place—and this is really more important—"water" (as also *eau, aqua*, etc.) *sounds* like water, whereas H_2O does not. Not only do historical truths touch our senses and our minds differently from scientific truths: words touch us differently from scientific formulas, because we are, literally, more *involved* with them. The historian must understand this not only because of certain literary requirements of his craft, not only because dull

[13] When, incidentally, it was meaningless to us, all geology notwithstanding. It is *we*, much later, who invested rocks with geological attributes.

history is usually bad history: but because history is spoken and written, taught and *thought* in our common everyday national languages which, in turn, are historical and not scientific phenomena.*

It may be argued that the historian's task is analysis rather than narration: but this is something quite different from saying that he must define rather than describe. Rather, he ought to agree with Dr. Johnson and Dickens to the effect that definitions, and especially definitions of words, are tricks for pedants: because words are not static, they are dynamic; they are not watertight categories, they are historical realities, which is why even a dictionary discriminates as much as it defines. And when any word is thought of as a rigid category, a decay of its meaning and a corruption of thought inevitably results—which, as we have seen, is what happened to "fact." It is not that words are better categories than are facts (words, too, depend often on their associations* and especially on their "context": the order in which words follow each other in English, for example, invests them with meaning); it is that words are not categories at all.

It is in this sense that the often criticized French realist aim for the *mot juste* acquires a highly important meaning. For the *mot juste* is not merely a literary equivalent of realistic representation in art. The literal meaning of *juste* suggests not only accuracy but propriety, justice, truth. *Mots justes: just* words: for words are not "tools of communication," they are not interchangeable units of expression; in a sense, every word is a metaphor, a luminous short symbol appealing through our imagination to our minds, enabling us to perceive its meaning in a flash; and thus the simplest phrase is pregnant with meaning, because of the vital, profound, and *historical* assumptions already inherent within it. This is something quite different from what the semanticists or the specialists of analytical linguistics tell us. For, if words are not mere tools, neither are they mere symbols. They are *representative* realities; they remind us of the inevitable connection between imagination and reality.[14] We must constantly keep this in mind in our times when our Western languages are profoundly threatened

---

[14] The German language makes a fine distinction between *Dar-* or *Vorstellung* (presentation-representation) on the one hand, and *Stellvertretung* (substitution-representation) on the other.

by democratic anarchy, by international abstraction, and by technological nominalism, amounting to degenerative and inflationary
practices; we must remember Montaigne's admonition to the
effect that the generalization of lying would by itself dissolve the
fabric of society. The corruption of speech involves the corruption
of truth, and the corruption of truth the corruption of existence:
the debasement of words means the debasement of speech which
is the debasement of our most human *and* historic gift.*

This chapter is not, however, a treatise on the nature of words: it
has nothing to do with linguistic analysis or with semantics. All
I am saying is that the historian inevitably deals with words, and
that this is an awful responsibility, especially in these times: that he
must be aware of the terrible beauty and power of their suggestive-
ness. Very early in my career I learned in practice most of the things
that I have been writing about in this chapter, even though I may
not have understood their philosophical implications: I learned
that my principal problem, in writing and teaching, involved
choices of words, and that often this involved not merely a question of their suitability but a moral decision of sorts. For this
weighing of words means something more than the ability to write
clearly and well—which, of course, is no mean task—it means not
so much the necessary cultivation of an extensive vocabulary as the
necessary cultivation of a sensitivity to the reality of language and
of the effects of rhetoric. The cultivation of these sensitivities will
eventually enrich the historian's understanding of not only his
craft but of the residues of the past with which his mind enters
into contact—sensitivities which may range from the necessary
knowledge of the rhetorical peculiarities of certain people and of
certain periods to an increasing awareness of the circumstances
of certain documents[15] and perhaps even to an appreciation of the
curious relationship between the forms of words or of names and
what they represent.[16] In any event, historianship is a descriptive
craft, and it is because of this involvement of words that it is

---

[15] This involves, among other things, what I may call the five questions inherent in the hermeneutical analysis of documents: who says what, and how,
and why, to whom? We never know the answers fully: but note that the *how*
and the *why*—these *par excellence* historical questions— are also the most personal questions, since they inevitably relate to the *who*.

[16] Think how the very shape and the sound of a name like Bismarck befits
the character of its wearer!

governed by the *esprit de finesse* rather than by the *esprit de la géometrie*, which is why every historian worth his salt soon learns by experience what Tocqueville, who admired Pascal, meant when he wrote: "Ces sont les nuances qui querrellent, pas les couleurs"— Shades of color, though close in their appearance, may clash—but of course, since they are different in purpose.

Among other things the historian must be aware that expression has a nationality even if thought may not.[17] The same statement, the same word may have a slightly (and at times profoundly) different meaning in different languages, beyond the dictionary synonyms: *to win* is not *siegen, honour* is not quite *honneur* which, in turn, is different from *Ehre, Wissenschaft* is not *science* in English, *common sense* is not *le sens commun* but *le bon sens . . .* in a way.* If the historian does not know these things he may be courting trouble.[18] This is one of the reasons for my insistence that in our developing era of truly *inter-national* history the person who attempts to write about the history of another nation be impregnated with the knowledge of the national culture and the national rhetoric of the people whose deeds and expressions and words he will describe. This is, too, why I, for one, look forward to the development of international history in a round-robin manner: not to international history written by international experts in an international language but to a situation when we should have good and meaningful histories of *every* civilized country in *every* civilized language. Those historians, then, who have ever addressed themselves to comparable tasks will know, as Owen Barfield wrote, that "anyone who has been to the trouble of learning a foreign language after the age at which he had reached a certain

[17] I say "may" because thought, too, very often has a nationality—not because of race or heredity, however, but because of the way in which memory is impregnated by language: the expression reverberates "back" into thought.

[18] Not only the historian. For example, it seems that one of the causes of the deep misunderstanding concerning the disposition of the French fleet after June 1940 arose between the Vichy French and the British governments from the slight difference between the French word *"contrôle"* and the English "control." Article 8 of the Franco-German armistice included the phrase: *"Le gouvernement allemand déclare solennellement qu'il n'a pas l'intention d'utiliser pendant la guerre à ses propres fins la flotte de guerre française stationnée dans les ports sous contrôle allemand. . . ."* Whereas "control," in English, is more powerful, it suggests directing, restraining; in French *"contrôle"* suggests not much more than verification.

degree of aesthetic maturity, will know that aesthetic pleasure arises from the contemplation of quite ordinary expressions couched in a foreign idiom. It is important, then, to note that this is not, in so far as it is aesthetic, the pleasure of comparing different ways of saying the same thing, but the pleasure of realizing *the slightly different thing that is said."*

No two people ever say exactly the same thing. There is no *perfect* communication between two persons: but this is exactly why their communications are *pregnant* with meaning. As Ortega y Gasset put it: "Perspective is one of the components of reality. Far from being its deformation it is its organization. A reality which would remain always the same when seen from different points is an absurdity."[19] This is a twentieth-century recognition,[20] a condition which is important for us to keep in mind as even the more intelligent historical thinkers among us cannot quite detach themselves from the terminology of objectivity. "It does not follow," Professor Carr says, "that, because a mountain appears to take on different shapes from different angles of vision, it has objectively no shape at all or an infinity of shapes."[21] But the more

[19] In *The Modern Theme* (1923). Earlier he wrote: "Reality cannot be observed except from the point of view to which each of us has been inescapably assigned in the universe." (I would quarrel only with the "inescapably"—see below, p. 166.) "That reality and this point of view are correlative, and just as reality cannot be invented, so the point of view cannot be feigned either." "Truth, the real, the universe, life—whatever you want to call it— breaks down into innumerable facets, into countless planes, each one of which slants towards one individual. If the latter has known how to be faithful to his own point of view, if he has resisted the eternal temptation to exchange his retina for an imaginary one, what he sees will be a real aspect of the world." "And vice versa: each man has a mission of truth. My eye has its unique place: the part of reality that my eye sees is seen by no other eye. We are irreplaceable, we are necessary" (1916).

[20] "It was first thought in Spanish towards 1914," Ortega wrote in 1932. Let me add that this is so ingrained in our minds that if we were to read the accounts of two different observers who, situated at different points, described an incident in the very same words, we would instantly suspect them of dishonesty, of plagiarism.

[21] By a curious coincidence one of the most telling illustrations in Owen Barfield's philosophical essay *Saving the Appearances* (London, 1957), dealing with the shortcomings of scientific assumptions, mentions mountains: "The economic and social structure of Switzerland is noticeably affected by its tourist industry, and that is due only in part to increased facilities of travel. It is due not less to the [condition] that . . . the *mountains* which twentieth-century man sees are not the mountains which eighteenth-century man saw."

objective our concept of the shape of the mountain, the more abstract that mountain becomes. For the existence of the mountain was meaningless until men appeared on the scene, saw it, called it a mountain. Much later in history they conceived of it as an objective fact.

During the nineteenth century and after, many thinking people believed that the establishment of objective facts would necessarily lead to increasing realism, justice, honesty, the widening reign of truth. This was a considerably decent as well as a considerably fallacious assumption, and it was part and parcel of a phase in the historical development of human consciousness. It was a decent assumption, most useful at a time when certain corroded myths still prevailed, and at least for a while it contributed to making more intelligible the communication of certain truths among men. We must not, therefore, rejoice simply in the slowly spreading recognition of the inadequacy of the category of "fact," in the crisis of this once so solid and hard intellectual currency. The recognition of its inadequacy, like our belated recognitions of other bourgeois illusions and ideals, is not sufficient unto itself: it must be complemented by a new respect for words, and by the comprehension of the inevitably moral element within every kind of human expression. Now when we may face all kinds of breakdowns in human communications this danger exists as much because of our *still* exaggerated respect for facts as because of our *increasing* disrespect for words. Facts are not more important than are words; indeed, they are inseparable from words, because we speak and think in words.[22] In the beginning was the Word, not the Fact; history is thought and spoken and written with words; and the historian must be master of his words as much as of his "facts," whatever those might mean.

(5) Historians and novelists: their similarities

It remains for us to consider the relationship of history and the novel—or, rather, of the historian and the novelist. If every fact is, to some extent, a fiction; if the historian must be master of his

[22] Except in the sense in which Piaget means it when he says, referring to the psychology of children, that *the sentence is earlier than the word*—including the uncompleted sentence, because of its potential meaningfulness.

words as much as of his facts—is there anything left to distinguish him from the novelist? Let me assure my historian colleagues: they have nothing to fear. My argument implies not the fictional nature of history: it suggests, instead, the historicity of fiction. Surely the difference between the historian and the novelist is narrower than what we may have been accustomed to think: but this has happened because of the growth of historical consciousness in the West, because historical thinking affected the novelists more profoundly than the novel affected historianship.

The effects of the latter are, however, far from negligible. There are at least four ways in which the novelist has produced valuable evidence for the historian. In the first place, the novelist frequently furnishes actual historical "material": vivid details about the past, many of which details are historically verifiable, since the seriousness of the novelist's re-search of the past is at times comparable to the historian's. Moreover the novelist, through his art of selecting, ordering, and describing such details, may draw the historian's attention to "overlooked" aspects, problems, periods. The classic examples are Scott, Balzac, certain books of Dickens. Thoughtful historians pointed out Scott's merits. The *Comédie Humaine*, taking place between 1792 and 1840, is chock-full of all kinds of historical details. In his preface to *Barnaby Rudge* Dickens stated his historical intentions: "No account of the Gordon Riots having been to my knowledge introduced into any Work of Fiction, and the subject presenting very extraordinary and remarkable features, I was led to project this Tale." (Not only did *Barnaby Rudge* turn out to be a good tale; it also preceded the first professional historical monograph on the Gordon Riots by almost a century.)

In the second place, the novelist's description of certain contemporary scenes which he himself witnessed is often first-rate historical evidence. "Fiction is often an aid to history," Alfred Duff Cooper wrote, "and the penetrating eye of genius can discern much that remains elusive to the patient researchers of the historian." I have often thought that Stendhal's—rather than Hugo's—description of Waterloo in the *Charterhouse of Parma* ought to be required reading in our military colleges, since it is such a powerful corrective to abstract schemes of battle orders as well as to the false image of the nineteenth-century battle in the form of one long *mêlée* among brightly uniformed soldiers, punctuated by the flashes of bayonets, the sabers of cavalry charging, and the Beethovenian sound of cannon in the background, always booming in major.[23] Maupassant's brilliant short story *"Coup d'état"* ought to be printed in our dreary readers in political science, because of its superb description of how unrevolutionary certain revolutions have been, because it is such an important corrective to such clichés as: "the government was overthrown," "the people rose against the established order," etc.,[24] which cloud the brains of young students, as the thoughtless repetition of these hollow phrases in their examination papers attests. On the level of social and intellectual history a novel such as *New Grub Street* is full of historical evidence not only about London in the 1880's, about how certain people lived, and about the conditions of literary life at that time; it also reveals a whole category of late Victorian sensibilities.*

Thus, in the third place, not only the novelists' description of contemporary scenes but their description of certain fictitious characters and events may serve the historian under certain circumstances—when, for example, these are prototypical representatives of certain contemporary realities. I suggested earlier that this function of the novel is peculiarly apparent in the cultural history of the United States: but this is generally true: Dr. Grantly, Madame Bovary, George Babbitt, Constance Baines are *potential* historical characters. I am not saying this in the vein of trite literary criticism, contrasting the "real flesh-and-blood characters" of the novelist with the paper-and-paste figures of the research professor: what I am saying is that the existence of the type of, say, M. Homais belongs to the history of the nineteenth century, and that an understanding of the particular circumstances of Emma Bovary's problems and tragedy is well-nigh a requirement for those who wish to understand her "times" is but a consequence of this condition, which is something more than our reactions to the novelists' evocative description of "atmosphere." Fictional

[23] In 1813 Stendhal watched the Battle of Bautzen from a hill: "From noon until three o'clock we had an excellent view of all that can be seen of a battle—that is, nothing at all."

[24] Thus *The Leopard*, the Prince of Lampedusa's historical novel, written nearly a century later, tells us more about the 1860 "revolution" in Sicily and about the fraudulent nature of the Garibaldian plebiscite than what liberal historians had told us before.

characters may represent prototypical tendencies and potentialities that did exist in the past, tendencies about the existence of which actual historical evidence is available elsewhere. A deliberate exaggeration, a satire may be a guide to historical understanding; and the sensitive historian may indeed include it in his writing for the sake of illustration. On page 139 of his excellent history of 1940, *Operation Sea Lion*, Peter Fleming cites an actual asininity, a bureaucrat's statement at the time, to which he then adds this judicious footnote: "For a satirical pastiche—from which the above sentence might well be taken—purporting to describe the religious activities of the Ministry of Information in 1940 see *Put Out More Flags* by Evelyn Waugh (London, 1942). This novel is an excellent guide to the atmosphere of the period."

If certain statistics are historical documents, so are certain characters composed by the novelist out of imagination as well as of reality—of historical imagination and historical reality.

Finally, in the fourth place, literary history belongs within history; it is not merely its cultural appendix, as Trevelyan put it, "like the tail of a cow." On the one hand, great literature has had an enduring influence—though often only in the long run. On the other hand, the evidences of the short run, too, are significant: the very history of books, very much including novels, the circumstances of their publication, their critical or popular success, their acceptance, and sometimes their rejection. A novel may articulate, generate, reflect, speed up, slow down currents of opinion; social and cultural tendencies. Sometimes these relationships are traceable: *Werther* and Scott come to mind: and recently the excellent Nirad C. Chaudhuri wrote how,

reading *A Passage to India* some time ago I was led to think not only of the final collective passage of the British from India but also of Mr. Forster's contribution to that finale. Such an association of ideas between a novel and an event of political history may be objected to, but in this case I think the association is legitimate. For *A Passage to India* has possibly been an even greater influence in British imperial politics than in English literature. . . . the novel helped the growth of that mood which enabled the British people to leave India with an almost Pilate-like gesture of washing their hands of a disagreeable affair.

All of this may be rather obvious. But let us now look at the less obvious side of the relationship: at the historicity of the novel. "Readers of Alexandre Dumas may be potential historians," wrote the French historian Marc Bloch. "A slice of life" is not enough for a novel, wrote Balzac one hundred years before Bloch. "History begins in novel and ends in essay," Macaulay said. Consider what Maupassant wrote in his only essay (disguised as his preface to *Pierre et Jean*). The aim of the realistic novelist "is not to tell a story, to amuse us or to appeal to our feelings, but *to compel us to reflect, and to understand the darker and deeper meaning of events. . . .*" A historian could have written that. The functions of historians and novelists overlap; their dependence is mutual; their approach is much the same—description, in prose, always the description of some kind of *past* (for even the utopian novel projects the reader in time beyond the "events" narrated by the author in "retrospect"). In the broad sense every novel is a historical novel.

The novel was a typical product of the Bourgeois Age. Literature in almost all of its known forms was either created or first perfected by the Greeks: the novel is the only exception. If this is one of the reasons of its possible demise, this was one of the principal reasons of its emergence two hundred years ago. Not only was the novel a "transitory response to certain conditions";[25] more than that, the novel may have been a manifestation of the development of historical consciousness. For the once customary view of equating the novel with narrative, seeing in it a prosaic form of the epic, is mistaken. "The novel and the epic," wrote Ortega y Gasset in 1914,

are precisely poles apart. The theme of the epic is the past as such: it speaks to us about a world which was and which is no longer, of a mythical age whose antiquity is not a past in the same sense as any remote historical time. It is true that local piety kept gradually linking Homeric men and gods to the citizens of the present by means of slender threads, but this net of genealogical traditions does not succeed in bridging the absolute gap which exists between the mythical *yesterday* and the real *today*. No matter how many real yesterdays we interpolate, the sphere inhabited by the Achilleses and the Agamemnons has no relationship with our existence, and we cannot reach it, step by step, by retracing the path opened up by the march of time. The epic past is not *our* past. Our past

25 Harold Nicolson in 1954: "Whereas the other branches of literature are some 3,000 years old, the novel is little more than 200 years old. It is legitimate, therefore, to contend that the novel is not a permanent form of literary expression, but a transitory response to certain conditions."

is thinkable as having been the present once, but the epic past eludes identification with any possible present, and when we try to get back to it by means of recollection it gallops away from us like Diomedes' horses, forever at the same distance from us. No, it is not a remembered past but an ideal past.

Coming out of history, the novel grew with history. Its emergence was contemporaneous with the development of professional historiography (the modern novel begins to flourish after 1750, the Göttingen school of modern historiography around 1770; by 1780 there are best-seller novels, by 1800 history and *Geschichte* appear as independent disciplines). *Wie es eigentlich gewesen* could have been Tolstoy's or Zola's motto besides Ranke's. The nineteenth century was the golden age of the novel. It was then impregnated with the consciousness of history. Not only are *Old Mortality, Les Chouans, A Tale of Two Cities, The Charterhouse of Parma, War and Peace* historical novels; so are *César Birotteau, Martin Chuzzlewit, Lucien Leuwen, Sentimental Education*. Let me pause here for a moment. Let me remind my readers of what I suggested in Chapter I about the shortcomings of Tolstoy's view of history. Flaubert's *Sentimental Education* is more *historical* than its contemporary *War and Peace*, even though the latter is a "historical" novel while the former is not. For the "history" in *War and Peace*, no matter how marvelously dramatic and explicit, is superficial, whereas the history in *Sentimental Education* is implicit and more profound: Flaubert's description of 1848 is, historically speaking, more meaningful than Tolstoy's of 1812, because Flaubert described how people thought and felt at that time; his novel abounds with paradigmatic descriptions of changing sensitivities, of mutations of opinions and of attitudes.[26] In spite (or, perhaps, because) of Tolstoy's penchant for writing a "scientific" history, *War and Peace* reflects a kind of ideological, rather than historical, thinking. Flaubert, without knowing it,[27] was the more profoundly

---

[26] For example: how good bourgeois democrats became disillusioned with democracy, in Fréderic's conversation with Deslauriers; or Flaubert's description of Sénécal, the first prototype of a modern Fascist. It is because of these matters that *Sentimental Education* merits a certain place on a reading list for a nineteenth-century European history course, whereas *War and Peace* does not.

[27] His attempt at an epic "historical" novel of antiquity—*Salammbô*—is a failure.

historical writer of the two, because of the way in which historical thinking had penetrated the Western mind by 1850. More and more after that time the great serious novels become historical sociographies, a development reaching its peak after the turn of the century. Arnold Bennett was not a better novelist than Laurence Sterne, Thomas Mann than Goethe, Roger Martin du Gard than Victor Hugo: but the former are novelists of a different kind: their minds are soaked with history: *The Old Wives' Tale, Buddenbrooks, Les Thibault* are grand bourgeois novels, historical novels, more "deeply" historical than their forerunners; so, of course, is *Remembrance of Things Past.*

In the twentieth century, then, the crisis of the novel and the crisis of historiography set in. What are some of the reasons for the decline of the "classical" novel? It may be worth while to sketch them briefly: the very problems of the modern novel are relevant to the problems of contemporary history, since they involve the changes in the texture of history as well as in the structure of events.

First, what people still call "Fact" has become often stranger than what they call "Fiction." By this I am not referring to space technology or to the—all the contrary assertions notwithstanding—juvenile genre of science fiction. On the one hand, I am thinking of such overwhelming matters as life in Auschwitz, for example, about which a novel could hardly make much sense, since the realities there were almost always more monstrous, fantastic, frightening than what the novelist would imagine. I am also thinking of the increasing volume of unrealistic madness—unrealistic rather than surrealistic, and madness rather than nonsense—that rises around us every day, evident in all kinds of advertisements, slogans, publicity handouts, public statements, technologized jargon, juvenile lingo, popular music, etc., one of the principal characteristics of this stuff being that it can be neither satirized nor parodied, since it consists not of a distortion of its hidden reality but of the exaggeration of its essential senselessness. On the other hand the necessary imagination of the novelist falters not only in face of monstrosities but also in face of the deadening accumulations of nonsense in this age of universal literacy when we encounter such banalities in conversation, such mistakes in rhetoric, such bloopers in the paper of a student that their accurate record would result in an unreal impression of exaggeration. A few years ago I was quartered in a dining car with two businessmen whose conversation, mostly about college sports, I couldn't help but overhear. For a few minutes every one of their phrases and near-automatic responses was a cliché; I could mentally predict nearly every retort they were about to utter. It then occurred to me that had I recorded this standardized dialogue and included it in a story the result would have been not only dull but unreal: moreover, it would have told us little that was important about the persons who uttered them, since such automatic responses are not necessarily marks of inner simplicity; instead, they may hide all kinds of entanglements of thought and rhetoric.[28] It is difficult to describe people whose expressions are not really their own; it is much more difficult to describe a grunt than a witticism; and since the difference between contemporary middle-class and working-class standards of morality is yet to be demonstrated, it is yet to be demonstrated that a particularly interesting novel could be written about truckdrivers, just as it is yet to be demonstrated that a history of the Pennsylvania Trucking Association would be particularly worthwhile to write . . . and to read.

This brings us to another reason for the decline of the novel, whose standard themes, in the Bourgeois Era, involved always, in some way or another, the relationships of the inner lives of persons with the external order of society. Yet large portions of this relatively stable outer scaffolding of society are now being dismantled— a development corresponding to the relative formlessness of the democratic texture of history—which means, among other things, that the principal topics of the classical novel, involving social relationships, social ambitions, social aspirations, because of the increasingly fluid characteristics of society, have become increasingly meaningless.* It is, therefore, not so much the influence of Freudianism but this growing meaninglessness of social bonds

[28] Butterfield: "The historian, like the novelist, is bound to be glad that it takes all sorts of men to make a world. Like the novelist he can regret only one kind—the complete bore—and take care not to describe him with too great verisimilitude." Maupassant: "The realist, if he is an artist, will endeavor not to show us a commonplace photograph of life, but to give us a presentment of it which shall be more complete, more striking, more cogent than reality itself. To tell everything is out of the question: it would require at least a volume for each day to enumerate the endless, insignificant incidents which crowd our existence. A choice must be made—and this is the first blow to the theory of 'the whole truth. . . .' Whence I conclude that the skilled Realists should rather call themselves illusionists. . . ."

which forces the novelist of the twentieth century to contemplate increasingly the individual's relationship with himself.

For it is this evolution of self-consciousness which is perhaps the principal reason for the crisis of the novel, as it involves, in the end, the consciousness of the narrator. Thus the collapse of the once inflated category of objectivity has affected the novelist as he has become aware of the artificiality inherent in the impartial, detached stance from which an invisible narrator related what third persons have done and thought and felt. Thereafter novelists, in the twentieth century, resorted to all kinds of devices to make their stories plausible: by establishing the position of the narrator in the first person singular, inside the brain and the nervous ganglia of the protagonist, inventing a storyteller within a storyteller, and in the end, novels about the writing of novels.[29] There is, however, reason to believe that most of these experiments lead—not in the least because of their increasingly difficult readability—to a dead end.

The novel is affected more deeply by the cultural crisis of the twentieth century than is historiography. Whereas in the nineteenth century the novel was both a narrative *and* a descriptive form of art, in the twentieth century the dissolution of this once unitary endeavor set in, in two directions. Two new principal genres may be emerging, one stemming from the narrative, the other from the descriptive propensities of writers. To put it in other words, the first tendency moves toward poetry, the other toward history. Most of the recent experiments of absurd, comic, involuted, "new" novels represent attempts at grappling with poetic language. Few of them have proved to be enduring, even though they are evidences of a deepening sense of consciousness, of the development of that "internalization" which, as we have seen, is a development complementary to that of historical consciousness: the internal dialogue of *Ulysses* is an early example of this.[30] The

[29] I found a relatively successful "solution" in Jean Dutourd's *Les horreurs de l'amour* (1963), written, it may be said, in the *second* person singular: the relationships of third persons are reconstructed through a running conversation between two friends, a technique which could, I believe, be applied to the description of certain historical problems by an audacious historian someday.

[30] Since, however, it is meaningless—for us, that is—to deal with the consciousness of even the most isolated person without some reference to his historical situation, we must consider how even novels such as *Ulysses* or *Miss Lonelyhearts* are historical, "dated" in a sense—which does not weaken but sharpens their isolated impact. As I think of them I know that I have these impressions: "Dublin 1904," "New York *circa* 1931," in mind.

"new" novelists may one day successfully break through to a new genre, but perhaps only on the condition that they cease to be novelists—that they be able to produce a new form of meaningful poetic narration[31] not description.

For the latter leads, more and more, toward history: toward historical writing of *some* kind. Of course professional, scientific, objective historiography, a typical expression of the spirit of the Bourgeois Age, no more exhausted the function of history than the nineteenth-century novel exhausted the function of prose: still I believe that the most important factor in the demise of the classical novel consists in its absorption by history. By the middle of the twentieth century, the standards of literary "fiction" have been gravely affected by anarchy and confusion, and talented prose-writers who a century ago would have been attracted to novel-writing have turned to historical writing. It is symptomatic that Disraeli was a novelist and Churchill a historian; the growth of popular interest in good history rather than in good "fiction" is significant; it is, as we have seen, yet another mark of the growth of historical consciousness, this appetite of people for historical reconstruction which to them now represents a certain kind of reality, a phenomenon which is evident in, among other things, the recent decline in the popularity of flamboyant "historical" novels and in the recent rise of interest in the "documentary" genre. With all its shortcomings, the documentary genre represents something that is much more than a serious journalistic technique. The "documentary" is but one manifestation of the unfolding of historical literature of all kinds, all attempts at reconstructing some portion of that unique kind of reality which is the historical past: and if such attempts are manifest in cheap work such as *The Day Lincoln Was Shot,* they are manifest, too, in the higher crudities of Mary McCarthy's *The Group,* as this authoress aims at rendering the intellectual sociography of a certain place, at a certain period, in the cultural and ideological history of the United States. During the last twenty-five years this kind of literature

---

(Also, in our historical situation we must understand why the stream-of-consciousness method of recreating human realities is very incomplete. *It is incomplete because people do not necessarily think in the way they speak.* The verbalization of the subconscious is considerably artificial.)

[31] I. Isaacs in his important study of the twentieth-century novel (1950): "We are witnessing the reconquest of the novel by poetry, and the reconquest of the drama by poetry, for both of these forms were originally in poetry."

has appeared in every civilized language. I said earlier in this book that historians must take this new "documentary" genre, with its variations, into account. So must the remaining novelists. To say, as Truman Capote said, that the historical reconstruction which he had attempted in a recent book (*In Cold Blood*) amounts to a new kind of novel, the "nonfiction novel," is shallow; it is not enough. We are witnessing the reconquest of the novel by poetry on the one hand; its conquest by history on the other.

(6) Historians and novelists: their differences

The "documentary" deals with people *in* history, rather than with "historical" people. This is a result of the change in the texture of history; of the evolution of the democratic landscape. In the old historical novel human actors were the protagonists, history provided the background. Increasingly, however, history became the protagonist, while the fate of the people involved in it provide the illustrations. Two hundred years ago, as he set out on his *Age of Louis XIV*, Voltaire wrote: "The principal figures are in the foreground; the crowd is in the background. Woe to details! Posterity neglects them all; they are a kind of vermin that undermines large works." A century later the monumental Balzac, standing halfway between Voltaire and Proust, no longer depicted history in a straight line: he explored it in depth; he described entire categories of social aspirations, of classes, of social and political opinions through his prototypes of character, among whom his secondary ones were as important as were his protagonists to his portraiture of history. In the twentieth century, then, the Historical Background became Historical Foreground.*

A historical novel of the "documentary" variety, Plievier's *Stalingrad,* for example, is the exact reverse of the older historical novel: the entire plot is History, the characters only faintly represent political or social classes or opinions, they are overwhelmed by History. There is a danger here. When people are thus overwhelmed, this means that their freedom of will is hopelessly curtailed, that their aspirations are crushed, that they are supernumeraries, not responsible actors. The result is the confusion of what is imaginary with what is real, instead of a proper understanding of their correspondence, of their complementarity: imaginary matters are introduced, illegitimately, into past realities in the "name" of History. There exist now documentaries in the form of "historical" novels where *actual* persons are made to appear and talk fictitiously for the specific purposes of the author: History is the foreground but it is a false and twisted history.

That history should not be thus falsified is obvious. What is less obvious is the problem of potentiality which is involved in the reconstruction of the past. This is a problem which the modern historian must consider, for it is not only a particular problem for the novelist. It is a particular problem for our times, even though Aristotle dealt with it in his classic distinction between poetry and history. "The poet and the historian," he said in *Poetics* (IX, 1), "differ not by writing in verse or prose. The work of Herodotus might be put in verse and it still would be a species of history with meter no less than without it. The true difference is that one relates what has happened, the other what may happen. Poetry, therefore, is a more philosophic and higher thing than history; for poetry *tends* to express the universal, history the particular."

By emphasizing *tends* I tried to suggest that perhaps not even Aristotle made the categories absolute. Midway between poetry and history, then, the classical novel tended to express not quite *what has happened,* not quite *what may happen,* but, rather, *what might have happened.* And this tendency was relatively new: part and parcel of the evolving historicity of our thinking. Later, because of the development of universal literacy on one level, and because of the intrusion of considerations of consciousness on the other, the novelists' "types" represent types of thought rather than of class or temperament or breeding. An early example of this is Flaubert's unfinished satire, *Bouvard et Pécuchet* (which was to be an illustration of its author's project for a satirical dictionary of *Idées Reçues*). Ezra Pound was probably right when he wrote that *Bouvard et Pécuchet* "can be regarded as the inauguration of a new form which has no precedents." Since we compared Flaubert with Tolstoy at one point, it is perhaps legitimate to compare *Bouvard et Pécuchet* with Dostoevsky's idea-novels. In the former ideas are laughable, in the latter they are always deadly serious: "deadly" is the right word; for Dostoevsky, who otherwise extols the power of the human spirit, is still under the impact of

Russian fatalism: the ideas are overwhelming, their influences are fatal. While Dostoevsky describes what ideas do to men, Flaubert describes what men do with ideas: and perhaps the latter may be more significant—certainly for the historian. True, *Bouvard et Pécuchet* is a satire: carrying the logical absurdities of the two characters to petty extremes, Flaubert wanted to demonstrate the consequences of "types of opinion." But this kind of demonstration of what could have happened, whether in satire, political novel, parable, or history, has an especial appeal to us, as it describes not so much what certain people have done but what they wanted to do, what they were capable of doing: a consequence in the change of the texture of history when outstanding persons form the foreground no longer, when tendencies and potentialities are as significant as are certain "facts," and thus the author employs "types of opinions" to represent them.

The modern historian, too, cannot altogether exclude the contemplation of potentialities. While potentialities by themselves, without their actual expressions, cannot constitute historical evidence —this being one of the few complete correspondences between historical and legal evidence, at least in the Western world—history and law are different in their purposes. The purpose of law is to maintain justice; the purpose of history is to establish truth. What Dwight Macdonald wrote about the relationship of lawyer and novelist is worth noting by historians: "A lawyer qualifies negatively —so he can't be caught out later; but a novelist qualifies positively— to make his meaning not safer but clearer. . . ."[32] So must the historian. His recognition that reality encompasses actuality and potentiality,[33] reflects his necessary propensity to see things with the eye of the novelist rather than with those of the lawyer.

"A great historian," Macaulay wrote, "would reclaim those mate-

[32] In his review of James Gould Cozzens' *By Love Possessed*. Macdonald: "Truth is a slippery fish, and often it cannot be caught by the coarse meshes of the law." Butterfield: "History would be forever unsatisfying if it did not cast a wider net for the truth; for if in one aspect it is the study of change, in another aspect it is the study of diversity."

[33] A. A. Milne: "The Baconians, who hold that . . . it was Bacon who wrote Shakespeare, have given us what they consider to be factual evidence of their theory: anagrams, cryptograms, parallel passages and the like: but they have never offered us any artistic evidence. They have never recreated for us the true story of the Great Imposture. They have begun at the wrong end; trying to prove that it did happen, before they had proved that it might have happened."

rials which the novelist has appropriated." The contemplation of potentialities, however, is one thing: their legitimate description another. Here we arrive at the still prevalent, essential difference between historians and novelists.

In the first place, the historian may not invent imaginary characters.

In the second place, the historian, like the novelist, *may* describe what might have happened (and not only what happened): but only on the basis of actual evidence.

In the third place, the novelist, by creating his characters, may attribute motives to them: indeed, his description of their intentions may be even more important than the description of their actions. The historian, on the other hand, must proceed on the basis of the primacy of actions. The novelist must, of course, make the connection between motives and actions plausible: but he does not sin by inventing motives for his characters. The historian does. To illustrate moral issues, therefore, the novelist may invent plausible potentialities; this the historian cannot do.

Thus the task of the historian is the more difficult one.

But this has been recognized by the novelists themselves. Maupassant acknowledged that the novelist may—nay, he must—deliberately change things, "correct" events, juggle their sequence.[34] That this the historian must not do is a truism. What is not a truism is that, therefore, the very artistic task of the historian is greater, because his restrictions are greater. Mencken said in a quip that the historian is a frustrated novelist: but one must read Tolstoy to find how, rather, the novelist may be a frustrated historian. It is easier to write a mediocre history than a mediocre novel. It is more difficult to write a great history than a great novel. Certainly this is the reason why, in the last two hundred years, there have been more great novels than great histories. Probably this is why the Western world is yet to see the appearance of a truly classic historian, a historian Dante, a historian Shakespeare.[35]

---

[34] "What the realistic artists say is this: 'The whole truth and nothing but the truth.' Since the end they have in view is to bring out the philosophy of certain constant and current things, they must often correct events in favor of probability and to the detriment of truth: for *le vrai peut quelquefois n'être pas le vraisemblable.*"

[35] Macaulay: ". . . to be a really great historian is perhaps the rarest of intellectual distinctions."

IV

THINKING ABOUT CAUSES

or the structure of events

(1) The consequences of events

"The structure of events:" I brought up this phrase earlier in this book. I said, for example, that with the change in the texture of history we must consider how such things as the coming of a revolution, the pressure of public opinion, the impact of a book may tend to develop in different ways, for a variety of reasons, among which the practices and the rhetoric of publicity play disturbing and confusing parts; and that the historian must recognize these conditions, if for no other reason than to avoid the degeneration of phrases such as "the people overthrew the regime," "the President decided," "the Left demanded" into empty clichés. Yet these things suggested the problem of the authenticity, rather than the structure, of events; and now I must venture further: for what I mean by the problem of the structure of events is that our contemporary historical experiences ought to lead us to a reconsideration of how and why events happen; that we literally ought to re-search our notions about their causes and their consequences.

But this is a very large order. Let me then, begin by moving forward backward: with the consequences, not the causes, of events. We remember but a very small portion of the past: but this includes an enormous amount of events: the mere account of what a single person may have seen, heard, done, thought on a humdrum day might fill thousands of pages. The historian, therefore, must be selective by necessity as well as by choice. He will be interested principally in such events which have consequences. Of course all events have consequences: Cleopatra's nose as well as a peasant's sneeze may alter—indeed, in some ways they do alter—the entire course of human history. Obviously, however, some events are more important than are others. But who will judge their importance? and when? Let us compare two judgments, the first by an enthusiastic contemporary ("This is the most important thing that a President has ever said on the subject of . . ."), the second by a historian in restrospect ("The President's speech of . . . was largely meaningless"). Historically speaking, we judge an event through its consequences: but these judgments will vary by personal perspective and through historical experience. There is nothing new in this condition—except that we must be honest enough to recognize and admit it, especially in our times when another factor intrudes: through increasing communications we are informed of more and more events, while at the same time the authenticity of many of these is questionable.

For this reason alone it may be worthwhile to speculate a bit about the relative importance of certain events. Let me, thus, play around a little with the simplistic idea of drawing up a certain hierarchy among contemporaneous events, classifying them according to their consequences. In *1914*, for example:

(A) The First World War broke out.

(B) The Panama Canal was opened.

(C) Ford installed the first automobile assembly line, and offered the then extraordinary daily wage of five dollars.

(D) Mussolini broke away from the Italian Socialist party and embarked on an independent political career.

(E) For the first time more than one out of one thousand Americans were divorced.

The order of importance attributed to these five events will, of course, depend on the historian's perspective as well as on the purpose of his exposition. For a historian of the United States the Panama Canal opening or the Ford assembly-line business are more important than what Mussolini did, *in 1914*; for a historian of California *1915* suggests not the Dardanelles but the San Francisco Pacific Exposition; for a European historian *1912* may suggest the Balkan War or the Haldane mission, while for a Chinese it is the year of their revolution.

Not so obvious is the order of importance for the general historian. If one were to write a general history of the Western world in the twentieth century one could reasonably proceed with the above-listed—A, B, C, D, E—hierarchy in mind. But since we see the present through the past and the past through the present, a historian writing in 1935, when Mussolini and Fascism were riding high, could understandably and, indeed, justifiably, proceed on the assumption that Mussolini's break with the Socialists was a more important event in the history of the western world than was Ford's financial decision. We think less of Mussolini nowadays: moreover, the argument of which event was the more important one of the two may be somewhat abstract, involving as it does two very different matters; it is like comparing apples with pears. But let me now shift the question a little, and consider not so much the relative *importance* as the relative *significance* of these events. In that case it is arguable that even now, when Mussolini no longer exists while the Panama Canal certainly does exist, that turning-point in the former's career in 1914 was more significant than the inauguration of the great canal which was about to be opened anyhow. For historical importance and historical significance are not the same things: while the opening of the transisthmian canal or the first automobile assembly line in 1914 are important rather than significant events, Mussolini's turn from international socialism toward a nationalist ideology, or the sudden jump in the American divorce rate—"minor" events, these—are significant rather than important.

They are significant because they mark the appearance of tendencies that were to become eventually important:

President Garfield was assassinated in 1881—the impact of this event was greater than its importance or its significance. (The event was sudden and horrifying: but the act by a deranged man had little political meaning.)

The famous editorial of the London *Times* on September 7, 1938, suggested that the Czechs ought to cede certain Sudeten territories to Germany—the significance of this was greater than its impact or its importance. (It was thought that the *Times* represented British official inclinations; but these inclinations had been evident for some time; and the editorial had not been suggested by the government.)

Certain German measures directed against Poland during the Polish-Russian war of 1920 had less of an impact but were almost as important and surely more significant than the reactions of France and Britain to that war. (The Germans failed to affect the outcome; but their attempts to tilt the military balance against the Poles could have become as decisive as the actual military aid that the French gave to the latter; and these German actions suggested, too, the later developing collusion of German nationalist and Russian Bolshevik interests at the expense of Poland.)

The American military decision in 1943 to land in Normandy and drive straight toward Berlin—its impact and its importance were both greater than its significance. (It directly involved the grand strategy of America, Britain, Russia; it foreshadowed the coming total defeat of the Third Reich; but it was in line with the overwhelming American strategic and political concept of the war both before 1943 and after.)

During the presidential campaign of 1952 the Republican Party adopted the slogan of the "liberation of eastern Europe"—the impact and the significance of this was greater than its importance. (It had an effect on American voters of central and eastern European origin; it marked the sliding of Republican "isolationism" into the seemingly opposite extreme of interventionism; but it was not meant with full seriousness and it was not translated into a general policy.)

It will now appear that while an *important* event has an immediate impact as well as consequences, the consequences of a *significant* event are more important than its impact. Conversely, while *insignificant* means something too small to be significant, too ephemeral to indicate a tendency, an *unimportant* event is one without an appreciable impact.

It is not my purpose to establish categories for a classification of events. All such categories leak. Historical life is infinitely stronger and richer than historical theory. I am interested not in the external classification but in the internal structure of events: and I indulged in this somewhat primitive speculation of "what is significant" only because this may lead us to the necessary consideration of what tendencies mean in history—something which is especially meaningful in democratic ages, when the sensitive historian must work with all kinds of materials, wherein he will discover new varieties of significance:

In the summer of 1642 the Queen of England (Henrietta Maria) told the Dutch Ambassador (Heenvliet) that the citizens of London no longer raised their hats when she and the King were driving through the streets.

In April, 1789, weeks before the meeting of the Estates-General and nearly three months before the event of the Bastille, Parisian workers wrecked the factory of a M. Reveillon during a large popular riot.

July 22, 1789: not until eight days after the fall of the Bastille would a moderate (Lally-Tollendal) stand up with enough courage to speak out in the Assembly against the excesses of mob rule.

In 1923 Communist seamen of Western nations who quit their ships in Russian ports were arrested and deported by the Soviet Russian security police, even though their desertion had been solicited and arranged by an agency of the Comintern.

American clothes, expressions, jazz were becoming popular among young people in Moscow in the summer of 1952, that is, at the height of anti-American and anti-cosmopolitan agitation, and nearly a year before Stalin was to die.

In 1830, crowds in Paris burned a church after the July Revolution; but in 1848, crosses were carried by some of the proletarian demonstrators and the slogan "Jesus the Supreme Workingman" appeared.

In 1936, when the Austrian government depended almost exclusively on Italy's good will and when the Austrian press was praising Italy every day, a large Viennese crowd shouted anti-Italian political slogans during a soccer game.

In 1943, at the height of the democratic world war against Hitlerism, masses of white workers attacked Negroes in Detroit; also, in certain parts of Boston, Jews were frequently assaulted by groups of Irish youths. The Detroit race riot was reported by the press; the Boston occurrences (because of careful Jewish intervention) generally not.

What about these random events? What do they have in common? Why are these expressions of working-class behavior, or bourgeois cowardice, of emotional nationalism, of religious or racialist inclinations, significant? Their immediate impact was small; they were not headline events. And yet their significance transpires[1] in retrospect—because of the consequences they suggest. They are relatively early, relatively unexpected symptoms of popular inclinations, rather than of public opinion: and it is exactly their divergence from the established categories of the public opinion of their time that makes them significant. Note the necessary qualifications of timing in every one of the above-listed events: "already," "at a time when," "not until," "well before." That there were divergences between international Communist and Russian state interests was obvious by 1939 when Stalin drank a toast to Hitler and deported German Communist refugees: but what is significant is that such divergences had appeared as early as 1923. On a big surface a small crack may be significant. Tendency, not size, marks significance: a 20 percent increase in Nazi votes in a German working-class district in 1930 was more significant than a 20 percent increase in Marxist votes: first, because in retrospect this indicates something that was to lead to 1933; second, because of the unexpectedness, the "newness" of that event, since contrary to the projections of experts and to the accepted categories of political thinking at that time it was not Marxism but something very different from Marxism that was about to profit from economic depression and social distress.

The word *tendency* suggests inclination, proneness, propensity toward something: thus it is preferable to *drift* and *trend*, historically speaking: *drift* implies helplessness, a lack of will; *trend* a scientifically determinable, compelling, and within a certain time, unwaver-

[1] "Transpire: to escape from privacy to public notice" (Johnson).

ing movement, while *tendency* implies at least the presence of certain elements of consciousness and of actuality. It is through a tendency that events are formed out of mere sentiment. This is why in political life, for instance, the historian's research into "facts" must be complemented by his recognition and description of social, ideological, national, racial, religious tendencies which are often reflected in significant events of all kinds: and it is thus that the historian's task has become more difficult, and also more perilous. Often, unusual powers of insight and a fine sense of proportion are needed in order to find and to describe plausibly what is important and what is significant, historically speaking. We have seen earlier that despite of the "openness" of our archives much of the significant evidence does not appear on the surface;* we have also seen that the general historian may no longer describe the history of active elites without referring to the large passive majorities because, even when these majorities have not become much less passive, the activities of important minorities have become much less formative, unduly entangled as they are with their divination of popular tendencies. Yet we shall see that in dealing with processes during which sentiments crystallize into tendencies, there is the grave danger of skidding into the realm of the unconscious: and the historian must refuse to meddle with theories of the unconscious. Historically speaking, what is potential and what is unconscious are not necessarily the same things. We cannot solve these modern historical problems by a definite separation of actuality from potentiality: in historical life we can distinguish but we cannot altogether divorce form from content, activity from passivity, minorities from majorities, actualities from potentialities. Tendency encompasses potentiality and actuality together. (Acton's famous phrase is almost always misquoted: not "Power corrupts" but "Power tends to corrupt" is what he said.) Human potentiality may express itself in all kinds of conscious acts, even though their actor may not be aware of his real motives. And when human potentiality manifests itself, this forms part of the actual historical evidence. It may be difficult to gather, to arrange, to explain, to describe plausibly this kind of evidence. But it is a large and often important part of the evidence with which the modern historian has to deal.

We have seen earlier that manifestations of shifts in public tastes and in popular sentiments in democratic societies may be very complex: this, for example, is the reason why it is easier to understand and to describe the origins of the July, 1830, than of the February, 1848, revolution in Paris: the former was bourgeois rather than democratic, the latter democratic rather than bourgeois in its character and inspiration, the former having been inspired by acute political indignation, the second by more vague but also more widespread sentiments of dissatisfaction and even of boredom. "In the last resort," said Burckhardt, "the impulse of great periodical changes is rooted in human nature, and whatever average bliss were granted to man, he would one day (indeed, then more than ever) exclaim with Lamartine: *La France s'ennuie*." Tocqueville understood this peculiar compound of dissatisfaction and boredom better than most of his contemporaries, and certainly better than Lamartine; he had spoken about it in his prophetic speech in the Chamber a month before the February revolution broke: this aristocratic historian was profoundly aware of the significance of popular tendencies.

Of course, not all manifestations of popular sentiment are significant: to be significant they must suggest change as they relate to movement. The historical description of tendencies is inseparable from the description of their movement.[2] The very life of tendencies —their often curious emergence, their often no less curious demise, their reappearance, their emerging into the daylight of consciousness, ducking down, trailing for long years underneath, rising up again—illustrates that the study of history must be the description of movement, not the examination of static defined portions of the past.

The difference between the mere momentum of progress and real change is *the* difference of significance, the latter suggesting either the emergence of a new tendency or a change in the direction of a tendency or an important increase or decrease in its crystallization.

[2] Otto Brunner, *Neue Wege der Sozialgeschichte:* "Vielleicht ist es mir doch gelungen, spuerbar zu machen, dass in diesen uns so fernliegenden Dingen *Tendenzen* [my italics] sichtbar werden, die auch die Gegenwart bestimmen. Und das ist ja die Aufgabe des Historikers; nicht aber totes antiquarisches Wissen zu vermitteln. . . ." ("Perhaps I have succeeded, after all, to suggest the visible existence of tendencies in these matters of long ago, tendencies which have a meaning for the present, too. And this is indeed the historian's task, not the communication of dead antiquarian stuff. . . .")

This is where so many projections of modern experts, with all of the vast information at their disposal, go wrong, as they almost always predict the continuation of what seems to be going on. Our newspapers, too, suffer from this kind of shortcoming: they, too, fail often to understand that such items as Air Force Logs Ten Millionth Mile, City Official Assails Corruption, Khrushchev Extols Communist Power in Policy Speech, 350,000 Down with Flu, are often *not* news, precisely because they are continuations of what has been going on: whereas it *is* news if the speech of the city official signals a split within the party ruling City Hall, if the Khrushchev speech is sharp after a softening period, or the reverse, if the increase in the influenza cases is sudden. News is history: but it is history only if it is new: it is interesting only when it suggests change, and significant change: for a difference that does not make a difference is not a difference, not in history and not even in statistics. If the rhythm of progress is regular, routine, predictable, it is not really change: for movement and activity do not mean change by themselves, since laziness of mind and atrophy of will may manifest itself not only in lethargy or passivity but also in the inability to diverge from routine.

The desire for change is a fundamental human characteristic (curiosity rather than carnal desire may be a source of passion). Real change always contains a minimum of unexpectedness, and this expectation of change is an essential ingredient of our reactions to sight and to sound; indeed, it is an ingredient of our sense of music and of poetry: whenever we listen to anything, we are, in a sense, constantly expecting. It is not only that we grow tired of routine, or that uniformity is boring; it is that our interest often depends on our conscious or at least half-conscious anticipation of something that is unexpected and, therefore, new. It is thus that actual events are born out of potentialities: they are not isolated "facts"; the wish is the father not of the "fact" but of thought; and tendencies are the mothers not of facts but of events. Note once more the sense of flow, of movement, suggested by the word *event*. "Only in movement, with all its pain, is life," said Burckhardt. "It is always in men's souls that we may find the symptoms of forthcoming events," Tocqueville wrote. "I enjoyed the luxury of our approach to London," Boswell wrote in March, 1776, having anticipated in a rumbling post-chaise "the high and varied intellectual pleasures which that metropolis, which we both loved so much, furnishes. I experienced immediate happiness whole whirled along with such a companion, and said to him: 'Sir, you observed one day at General Oglethorpe's that a man is never happy for the present, but when he is drunk. Will you not add—or when driving rapidly in a post-chaise?' JOHNSON. 'No, Sir, you are driving rapidly FROM something, or TO something.' "

In history, too, anticipation may be already part of the event: and for the event to be eventful it must be important or significant, that is, different. We judge events by their consequences, for a variety of reasons . . . one of these being that the anticipation of consequences may be among the causes of certain events.

(2) The happening of events

But let us move backward slowly: before speculating about causes, let us proceed from the consequences of events to how—not yet why—they occur.* This, of course, is arbitrary to some extent: just as the present and the past cannot be altogether separated, how? and why? are often inseparable, too, because of the vivid connections of thought and life, and because of the nature of words functioning in language, whereby in every historical description of how something happened the why is somehow implicit. Still, how is the relatively simpler question of the two: it is not the human and the historical question par excellence. Up to this point, for example, we encountered no particular uniqueness in the structure of historical events: if we judge an event by its consequences, so do we judge a piece of machinery on its working effects. But now, as we come to the "happening" of an event, we face an altogether different phenomenon. An event is something that comes (and more than often suddenly, rather than gradually) into our recognition. What happens is almost always involved with what people think happens. Without going into this matter deeply enough to grapple with philosophical and phenomenological questions of human perception, let us simply note that we touch upon something here which demonstrably shows the great difference between human affairs and the physical laws that govern our environment—and which, then, furnishes one of the decisive arguments against historical materialism.

For it is only in a very limited sense that material conditions directly affect our lives. Historically speaking, there are no isolated or isolable material conditions. Political oppression, social discrimination, material deprivation, even suffering, even pain—they are not measurable, and they cannot be separated from their recognitions. Millions have suffered through history; but their sufferings become historical only when they themselves recognize their suffering, and when they consequently realize that their conditions may be changed. In the physical world we can predict accurately at what point of temperature or pressure the tight lid will blow off the steaming kettle; in the historical world, explosions, revolutions, riots often break out not when the oppression is strongest but when it has already begun to lessen: when, on the other hand, the recognition of the desire for change has gathered sufficient momentum, when the very idea of the intolerability of oppression has already become an accepted idea, and perhaps even part of the public rhetoric. "Intolerable" is what people no longer want to tolerate. This is a simple truth, almost a platitude: but what is not a platitude is *when* and *how* and *why* people find something to be intolerable: that, indeed, is a very complicated matter. It involves the movement of ideas, compared to which the economic interpretation of history is primitive nonsense; and it involves questions of consciousness within the human mind, compared to which a chemical analysis of the latter's mechanism is even more primitive nonsense.

Up to this point these may be assertions by a neo-humanist, insisting that human beings are different from all other living beings because of the way in which their mind participates in the universe —an important enough argument. But I am writing about history rather than philosophy, which is why I cannot simply assert the unpredictability of the human spirit, leaving it at that. For one thing, this emphasis on nonmaterial conditions is not a restatement of some kind of Platonism: it depends not on philosophical arguments but on historical experience. For another thing, there exist, after all, certain differences between the reactions of an individual person and the reactions of groups of people to certain events. Adequate measurements, in certain fixed conditions, may accurately predict at what turn of a vise a piece of clamped metal will break. Through similar measurements it may be predictable at what turn of a certain thumb-screw a certain bone of a certain finger of a certain man will break: but at what turn (if at all) will he cry, scream, bite his lips, plead for mercy, defy his torturers, betray his friends, confess truth, confess untruth, say nothing?[3] All this is hardly predictable at all (certainly it is not predictable in disregard of the person's character and of his historical situation). Yet the reactions of great numbers of people are, at least in the short run, perhaps a little more predictable—though they are far from being altogether predictable— than are the reactions of individual persons. This happens not so much because "the law of great numbers will prevail," which is a platitude saying little, if anything. It happens because even while there is a great deal of similarity between the behavior of human societies and the behavior of individual persons, this similarity does not altogether amount to an analogy (a nation, like a person, may have a character and even certain organic functions but it does not possess a soul). It is always in the case of individual human beings that the inseparability of mental and physical, spiritual and carnal factors appears clearest (real heroism, like real evil, is always individual, never truly collective). The reasons why revolutions tend to break out after their so-called principal "cause," that of the oppression, has started to lessen, are many: they cannot be attributed merely to mass opportunism (even though that surely plays a role in most actions of human groups) or simply to historical unpredictability. Save perhaps in extreme conditions, the difference between individual and collective reactions exists because of the way in which ideas move. This movement of ideas—their generation by public rhetoric, their timing, the time lag between the recognition of the oppression and the outbreak of the revolt, the crystallization of sentiments into ideas—is a cardinal condition involving the structure of historical events, not quite identical with the reactions of individual persons: yet here, too, the successful evocation of responses has often surprisingly little to do with material circumstances.

To sum up: ideas—all sorts of ideas—are not the superstructures but the most important components of the very structures of human events: and this is not merely a reassertion of the now old-fashioned argument about the primacy of the spirit over the flesh but a recog-

---

[3] All of the recent talk about "brainwashing" notwithstanding, it seems that no drug can do more than weaken the resistance of a prisoner—which resistance, incidentally, is far more a matter of self-consciousness and less a matter of physical vigor than what people are inclined to think.

nition—a historical recognition—of the way in which the human mind inevitably interferes with the causality of events. Different people who experience the same things may think about them differently: and this thinking influences not only the consequences but the very experience of the event itself. (I touched upon some of these things in the foregoing chapter about the inevitable mental construction of *fictio* and of perspective; and in the very first pages of this book I suggested, too, that the consciousnesses of people born and raised in different civilizations may be different.[4]) A kind of governmental interference, certain forms of arrest or of censorship, which may be repellent to Englishmen in the twentieth century may be accepted by Russians at the same time without their thinking much about it; and millions of Frenchmen who in their youth had paid large taxes decreed by Napoleon I convinced themselves that a fractional increase in taxes was extremely injurious when these were imposed by the government of Louis Philippe. It is usually easier to convince people that they are mistreated than that they are treated well: on the other hand, it is sometimes difficult to convince people who are mistreated that they are being mistreated at all. The process of conviction takes a lot of rhetoric and not a little time.

These are generalizations. They deal with the human condition. Do they have anything particular to tell us in our historical situation? I believe that they do—because of the evolution of our consciousness (which, contrary to what Darwinism and modern biology tell us, may be the only kind of meaningful evolution there is). By this I mean that as our recognition of the involvement of mental factors within physical factors increases, this very involvement itself tends to burgeon and grow. The evolution of consciousness and the evolution of societies proceed together. (One should not, perhaps, speculate whether this evolution bodes good or ill: in any event, the future of the human race may depend on the answer to this question. Somewhat more historical, but no less difficult, is the question whether the increasing influence of ideas has been cause or consequence of the evolution of modern democracy.) In any event, it is a common mistake to think that democratic societies are overwhelm-

---

4 That is: we must consider the historicity of our consciousness. By reflecting on their experiences in different ways, people learn from these experiences in different ways: the very meaning of these experiences becomes transmuted in retrospect, and this quality of retrospective thinking depends to a great extent on the accumulated habits of its practice.

ingly materialistic, and that, consequently, the study of material conditions is more important in our times than the history of ideas which may have been principally important during aristocratic ages. The opposite is rather true: the relationship between, say, bread prices and peasant riots in past centuries seems to have been more direct than the relationship between economic conditions and popular discontent during the last one hundred years.

(3) Thinking and the history of ideas

Let me repeat: the recognition (or, in other words, the self-consciousness) of thinking leads to its increasing intrusion into the structure of events. The movement of ideas is paramountly important in the history of democratic peoples—which is perhaps one of the reasons why the great historians, during what was otherwise an age of materialism, became more and more interested in the historical function of ideas.[5] But not only the portent and the extent of ideas: their movement, too, is different from the history of ideas in the past—one of the differences being that ideas in democratic ages may move remarkably slowly. This was not foreseen by Acton,[6] though it was foreseen by Tocqueville.[7] I have touched upon this phenomenon earlier;[8] its sources are many and varied, including not only universal literacy and education but the practices of public rhetoric whereby the movement of ideas often depends on publi-

[5] Burckhardt: The history of ideas is the "great general task of the historian, what we really have to do." Maitland: the essential matter of history is not what happened but what men and women thought and said about it. Acton: "To exhibit the course of ideas and the course of events in their parallel progress, and their action on each other, is a principal function of the modern historian. Still it is rather a desideratum than an achievement of our time . . . history . . . must be studied as the history of the mind. . . ." Huizinga in his "Historical Ideals of Life" on the Russian Slavophiles in the 1850's ("then still primarily a romantic literary group"): they dealt with an agrarian system that was to be set up after the impending abolition of serfdom, "an important example, because it pertains to an economic situation erected as a direct result of an historical idea."

[6] "What chiefly distinguishes the modern historical art from that of the ancients is that the history of ideas is now understood in its bearing on the history of events." Unquestionable. "Formerly . . . the connection was less visible; the movement of the mind was less rapid, ideas were not so easily interchanged, their consequences were not so quickly developed as now. . . ." Questionable.

[7] See above, p. 90.

[8] See above, pp. 41–45; also below, p. 314.

cized evidences of opinions, tastes, sentiments. There are many evidences to the effect that during the increasing fret and fuss of a mechanical civilization the reflexes of individuals may have become quicker while, at the same time, the movement of ideas has become slower. The portents of these seemingly (but only seemingly) paradoxical developments are of great importance: with the increase of *external* communications critical breakdowns of *internal* communications occur. Texts and pictures may be flashed across the world in seconds, tens of thousands of people are transported across continents in hours: but the movement of ideas, together with some of the most essential forms of human communications, are slowing down, breaking down.

Through such phenomena as "time lag" or "momentum" the public progress of ideas, from their first recorded articulations to their eventual public acceptance, has become extremely cumbrous. "Time lag" means that an idea, a proposal, a policy may be finally recognized, accepted, adopted, and acted upon at a time when the conditions that had led to its original proposition have already changed; "momentum" means that the dead-weight impact of an accepted idea may roll on and on, influencing men and events long after its original rational springs stopped flowing. There are innumerable examples of this phenomenon: let me choose some from the history of democratic foreign relations.

In the 1920's American liberal and radical intellectuals began to criticize the Versailles Treaty together with America's intervention in the First World War. This was, at the time, a rather normal and predictable intellectual reaction against some of the crudities and the exaggerations of wartime patriotic propaganda; and it was part and parcel, too, of the "debunking" climate of intellect in the twenties. A little later serious writers and historians were settling down to write the "true" history of America's Road to War. Some of these substantial books were completed and published by the mid-thirties—for example, Walter Millis' *The Road to War*—at the time when Germany was on the march again. By that time, too, the ideas of the intellectuals of the twenties in regard to historical "revisionism," about the sinister forces behind America's intervention in 1917, had finally filtered down to the level of mass newspapers and of congressional politics. The congressional investigations of the international bankers, war profiteers, munitions-makers, and propagandists of 1917 began in 1934; three years later Congress passed a stringent Neutrality Act, the belated reaction to 1917—at a time when Roosevelt himself grew anxious about Hitler and Mussolini, and when the convictions of many intellectuals, together with part of the American press, about the virtues of isolationism and pacifism were beginning to fade. Still the momentum of the by then popularized antiwar ideas and the publicity generated around the Neutrality Act had a powerful influence on people; and the image of this kind of an "isolationist" sentiment had powerfully affected Roosevelt's calculations and his politics.

This chain of examples could be continued until the present. Let me only mention the "inside" history of an important turning-point. In January, 1945, Senator Vandenberg, the then isolationist Republican leader, made a speech in the Senate renouncing isolationism and espousing the United Nations. This event was hailed by the press and, later, by historians, signaling it out as one of the most significant milestones in the history of American foreign policy. It was more than a decade later that I read in an article of *The Reporter* magazine about the confessions of an anonymous journalist who in early 1945 had written Vandenberg's famous speech, *after* this politician had convinced himself of what to him seemed to have been a definite and irreversible turn of American public opinion from isolationism to internationalism.

Around that time Churchill, worried about the future of Europe, thought that the time had come to stand up to the Russians. His ideas met with suspicion, misunderstanding, and even occasional scorn among the American political and military elite whose ideas of the world were quite different from Churchill's: for, among other things, they regarded the American democracy occupying a midway position on the world ideological spectrum between the rough pioneer Soviet Union represented by Stalin and the Toryism of a Britain represented by Churchill. This then current American ideology was exemplified, for instance, not only by General Eisenhower who on a crucial occasion of world history succeeded in obstructing Churchill's plans, whereby not the Anglo-American but the Russian armies were to occupy Berlin, Vienna, Prague; as late as 1946 Dean Acheson publicly disassociated himself from Churchill's "extreme" warnings against Russian ambitions when the latter had spoken at Fulton, Missouri. Less than a decade passed. By 1953 Churchill concluded that the time had come to negotiate with the Russians anew, in order to attempt the rectification of the division of Europe: but he was opposed by the very same personages in the United States who had obstructed his plans seven and eight years earlier. *Then* he had been regarded as too tough on the Russians; *now* he was suspected of having become soft on Communism. (These views, widely shared throughout the spectrum of the American establishment, were reflected, for example, in *Time* and *Life,* which in 1944 had sharply criticized Churchill as the latter intervened in Greece to crush a Communist rebellion, while in 1953 they suggested that, in wishing to negotiate with the Russians, Churchill was becoming "senile.") Now, it is instructive to observe that in both instances Churchill proved to have been right and the American elite wrong: but this may be illustrated best not through argument of comparative political philosophy but through historical experience, an experience involving "momentum" and "time lag." On both occasions Washington finally came around to adopt policies largely in accord with Churchill's earlier diagnoses, about four to six years after Churchill had put these forth—but this standing up to the Russians by 1947, and this willingness to try out coexistence by 1959–1960 became American policies at a time when their optimum opportunities had already passed.

Thus did the ideas of young, informal, radical, democratic America move slower than those of the old Tory Churchill. Of course politics has always involved, in a way, the art of timing ("Burke is a wise man," said Fox, "but he is wise too soon"). But what is peculiar to our times is that the movement of ideas in democratic societies *appears* to be rapid when in reality it is tortuous and slow. When the validity of an idea is considered together with its public image (that is, with its preconceived intellectual respectability), this means that it will receive recognition only when it is but barely "ahead" (meaning, sometimes, that it is really "behind the times"), or, in other words, when it does not really suggest significant change. This condition, too, has been always true to some extent. I think it was Stendhal who said that wit ought to be but two degrees above the level of the public mind; "if it is five or six degrees ahead, it gives them an intolerable headache." In democratic societies, then, all appearances notwithstanding, conformity to certain ideas counts even more than does conformity of behavior: and since it is more difficult to detect, especially in retrospect, the temporary prevalence of certain opinions than to find recorded manifestations of social behavior, the task of the historian of democratic ages is especially difficult.

Here, then, is an illustration of these subterranean difficulties through another example taken from the 1944–1945 period. I write "subterranean" because, for once, this example will deal with a current of thinking which, though surprisingly widespread, hardly emerged on the political surface—because of its divergence from the mainstream of the accepted opinions and accumulated public ideas of the time. We have seen that the Russophile tendency of American foreign policy during the last war reached the zenith of its momentum in the year 1944. This was manifest in many matters, among them in the above-mentioned misunderstandings between the American elite and Churchill; it had protean manifestations in the press, movies, education, the arts; this was the height of the anti-Fascist ideological crusade; it was, for example, in 1944 that the Morgenthau Plan for the severe chastisement of Germany was adopted by Roosevelt and the government, to be abandoned in 1945. Indeed, future historians who may attempt to describe and to justify the world political decisions of the American government of that period, will probably explain and perhaps even excuse some of these by evoking this context of the then prevailing climate of opinion, evidences of which may be culled from a very wide variety of contemporary sources. Now, what is interesting is that in 1944 a countervailing current of American opinion and sentiment actually moved beneath the surface. There is evidence suggesting that in 1944 a surprising number of Americans were beginning to mumble their worries about Russia, while they felt surprisingly sympathetic toward Germany. This is the kind of subterranean evidence which it is difficult to record and to detect in a democratic society where the surfaces are extraordinarily thick: but it does nonetheless exist: and its expressions range from personal reminiscences to fragments from the diaries of foreign observers.[9] To me this 1944 example tells a

[9] Examples: in certain letters-to-the-editor in small-town papers (where such letters on world affairs, because of their relative scarcity, are less likely to be ignored by the editor); more significantly, in random books by foreign observers, to wit, J. Dutheil, *The Great American Parade* (New York, 1949), passim; in the memoirs of Jan Ciechanowski, *Defeat in Victory* (New York,

number of things: first, that the history of ideas must include all kinds of ideas; second, that the movement of the ideas prevailing among political and intellectual elites in a democracy may be in profound disaccord with the sentiments and opinions of large masses of people; third, that consequently those who are obsessed with the importance of public opinion may underestimate the capacity of the people to understand the need for sudden changes in policy (I am not saying that the Germanophile current in 1944 was exceptionally intelligent or even that it was very reasonable: what I am saying is that it indicates the then existence of far more *potential* support among the people for a determined policy confronting Stalin than what was actually believed at that time); fourth, that the inclinations and the sympathies and the antipathies of people toward certain nations are more concrete realities than are their professions of ideologies (for the receding tide of Russophilia and of Germanophobia in 1944 did not necessarily suggest the appearance of pro-Nazi or authoritarian sympathies).

But the proof of the pudding is in the eating—and also in the digestion that follows the eating. This 1944 countercurrent, significant though it may have been in the long run (it indicates some of the sources of the relatively rapid crystallization of American popular anti-Communist ideology by 1947), did not make much of a dent in the massive surface of congealed ideas and interests at the time. The movement of ideas in democratic times is slow not because democratic societies disdain them, but because they respect them too much. In the United States respectability, social and even professional acceptance, on all levels, and among all kinds of groups (very much including the self-professed nonconformists), depends not so much on personal habits as on the public avowal of certain

---

1947), significant because the purpose of this author, the Polish ambassador in exile, was to illustrate undue American leniency toward Russia, not Germany: his conversation with Justice Frankfurter, p. 266; pp. 285–286: "the sudden appearance in political circles and in some sections of public opinion of a movement of sympathy for the Germans" (May, 1944). . . . "In some American circles, *especially outside Washington* (my italics), pro-German sympathy was growing because of increasing fear of Russia and of communism. . . ." H. Montgomery Hyde, *Room 3603: the Story of the British Intelligence Center in New York during World War II* (New York, 1962), p. 203: in the fall of 1944 public opinion in America "was beginning to favour a lenient peace with Germany. . . ."

opinions. For Americans respect and fear ideas very much indeed: the power of abstractions and of theories, of intellectual categories and of accepted opinions dominate their minds and their lives. Americans acquire and exchange things with great rapidity; their possessions and their sense of possession are extraordinarily impermanent, which surely is not the mark of a materialistic people. But while the movement of goods in America is extraordinarily quick, the movement of ideas is extraordinarily slow, suggesting that it is not certain things but certain ideas which are especially dear to Americans, since they won't let go of them easily. For it is those people who do not recognize how much they are influenced by ideas who find it especially difficult to escape the hold of those ideas; while, on the other hand, their intellectuals tend to regard their categories of ideas as social commodities, in order to assure other people (and very much themselves) that they possess certain kinds of opinions and ideas which are different from those of the common herd of men.

Our difficulty then, is with the word *idea*. Many people think of life as a dark stream of blood and sweat, of emotion and excrement, above which hovers the brighter, fragile, immaterial sphere of ideas, above which, in turn, stand certain theories, the constructions of Great Minds, systems of ideas which had been stuck together by them. Life, Ideas, Theories—three stages of an ascending hierarchy. But this is all wrong, of course: ideas are inseparable from human life, since man is the only living creature who knows that he lives while he lives. On the other hand, the more theoretical a theory, the less true it is: indeed, it may be said that theories are part of our ideas rather than ideas being parts of our theories (when theories influence history they act upon our lives through our ideas of them). But definitions, again, will be of no use here: it is not only difficult, it is senseless to establish different categories for opinion, theory, ideology, *idée reçue*, *idée mère*, idea. Nor is it very practical for us to insist that *idea* (as also *theoria*) originally meant *seeing, vision* to the Greeks. It may be a little more useful to keep in mind that the word *idea* first appeared in English in its modern sense only in the seventeenth century; for it is only then that western European consciousness became aware of its distinct existence in the real world (the word *real*, at least in its legal sense, had appeared in English much earlier). And now, three centuries later, we must broaden our somewhat insubstantial and perhaps unduly intellectualized sense of the word *idea*: we must liberate our minds from its categorical notion: when we consider history in a wide sense, we must consider the function of ideas in a wider sense, too: for when I insist upon the intrusion of ideas in the making of events, I mean all kinds of ideas, mental constructs in the possibly widest (and deepest) sense of the word. I have argued that with the evolution of consciousness, and possibly with the evolving democratization of the world, the influence of mental constructs in the formation of events increases. But these mental constructs are not categorical superstructures or interpretations, they are inseparable from historical life itself: for, if it is foolish to ignore the influence of ideas on the "making" of historical events, it is also foolish to ignore the influences of historical life on the making of theories and on the management of ideas. To put it somewhat primitively: not only do ideas influence everyday thinking, but everyday thinking, too, influences ideas and interferes with them. This is what I meant in the foregoing chapter when I said that, historically speaking, it is perhaps even more interesting what people do to ideas than what ideas do to them.* As H. C. Allen wrote in his *Sixteenth Century Political Thought:* "Men are constantly engaged in an, on the whole highly successful, effort to adjust their ideas to circumstances and also in an effort, very much less successful, to adjust circumstances to their ideas"—of which two processes the first has been, by and large, ignored by Dostoevsky and by many modern intellectuals.

If, therefore, history is principally the history of ideas, this is true only if we consider *idea* in the broadest possible sense. Particularly in democratic ages the history of ideas involves something much more than *Geistesgeschichte, Ideengeschichte,* intellectual history. It is no longer sufficient to search back for the pedigree of certain ideas (even though this is still one of the most estimable tasks of the modern historian); this tracing of their history can no longer remain separated from the process of their dissemination, leading to their eventual public acceptance. This task is, of course, complex and at times exceedingly difficult; the history of ideas, of intellectuals, of public opinion, of popular sentiment, of politics, and of societies overlap and merge. This is the source of the many varieties of significance that I mentioned earlier: but this is, too, a process which we observe and experience in our daily lives in this century, which is the reason why we are not only, as I said in the beginning of this book, all, historians now; we are, all, cultural historians. The history of ideas has become much more than intellectual history;* it is more than a branch of history: it is general history, perhaps especially in our times. The modern historian should never—a strong word, this—treat ideas categorically, since such a treatment, with its implicit exaggeration of the directness of the function of certain ideas, will only lead to their divorce from reality in retrospect[10]—which is, too, why too much importance should not be attributed to the history of the intelligentsia.[11]

We must, therefore, guard against the unreasonable separation of ideas from historical life on the one hand, and against the unreasonable exaggeration of the importance of certain categorical ideas on the other. Consider, for example, the disastrous preoccupation by Americans, during the cold war, with the ideology of Communism (an obsession which obscured their recognition of certain realities of Russian state power and of Russian national ambitions); their unwarranted fear (rather than disdain) of Communist ideas, their obsession with the dangers of Communist indoctrination even when experience showed that the vast majority of people in the Western democracies, and perhaps especially Americans, were impervious to Communist propaganda, and when it was evident that not the appeal of Communism but the brute armed forces of Russia had created the Communist regimes in eastern Europe. It is thus that certain people attribute an exaggerated importance to the power of certain categories of ideas and isms, like Communism, frozen for a long time into a gigantic block by its admirers and enemies alike,* even though such categories of ideas no more pre-empt the real history of ideas than the activities of professional intellectuals pre-empt the sphere of creative mental activity.

Let me, for the last time, invoke the example of Churchill. In

[10] As Veronica Wedgwood put it in her Introduction to *The King's War:* "Theory and doctrine are more often the explanation of actions already envisaged or performed than their initial inspiration." When Bagehot said that "what impresses men is not mind, but result of mind," this was not merely a Victorian expression of English pragmatism; this is still true today, when our situation differs only in the respect that an increasing variety of intellectual occupations have become profitable—and, therefore, more respectable.

[11] A word that the *Concise Oxford Dictionary* "with a touch of possibly unconscious irony" (Richard Hare) defines as "that part of a nation (especially Russian) which aspires to independent thinking."

1918–1919 he was one of the earliest arch-foes of Communism. Less than two decades later he had not let his anti-Communism stand in the way of his conviction—both before and after the Nazi-Soviet Pact—that Russia ought to be sustained and supported against Germany. In turn, in 1944–1945 he did not let his admiration for the Soviet Russian war effort interfere with his belief that the time had come to limit Russia's imperial progress in the middle of Europe. Then, in 1953–1954, as we have seen, he became the principal advocate of the idea of negotiating with the Russians anew. This disturbed Eisenhower who, under the prodding and guidance of Dulles, remained "steadfast" in his anti-Communist ideas and beliefs (whereby, incidentally, a great diplomatic opportunity, perhaps the last one to modify the unnatural division of Europe, passed). My point is the falsity of the contrast between the then "steadfast" Eisenhower and the "erratic" Churchill,[12] since the true contrast exists on another level: between Eisenhower's ideological and, consequently, insufficiently historical, thinking and Churchill's historical and, consequently, nonideological mind.[13] Eisenhower's foreign policy in the early 1950's is a telling example of what happens to democratic statecraft when political ideologies are elevated to the force of moral principles. And, turning from Churchill the statesman to Churchill the historian, let me for the last time point out that kind of intellectual confusion which befogs the mind when ideologies are mistaken for historical thinking. Writing about the history of the First World War and after, Professor A. L. Rowse said that at least in one respect Churchill's historianship was inferior to Trotsky's: for the former, unlike the latter, had "no philosophy of history."[14] This is the kind of think-trap into which

[12] Margot Asquith: "One can only influence the strong characters in life not the weak."

[13] John Morley about Burke (with some exaggeration): "He changed his front but he never changed his ground." The old Metternich once told Donoso Cortés: Categorical ideas are "like a fixed gun whose muzzle thrusts through a narrow opening in the wall of a fort. It is dangerous for those who stand or move along the line of its trajectory. Principles, on the other hand, may be compared to guns that turn around their own axis and which may thereby fire at untruth in every direction."

[14] Written first in 1933, this statement stood unchanged in the 1947 edition of Rowse's *The End of an Epoch* (pp. 282–283); and Professor Carr in 1961 found it sufficiently exemplary in its wisdom to cite it, with approbation, in his *What Is History?* (pp. 20–21).

otherwise judicious intellectuals may fall. It springs from the inability to distinguish between Philosophies of History, such as Trotsky's, and the kind of historical thinking which Churchill possessed: for what Professor Rowse meant was that Trotsky had a systematic theory of history while Churchill had none—which, then, is exactly why Churchill was the better statesman *and* also the better historian.[15]

It will now appear that my emphasis on the importance of ideas is not at all a reassertion of the older kind of German idealism. To say that history is "made," at least in the short run, by what people think happens, contains the germs of something different from the neo-idealist statement (Collingwood's) that history is nothing but the history of ideas. We must keep in mind that no idealism exists in the abstract, that every philosophy of idealism is also a historical phenomenon. Among other things, we ought to distinguish between "pre-materialistic" and "post-materialistic" idealisms. In the preceding chapter I said that we cannot go back to the prescientific idealism of a Berkeley. Neither can we return to the earlier Germanic philosophy, to the Hegelian universal-spiritual or to the Kantian transcendentalist kind: *our* historical view of the function of ideas (like our physical concept of the character of atomic particles) must consider their existence inseparably from their tendencies and from their movement, and not in a sense which is categorical (and which tends consequently to be static). A thinking person in the twentieth century, having experienced the enormous amount of nonsense propagated around us by popularized scientism (for even if "materialism" is no longer a fashionable term, it is merely disguised by sophisticated wrappings), ought to have an altogether different realization of the importance of ideas than, say, a philosopher of Hegel's time. I say "realization" because we must supersede the already outdated

[15] Not only did Trotsky's bad luck or lack of guile defeat him in his struggle with the craftier Stalin in the 1920's, but whatever Trotsky's mental powers may have been, his penchant for ideological thinking gravely compromised his view of historical realities. This is revealed, among other things, by the lately published Trotsky diaries of the 1930's. Disillusioned with Stalinism, living in the midst of the free world, with vast sources of information at his disposal, his understanding of the European situation, including Hitlerism and Fascism, was extraordinarily fuzzy and feeble. The vision of the "Prophet" (*vide* the book titles of his present admirers) degenerated into the babbling of an intellectual bore—at a time when the real prophet was the unphilosophical Churchill.

popular antithesis of the nineteenth century: for it is not idealism
and realism but idealism and materialism which are antitheses.*

I shall not yield to anyone in my advocacy of idealist philosophies:
but I do have serious reservations against considering history as if
it were nothing but the history of ideas. In Chapter I of this book
I mentioned the first wave of what I like to call a "post-materialistic"
reaction among historically conscious philosophers, and I even ventured to suggest certain dates—1874–1941—marking its emergence
and subsiding. This is not the place to list the principal figures during
this important phase of European intellectual history (especially
since it was more widespread than what many people think) or even
to sum up their distinct and respective contributions. But I wish to
say that the contributions of certain philosophers—for example,
Nietzsche, Bergson, Ortega—were, for once, more realistic and,
consequently, more meaningful than those of the historians who
were speculating about these matters—for example the neo-idealists
from Rickert through Croce to Collingwood. I am far from denying
the serious and important contributions of the latter: they have
reminded us, in different ways, of certain limitations of objectivity
in history, together with the inescapable condition that the past
and the present are not separated in our minds. There are, however,
all kinds of dangers inherent in the tendency to take ideas *too* seriously. When, for example, Professor Oakeshott says that "history
is the historian's experience. It is 'made' by nobody save the historian: to write history is the only way of making it," I understand
what he means; but I know, too, that he is separating the idea of
history from history: or, in other words, he is distinguishing between
the past and the reconstruction of the past in the historian's mind
which, according to him, alone is "history." In spite of my deep-
seated sympathy with much of the neo-idealist position, it is this
separation of "the past" from "history" which I cannot accept.[16] It
suggests a notion of history which, though deep, is too narrow. My
readers may recall the—intentionally somewhat simple—statement
about history that is my preference: history is the remembered past,

[16] There is, namely, an implicit contradiction between Oakeshott's statement
and Collingwood's statement to the effect that the past is not dead but "in some
sense is still living in the present." This is very true: it is only that the presence
of the past in the world and in our lives is something that is both more widespread and deeper than the process of reconstruction which goes on in the
historian's mind.

meaning all that we remember of the past, in every possible way, the corollary of this being that the entire past of mankind is history, at least potentially so.

What the neo-idealists have been tackling are the conditions in which history appears in our minds. This *is* a very important issue; of course we must consider this factor of human consciousness very seriously, and it is with this question of the knowledgeability of history that I shall have to deal in Chapter VI of this book. But here I am dealing with a simpler question: not how history is "made" by the historian but how the events of history are "made" by their participants: or, in other words, not how the "past" is spun out of our minds *post facto* but how the past is made by people into their "present."

(4) Thinking about causes

And now we must shift the emphasis from the *how?* to the more important and the more difficult *why?*—which, however, is not a sudden transition: in a way everything with which we have been dealing involved the problem of causes. Much has been written about the problem of causality by philosophers. Unfortunately we do not yet possess a single volume dedicated to the questions of historical causality—perhaps because of the oceanic width and depth of such a subject. For, in a way, this is the most profound subject in the entire world: or, in order to remain true to the basic thesis of this book, that the subjects of this world may be understood best through their histories, in the *history* of the entire world. Since men are historical beings, they will periodically rethink their concept of causes. Nearly one hundred years ago Taine wrote: "Renouveler la notion de cause, c'est transformer la pensée humaine"—"the renewal of the notion of cause means the transformation of the thinking of mankind." I shall try to write about this as simply as I can.

History may be characterized by the absence of laws and by the multiplicity of causes. Every human action has endless consequences *because* it has an endless number and variety of causes, some of which reach back far into the past. What was the cause of what happened to Louis XVI on January 21, 1793? The blade, the guillotine, the executioner, the death sentence, the tribunal, the revolution; the French temperament, the republicanism of the eighteenth

century, the hatred for the absolute monarchy; Samson, Dr. Guillo-
tin, the opportunism of Philippe Egalité, the venality of Danton, the
ideology of Robespierre, the inadequacy of Turgot, the afternoon
sun at Varennes, the original sin of Adam and Eve . . . they are, all,
among its causes, many of which we do not know and cannot know
and will never know. Obviously, again, our knowledge is limited;
and we must be selective. Is there, then, a hierarchy of causes?
Yes and no. It is at least arguable that the execution of Louis XVI
was a more important event than the execution of André Chénier or
than the monetary inflation of 1793—a primitive statement, arguable
only in view of its worldly consequences. But what is not arguable is
that among the causes of Louis XVI's death the blade of the guillotine was a more important cause than the opportunism of the Duke
of Orléans or than the fall of the Bastille, because such an argument
would make no sense at all: we would be speaking of different kinds
of causes, and this is exactly what makes their discussion so difficult:
we cannot even indulge in the earlier speculation about "important"
and "significant" causes: we cannot categorize them this way at all.

We can, however, discern certain unexpected things about the
functions of causes in the structure of human events. Let me return
to the primitive illustration which I employed a few pages earlier,
when I wrote that in the physical world we can accurately predict
when and how (which, in this instance, also means why) the lid
will be blown off by the steam in the boiling kettle, whereas this
kind of thing is not predictable in the historical world, where, indeed, explosions tend to occur not when the pressure is greatest but
when it has already begun to lessen. Now, one of the principal—
indeed, perhaps *the* principal—cause of this human phenomenon
lies in the circumstance that while in the physical world the pressure
comes from the kettle, in the historical world it comes from the lid as
much as from the kettle, by which I mean that while in the physical
world the steam generated by the heat in the kettle presses upon
the passive body of the lid, in the historical world the pressure is
generated, among other things, by the lid thinking about itself. For
it is through its thinking, and through its consciousness of itself (no
matter how vague or uncrystallized the latter may be) that the
human mind, intruding into the causal sequence of events, entangles
and complicates it. The mechanical causality of the universe is forever disrupted by the human mind.

I said "mechanical causality": for here we are already at the very heart of the matter. Throughout this book I have been arguing about the essential differences between the scientific and the historical world-view: but nowhere is this as simply, and as cogently, demonstrable as when it comes to a comparison between scientific and historical causalities.* For, no matter how sophisticated and complex the scientific method may have become, its notion of causality has remained, by and large, a rather primitive one. The very essence of Newtonian physics, and nearly all of the practical applications of the scientific method, depend on the condition that the same causes must always produce the same effects, which in historical life—in *real* life—is not so at all. Still, the meaning of this human condition, observable though it is through common sense and by everyday experience, has been obscured through more than a century by the immense prestige accorded to the natural sciences. It is thus, for example, that modern sociology, and political science, with few exceptions, still proceed on the assumption that certain methods borrowed or adapted from the natural sciences may eventually lead to the finding of causal laws for the explanation of human occurrences* —even though two centuries have passed since Hume's naïve postulate which I mentioned earlier in this book ("The same motives always produce the same actions, the same events follow from the same causes"). It is true that some of the more sophisticated professional spokesmen of the so-called social sciences will now, in the second half of the twentieth century, pretend to deny the primitiveness of this kind of causality, as they talk of laws of probabilities not of certainties; but we should not believe their protestations too seriously. The essence of their arguments does not go a whit further than that of Tolstoy's speculations a century ago as he, at the end of *War and Peace,* ranting and raving about the inaccuracy of history, invoked the mechanism of the locomotive in order to exemplify the kind of causality which, to him, should have been—but, alas, wasn't —the ideal model of historical knowledge.[17]

In other words, while the natural scientists and their social scien-

---

[17] Not only could Tolstoy's mind not conceive of any other kind of causality but a scientific one—a rather Russian ahistorical attitude (see above, pp. 26–27; also below, pp. 220–221). While he was acutely and painfully aware that history is written by human beings, he overlooked the common-sense condition that so are locomotives invented, built, and driven by human beings, that it is the engineer who "governs" the motion of the locomotive.

tist brethren may have lately become somewhat less sanguine about
the potential certainty of physical and social laws, most of them
have not yet given much thought to the essential narrowness of the
still prevalent notion of cause. Now, as every undergraduate student
of the history of philosophy knows (or ought to know), until the
eighteenth century philosophy used to distinguish between four
kinds of causes: the *causa formalis* (the form or essence of a thing),
the *causa materialis* (its material consistence), the *causa finalis* (the
purpose for which the thing was created),[18] and the *causa efficiens,*
which alone and exclusively is the modern mechanical concept of
cause. Still, a restoration of these ancient philosophical categories
will not do. We must, again, proceed from a post-mechanistic, not
from a pre-scientific, viewpoint: a perspective which will derive from
our recognitions of our historical consciousness to the effect that historical causalities function differently from mechanical causalities;
that, for example, our consciousness of a past event modifies its
effects in the present[19] (a function which, in another sense, illustrates, as Henri-Irénée Marrou put it, the capacity of a certain kind
of historical knowledge to "liberate the mind from past burdens").*

It is not enough to accept the social scientists' nowadays somewhat
cautious admission that causal laws represent probabilities rather
than accurate certainties, since it is easy to keep this, largely rhetorical, limitation in one's mind (preferably in the back of it) while
one goes on with the task of categorizing and defining these laws.
Yet, as mechanical causality and historical causality are not the same
things, mechanical probability and historical probability are not the
same things either. In the terms of modern physics the probability
function of atomic particles represents, in Heisenberg's words, a
definite tendency for events. But human beings, while governed by
their tendencies, can also supersede them: and it is therefore that
probability in historical life transcends mathematical categories.
When I say that the outbreak of a great European war in 1914 was
probable I mean not only that this was *not 100 percent certain:* I
also mean that this was *not at all inevitable.* Probability, in this ex-

---

[18] Coleridge: "Snuff! Perhaps it is the final cause of the human nose." (There
is at least one instance in which the *causa finalis,* suggesting purpose, survives
in present English usage, i.e.: "Blood shed in the cause of liberty.")

[19] A recognition of this function in itself suggests the nonsense of those now
widespread concepts of consciousness according to which the latter itself is
caused by the mechanism of chemical agents within the body and the brain.

ample, represents an indefinite tendency, rather than a position at number 75 or 80 on a scale of Certainty that ranges from the 0 of the Impossible to the 100 of the Inevitable. After all, every one of the major crises of 1905, 1908, 1911, 1912, 1913 passed without the eruption of a great European war; in every one of these crises there existed "causes" for war which were stronger and more serious ones than the assassination of an unpopular archduke; and as late as June, 1914, few people thought and acted as if a European war had been inevitable. But, among other men, the Austrian foreign minister chose war in 1914 (only, he chose not the kind of war that resulted). When we say that he was one of the men responsible for what happened in July, 1914, we say this because of the consequences of his acts and not because of their causes. Berchtold was a free moral agent: we can describe his words,[20] his acts, and even some of his purposes: and while it is because of this kind of human evidence that we can assert his responsibility for the consequent catastrophe, we cannot categorically determine his share thereof— not only because other men and other forces were also at work but principally because we know more about his purposes than about his motives. It is thus that we can understand some of his limitations (among them the condition that Berchtold comprehended but the first half of a very important truth, which is that while it is helpful to know what it is that one wants, one must also understand the consequences of what one wants).

But let me return to the essential human condition whereby thinking interferes with causality: for this interference may involve not only the mechanical function but also the time sequence of events. The same causes moreover, do not necessarily produce the same effects; certain causes do not necessarily precede effects. Both its anticipation and its consequences are parts of the structure of the historical event—in retrospect as well as when it happens. As we recall some kind of hopeful and happy event in the past we may remember it together with its delightful anticipations, which are not altogether

[20] His words, not only in the sense of their being expressions of his motives but in the sense of their being formative factors on his thoughts (and on the thinking of others) and, consequently, on the shaping of events. For Berchtold's rhetoric, in 1914, was very German; this smart and cosmopolitan Austrian aristocrat was neither the first nor the last German-speaking (and consequently German-thinking) statesman who courted catastrophe by wishing to show that he could talk as Prussian as any Prussian.

subconscious or irrational ones;[21] and we surely remember them together with their consequences (which is not the way we thought about them *then*). A primitive example of this interference is the kind of nervous behavior (blushing or giggling or perspiring, for example) which is generated by a person's nervous and fear-ridden anticipation of this kind of unwilled reaction. On a more conscious level it is obvious how fear may be caused by the anticipation of fear: as Stendhal put it, "Fear is never in the danger itself, it is in our own selves"; and both St. Teresa and Flaubert said something about courage being the willingness to overcome our own fear—a statement infinitely more profound than Hemingway's curiously Byzantine and American fatalistic and mechanical "definition" of courage being "grace under pressure" (enthusiastically cited, alas, by John F. Kennedy in the Preface of his *Profiles in Courage*). There are many forms of neuroses which are caused, at least in part, if not principally, by the anticipated knowledge of the existence of neurosis (in the case of certain people, for example, whose nervous breakdowns may be considerably consequent to their knowledge that these are recognized possibilities of behavior and of experience in a certain historical and social situation). I do not know—indeed, nobody knows—whether there are fewer or more unhappy marriages in the twentieth than in the nineteenth century (I suspect that there is no great over-all difference); I believe that one of the principal (if not *the* principal) causes of the increasing number of divorces—and, in some cases, even of marital unhappiness—in the twentieth century is the anticipated knowledge that the "solution" of divorce exists.

Anticipation leaps across past and present. And thus "the pull of the future" may function as a "cause," a component of events. That which will be is to some extent the cause of that which is. What is going to happen tomorrow is already to some extent the cause of what is happening today; indeed, of what has happened yesterday. We are not merely the products of the past; we are also the creators of the future—and let me now add something to these common-sense

[21] When Pascal said that the heart has reasons which reason knows not he did not say, as it is too often believed, that the heart is altogether different from the mind: he said that the heart has its own particular variety of reasons. Or, as a modern French genius, Raymond Radiguet, wrote: "True presentiments take shape in depths not fathomed by the mind. And thus, at times, they cause us to perform acts which we interpret in quite another manner."

statements—we are products, and creators, of the past; and also creators, and products, of the future. Hence the inadequacy of the still prevalent concept of mechanical causality as it depends on the absolutely irreversible sequence of time, whereas in historical life events are not only "pushed" by the past but "pulled," too, by the future; desires, aspirations, anticipations, expectations, perceptions, premonitions, purposes, all play their parts, suggesting questions that are as much historical as they are metaphysical ones. They should be pondered by the professional historian for many reasons. For one thing, they bear directly not only on his concept of the past but on the "method" of its reconstruction, that is, on his "research." We do not search the past: we research it. Few documents are, strictly speaking, unexpected "finds." In more than one way we find what we are looking for. True, what we are looking for and what we find are not the same things, since our minds are affected and changed by the smallest "find"; but, still, the "find," more than often, was the result of the pull of the future, caused as it was by our purposes.

Our purposes are more important than our motives. I am coming to this distinction in a moment. At first sight there seems to be something quite unhistorical in this emphasis on the attraction of the "future" (purposes) rather than on the pressure of the "past" (motives). Yet our recognition of the former is deeply involved with the development of historical consciousness, superseding some of the categories of deterministic scientism. Of course Darwinism and positivism were already the consequences of the spreading of a historical consciousness and not only of the scientific method: to study the nature of man through his origins,[22] to explain his present by the past involved a kind of historical thinking that had been largely unfamiliar to the medieval mind. Still this kind of historical thinking was inadequate, for many reasons, perhaps principally because of its acceptance of the fundamentally unhistorical premise of mechanical causality, according to which, for example, every human action is nothing but a reaction—a kind of logic which leads to the unilateral assertion of automatically functioning motives, eliminating the recognition of personally generated purposes. The historian of the twentieth century must overcome these habits of

[22] Anthropology deals with the future of the past, but historical thinking involves the future of the past together with the past of the future.

mind: he must understand the greater and higher complexities of historical causalities. Perhaps this is one of the reasons why his main task now is cultural history, involving as this does, among other things, the ideas and the tendencies and the aspirations of certain people at a certain time—which is history on a high human level of comprehension, the furthest away from animal nature, since its inquiry into causes involves not only answers to *how?* but also to *why?* —and, moreover, *why?* not only in the sense of *wherefore?* but of *whither?* too.[23]

(5) Motives and purposes

The word "motive" suggests something more personal than what is suggested by the word "cause." There was a time, long before the "invention" of psychoanalysis, when the profoundest students of human motives were certain aristocratic writers, or men whose creative genius functioned together with their great knowledge of the world; and it is still true, in more than one sense, that what La Rochefoucauld or Shakespeare did not know about human motives is hardly worth knowing. Since that time, and especially during the twentieth century, our self-consciousness has developed further: or, in other words, more and more people have become introspective in more and more ways, a development which is a concomitant of the historical evolution of consciousness. Yet this will not explain the enormous influence which psychology (or, rather, the terminology of psychology) has acquired in the modern world, and perhaps especially in the United States. This development would have surprised Stendhal, and perhaps even Tocqueville. To discuss the cultural and historical causes of this development does not belong here, where I am writing (I hope for the last time in my life) about history in general, instead of describing it in particular. Yet I shall venture to say that the appeal of modern psychology for democratic societies may lie not so much in its promotion of introspection as in its capacity to categorize and to attribute motives. This happens, as we all know, through the medium of a pseudoscientific vocabulary, the apparent sophistication of which obscures its far from sophisticated notion of the relationships of causes and effects in human and

---

[23] Huizinga: "For history the question is always 'whither?' History . . . is the teleologically-oriented discipline *par excellence*."

historical life. In other words, the same people who claim to identify more and more varieties of human motives may also understand less and less about their functioning. Yet it is the latter, indeed, *only* the latter, with which the historian ought to be concerned.

Now my purpose is not only to suggest the limitations of the historian's craft when it comes to the attribution of human motives but also to point out how these attributions derive from the earlier discussed primitive concept of causality, a concept which not many of the great prophets of psychoanalysis seem to have been able to transcend (one notable exception being the Viennese Professor Viktor Frankl). For not only Darwin and Marx but Freud, too, had an unduly narrow notion of the functioning of causes in human nature—whence their unduly broad emphasis on certain motive factors. This paradoxical duality is symptomatic of the modern intellectual confusion. While, on the one hand, modern psycho-analytic insight into certain human motives is complex and, on occasion, profound, the resultant categories are simplicist and, on occasion, vulgar: since often behind the psychoanalytic rhetoric lurks not the necessarily amateur (in the best and broadest sense of that term) analytical interest in the mysteries of mind and soul but the professional (in the narrow sense) desire to define and categorize and, consequently, attribute motives. Such categorical imputations of syndromes of intentions and of typical motives imply a grave limitation of the potentialities of the human spirit. This was not, of course, what Freud had intended; but the Freudian formulas have been exploited, the Freudian terms employed, and certain exaggerated Freudian implications have been further exaggerated in frequently preposterous applications in a now fantastic variety of intellectual endeavors, ranging from literature to mass motivation research. Whatever merits modern psychoanalysis may have had in contributing to the increasingly introspective direction of literature during the first quarter of the century, most of its refinements have been washed out by the torrents of exhibitionist subjectivism funneling into the mainstream of the present cultural chaos. In any event, just as "openness" and "freedom" in the portrayal of sexual matters, very much contrary to what the intellectual purveyors of popular psychoanalysis and of pornography have been saying, do not seem to have simplified the lives, reduced the complexes, or lessened the inner conflicts of people, so, too, the increasing habit of ascribing motives to people does not seem to have led to a particular sanification of our view of human nature. Rather the contrary has been happening: the preoccupation with motives may have contributed to the breakdown of true communications between persons; and, most lamentably, it contributed to a general climate of suspicion among people. For not only, as Harold Nicolson once wrote, is the attribution of false motives "the most pestilential of all symptoms of frightened ignorance," but suspicion and categorization go hand in hand too, both of them reducing human realities to terrible simplifications. It is easier to define human actions by coupling them with categorical motives than to describe them with all of their illogical complexities: the former is indeed an easy way out, a mental shortcut at the expense of thinking and of charity, reflecting as it does, despite all of its rhetorical sophistication, an inadequate and unhistorical understanding of human nature.

The unreasonable and illegitimate attribution of motives is, thus, one of the most widespread intellectual practices of our times. I need not illustrate its totalitarian applications. They are, in any event, among the fundamental characteristics of the ideological mind.* Nor is this the place to illustrate the influence of the psychoanalytic terminology on the works of professional intellectuals. Still I must record the lamentable occasion which occurred during the writing of this book when, in 1957, the then president of the American Historical Association, at the end of a distinguished professional career, chose to devote his presidential address to the recommendation that historians adopt psychoanalytic techniques wholesale, presumably in order to penetrate the minds of people dead long ago.

Of course the historian cannot forego the observation and the description of human motives altogether: but he must be aware that there is *a legitimate distinction between expressed and unexpressed motives.*

Here, then, we find one of the few close correspondences between the regimen of law and the quest for historical truth. It is a central tenet of the Judaeo-Christian and Western concepts of justice that only human actions, deeds, and words but not unexpressed intentions are subject to human law; that potentialities and inclinations, when they are not expressed in deed or in word, do not constitute admissible evidence. Motive, according to the best authorities of

English and American criminal law, is not essential for the definition of a crime. The law, of course, refers to motives: but in doing so it refers to evidences of intentions already expressed. These limitations are equally valid for the historian and for the administrator of justice: neither may judge motives apart from their actual expressions, or apart from their actual consequences.

These principles have been cast aside by certain totalitarian states where certain officials tried to ascertain the *potential* conformity of certain citizens. But these principles are endangered among ourselves, too. For the essential difference between democratic and totalitarian systems of justice is not that in the former everybody is innocent until proven guilty, while in the latter the opposite tendency may prevail.[24] The difference beween them is, rather, that the latter will construe all kinds of potentialities as "evidence" while the former will not.

"Intentions," said Dr. Johnson, "must be gathered from acts." "The persons we see moving about us do not divulge to us the motives from which they act," wrote Maupassant, "we cannot lay a finger, one by one, on all the secret evolutions" of other persons' minds, on "all the mysterious pleadings" of their instincts "which are not the same as ours. . . ." "The truth is," said Napoleon, "that men are very difficult to know and that, to avoid mistakes, they must be judged only by their actions. . . ." There are "two very distinct elements" in history, he said,

material fact and moral intent. Material facts, one should think, ought to be incontrovertible; and yet, go and see if any two accounts agree. . . . As for moral intent, how is one to find his way, supposing even that the narrators are in good faith? Suppose I have given an order: who can read the bottom of my thought, my true intention? . . . I have found it very

[24] Acton: "The maxim that a man must be presumed to be innocent until his guilt is proved was not made for [the historian]."
The reason for this is that whereas the judicial process is closed with a definite judgment, the historical process is not: it is always subject to revisions. The historian, it may be said, specializes in multiple jeopardy. Moreover, while legal justice by necessity deals with infractions of already existing (and usually codified) laws, the sphere of historical judgment is infinitely greater, embracing the entire moral sphere of human actions. There are many human acts that are not susceptible to proper judicial investigation (to some extent this is true of the war crimes trials)—which does not at all suggest that they are not condemnable. The ultimate purpose of legal knowledge is justice; the ultimate purpose of historical knowledge is truth.

difficult to assert with any degree of truth what was my whole and real intention.

The historian must not meddle with unexpressed motives;* and he must not dabble with theories of the subconscious. It is enough for him to know that subconsciousness exists, and that there is no clear line dividing what is conscious from what is subconscious. He must limit himself to describing the expressions of persons, dealing with their subconscious motives only when these are reflected in personal acts or words, in which event he must *describe* these things and not *ascribe* them to psychological categories. And the human personality consists of something else than of a double layer of conscious *plus* subconscious: by focusing upon the latter we do not really get "to the bottom" of things: as Professor Wilhelm Hennis put it, "what is being babbled out during psychoanalytic treatment does not reveal the 'real' or the 'true' character of the man. That he is in his wholeness, with all of his efforts to be himself, to be what he thinks he should be." Throughout this book I have been arguing that everything is potential grist for the historian's mill: but this "everything" must consist of acts that are more or less conscious ones. (More or less: because such things as gestures, facial reactions, slips of the tongue, are obviously worth recording or observing on occasion. But these must be handled by the historian with particular scrupulousness and care: for they are largely, but not wholly, unconscious expressions of motives.) The record of a person's dreams, for example, is not the business of the historian: such evidence would make sense only if people *did* things in their dreams, whereas things *happen to them* in their dreams: a record of a person's words uttered either under hypnosis or during psychoanalysis is illegitimate evidence, too. Not only does the rendition of such expressions involve serious moral questions; but they, too, lack sufficient historicity.

What historians nowadays call "the psychological factor" is, of course, important: but it cannot be treated as if consciousness were merely an intellectual superstructure. ("Character," said Emmanuel Mounier, "is not a fact, but an act.") Sir Lewis Namier's statement that "mass psychology is the most basic factor in history" is not much of a truth. "Very seldom," Namier wrote, "do we come across in history powerful political movements, such as the revolution of 1688, planned and executed with a clear purpose: this was a rising of politically conscious men. . . . It is hard to believe that on the Paris barricades men died in 1830 in order to preserve the Charter, or in February 1848 in order to obtain an extension of the franchise." Of course *that* is hard to believe; but why should we believe *that?* "In most cases," Namier says, "the essence of political mass movements is shrouded in darkness." In most cases the essence of personal motives is shrouded in darkness, too. There are discrepancies between people's motives and their acts; there are even greater discrepancies between their acts and the consequences of their acts. The discrepancies do count, but motives alone do not count.* The historian must agree with the axiom that it is better to do the right thing for the wrong reason than to do the wrong thing for the right reason:* for not only is the road to Hell paved with good intentions, but, too, the road to Paradise wends its way between bad intentions, between intentions that had not ripened into acts.

"It is futile to judge a kind deed by its motives," wrote Eric Hoffer, the American populist philosopher. "Kindness can become its own motive. We are made kind by being kind." One single word sums up and illuminates the historian's craft, Marc Bloch wrote: "to understand," *comprendre.* Perhaps one cannot really hate and understand another person at the same time: and here the Christian principle of the primacy of charity[25] accords with the very methodical requirements of the historian.* His understanding of motives will always be limited. But while even a limited understanding of the motives of another human being is an achievement, a definite judgment of his motives is always questionable, and their categorical attribution from insufficient evidence is in every way—morally, historically, practically—misleading and wrong.

The historian must understand the difference between a motive and a purpose. The former is an inward thing, pointing at the past;

---

[25] Bernanos, in *Last Essays:* "Justice, without love, quickly becomes an enraged beast. . . . They have let loose justice without God in a world without God, and it will not be stopped—I say this with no eloquence; I wish I could find simpler words—until it has ravaged the earth." "The instinct for justice . . . is perhaps the most destructive of all . . . [it] isn't really justice any more than the sexual instinct is really love; it isn't even the desire for justice, but rather a savage lust, one of the most powerful forms that man's hatred of himself takes. The instinct for justice, when equipped with all the resources of technology, is capable of laying waste to the earth itself."

the latter suggests the future, an outgoing thing and, therefore, easier to ascertain. Motive and purpose are much confused nowadays. It is, among other things, on this point that the relativistic or subjectivistic thesis expounded by Charles A. Beard, among others, fails: for, while some of the historian's motives may be formed by his past, his purposes are not necessarily determined by his past at all: the historian, like everyone else, is not merely the product of the past, indeed, not even of *his* past. Those who have lately rediscovered, with Professor Carr, that "before you study the history, study the historian" (which is, really, what happens when historians look at each other's writings) ought to be a little more careful when they say this: they ought to understand very clearly the difference between the attribution of motives and a statement of purposes—a distinction involving the very ethics of that critical rhetoric which is at the core of the discipline of the professional historian. Suppose that I were to write a history of my native country during the last phase of the Habsburg Monarchy in which I should endeavor to correct the generally accepted bleak picture of Magyar government and society at the time. There would be a world of difference between these two critical statements by reviewers: "Lukacs is, of course, a Hungarian, . . . etc.," and "Lukacs' purpose was to extol the role which Hungary played, . . . etc." The first of these statements is unanswerable, while the second is not; the second can be discussed indeed, the first cannot be discussed at all.

The historian's principal question, *why?* refers to causes and motives and purposes: but we have lately expanded our interest in motives at the same time when our interest in purposes has faded, and when the meaning of cause has shrunk.[26] This has been, by and large, a regrettable development. We must, therefore, rethink these things anew, keeping in mind, among other things, that the function of human tendencies is existential rather than causal; they may or may not cause a specific kind of behavior, a particular act, or thought, or kind of judgment.

"The great abstract law of mechanical causality," wrote Haeckel

---

[26] The meaning of "purpose" has narrowed, too, to some extent (the original version of the maxim read: "man *purposes* but God disposes"). Until the end of the eighteenth century, cause and purpose were closer to each other than cause and motive.

in 1899, "now rules the entire universe, as it does the mind of man." But this is old-hat now.[27] For if there is one principal philosophical lesson deriving from our historical experiences in the twentieth century, this is that mechanical causality tells us little about human nature and human behavior and that, consequently, the connecting of human motives with human acts through the categories of the *causa efficiens* obscures rather than enlightens human realities and the structure of human events.

Appendix to Chapter IV. A note on symbolic elements

Our historical thinking is often attracted by symbolic elements in events. Let me say something about these "elements" of symbols, coincidences, correspondences—without, however, unduly extending the meaning of "symbol," in order to avoid those slippery slopes of language and logic where linguistic or philosophical "definitions" of symbols may lead.

Let me begin with the obvious. There exist events provoked by symbols, there exist symbolic events, there exist symbolic coincidences. Stalin's monument in Budapest, pulled down by the Hungarian revolutionaries in 1956, has not been replaced, even though the Rising was crushed. Napoleon's Vendôme column was re-erected twice after it had been pulled down. All kinds of monuments, all kinds of names may be symbolic, historically speaking—or, rather, historically thinking—so also are, of course, their changes. We know some of their causes; we know to some extent why certain things happened and why they were symbolic. It does not take much imagination, for example, to see why Stalin's monument in Budapest was a hated symbol, and why thousands of people were drawn to its destruction during the first feverish evening of the Rising even when there were so many other things to do.

Then there exist events and matters whose correspondences are recognizable but the causes of which are extremely complex and subtle—

[27] The date of this statement is symbolic. See below, Chapter VII, pp. 294–295.

though they *are* historical. They are historical because of the historical factor influencing all human behavior, including that of imagination. (Consider the tremendous importance of the symbolic element in sexual choices, and even in certain forms of lust.) By "all human behavior" I am inclined to include even physiognomy: it is not only that there exist English faces and Spanish faces; there is such a thing as a medieval face or a bourgeois stance, and I am not merely referring to different clothes, fashions, cosmetics, hairdo. There is more than the difference of two races, there is the difference of two historical epochs, of two worlds, in the faces of an Elizabeth of England and of Isabel la Católica. The difference in the countenances of Lincoln and of Eisenhower is the historic difference of two Americas. And, then, doesn't Theodoric's Ravenna tomb *look* like a Gothic chieftain-emperor's face: round, cylindrical, helmeted, tight-lipped, stolid, severe, monumental? A William and Mary high chair *looks* like people of the William and Mary period, a Charles II chair *looks* like Charles II with that pseudo-baroque wig on top, Duncan Phyfe chairs *look* like Dolly Madison. On page 608 of Volume IV of the *History of The Times* there is a photograph of Northcliffe and Steed on the deck of the *Aquitania* in 1921. It is a period picture: but not only because of *Aquitania* and Northcliffe and Steed: behind them an unknown man gazes out, in a *stance* typical of that period. . . . Of course a certain amount of imagination may be needed to recognize such things: but it is through its historicity that this kind of imagination is connected with reality; it does not exist in the abstract. National characteristics, for example, are reflected even in the standardized products of mass manufacture: on page 21 of Kennan's *The Decision to Intervene* there is a photograph of a Russian locomotive, which I recognize thus, even though I have not seen such a Russian locomotive before—meaning that one can recognize its Russian form, and see that it is not a French or a British or a Swedish locomotive. . . . These are ultimately historical rather than national factors. Not only do American automobiles tend to look American: there exists a resemblance in the faces and frames of Henry Ford and Calvin Coolidge and the gaunt Ford Model A, quite different from the corresponding physiognomies of the fat Buicks and Oldsmobiles of the 1950's and of that bumbling General Motors statesman Charles Wilson. Consider the red two-decker streetcars of England, with their English spinster-look, or that Edwardian look of British locomotives, smooth, portly, moderate, with Great Liberal Wheels. . . .

Such correspondences exist in an endless variety of forms. Sometimes not only the handwriting of a person but the very typography of a document is full of symbolic meaning. But do we know why? There are, of course, causes operating here: the sensitivities of a period, the historical factor of culture, the relationships between environment and culture (doesn't Mt. Fujiyama *look* Japanese?). They may even be described, in a suggestive fashion. But I must insist that our historical knowledge is existential rather than causal. There exist symbolic correspondences, and coincidences whose causes are entirely unknown to us: and yet we may find them worthy enough to include them in our historical accounts. Jefferson and John Adams dying on the same day of July 4, 1826, on the fiftieth anniversary of the Declaration; the imperial crown falling off the coronation coach of Napoleon I in 1804 and of Napoleon III in 1852. Of the one hundred Trees of Liberty planted in the streets of Paris in 1848 by the new republican government not one survived by 1849. These are "those dazzling coincidences that logicians loathe and poets love." For there is meaning to them, in retrospect; and this is why historians ought to love them, too.

Consider the *Titanic* event in 1912: the name *Titanic*, the titanic trust in the tremendous black-red iron ship, out of Ulster Belfast, built by the firm of Harlan & Wolff, symbolic of the monumental belief in Progress and Strength in an age dominated by the Northern and Atlantic Protestant Seafaring Races, by Capital and Science—and the fatal wound by the icy underwater jag of hostile nature, a cold flash of terror, a symbolic premonition of the historical catastrophe of the Bourgeois Age to come in 1914. The symbolic character of this event is recognizable in retrospect, but the connection between the two catastrophes of 1912 and 1914 could hardly be called causal at all: and yet sensitive historians have not foregone to suggest their connections. . . . In 1933 the delegates to the gloomy World Economic Conference in London met "in a vast, white and cold hall in South Kensington, shortly to become the Geological Museum"; this is how Lord Templewood described this event in his memoirs, but this symbolic coincidence was not produced by his pen alone. I find it faintly symbolic that Frederick Jackson Turner, the Progressive frontier historian, was born in *1861* and died in *1932*; I find it amusingly symbolic that the official transfer of Alaska from Tsarist Russia to democratic America was executed in 1867 by a General Rousseau of the U. S. Army; I find it mildly funny that *The Masses* magazine was founded in Greenwich Village in New York in 1911 by a man named Piet Vlag,[1] for the very shape and the sound of this radical's monicker is suggestive. Ask any author about the symbolic element in names; consider but the social and historical cognomology practiced by Balzac. *Nomina sunt omina*: I find the bibliographical item on page 377 of the paperback edition of Hofstadter's *The American Political Tradition*:

---

[1] Alfred Kazin: "as a vehicle for the growing co-operative movement, but (*The Masses*) soon passed into the hands of a gay Socialist group" (unintentional humor?).

"Hoover's relief work is surveyed in Part I of *American Food in the World War and Reconstruction Period* (Stanford 1931), edited by Frank M. Surface and Raymond L. Bland, a mine of information" very funny. But it is more than funny. It is symbolic of something beyond being merely funny.

Omina: I am not suggesting here a triple hierarchy in the structure of events, I am not saying that to the earlier suggested "important" and "significant" events we should add a third, "symbolic" category. I have mentioned the existence of symbolic elements only in order to illustrate that such things, too, belong within our historical knowledge, since we can recognize them even when we do not at all know their causes, even when they may be the results of wholly nonhistorical forces (that extraordinarily severe winter of 1788-1789 in France; that rainstorm on the night of 8-9 Thermidor; the wind toppling the golden eagle from the roof—or was it the gate?—of Schönbrunn Palace the night the Eaglet, Napoleon II, died). Why include such a thing as the latter—an event without historical causes, and without consequences—in any historical account? Because it gives an added meaning to events . . . through our minds.

There is no such thing as an event that is *merely* symbolic. A symbolic event is historical as it is representative of something, of some fragment from the past: and it becomes representative through our imagination which is, properly speaking, not merely psychological but historical.

V

✤

ABOUT HISTORICAL FACTORS

or the hierarchy of powers

(1) The proper study of history is . . . what?

The past; the remembered past; the recorded past. History is less than the first while it is something more than the last. But "the remembered past" harbors difficulties, too. For one thing, there is a difference between what we remember and what we think we ought to remember. We do not have much control over what we remember (though we have more control over it than what many modern psychologists imply); and we are often more conscious of what we want to know than of what we know. But what portions of the past are especially worth knowing? This depends, of course, on one's purposes: it is not the same for different people living in different times. Our historical interests are subject to change. There is, moreover, a difference between a "portion" and a "period" of history.[1] In any event, certain portions of it are better discernible and more intelligible than are others.

Why is this so? Why is a history of the United States in the nineteenth century a more intelligible and more meaningful "portion" than a history of North America? or, in the twentieth century, a history of Philadelphia rather than that of Pennsylvania? Because

[1] Perhaps it may be said that we remember "portions" of the past: whereas, whenever we think that we ought to reconstruct something historically, what we are striving for is the mental reconstruction of a certain "period."

171

the aggregates represented by the former of these pairs are more unique than are those of the latter. History is the history of human communities, and these communities must be, in more than one sense, particular and real. (Civilizations, Spengler declared and Toynbee preached, are the only more-or-less self-contained and intelligible units of history: yet what Spengler and Toynbee demonstrated, in their different ways, was that it was easier for them to write *about* this kind of history than to write it, to compare certain historical aspects of civilizations than to describe their histories.) This is why books and courses in the history of the entire globe—World History—are still largely unmanageable. This is why a history of Eurasia (a real continent) would be, to a large extent, meaningless, while the history of Europe (a mere idea of a continent) is potentially meaningful—though only on certain levels, and perhaps only during the last few hundred years. For even Europe seems to be a community only when it is being regarded from the distance of another continent: for long centuries "Europe" existed only in the sense of a geographical area. Anyone attempting to write of recent European historical developments in some depth even now will encounter inevitably the problem of the diversity of Europeans, of how the continued existence of different national cultures and of different national conditions makes it very difficult for the historian to generalize about Europe, to proceed from the particular to the general.

The proper study of history includes, principally, persons rather than social types, nations rather than classes, cultural rather than economic units. A history of science must be a history of scientists, a history of technology of the inventors, producers, and managers of technology: for the more the emphasis lies on the technical changes and the less on the human conditions and characteristics of their propagators, the less historical—and also the less interesting—the account. Of course everything is potentially interesting: it can be made interesting, possibly even the history of the aluminum industry in western Ohio. A good economic history is better than a bad political history—that goes without saying. It is only that the good economic history is the one in which the human element is sufficiently emphasized and, therefore, real. For, generally speaking, the history of technologies *is* less interesting than the history of nations, and the history of economics *is* less interesting than the history of wars. Less interesting, because less real, and, consequently, boring; for, at least in one sense, the more boring something the less true it is.

This is not a facile statement. The reason behind it is the obvious condition of history being man's knowledge of man *par excellence*. Historical knowledge is inevitably anthropomorphic; consequently the more the organism of the object of our historical research resembles human characteristics the greater its historicity, and the more interesting to us it is. We cannot really escape this condition. The histories of modern nation-states, for example, are not only among the relatively most intelligible "portions" of historical research: their histories are interesting because there exist considerable similarities, though not analogies, between the characteristics of certain communities such as modern nations and of the characteristics of human persons. "The life of nations," reads one of my favorite passages from Proust, "merely repeats, on a larger scale, the lives of their component cells: and he who is incapable of understanding the mystery, the reactions, the laws that determined the movements of the individual, can never hope to say anything worth listening to about the struggles of nations." We must, of course, be careful not to indulge in drawing biological parallels between nations and persons: we must not attribute "souls" to nations. Communities are not organisms, they are aggregations. But not only do national characteristics, such as "mercurial," "temperamental," "steady," "stolid," "imaginative," "unimaginative" exist; some of the functions of these characteristics do resemble certain functions of personal characteristics. A community, like a person, may be "humiliated," "downcast," "ashamed"—metaphors which cannot be applied to economies and rarely to civilizations. And this is a condition which reflects not only superficial appearances but deeper reactions, too: it may not be unreal, for example, to suggest that on certain occasions the military conquest of a nation by another may result in psychic conditions which, without being analogous, may resemble the results of a sexual conquest, since the sexual act does mean the imposition of the will of one participant on another, involving at least a partial acquiescence or even the collaboration of certain elements of the latter, and, as even Freud would say late in his career, the temporary creation of a community between two autonomous persons. It is from these recognitions that the ensuing speculations about the relative hierarchy of certain historical factors issue as a matter of course.

(2) *About economic history*

What follows are occasional, though not necessarily disjointed, observations concerning certain "aspects" or, as they are nowadays called, "fields" of history.

These observations must, by their nature, be existential rather than philosophical. It is true that any kind of comparison of the relative importance of, say, economic vs. political history will necessarily involve the metaphysical argument whether man is principally an economic or principally a political being. But this is not the place for such a discussion: for one thing, it is very difficult, if not altogether impossible, to convince people about such fundamental matters within the limits of a chapter or even of a book. On the other hand, the limitations of certain "fields" of research may be demonstrated on the historical, rather than on the philosophical, plane of argument—and this is what I am attempting to do.

Economic history, it is generally believed, is a very important "field"—or, perhaps, "level"—of historical studies: it is the bedrock for the structure of general history. The present interest in economic history reflects an increase in the seriousness of historians, a concern to get beneath the surface, a deepening of our quest for understanding the past, an *approfondissement*, as the French say, *de l'état actuel de nos connaissances*. Yet the trouble with much of modern economic information is that it is abstract rather than solid, and superficial rather than profound. This is perhaps one of the reasons why most of our economists have been rather incapable of explaining much about the historical movement of events. I am not only referring to the present ways in which famed economists and public statesmen such as Professor Rostow dazzle the mind by devising historical periods such as The Economic Take-Off which, according to them, are *the* decisive events in the histories of nations. Apart from the frequent follies of modern economists, there is ample evidence in modern and contemporary history to show that the so-called economic factors were less decisive than they may seem at first sight. The First World War; the Second World War; Mussolini, Hitler, Stalin; the Russian Revolution, the Hungarian Revolution; the cold war, the end of the European empires—they are not explainable on an economic basis, by a principally economic interpretation of their origins. Obviously, economic conditions are historical factors. It is only that their operations are less direct, less profound and, often, less powerful than what we have been accustomed to think.

I think that this will appear even in those instances of history where the economic interpretation of motives is generally recognized as principally valid. Most thoughtful people will dismiss the Marxist idiocy according to which Hitler was a tool in the hands of monopoly capitalism. Still, it is true that most German industrialists and capitalists supported Hitler in 1933, just as one of the principal, if not *the* principal, factor in the foreign policy of the Chamberlainites until 1939 was their fear of Communism. But this preference of Fascism over Communism evinced by most German and by some English capitalists was something more than an economic preference; it was involved, on a deeper level, with their social, political, national convictions: they were afraid of the social consequences of Communism rather than of the diminution of their personal profits. There are innumerable examples in the "pragmatic" and "materialist" English-speaking countries which illustrate that the most rabid and anxious opponents of Communism are to be found among people who have very little capital of their own, and consequently very little stake in the economic order which they profess to preserve; on the other hand, some of the most influential advocates of pro-Soviet foreign, or pro-Socialistic domestic, policies have come from among the principal capitalists of the British and American empires. Let me go so far as to say that there are no economic motives: there are only economic acts.

But my argument involves not only the impossibility of isolating economic motives. It is addressed to the limitations of reconstructing economic acts from economic records. This is a more complex matter, since it inevitably impinges upon economic thinking. A person may not act as a capitalist, just as Stalin often acted in a very different manner from that of a Marxian Communist: but as long as one person thinks that he is a capitalist, or that he is a Communist, this will have an important influence on their actions. There may be no such thing as an economic motive, but there surely are things such as economic ideas. Yet the latter are usually categories which, by their very nature, are often systematic abstractions. For, unlike the material realities of this world, economics are human formulations. This is perhaps the most important thing that we have learned—or, rather, that we ought to have learned—from the history of the last fifty years. A statement such as the one made by the president of the British Board of Trade in 1914 (Walter Runciman, a Liberal M.P.; perhaps significantly a principal Chamberlainite in 1938) that "no government action could overcome economic laws and any interference with those laws must end in disaster" is inconceivable now not only because the ideal of Free Trade is dead but because the idea of Economic Laws as if they were something like the Laws of Nature is even more dead. This notion of economics as a mental construction, indeed, as a *fictio* in every sense of that word, may be hard for many people to accept, but accept it they must if they want to think sensibly about the functioning of economic factors.

For it is the functioning, rather than the measurability, of economic factors which should be of interest to historians as well as to economists. Whatever may be the merits of the new science of Econometrics (not to speak of "Cliometrics"—this obscene word having been recently proposed in order to describe historical quantification), their practitioners would do well to keep in mind how many economic data are the results of human abstractions. I have written earlier about the illusion inherent in the notion of Hard Facts: but let me now add that of all facts economic facts are among the softest kind. (I cannot, for example, conceive of any economic fact that is as solid as a demographic or an electoral datum, a birth-rate statistic or a percentage among voters.) And the reason for the softness inherent in most economic data is that they are not only inseparable from their interpretations but that they are the results of interpretations. They are statistical answers not only of pre-existing questions but of preconceived definitions; and, moreover, of definitions which are far from being solid or leakproof, a good example of this being the now fashionable figure of the Gross National Product, the very computation of which depends on questionable categories and variable definitions by econometricians. But, then, even the value of a stock, or of a currency, depends not so much on the actual and computable assets and liabilities of a corporation or of a nation as on what the public thinks their value is. The principal factor in the development of such a *prima facie* "economic" event as the American depression beginning in 1929 was a loss of confidence, that is, a change in mentality (just as the American recovery beginning in 1933 was the result of the national recovery of confidence). What counts, often, is the popularity of an economic idea, rather than the "measurable" economic condition: indeed, changes in the first so often lead to changes in the latter that one is left to wonder whether the causalities of economics may not furnish *the* principal illustrations for arguments against materialist or determinist conceptions of the structure and sequence of events. But, then, no economic idea is ever purely economic; it is inseparably interwoven with political and social preferences and tendencies. The history of the twentieth century is full of examples where all kinds of personal influences or psychological maneuvers resulted in actual economic changes (Roosevelt's first radio addresses, Hitler and the German money, de Gaulle's mathematically meaningless but psychologically most effective push of the decimal point two digits to the left, lopping off two zeroes from the franc).[2]

During the nineteenth century historians erred by generally neglecting the history of economic factors. We have become more sophisticated, not only in the sense that economic history made great advances and attracted a few master historians, but in the more important sense that our notion of history has become broadened so that in our times the general historian feels compelled— and, let me hasten to add, rightly so—to begin his description of a period or of a society by some of their economic conditions and developments. This is all to the good. Only, the historian must be

[2] *Re* inflation. In 1919 the dollar was worth dozens of German marks, in 1923 billions, in 1924 four or five. Leaving aside the point of the "old" and the "new" Reichsmark, not only does the wild extreme of 1923 give us a fantastically distorted picture of the—admittedly difficult—state of the German national economy in that year, but also, no serious historian will say that Germany was weaker in 1923 than she was in 1919. Moreover, while it is true that the German inflation was a very serious thing, and that it was involved with many disastrous social, political, cultural consequences, in retrospect it seems that neither the inflation of the early twenties nor the depression of the early thirties fundamentally deflected the course of German history after World War I; with or without inflation, with or without depression, the recovery of German national power and of German national confidence is discernible after 1920. I am not saying that these economic catastrophes made no difference at all: I am only saying that they made less difference than what we have been accustomed to think. (Consider, too, the experiences of France in the 1790's, the United States in the 1770's, Greece in the 1940's; these disastrous inflations harmed these nations relatively little in the long run; their power and prestige and prosperity rose steeply after these chastening experiences.)

very much aware of the limitations of economic data—and especially of certain data of recent times. All of our computers, all of our statistical information notwithstanding, there is reason to believe that the meaning of economic data decreases with their accumulation; that, historically speaking, many of these recent data are less meaningful than are certain data of the past. The information produced by Marc Bloch and his colleagues about medieval France, the household accounts[3] presented by historians such as Eileen Power in her *Medieval People*, are wonderfully telling things. A study such as J. Singer-Kerel's on the cost of living in Paris during the nineteenth century tells us very much, since the costs of living, *les coûts de la vie*, are inseparable from *les goûts de la vie*, the ways of living, from the prevalence of standards and tastes and aspirations. I read Boswell's detailed accounts of his expenditures in London of little more than two hundred years ago. They are marvelously illustrative. But let us suppose that an eager researcher gets hold of the tax returns and checking accounts of an American public figure in the 1950's. They will, I think, tell him much less about such a person's tastes and habits and problems, about his way of life, including perhaps his financial ups and downs, than what a cursory reading of Boswell's Diaries tells about these things of two hundred years ago. The reason for this lies in the complexities of modern records of accounting, which may obscure even more than enlighten us about their underlying realities, just as the most detailed legal account of a corporation fight may tell us very little about the personal factors which are inevitably involved. The more the economic data—or, rather, the more *demand* for economic data, by impersonal agencies such as governments, industries, accounting firms, all kinds of organizations[4]—the more complicated the accounting which, after a while, becomes a closed system of its own, and consequently less and less meaningful, historically speaking. An example of this is a figure such as the "national debt" which in the twentieth century has become not much more than an abstract item

---

[3] In his *Neue Wege der Sozialgeschichte* Otto Brunner made a very important distinction between the older "household" economics and the newer accounting-economics.

[4] During the nineteenth century the principal productions of bureaucracies were verbal formulations. In the second half of the twentieth century they prove themselves by producing more and more "data."

within intra-national accounting.[5] Meanwhile certain international financial transactions have become abstract, too, in the sense that the movement of monies that they register are often transfers on the level of bookkeeping, not physical transfers from one country to another. This does not mean that they are meaningless: it means, however, that what happens during such transactions is something quite different from what we are told happens and that, consequently, some of their portents may be different, too, from what one would expect. As in much of contemporary political science, the old terms no longer fit the newer realities.

The development of the twentieth century has been marked by inflation which has affected every nation, to various extents. The historical meaning of this over-all development may be summed up by saying that money has become more available while it has become less valuable—and, consequently, less important. What this means for economists is that a new science of economics is necessary for a new world: but this is, as yet, far from forthcoming. What this means for historians of the twentieth century is that they must be especially aware of the illusory nature of "purely" economic conditions and of the limitations inherent in many economic records, because they must recognize the increasingly papery characteristics of an increasing number of economic transactions, the new realities of which accord less and less with the traditional meaning of economic relationships. A modern and popular economics textbook, lying before me, defines *demand* as "desire backed up by ability to pay." Yes: but what is "desire" and what is "ability to pay"? In 1966 the meaning of these things—consider only the widespread existence of consumer credit—was something quite different from what it was in 1866. What do *ownership, property, possession* mean in a society such as ours where most people are no longer employed in production but in administration, and where the principal purpose of the national economy is to produce employment rather than durable

---

[5] A. J. P. Taylor wrote about England after World War I that the National Debt "did not diminish the wealth of the community at all, just as an individual does not impoverish himself by transferring some of his money to a No. 2 account. The war had been paid for while it was being waged, and the Debt was a book-keeping transaction, its only real cost to the community being the salaries of the clerks who handled it. Its significance was purely social. . . ."

Another chestnut which journalists cannot seem to do without is that of a nation, or an economy, "on the verge of total bankruptcy." Nothing like this ever happens. Not in Rhodesia; not in Indonesia; not in Egypt.

goods? In 1966 many more Americans owned their houses than at any time before in history: economic facts such as this are often employed proudly by public speakers in order to extol the merits of the American "people's capitalism." Yet what do these statistics of ownership mean when, at the same time, the average American family moves every three or four years, when no more than one out of twenty Americans expect to pay off their mortgage and fully own the house they occupy at the present, when not one in a hundred expects to be able to hand over his house eventually to his children? Surely in the second half of the twentieth century in the United States at least the very sense of the ownership of material goods has changed, together with the increasing impermanence of possessions: but, then, even a century ago *ownership, property, possession* meant something very different in the Dakota Territory from what they meant in the Touraine.

(3) About social history

This is what I mean when I say that instead of studying history in terms of economic developments we must attempt to understand economics in terms of historical developments. This, too, is why no line separating economic from social history can be drawn. The movement of materials in and out of a man's life, the record of his possessions and of his management thereof is meaningful only because of his relationship with other human beings. The economic history of a man is an inseparable part of his social history. Let me illustrate this. X, the famous late-Victorian politician, switched his party allegiance in 187—, an event which led to all kinds of then unforeseen consequences in national politics. The records about this event having been fragmentary, X's motives have been debated by historians ever since. But now, nearly a century later, Alpha, a young historian, rummaging among private papers, discovers a set of letters and private memoranda, which furnish the Decisive Evidence. X was in debt to Y, to that great gray eminence of a banker who was beginning to press him; shortly thereafter he turned to become a National Liberal, and he came out in support of the Railways' Act from which the financial interests controlled by Y and his friends were to profit. Very well: let Alpha make his career. Still, after all is said, the attribution of the economic motive to X is not enough, not even in such a clear-cut case. X joined the National Liberals because he was in debt to Y; but is this "because" enough? Why was he in debt? Why was he in debt to Y? He *was* greedy: but why?[6] He wanted to cut a large figure in the world; he wanted to impress a certain woman; a set of people had snubbed him earlier; he wanted to identify himself with the *grand monde*; he wanted a town house, a carriage. And, still: why? Why did he want a certain kind of carriage and a certain kind of town house and a certain kind of club membership and a certain woman? We can never, of course, know the full answer to these questions: but we are, in a sense, back at the historiographical problem of motives vs. purposes. We do know something about the latter—from certain records of X's acts and words, from the surviving expressions of his ambitions and aspirations, which were personal as well as historical ones, since not only certain traits of his personality but even some of his intimate desires may not have been altogether inseparable from the habits, fashions, standards, and ideas of his times, that is, of a particular culture in a certain historical period.

In a sense, therefore, social history is the largest portion of cultural history. There are many problems about this field, however. The first is its relationship to sociology, a problem which I tried to dispose of in Chapter II with the summary statement that history can never become sociology, even though it must become more and more sociographical[7]—meaning that the purpose of the conscientious historian as well as of the intelligent sociologist must be the

[6] Aristotle: "The acquisition of money in excess of natural requirements is incompatible with economic activity."

[7] Beginning with demography. For demographic data (but not demographic projections) are perhaps the richest mine for the modern historian, for two reasons at least: first, because the records of such things as birth, death, marriage are seldom disputable, they are closest to the nineteenth-century ideal of Solid Facts; second, because the transmission of life and the choices of people for their habitations involve the basic phenomena of all historical life. The fluctuations of the rate of birth, marriage, illegitimacy, suicide, divorce, of the movements of populations are, or rather ought to be, of central interest to the historian, even though the causalities which they involve may be extremely complex and profound, discernible only with great difficulty. The relationship between birth rates and material conditions is, for example, very different from what sociological "reason" suggests. Why is the birth rate so high in the Soviet Union, with its chronic and miserable conditions of housing? Is there any relationship between the decline of the birth rate in western Europe and the introduction of contraceptive devices? Not very much; the birth rate dropped in these countries decades before the manufacture of contraceptives began.

description of societies rather than their categorization according to so-called laws, and that this description must be historical in the sense that it must focus on movement—that is, on the origins, developments, and changes of social habits and other social phenomena. *

These phenomena include things such as classes which are for the social historian what states are for the political historian. It is here that the second problem, that of the terminology of social history, arises. This terminology must be historical, not sociological; it must depend, as much as this is possible, on the vocabulary of everyday language. But it is not enough to say this. The social historian faces certain difficulties which are peculiar to his subject. Classes, for example, are more fluid and, therefore, more elusive realities than are states which do have, after all, a concrete and geographical basis. And, as Professor Alfred Cobban wrote in a magisterial manner, historians have not been very accurate in writing about classes, since they have "borrowed their vocabulary, and therefore the presuppositions of their history, from the Marxian analysis, and continue to use the same terms even when their researches call for something different."[8] This does not mean that we should acquiesce in the defeatist thesis proposed by Professor Seignobos, that class terminology necessarily rests on a "mythological" vocabulary; it means, however, that we ought to reconsider the accuracy of the old categories and, with new materials at hand, we ought to be more precise about them. For example, the dominant "bourgeois" character of the Huguenots or of the Louis Philippe regime "deserve," in Cobban's words, "a little more investigation before we can take it for granted." Furthermore, we must keep in mind that the trouble with the old categories lies often not so much in their wanting accuracy as in their static character, for the very notion of class is dynamic rather than static. In the eighteenth century, for example, *manufacturer* in England meant industrial worker, whereas in France *ouvrier* meant what we now mean as manufac-

---

[8] There is, for example, widespread confusion of status with function; and, as Professor Cobban writes ("The Vocabulary of Social History"), "function [is] interpreted in a single and restricted sense. An official, because he lives on a salary and has no share in the ownership of the means of production, is a wage-earner and therefore a proletarian; a poor shopkeeper, or even a peddler, is a capitalist. This is to ignore their level of remuneration, the way people live, and—most important of all—the way they feel. . . ."

turer; as Cobban put it, thereafter "the English term has gone up in the world and the French one down." I have tried to suggest earlier the difference between *bourgeois* and *middle class,* since the former term is the more dynamic one of the two. It refers to an entire sphere of functional and historical aspirations which are altogether missing from the more static and sociological term of *middle class.* These aspirations reflect tendencies which are different from the material conditions that are registered by economics: for, to a considerable extent, social history is not only the history of movements, it is the history of aspirations. Not only is what happens often inextricably involved with what people think happens; what people are is involved with what they want to be.

Typical of the Bourgeois Age was the powerful impulse of social ambitions. That Rastignac was a rake, Josiah Bounderby a pompous ass, Emma Bovary a fallen woman will be evident to readers a hundred years from now. What they may find difficult to comprehend is the exaggerated importance that certain characters of Balzac as well as of Flaubert, of Jane Austen as well as of Trollope, attached to social ambitions. At least for three centuries in the West such social aspirations were among the profoundest personal—and, consequently, historical—factors. It is because of their deep complexities that they have been described by master novelists rather than by historians. For, even if we recognize the powerful element of emotions and sentiments in politics, we can see that political ambitions are more or less rational ones, whereas this is less true of social ambitions, at the sources of which we find the gnarled roots of Vanity, luxuriating in cavernous recesses of the human spirit: and it is therefore that the penetrating eye of the novelist may furnish some guidance here to the cultural historian. For the social element is something more than environmental influence; it does not only surround, but through images and ideas it intrudes into the private spheres of thought and personal choice, including even the deep sphere of sexual choice. It is a mistake to categorize Madame Birotteau as having been the victim of her social, and Madame Bovary of her sexual, ambitions. There is a very close connection between these two things. They are involved with each other through personal aspirations generated by certain ideas through imagination. I shall have to return to this point once more in the following chapter; let me only suggest here that, just as the Industrial Revolution was the consequence of certain ideas, the modern Sexual Revolution has been social rather than sexual. It is especially in our democratic times—consider, for example, the marriage habits of young people in the United States—that this primacy of the social over the merely sexual element so often prevails. It is only because of the peculiar intellectual confusion of our times that it has been seldom so recognized. But we ought to recognize that if the so-called Sexual Revolution in the twentieth century has been a revolution at all, it has been a social revolution, a leveling revolution; for sexual ambitions are almost often inseparable from social aspirations, just as sexual frustration is often social frustration, existential frustration, the sense of a personal failure within a society.

Meanwhile we face a new situation. The social historian of the second half of the twentieth century will have to consider the weakening of traditional social ambitions—at the very time when the impact of mass society on the individual is very strong, when social conformities of various kinds have become pervasive. We may face new phenomena of social history. Not only are "classes" difficult and, in retrospect, fragile historical categories: we may be moving into an era of a certain classnessness, at least in the traditional sense of the word. Surely many of the older class distinctions are dissolving, as we may be moving toward a neo-medieval society based on status rather than on contract, on recognized professional rank rather than on distinctions of birth or of wealth. Still, the momentum of accepted ideas is very strong, for people will think in terms of classes even when the realities of the latter may no longer function. (In any event, one of the most complex and most interesting factors within social phenomena is the discrepancy which almost always exists between two perspectives of one's position on the social scale: between the position in which a person sees himself and the different position to which others may assign him in their minds.) Moreover, with the gradual dissolution of class boundaries in many national societies, the desire for a kind of group self-identification has replaced the older personal propellant of social ambitions: we have a new type of person who wants to rise with his group, and almost never beyond it. This is altogether different from the bourgeois aspirations, this social phenomenon of the Organization Man, or Mass Man, or whatever we may call him; in any event, there are complex personal problems latent within his rootlessness,

within the degeneration of his aspirations, and within the super-
ficially manageable character of his ambitions. Some of the most
telling observations of this structural change were made not by
sociologists or by social historians but by the Italian-German theologian Romano Guardini. In a little book, characteristically entitled
The End of the Modern World, and again characteristically, written
not during the desperations of the Hitler era but amid the flourishing prosperity of Adenauer's West Germany, Guardini said that the
era of Mass Man is already succeeding that of the Modern Man,
but that this mass "is not debased and decayed essentially as was
the rabble of ancient Rome. The mass has assumed a genuine form
of existence in human history." But with the "loss of personality
comes the steady falling away of that sense of uniqueness with
which man had once viewed his existence, which had been the
source of all social intercourse. . . ."

Still we cannot conclude that while political history was the history *par excellence* of the Modern Age with its bourgeois characteristics, social history is the history *par excellence* of the mass
democratic age now developing. The description of societies, of
their habits and of their ideas, has become more and more important
—on the condition that such a description retains its historicity—
as long as it remains "history" rather than "social."[9] The constant
danger which social historians skirt is the tendency to gloss over
what is unique and exceptional and resistant to the pattern of general developments. Of course we live in a world where we are more
acquainted with the large than with the small: but "more" does not
necessarily mean "better." The historian must remain introspective;
he must avoid Comte's original error of trying, as Maxime Leroy
put it, to explain "l'homme par l'humanité" and not "l'humanité par
l'homme." There is no history to *every* categorized aggregate of
individuals, so dear to the social scientist: there is not much history
in the story of Tall Men or of Young Businessmen: there is history
in the story of the Young Turks.[10]

[9] This is why even such an otherwise interesting social history of England
between the wars as *The Long Week-End,* by Robert Graves and Alan Hodge,
with its journalistic *petite histoire* and coterie gossip, is often defective.

[10] The history of certain minorities may be significant: but this significance
resides in their quality (Spanish Jews, Huguenot minorites in exile and in
France, etc.); as Américo Castro said, the importance of the Hispano-Hebrews
(about 4 percent of the Iberian population in the fifteenth century) "consisted
in the quality of their work and not in their numbers."

(4) About political history

History is still principally the history of states and of governments. The now so respectable emphasis on economic and social developments obscures this fact. Yet the history of what used to be the governing classes no longer explains almost everything about domestic politics, just as the account of the relationships of states no longer explains all about foreign politics. The texture of history has changed, together with the structure of politics, in our democratic age. I shall not belabor this argument further, having devoted to it the second chapter of this book; I have little to add to what I said there about the problems of historiography and about the deteriorating authenticity of records in the democratic epoch in which we now live. Apart from these problems the practice of political history, especially in dealing with subjects after 1650 and before 1945, is relatively (but only relatively) in not too bad a shape. The main reason for this condition is that, all of their verbal respects to economics and to sociology notwithstanding, most historians are still interested principally in politics—indeed, it is probably because of their political interest in the past that they took their degree in history and not in economics or sociology.

There are, however, certain matters which may be worth mentioning at this point. There are many signs which suggest that the importance of local politics is decreasing: an alarming symptom for the future of traditional democracy. For one thing, the destruction, and not only the temporary defeat, of entire nations has now become possible because of atomic weapons, whereby foreign policy is literally a life-and-death matter for their governments. For another thing, the domestic life of peoples is influenced increasingly by administration rather than by legislation, permanent governmental agencies having become rather more important than even parliaments and other more traditional bodies. The most drastic curtailments of personal liberties and of traditional civic processes may be expedited by such agencies through their routine evolution —I need only to refer to such things as telephonic and electronic eavesdropping. Indeed, halfway to 1984, when this is written, the great danger in the West is no longer the possibility of the totalitarian and antidemocratic regime of a political Big Brother but, rather, the increasing regime of a totalitarian democracy, by which I mean the evolution of a society in which universal popular suffrage, including a minimum of party choice, exists, but where freedom of speech is hardly more than of theoretical value for the individual, whose life and ideas, whose rights to privacy, to family autonomy, and to durable possessions are regimented by government and rigidly limited by technology and by mass communications. It will be difficult for a future historian to trace exactly the shapeless stages of these evolutions. In any event he will have to be exceptionally discerning in order to avoid becoming entangled in the thicket of antiquated adjectives—liberal, conservative, reactionary, progressive, Rightist, Leftist—which may obscure rather than enlighten his path.

This brings us to the problem of our political terminology. For not only is a "new science of politics necessary for a new world," but a now antiquated terminology may obscure our view of the historical developments of politics after 1914—indeed, perhaps during the last one hundred years. Since this is not a treatise in political theory I must sum up my argument as briefly as I can. We are still using the categories "Left" and "Right" even though they are often outdated and inapplicable. Here are a few examples. Has the United States been moving to the "Right" or to the "Left" during the last twenty years? Has the Soviet Union been moving to the "Right" or to the "Left" since Stalin died? Was Hitler more "Rightist" than Mussolini, or less? These questions are unanswerable: the categories do not fit.[11] Of course they never fitted exactly, not even in the more remote past; still, Left and Right *were* relatively meaningful designations during the nineteenth century, whereas recently they have become meaningless in an increasing number of instances. And even less useful than "Left" and "Right" are the categories "conservative" and "liberal," especially as they are employed in the United States. I am not only referring to the evident transmutation of ideas whereby the liberals, the earlier champions of free enterprise, in the twentieth century became the champions of the welfare state. I am referring to the condition that whereas the principal dialogues in the nineteenth century occurred indeed between relative conservatives and relative liberals, the principal relation-

---

[11] I remember hearing Edward R. Murrow refer to Joseph McCarthy in 1954 as someone "to the Right of Louis XIV." Thereupon I had to turn the radio off.

ship in the twentieth century involves two elementary political tendencies of quite another order: they are not liberalism and conservatism; they are nationalism and socialism. They, and their relationship, are the principal political phenomena of this century. For example, National Socialism has been the common denominator of the principal totalitarian regimes during the second quarter of this century, a fact which has been deliberately obscured by the Communist,* and regrettably, by the frequent liberal attribution of the adjective "fascist" to all totalitarian regimes of the non-Communist variety. Yet, for once, the German term National Socialism was a precise one. While it is nonsense to call Hitler a Brown Communist or Stalin a Red Fascist, it makes a lot of sense to recognize that, in one way or another, Hitler, Stalin, Mussolini were, all, national socialists. So were (and are), in their ways, Nasser, Tito, Perón, Gomulka, Father Coughlin, Joseph McCarthy, Castro, Nehru, Sukarno, Mao Tse-tung, Ho Chi Minh, and others: nationalist socialists or social nationalists, all of them. Our political analysts and theorists have consistently underrated the influence of the national factor upon socialism, even though this should have been evident as early as 1914 when the nationalism of the masses, including the working classes, proved so much stronger and enduring than the rational exhortations of the suddenly few spokesmen of the international Socialist ideology. After World War I German National Socialism was but an extreme manifestation of this worldwide conjunction of nationalism and socialism, a phenomenon which, I repeat, is recognizable *not* only in its totalitarian varieties. (I have often thought, for example, that it is by these terms that the ideological mysteries and complexities of the American two-party system may be explainable to Europeans in the twentieth century, since it may be said that among our two national welfare parties the Democrats have, by and large, emphasized their socialist rather than their nationalist programs, while the Republicans have been, generally speaking, nationalists rather than socialists—even though, of course, they would not admit this.)

They would not admit this. The United States, as every other nation, has been moving in the direction of a welfare state during the last sixty years at least. This has involved legislation and administrative practices of the kind which in other nations are called "Socialist"; in the United States they weren't. Americans have strenuously avoided this adjective; but, then, in this evolution of an American socialism the role of American Socialist parties was minimal. This should illustrate the importance of political terminology, and perhaps of rhetoric in general. Since the American people rejected (and they still reject) the word "socialist," and since what happens in the short run is inseparable from what people think happens, the legislation of the New Deal, for instance, was *not* socialist in the sense in which the legislation of British Labour or of Swedish Socialist governments *was* socialist. Of course this reluctance to call certain spades spades is a historical phenomenon involved with certain national traditions and national characteristics, including the reluctance of certain peoples to reconsider some of their ideas. As early as 1881 John Morley, referring to the English Factory Acts, wrote of "the rather amazing result that in the country where socialism has been less talked about than any other country in Europe, its principles have been most extensively applied." Two generations later, however, the word "socialist" (and not merely "Labour") has become more acceptable even in England. It is not inconceivable that, in the long run, future generations of Americans may recognize the socialistic transformation of American society, but this would involve a change in accepted ideas together with a change in the general political climate of the country. The course of the world, as Lord Percy of Newcastle wrote, is still "determined by what people believe," but it is also true that political terminology is not a mere matter of names, that, as René Rémond put it, "the changing fortune of certain political terms indicates corresponding changes in the fortune of certain political formations." Consider the recent fortunes of the political adjective "conservative" in the United States. As late as 1952, when the popular reaction against the liberal ideologies and policies of the previous Democratic Administrations was in full swing, even Senator Taft shunned the word "conservative"; eight years later, however, "conservative" became acceptable, Nixon and even Eisenhower employing it approvingly on occasion, until by 1964, for the first time in American history, the presidential nominee of one of the two great national parties appeared as a "conservative"; by 1965 Conservative third parties were forming, here and there, in the country. This antiliberal political reaction has had little to do with class-consciousness (the mainstay of "conservative" strength in the United States is to be found generally among the lower middle class), just as throughout modern history in Europe there have been "Rightist" and "Leftist" peasants, "Rightist" and "Leftist" bourgeois.

In any event, the vocabulary of politics is dynamic not static, and its historical study amounts to more than to antiquarian etymology. The growing acceptance or the increasing refusal of a term, the popularity of a new word, the change in the meaning of an old one, are reflections, symptoms, and sometimes even possible causes of political sentiments[12]—which, in turn, are almost always involved with some kind of a historical interpretation.

History, said the great English historian J. R. Seeley nearly a century ago, "is past politics and politics present history." This unilateral emphasis on the political factor in history marked Seeley's entire career as Regius Professor of Modern History at Cambridge; it was also fairly typical of the prevalent attitude among historians in the nineteenth century. (No chair for economic history existed, for example, in European or American universities before about 1895.) We know better now. The view prevalent among historians in the twentieth century tends to regard politics as if it were the superstructure—albeit a very important superstructure—of history, that is, largely a consequence of deeper, economic and social developments. There is no doubt, of course, that a narrow preoccupation with political history may give us a relatively superficial version of events. But throughout this book my point has been that the necessary deepening of our professional historical concerns (which, let me repeat, is but a consequence of the deepening of the general historical consciousness) may come about not so much by a shift of interest from the field of political history to the fields of economic or social history but, rather, from a deepening of our interest and insight in every one of these fields. Instead of substituting the principally economic for the principally political interpretation of history we ought, rather, to search deeper into the structure of political events and social developments, as indeed we must probe into the

---

[12] On April 17, 1788, Louis XVI referred to the *parlements* as "an aristocracy of magistrates." "Consider," Tocqueville jotted down in one of his notes, "how furiously they react to this word! . . . The word 'aristocrat' is often employed afterwards but for the first time in this [bad] sense. . . . What is the hidden power in that democratic element of the nation that these people who do not *see* at all clearly, confusedly *feel* that the most effective blow the King could score now [1788] is to call his adversaries *aristocrats*."

essence of economic data. For it is through this deepening of historical interests, too, that the historian discovers the arbitrary nature of the division of fields of historical research; as the English economic historian Clapham said, "it is at the overlapping margins of disciplines and sciences that the most important discoveries are usually made." Even about Seeley, G. P. Gooch wrote that "though no historian of his time took a more limited view of the province of history . . . it was not because his own interests were few." To historians such as Seeley, history was the school of statesmanship (his contemporary Droysen said that "the statesman is the historian in practice"); and historians, beginning with Ranke, "regarded history as concerned mainly with the life and relations of states." To the best of the old-fashioned political historians such as Seeley domestic politics were always subordinate in importance to foreign relations. I believe that in this they were right. Their concerns were not as narrow as it may seem at first sight.[13] They recognized the tremendous importance and influence of a subject—perhaps *the* most important subject in modern history—to a cursory discussion of which I must now turn.

(5) About the historical relations of states and nations

"There is no nation on earth," said Ranke more than a century ago, "that has not had some contact with other nations. It is through this external relationship, which in turn depends on a nation's peculiar character, that the nation enters on the stage of world history, and universal history must therefore focus on it." This *Primat der Aussenpolitik* is even now incontestable. The foreign relations of states are still more instructive than are their domestic politics. There is no general history without them. Even today the history of Europe, and, indeed, of the world, no matter how ideologically divided, is still the history of states and of nations, the United Nations, NATO, Common Market, or the Soviet bloc notwithstanding. The implication of something external, secondary, foreign in the

[13] The argument that the general view of history professed by a twentieth-century research historian, such as Namier, is necessarily deeper than that of Seeley's, is, therefore, not indisputable. ("English history," Seeley wrote, "always tends to shrink into mere Parliamentary history; and there is scarcely a great English historian who does not sink somewhat below himself in the treatment of foreign relations.")

term "foreign policy" is misleading: it is a mistake to think that foreign relations, save on certain critical occasions, are something extraneous, different, and not directly relevant to the main, domestic, internal business of governments, states, nations. As this book is written, the relations of the United States and the Soviet Union are more important than the relations of democracy and dictatorship, or of capitalism and Communism. I am not writing here a theory of international relations but I am compelled to draw attention to certain, nowadays often obscured and confused and overlooked, factors in these relations. They are the geographical and the territorial factor in the relationships of states, and the cultural factor in the relationships of nations, the first two being a more-or-less traditional, the latter a more-or-less recent and democratic, phenomenon.

About the geographical factor we may as well observe that it has not been very much affected by the Space Age. History is not only anthropomorphic; it is geocentric.[14] "The policies of all the powers," said Napoleon, "are inherent in their geography." Events in Mexico concern the United States more than events in Tibet, just as events in Poland are of greater interest to the Russian government than are events in Brazil. The brave new worlds and their brave new words notwithstanding, the United States would not risk a war for Hungary in 1956, and the Soviet Union not for Cuba in 1962. It was, it is, and probably it will always be easier to bombard Florida from Cuba than from the moon; and if tomorrow we should learn that the Russians planted their flag on Mars but were compelled to haul it down in East Berlin there is no question that of these two events the latter one would be more important, not only for the history of Germany and Russia but of Europe and of the world.

Geography circumscribes the limits, it governs the ambitions of states, it conditions the character of nations: it involves, however, not only the effect of environment on human societies, it involves—increasingly[15]—the effect, too, of human societies on their environ-

---

[14] Captain John Smith in the *Generall Historie of Virginia:* "for as Geographie without Historie seemeth a Carkasse without motion, so Historie without Geographie wandereth as a Vagrant without a certaine habitation."

[15] Hence the increasing importance of the "field" of human geography, and of historical geography (see Lucien Febvre, *A Geographical Introduction to History* (1924), a pioneer work).

ment. The geographical element in the relations of states, therefore, comprehends not merely proximity but possession. The term *real estate*, deriving from medieval usage, admirably suggests this strong and unique reality of territory. It is even now impossible to conceive of an autonomous community without some kind of a territorial base. The territorial circumscriptions of communities are clearer than are their social distinctions: a state frontier, an extraterritorial enclave, a capitulation, or even a modern air or naval base represent "horizontal" divisions that are not only visible on maps but, in many ways, more real than are the "vertical" divisions of society, things such as classes or corporations.

But geography, while it conditions, does not determine the relations of states and the interests of nations. There exist certain historically observable tendencies: the tendency for natural frontiers, for rounding off frontiers to seek alliances with one's "neighbor's neighbor," the dangers of sudden proximity (Russia and America bumping into each other in 1945, in the middle of Europe, when Germany was eliminated as a power). Still, all the appearances of *Geopolitik* notwithstanding, there is no such thing as a Newtonian rule of gravitation among the powers of the world. When the relations of states change, this happens because of their ideas of state and of national interests. These ideas are neither mechanical nor progressive matters. Not even technical progress determines (though it does, of course, influence) the character of these relations. Americans who have, after all, many reasons to regard history as if it were the Story of Progress, regard the progress of communications as if this technological development would by itself have caused the increasing American involvement in wider and wider affairs and areas of the world. American history textbooks have little charts showing how the Atlantic has "shrunk": in 1620 it took six weeks to cross that ocean, in 1820 three weeks, in 1920 six days, in 1960 six hours. . . . Of course today, in the age of the nuclear submarine, jet plane, transoceanic rocket, hydrogen bomb, America is more vulnerable than she was in the past. Still, as we survey American history, we may see that American involvements in the wars of Europe do not follow such a pattern of progressive increase. During the eighteenth century, indeed until 1815, America was involved in virtually every European and world war. During the nineteenth century she was not. During the twentieth century she chose to be involved again. Note that I said "chose": for geography, strategy, technology are important factors yet ultimately it is not science or fate but human choice that decides. Does the development of technology alter the relations of states and of nations? To some extent, yes; essentially, no. In 1914 the United States was safer from the danger of foreign invasions than one hundred years earlier when a British force could occupy Washington and burn the White House. Does the diminution of distances mean the diminution of ignorance with which the peoples of the world regard each other? To some extent, yes; necessarily, no. By 1914 millions knew something about other nations, other millions had visited other nations as tourists, but did this great increase of communications correspondingly decrease misunderstandings among nations? As in the relations of persons, proximity may lead to understanding or to contempt, to friendship or to enmity. *Not the instruments but the tendency of the relationship counts; it is not the technical conditions of distance but the direction of ideas and sentiments* that determines the relations of human societies, and of their component human beings.

The sentiments and the ideas of peoples remain the main motive force of nations. Even the totalitarian modern tyrannies are far from immune from their influences in the long run. It is these sentiments and ideas that are formulated into conceptions of national interest, which is not a fixed constant category adjusting itself automatically to ratios of geographical proximity and of military equipment. National interest, like self-interest, tends to produce its own rationalizations; but national interest, like self-interest, is produced by sentiments, inclinations, tendencies, ideas; national interest, again, is what people think it is, and there is more to it than meets the eye. It is certainly more than *Realpolitik* or *raison d'état*—especially in our democratic epoch, when the relations of states no longer preempt the wider and more complex influences in the relations of nations.

The modern term "international relations" is a misnomer; as I suggested earlier, it is almost always used for a study of supranational rather than of truly international history, since it deals with the relations of states rather than with those of nations. Both "nationalist" *Realpolitiker* and "internationalist" idealists often overlook the important historical condition that state and nation are not necessarily the same things. This is not the place to embark on the various historical origins of the two terms, except perhaps to suggest that if, as Figgis said, "the enduring work of the sixteenth century was the modern State," the enduring work of the nineteenth century was the modern nation. Now, it is true that during the nineteenth century state and nation became closer and closer; the old multi-national empires were about to break up, while the modern national states were crystallizing, which is perhaps why Matthew Arnold would call the state "a nation in its collective and corporate capacity." During the last one hundred years, however, the relations of nations have become more important, since in this democratic age the historical development of nations, in the broadest cultural sense, underlies as well as supersedes the histories of states. The latter no longer pre-empt the general histories of nations whose relations, in turn, have become something more than the foreign policies of their governments. With all of his emphasis on the foreign policies of governments, Ranke may have had an early insight into their truly international factor as he wrote that "we must understand the inner life rather than the abstract principle of the state."

I can only attempt to draw attention quickly, in passing as it were, to this enormous and important subject of the relations of entire nations, which by now encompasses all kinds of "foreign" relations, including literature, trade, translations, films, tourism, etc., all of them involved with the image which one nation has of another. This existence of national tendencies beneath state relations has not yet received the attention it deserves; and the preoccupation with political ideologies has only served to obscure its existence further. Obviously ideological sympathies may transcend patriotic loyalties. But this is not the end of the story. The allegiance of European and American Communist believers to Soviet Russia during the second quarter of this century was consequent to their sympathy for the Soviet state in its capacity as an ideological and political prototype. But, having focused their attentions and their hopes on that kind of thing, they failed to see from the beginning the existence of certain Russian national and historical characteristics which proved to be more real, enduring, and deeper than the ideological and political image of the First Communist State. The subsequent disillusionment of these Western believers was, therefore, to some extent predictable, even though few among them were brave or intelligent enough to admit this.

We tend to like or dislike persons rather than ideologies, whence the condition that the relationships of persons to certain nations may often be more significant than their relationships to certain ideologies, for national cultural traits may resemble personal traits more than do state political systems or ideologies. Since a nation is principally a cultural, while a state is principally a political, prototype, the tendencies of nations toward each other, the sympathies and the antipathies of certain nations, the rise and the decline of these sentiments, and the tendencies of certain people toward certain national cultures are on occasion powerful historical factors, very much worth our attention. It is possible that these factors functioned already during the religious struggles of the sixteenth century ("Calvinism," Burckhardt said, "was the Reformation of those peoples who did not like the Germans"). They are, in any event, more and more observable during the last one hundred years. Let me string out a number of examples. In the Russia of the nineteenth century Dostoevsky's Germanophilia and Turgenev's Francophilia were not superficial or accidental matters: they reflected significant inclinations of the Slavophiles and of the Westernizers. After 1917, then, as the excellent Wladimir Weidlé remarked, "it was German socialism which triumphed at the expense of French socialism through the revolution conceived and executed by Lenin."[16] On the other hand, as John Plamenatz put it, had Germany and not Russia become Communist in 1918, the attractions of Communism throughout central and eastern Europe would then have been much greater: because Russia and her culture enjoyed little respect among these nations at that time, while the prestige of German culture was much greater, and not only among Germany's allies. This German prestige was a very important factor in her fortunes and in the subsequent destinies of many Euro-

---

[16] This unusual but incisive view of the Bolshevik Revolution having been part of a deep-seated reaction of the Russian people against their cosmopolitan and Francophile upper classes was glimpsed, too, by such disparate people as Georges Sorel and Winston Churchill. In his *Reflections on Violence* Sorel wrote (1919): "When the time comes to evaluate present day events with historical impartiality, it will be recognized that Bolshevism owed a good part of its power to the fact that the masses regarded it as a protest against an oligarchy whose greatest concern had been not to appear Russian. . . ." In *The World Crisis* (1929) Churchill suggested that the Western Allies' failure to push the Dardanelles campaign through exacerbated the suspicions of the Russian masses against England and facilitated the coming of the revolution.

pean nations between 1870 and 1945. It may be even said that during these decades the lower middle classes in many parts of the world tended to be Germanophile, while the upper middle classes were Anglophile; this was evident among such different peoples and societies as Japan and Hungary, Rumania and Argentina, the United States and Turkey, Persia and Spain. Let me suggest, therefore, that while in a certain historical period there was such a thing as the "liberal" or the "authoritarian" type of personality, there was also such a thing, as say, a "Germanophile" or "Anglophile" personality, incarnating cultural rather than ideological preferences and inclinations. Even in the 1950's an American industrial worker would rather have his daughter marry a German than a Frenchman, if she was to marry a foreigner at all; for an American lawyer or banker, especially in the eastern United States, the converse may have been true. The so-called isolationism of many Americans in 1940–1941, and the McCarthyism of others in the 1950's often cloaked deeper, more hidden national and cultural preferences: relative Anglophobia and relative Germanophilia played their roles in these instances.[17] Among the American political elite the condition that, say, Walter Hines Page was an Anglophile and John Foster Dulles a Germanophile does not, of course, mean that they were disloyal Americans, British or German agents; it does not even mean that they were always conscious or even consistent supporters of these respective nations; it means, however, that on crucial occasions of their public offices their sympathies toward these nations were more significant than their recognized categories of having been Progressives or Republicans or Conservatives or isolationists or internationalists. (In a different vein the principal element, indeed, the largest common denominator, in the French armistice party in June, 1940, was not so much pro-Fascism or right-wing conservatism but Anglophobia.)

---

[17] Conversely, the Anglophile (and sometimes Francophile) sympathies of American humanist intellectuals in our times represented, too, something more than ideological preferences: they reflected historical inclinations toward certain cultural prototypes, since many of these people saw in Britain and in France still partial representatives of the ideas and of the culture of the Enlightenment; on the other hand the Germanophile (and often Hispanophile) sympathies of many American "conservatives" reflected not merely hidden sympathies for Hitler or Adenauer or Franco but their inclinations toward romantic, neo-medieval, and generally anti-Enlightenment cultural tendencies.

One could multiply these illustrations endlessly. But let me conclude with an example that should show the powerful interactions
of national inclinations and foreign policy. It concerns both the
internal and the external relations of Austria between the two
world wars. The history of Austria was then, in many ways, a
paradigm of European political developments during the twenty
years from 1918, when we can see in the dissolution of the Austrian
Empire the most important single consequence of World War I,
to 1938, when Hitler's absorption of Austria marked the first of the
great changes in the map of postwar Europe, leading to the outbreak of World War II in the following year. During the interwar
period Austria was a weak state, torn by internal dissensions. Particularly in the early thirties—the period which, in retrospect,
appears to us as the hinge of fate not only in the interwar history
of Austria but in the entire international history of the interwar
years—the Austrian people were divided between three factions
(whose origins go back to the 1880's), popularly known as "Blacks,"
"Reds," and "Browns": more precisely the Christian Socials (who
after 1931 turned toward a partially clerical-Fascist direction), the
Socialists, and the National Socialists.[18] In February, 1934, the
Christian Social government crushed the Socialists; in July, 1934,
the Nazis prematurely rose; but in 1936 the government had to
declare an uneasy coexistence with them; finally in 1938 Austria
became a Nazi state. Now all of these events depended very much
on the external relationships of Austria: more precisely, on her
relations to her neighbor states. The principal weakness of the
Socialists, who were the first to go under, lay in the condition
that they had no strong patron states abroad; on occasion, they
could count on sympathies from Czechoslovakia and France, but
these states were relatively uncommitted and relatively unpopular among Austrians. The principal strength of the Christian
Socials during the first crucial phase in 1933–1934 lay in the condition that they were supported by Mussolini's Italy which was,
strange as this may seem in retrospect, a great power, perhaps the
greatest in Europe, during those two years. It was, indeed, Mussolini who demanded that the Blacks crush the Reds in early 1934;

18 The history of this 1931–1936 period furnishes one of the arguments why
Nazis should not be simply called Fascists, since the two were opponents then,
with different ideas.

and Mussolini's threat of military intervention during the July, 1934, Brown Nazi *Putsch* contributed to the failure of that attempt. By 1936, however, Mussolini decided that Italy should align herself with Germany, and that Austria should not remain an obstacle to such an alignment; it was thereby that the fate of an independent Austria was about to be sealed; and in March, 1938, Hitler occupied Austria without any opposition on Mussolini's part. It would seem, therefore, that the destiny of Austria in the thirties was completely consequent to the relations of foreign states, and of the ideological alignments of these great powers. Yet this is not quite the case. The strength of the Austrian Nazi cause was very much enhanced by the condition that while most Austrians disliked Italy (the protector of their regime), they had strong affinities for Germany. Most of these Austrians were pro-German rather than pro-Nazi; indeed, it is often difficult to distinguish convinced Nazis from convinced pan-Germans during that period. This was a condition that both Schuschnigg[19] and Mussolini knew; and it facilitated the surrender of Austria to Hitler in the dramatic days of March, 1938.

(6) About national characteristics

The traditional ingredients of nationality are common language, common institutions, common culture, sameness of race, consciousness of history, consciousness of territorial limits, ancestral ties, permanence of residence. These are not categorical requirements: all of these eight ingredients need not always coexist: still, the majority of them must somehow coexist, in order to form nationality in the European sense. In the United States some of these ingredients do not exist, which is why being an American is still something different from being a Frenchman or a Pole. The American idea of nationality has been ideological rather than patriotic, populist rather than traditional, universal as well as distinctly particular in its portents, more superficial but also more generous than nationality in Europe. *Nomen est omen:* the United States of America, like the Union of Soviet Socialist Republics, is a general and open term;

[19] This last Catholic Chancellor of an independent Austria could not liberate himself from the notion of a "German" Austria; and traces of his admiration for Germany appear even in his diaries jotted down during his imprisonment by the Germans.

it suggests not a national society but rather something that is, at least implicitly, universal: like "Soviet citizen," "American citizen" marks adherence to certain political principles rather than a certain nationality; there is theoretically no limit to what it may include.

The "nation," evolving from *patria* and *natio*, has been a particularly European phenomenon. In most Asian languges an equivalent for the word "nation" does not exist; for Arabs as well as for American Indians the same word serves for "folk" and "people" and "nation"; so does, in a way, the Russian *narod*. Most European languages, distinguish, however, between "nation" and "people." In most European countries, especially in western Europe including England,* the sense of "nation" has been historical rather than racial, issuing from patriotic rather than folkish origins, with an emphasis on common land and common speech and common history rather than on common blood or common belief.

Patria carries the sense of a family, descent from a father; and *natio*, too, refers to relationship by birth. But early in European history this tribal sense was beginning to be replaced by something else: *patria* was becoming inseparable from a common place of settlement, which had not always been true of *natio*. No matter how atavistic the tribal bonds of the barbarian kingdoms after the fall of Rome may have been, they were not yet patriotic in this, post-Roman and early-European, sense; their laws as well as their territorial jurisdiction were fluid, resting not on soil but on blood. But when Pepin drove the Moors out of Narbonne in 759 he allowed the Visigoths of that region to live according to their own laws, provided that they stayed there; and during the next thousand years in the history of Europe the relationship to land became more important than relationships of blood.*

This is not the place to embark on the historical vicissitudes of these relationships: I have referred to the origins of *patria* and *natio* only because of my concern with the more modern phenomenon of the distinctions of patriotism and nationalism. While nationality, national ambitions, and national consciousness are discernible early in European history, nationalism, like the modern nation-state, is a more recent phenomenon, the result of the growing social homogenization of certain European peoples and of the development of their historical consciousness—or, to put it perhaps in two other words in intellectual shorthand, of democracy and of romanticism.

The history of the two modern terms reflects this condition: in England, for example, *patriotism* first appeared in print in 1738, *nationalism* more than a century later, in 1844.* This may explain why Englishmen of the eighteenth century, for example Dr. Johnson could not yet distinguish between patriotism and nationalism.[20] But to certain Englishmen of the twentieth century the distinction was more evident. "Nationalism," wrote George Orwell, "is not to be confused with patriotism. Both words are normally used in so vague a way that any definition is liable to be challenged, but one must draw a distinction between them, since two different and even opposing ideas are involved."

By "patriotism" I mean devotion to a particular place and a particular way of life, which one . . . has no wish to force upon other people. Patriotism is of its nature defensive, both militarily and culturally. Nationalism, on the other hand, is inseparable from the desire for power. The abiding purpose of every nationalist is to secure more power and prestige,[21] *not* for himself but for the nation or other unit in which he had chosen to sink his own individuality.

During the nineteenth century nationalism became an ideology: the older patriotic sentiments were often replaced by ideological nationalism. As Duff Cooper wrote, the jingo nationalist "is always the first denounce his fellow countrymen as traitors"—a statement worthy of Dr. Johnson.[22] Adolf Hitler was to incarnate this tendency in the twentieth century. "By the time I was fifteen" (in 1904), he wrote in *Mein Kampf*, "I understood the difference between

[20] What he meant by the "last refuge of scoundrels" was what we mean by nationalism nowadays. Boswell: Johnson "did not mean a real and generous love of our country, but that pretended patriotism which so many . . . have made a cloak of self-interest.

[21] Harold Nicolson in his 1937 Rede Lectures (*The Meaning of Prestige*): for the German "his personal honour becomes fused with his national honour, and the resultant form of [nationalism] is far more inflammable than that old warm blanker which patriotism is with us." It is perhaps symptomatic that some of these distinctions have been expressed best by certain writers rather than by political theorists and, moreover, by patriotic rather than internationalist intellectuals, who comprehended the historic origins of national consciousness: for the condition that Germany, unlike England, became a unified national state only relatively late in history may explain much of the peculiarly distasteful character of modern German nationalism.

[22] The true patriot, on the other hand, is often the kind of thinking person who is bitterly critical of, because he is deeply concerned with, the faults of his own people.

dynastic PATRIOTISM and folkish NATIONALISM, even then I was interested only in the latter. . . . Germany could be safeguarded only by the destruction of Austria [Hitler's native country] . . . the national sentiment is in no sense identical with dynasties or with patriotism."

What was startling and new in the twentieth century was the emergence of a certain antipatriotism in the name of nationalism. In 1809 the peasant Andreas Hofer led the patriotic resistance of Tyrolean Austrians against Napoleon's Frenchmen and their Bavarian allies; in 1938 a Tyrolean by the same name became Hitler's Gauleiter. Before and during World War II throughout Europe "Nationalist" movements, blocs, parties, "National Opposition" were often the names of groups who worked against the legitimate governments of their countries, usually favoring an alignment of their country with Nazi Germany, and at times even the military occupation of their country by the latter. Of course there always have been all kinds of people, from traitors through ideological revolutionaries to persecuted minorities, who would welcome the occupation of their country by another power. But what is remarkable is the appearance of such tendencies in the form of a certain ideological nationalism, which was the result not only of modern nationalistic indoctrination but also of those conditions of modern society which make it possible for many people to be nationalists without being patriots.

Yet this may have been a transitional development, reminiscent of certain transitional developments during the sixteenth century when, as Burckhardt put it, on occasion *Glaubensgenossen,* coreligionists, felt closer to each other than *Landsmänner,* compatriots. For ideological nationalism is a secular religion. And in Europe at least, the era of ideological nationalism may have come to an end: its attractions declined steeply after the last world war. Still, the factor of nationality, all superficial appearances to the contrary notwithstanding, continues to prevail, in Europe as well as all over the world. And this is the reason why I found it necessary to distinguish between patriotism and nationalism, or between the patriotic and the ideological varieties of nationalism. My argument is that nations are one thing and nationalism another. The former not only preceded but they survive the latter. Nations and national consciousness are enormously important historical factors even now, in the second half of the twentieth century, with its mass ideologies, in this age of superpowers, of the United Nations, of a rapidly spreading superficial internationalism on a global scale. History does not repeat itself: the Greeks had municipal *patriae* but no real nations in the modern sense. The Argive or Corcyran local quislings called in outside armies even when this meant the extinction of the particular characteristics of their communities. But this is not what happened even during World War II and after. Not even Quisling wanted to see Norwegian nationality and independence extinguished; not even Kádár wishes to witness the absorption of his nation by Soviet Russia. Indeed, the strongest evidence of the enduring importance of nationality emerges from the historical development of Communist states in eastern Europe. I am not only referring to their conflicts of national interests, Rumania vs. Hungary or Bulgaria vs. Yugoslavia or China vs. Russia; I am referring to the personalities of their Communist leadership: from Trotsky through Stalin to Khrushchev, from Rosa Luxemburg through Bierut to Gomulka, from Kun through Rákosi to Kádár, from the 1920's through the 1940's to the 1960's the leadership in the Communist countries has become more and more typically national, reflecting a general historical development in a more national—though not always more nationalist—direction. For in Europe (as indeed in many other places in the world, including the United States) the meaning of nationality has become deeper, together with the development of some kind of a historical consciousness: it has entered the lives of many millions, penetrating their consciousness, transcending politics, through the democratization of societies and through the still powerful, only partially diluted, and occasionally emasculated national languages. On the one hand the world, in this age of television and air travel, is becoming more and more international (or, as we have seen, rather, supranational). But on the other hand, the democratic societies of the world are also becoming not less but more national, in depth rather than in extent, through the now developing consciousness of nationality as a cultural, rather than a racial, phenomenon.* Thus nationality is still the most formative historical factor in our democratic times, despite powerful influences and technological institutions working against it. Even now, "French," "Dutch," "Polish" remain both more important and more meaningful historical realities than categories of classes such as "proletarian" or "bourgeois," or than political categories, such as "liberal," "conservative," "Communist," many of which, as we have seen, have now become fuzzy and often increasingly meaningless.

In Europe the existing national states are now more homogeneous than ever before. They are settled down in their places; there are few outstanding frontier problems (this may have been one of the very few auspicious results of the last world war). The sovereign and independent national state may have had its day: but nationality continues to function, perhaps in a novel manner, corresponding to the change in the texture of history. Whether a truly united Europe will emerge before the end of the twentieth century is an open question; what is hardly questionable is that the era of wars among the national states of Europe is over. Wherever serious problems between nationalities exist in Europe—the conflict between Flemings and Walloons in Belgium, the South Tyrol controversy between Austrians and Italians, Transylvanian and Macedonian problems in eastern Europe—these involve the rights of nationalities (and, moreover, cultural rather than political problems) rather than questions about state frontiers: they are truly inter-national, rather than "international" (meaning inter-state, or supranational) questions. We may be still far away from the development of a strong decentralizing tendency which would be a reaction against the overcentralization in the present political structure of the world. This may not come until some horrible experience, such as an atomic world war, when the breakdown of the technological efficiency of overcentralized power and authority will become obvious. But even now the reactions of some of Europe's nations to the great intercontinental superpowers suggest that our nation-states may be acquiring certain of the characteristics of the former city-states, that their historical function may reside increasingly in the uniqueness of their national cultures,[23] in their traditional customs, habits, and liberties, maintaining their national identities together with the now unavoidable restrictions of their independent state sovereignties. The two countervailing tendencies now seem to be the increasing dissolution of patriotic traditions, the weakening of national cultures through the technological "Americanization" of the world on the one hand, and the further cultural crystallization of nation-

---

[23] Huizinga (1933): "Why do some intellectuals expect a concord of nations only through a melting down of national characteristics?" "Why this deep scepticism against a harmonious accord?"

ality on the other. Our grandchildren should know which of the two tendencies will prove to be stronger. Meanwhile we ought not overlook the existence of the second: for we cannot say really that Frenchmen have become less French, Finns less Finnish, Poles less Polish—and Americans less American—no matter what has happened to their states and nations in the twentieth century.

And this leads me to the question of national characteristics. Intellectuals have found it to be fashionable to ignore them nowadays. But this is a foolish thing to do: they'd be better off if they'd consider Henry Adams' admonition, as he called national character "the most difficult and the most important . . . of all historical problems."

The "historical problem" of national character consists of two complementary and reciprocal parts: national personality and personal nationality. There is such a thing as a national personality: a nation is not a person, but it manifests certain personal traits, especially since it is a more organic phenomenon than a state. Its character traits are nothing more and nothing less than tendencies: but these tendencies underlie, and on occasion supersede, other tendencies, other historical conditions. They are manifest in the history of politics: consider, for example, the differences between Russian and Polish and Yugoslav Communists. They are evident in the historical development of societies: consider, for example, the differences between English and Italian industrial workers, or between French *bourgeois* and Austrian *Bürger*. They are obvious in the historical unfolding of art: consider, for example, the differences between South German and South Italian baroque, or between German and Spanish "Victorian" architecture. They may be discernible even in the mechanical and standardized products of modern industrial mass manufacture. And the most meaningful reflections of these distinct tendencies of national character are to be found, of course, in the different national languages, the habits of which are veritable mirrors of national characteristics. I have mentioned the subtle differences of the "same" words in different languages earlier. Let me repeat here that expression does have a nationality, even while thought may not always have one. I say "always" because expression has a way of forming consciousness; it is therefore legitimate to speak of national mentalities, and of tendencies of national consciousness which are discernible on occasion.

National characteristics and a certain consciousness of nationality existed before the crystallization of most European national states. In the spreading of Protestantism, for example, national tendencies played important roles: certain people responded to Luther, others didn't. For, ultimately, the national characteristics of certain peoples are involved with certain religious and even spiritual inclinations (just as Weber and Sombart and Tawney attempted to demonstrate the connections between economic systems and religious ideas, we are in need of a historical investigation of the relationship between certain national characteristics and certain religious tendencies, of an inquiry into the inclinations of certain nationalities toward certain ideas).

For national character is inseparable from ideas: it is formed by geographical, social, racial, cultural, spiritual elements together. There is such a thing as a race, even though it is fashionable nowadays to deny this; however, race is a cultural, even more than a biological, factor, and this means that while we must recognize its existence we must understand, too, that the very function of its characteristics transcends deterministic causality (that, among other things, human beings may indeed acquire certain "racial" characteristics).[24] While this may be a complex development, its meaning is simple: national character is historical character: and this recognition is an intrinsic part of the evolution of our historical consciousness. Moreover, since history is a form of thought, national character is very much reflected in a nation's view of its own history, just as a person's autobiography—the expressions of his auto-historical thinking—his view of his own development and of his aspirations, affords us an insight into his character. On a more pragmatic level, then, just as the character traits of a person are best revealed in his dealings with other persons, the character of a nation is often best revealed by its actions and attitudes toward other nations[25]—whence the intrinsic significance of foreign policy.

[24] See below, Chapter VI, pp. 252 ff. Also, Christopher Dawson: the racialists are wrong in believing that "culture is the result of predetermined racial inheritance. On the contrary, it would be more true to say that race is the product of culture, and that the differentiation of racial types represents the culmination of an age-long process of cultural segregation and specialization . . ." especially among primitive peoples.

[25] It is significant that the two historians who perceived and, as E. H. Carr, too, noted, "emphasized most strongly the continuity of the French Revolution with previous régimes" were Tocqueville, who was Foreign Minister in 1849, and Albert Sorel, the diplomatic historian.

Thus it is not enough to say that we still live in an era of national states, and that the principal motive of their actions is still national interest. There is more to "national" than meets the eye: there is more to "interest," too. We may say of persons that the main motive factor of their actions is self-interest; but this is a truism. Take such different modern thinkers as Machiavelli, La Rochefoucauld, Bentham, Stendhal, Spencer, Tocqueville, Marx, Freud—yes, of course, this is what all of them say. But the better thinkers among them (Stendhal rather than Bentham, Tocqueville rather than Marx) do not leave it at that; they see deeper motives: fear and greed, guilt and ambition, all entangled; the best of them see vanity (a forgotten word nowadays) as the basic human motive. For what is self-interest, after all? Its formation comes from the concept of the self: an entangled thing, a complex thing, a tendency rather than a category, an aspiration rather than a constant.

The character of a person is formed as well as revealed by his own ideas of self-interest. These ideas change with time; they are often influenced by other persons; except in rare instances they cannot be accurately defined; they nonetheless exist. So it is with the interest of a nation: the character of a nation, too, is revealed by its own ideas of self-interest, by the nation's own image of itself, by its own concept of the place it would like to occupy, of the figure it would like to cut in the world.

Thus the geographical situation of a nation to a large extent defines its foreign policy, the conduct of which, however, is largely formed by the nation's character: thus the history of a state is governed by its concepts of state interest that reveal, in turn, certain important elements in the character of the nation. Britain's geographical situation is evident; but the conduct of British foreign policy has also reflected the willingness to mediate, to compromise, the tendency to pragmatism as well as the racial self-confidence that have been recognizable elements in the British character. Behind the Iron Curtain, did the Hungarian people rise in 1956 because of their economic conditions? No. Did they rise because they wanted to do away with the socialization of their industries, did they want to restore capitalism? No. Did they revolt because of their sense of deep injuries committed against their national interests? Yes. And were not their very ideas of their national interests, dissatisfied as they were with the initial Russian concessions, expressed in impulsive, occasionally heroic, and often unrealistic, demands?

Yes; for these actions (and their very rhetoric) reflected typically Hungarian national characteristics. The Hungarian Revolution turned out to be the way it was not because it was post-Socialist, national-Communist, crypto-Fascist or what not, but because it was a *Hungarian* Revolution—and, moreover, a Hungarian Revolution *in 1956.*

For these concepts of national interests are not always constant and not always consistent: national character may be tempered and conditioned by historical experience. (British self-confidence in 1960 may be something different from what it was in 1860; and in 1956 the otherwise impulsive, romantic, feckless Poles acted in a different way from their tragic revolutions in the past.)

National interest would be a constant factor, a geographically ascertainable, strategically predictable category, if human beings were the same everywhere. And human beings *are* essentially the same: but their actions and reactions are different when their ideas and aspirations are different.[26] There is still much truth in what Charles Evans Hughes said in 1923:

> Foreign policies are not built upon abstractions. They are results of practical conceptions of national interest arising from some immediate exigency or standing out vividly in historical perspective. When long maintained, they express the hopes and fears, the aims of security and aggrandizement, which have become dominant in the national consciousness and thus transcend political divisions and make negligible such opposition as may come from particular groups. They inevitably control the machinery of international accord which works only within the narrow field not closed by divergent national ambitions. . . .

This some what narrow argument must, however, be tempered with the more profound considerations proposed by Johan Huizinga in 1936:

---

[26] This is why, for example, A. J. P. Taylor's *The Origins of the Second World War* is defective in one of its main arguments. Taylor explains the origins of the war in terms of *Realpolitik,* but his concept of *Realpolitik* is too narrow: he treats history as if it consisted of the relations of states, and of states with more-or-less identical reactions: he ignores the effects of certain national tendencies. For example he says that in the 1930's the Poles were just as anti-Semitic as were the Germans: but he overlooks the condition that the Poles and the Germans were anti-Semitic in different ways, and that they pursued their national interests in different ways. Pilsudski was a nationalist dictator, as indeed was Hitler: but he was a different kind of nationalist dictator.

States will continue to set their course of action predominantly by their interests or what they think to be their interests, and considerations of international morality will drive them only a fraction of an inch off their course. But this fraction represents the difference between honour and loyalty and the jungle, and as such reaches further than a thousand miles of ambition and violence.

Thirty years later we may observe that these "considerations of international morality" have, after all, grown in international esteem. As the world has become smaller and more interdependent, wars have become more dangerous in their consequences, and entire departments in the governments of states are now busying themselves with propagating benevolent and successful national images to the world. True, these considerations may be systematically obscured through all kinds of ephemeralities through publicity, their images may be falsified; nevertheless they exist. This may be but one manifestation of the continued importance of national characteristics, and of their apparent resemblance to personal characteristics: for, if few nations can nowadays afford the reputation of being arrogantly indifferent to other peoples' considerations of their morality, this is because these considerations are inescapably anthropomorphic in their nature.

And now let me turn rapidly from the characteristics of nations to the national characteristics of persons, which is a very complex thing. The legal criterion of citizenship, the geographical criterion of the birthplace, the cultural criterion of language, the racial criterion of parental and ancestral heredity: every one of these categories may leak. There are exceptions to every rule. In many instances—the Macedonian Alexander who wanted to be a great Greek, the Corsican Bonaparte the Frenchman, the Austrian Hitler the German, the Georgian Stalin the Russian—the exceptions count indeed. Earlier I suggested that in the conflict between Trotsky and Stalin the factor of their respective national differences was decisive. Trotsky had his Jewish characteristics, Stalin his Georgian ones; and in the struggle for political power in Russia this was to harm Trotsky more than it harmed Stalin. But this is not all. Trotsky did not want to be a Jew, and Stalin did not want to remain a Georgian. The former did not in the least identify himself with Judaism or with Zionism; the latter not with Georgian nationalism; they succeeded, indeed, in incarnating certain Russian traits. Consequently Trotsky was Jewish and non-Jewish, just as Stalin was Georgian and non-Georgian, Hitler Austrian and anti-Austrian, Napoleon Corsican and French, Disraeli Jewish and English at the same time.[27] Both of these characteristics existed within their lives: and, historically speaking, the second, the direction of their aspirations and ideas, was more important than the first, even though we must recognize the existence of the functions of the first. The decisive element is often not so much what a person "is" but what he wants to be. (Ortega y Gasset: "Life is a gerundive, not a participle: a *faciendum*, not a *factum*. Life is a task. . . ." Tocqueville: "a serious spiritual business.") And this is true of entire nations, too, whose character traits are formed but not caused: formed by their histories, and by their consciousness of their histories.

In the history of the consciousness of nationality in Europe speech has often been thicker than blood; and in certain instances patriotic and cultural affinities and aspirations superseded even speech. I am not only thinking of multilingual Switzerland, I am thinking of the German-speaking Alsatians, with their developing affinities for France, or of such relatively recent instances as when after World War I certain Slavic groups along the then new German-Polish frontier opted for Germany rather than for Poland: a clear case of cultural-national preferences. There are many examples in the histories of European nations which strongly suggest the non-Darwinian and supra-biological realities of historical life: that cultural-national aspirations may become historical, existential, personal and, on occasion, even physical factors and that, consequently, acquired characteristics *may* be inherited.

A person is born with certain characteristics; he inherits certain tendencies; he acquires other inclinations through his life. Some of these are strong and enduring, others are ephemeral. Life consists of constant tensions: a person is formed, pulled, pushed by charac-

---

[27] Esmé Wingfield-Stratford: "It is only too facile a biographical lead to refer every thing to [Disraeli's] Jewish descent, but the popular conception of a Jew is, in fact, one that fits him a great deal less than Gladstone—since he was, as a man and a statesman, rather deficient than otherwise in the money sense—an out-and-out Romantic of the Byron, D'Orsay tradition; moreover, one who could have been described, throughout his career, as positively drunken with the love of his adopted country, a patriot of patriots. Where, then, it may be asked, does the Jew in Disraeli come in? And I would answer—in the quality of his patriotism. He loved England—but not quite in the English way."

teristics inherited from his father, by others inherited from his mother, as well as by his acquired personal desires, vanities, ambitions, obligations, loyalties, fears that are often consequences of his ideas of his own situation in the world. So with the history of nations. Human, and historical, life is a succession of choices, which every conscious human being has to make every moment. At times these choices are decisive: and their very quality will often reveal that person's character and decide his fate. But that fate is by no means prescribed: for he may supersede his inclinations, inherited as well as acquired ones. The decision and the responsibility are his: for he is a free moral agent, responsible for his actions.

It is here that the semblance of analogy between the nature of persons and the nature of nations breaks down, in spite of the superficial resemblance of their characteristics. I said that a nation is a more organic phenomenon than a state; but the nation is not a person; and, apart from the persons and the communities which compose it, a nation has no life of its own. Thus, while a person is responsible for his actions, a nation is responsible only in part; for a nation has but a halfway sort of claim to immortality. Men die and disappear from this earth while nations do not die for a long, long time; but while the soul of a man is liable to divine judgment and is immortal, the soul of a nation is not.

(7) About a certain hierarchy

It will be now evident that in this chapter I have tried to suggest a certain hierarchy of historical factors according to their relative importance: a hierarchy the order of which goes considerably contrary to many recent assumptions. This hierarchy is far from being universally valid: but I believe it to be applicable, by and large, to the history of modern nations. Whether in the history of eighteenth-century England or nineteenth-century Germany or twentieth-century Russia, I believe that the changing structure of their economies was less decisive than the development of their societies which, in turn, was less decisive than the history of their politics, including their revolutions which were less decisive than the nation's relations to other nations through peace and through war; and these very relations, then, reflected national inclinations toward certain ideas which were, in turn, more universal than national, since they reflected certain concepts about human nature that were ultimately involved with certain cultural and spiritual concepts of more universal portents.

There is, thus, an order of ascendancy inherent in this thesis: the biological, racial, political, cultural, moral categories corresponding to the ascending order of social categories—mass, people, state, nation, religion—and perhaps even with certain cosmological categories: atom, elements, earth, man, universe. I believe that there is much truth in this, except that it is too much of a neat little shorthand sort of philosophy: for I believe, too, that historians ought to comprehend the pragmatic wisdom of the Latin proverb *primum vivere deinde philosophari*, that is, historical life is not only stronger than theory, it is, too, prior to philosophy. A merely categorical assertion of these hierarchies, or their definition, will not do. The categories, through the function of their component tendencies, overlap. We find microcosms at the two opposite extremes, within the atom as much as within the universe, just as in the life of a person his "lowest" material interests are often inseparable from his ideas and aspirations, while material forces often play roles within his "highest" intellectual experiences.

Still, I found it necessary to insist on the relative importance of certain historical factors: to put it in one sentence, that the motive factors in the history of the world even now ought not to be sought in economic developments as much as within nations and ultimately within the minds and hearts of persons in the midst of nations. The history of contemporary American-Russian relations is a good example of this relative hierarchy, since such a history, dealing as it must with enormous and complex matters, encompasses economics, sociology, ideology, politics, strategy, nationality, culture, religion: not only the relations of the United States and the Union of Soviet Socialist Republics but also those of Communism and capitalism, of Marxism and democracy, of "East" and "West," of the Russian and American empires, and nations. Economically Russia and America have been growing more and more alike, as America was becoming a socialized welfare state, and Russia began to catch up with mass production. Yet in 1955, when these differences were smaller than what they had been in 1945, 1935, 1925, the hostility was greater than before. More important than the contest between Communism and capitalism was the ideological struggle between Soviet Marxism and American democracy. Yet the difference between the two political ideologies was not the cause of the cold war: were Russia a small country, like Yugoslavia, no matter how she may have been dedicated to revolutionary Marxism, the cold war would not have developed as it did. Thus the source of the cold war must have been national interest: America and Russia, two great world empires, bumping at each other in the middle of Europe at the end of the last world war, suspicious of each other's strategies. We are getting closer to the more important factors in the origins of the cold war: but this is not yet enough. This strategic view will explain many things but it will not explain many others: for, after all is said, American strategy during the entire cold war has seldom been aimed at the Soviet Union proper (as distinct from her satellites and other areas), while in turn Russia interfered only occasionally, and hesitantly, with the immediate American strategic neighborhood in the Western Hemisphere. The animosities of these two states have not been wholly the results of their altered strategical situation: they have involved, increasingly, the images which the two nations have had of each other. Thus in their competition for world leadership Russian suspicion and aggressiveness on the one hand, and the popularity of anti-Communism in the United States on the other, were national tendencies which have played decisive roles in the relations of these two great nations; and, in turn, these ideas themselves have often reflected all kinds of cultural developments, including even religious ones.[28]

Let me repeat this then for the last time: Russian industrial statistics are less important than the condition that the masters of Russia are Communists which, in turn, is less important than the fact that they are Russians, the masters of a long-standing empire and the children of a long-standing nation. The routine life of the Russian people depends on the development of their politics, but the national interests of the Russian empire are more important than

---

[28] The condition that within the United States the Catholic population increased in its numbers and in its influence was an important element in the popular development of anti-Communism as *the* American national ideology in the 1950's. On the other hand, the relative absence of a deep-seated Russophobia—as distinct from anti-Communism—among Americans, as well as the Russian people's liking for Americans, were no less important factors in keeping the "cold war" "cold" in the fifties, and in the general improvement of the relations of the two states later.

its official ideology, and this pursuit of Russian national interests depends not only on geographical circumstances but on national characteristics which, in turn, are formed by cultural and historical and sometimes even religious tendencies. Thus I seem to have narrowed the focus closer and closer, trying to penetrate deeper, peeling away the layers, getting down to what in the end may seem to be a very old-fashioned argument about national character, an approach which is not telescopic but microscopic in its direction. But the nature of human beings is such that close to the dark recesses of the human heart we find something universal again: for the human heart is a microcosm itself, reflecting the universe. "No man is an island"—these words of a poet, cited so often by superficial internationalists, have a meaning only because of the spiritual condition of man. The body of a man may be confined to a solitary island; but his heart and mind are not. A nation occupies a certain confined place in the world; but the origin and the effect of the ideas that form its conduct are ultimately supernational.

Let me now try to apply this argument to the history of history—say, to the history of the French Revolution. Many a historian found the analysis of the historiography of the French Revolution to be rather instructive: they investigated the politics of successive generations of French historians, the French Revolution For and Against. This *is* an instructive and intellectually enlightening endeavor: I believe, as does Professor Herbert Butterfield, that the historical study of the French Revolution may indeed be approached through the study of the historiography of the French Revolution. But now let me add my little bit as a nonspecialist and general historian. Instead of ranging the generations of radical and conservative, of pro- and anti-Jacobin, of republican and monarchist historians and evaluating them, let me take another approach in order to say that I believe that the exposition of the Revolution as a social movement (say, by Jaurès or by Mathiez) is less enlightening than its exposition in terms of politics and of political ideas (say, by Michelet or by Aulard), and that even more instructive is its exposition in terms of the persistent factor of foreign relations (say, by Albert Sorel), and that perhaps even more important is the consideration of the specifically French characteristics of the Revolution, together with its treatment as part and parcel of the greater and more universal ideas of the times (something that Tocqueville was about to try in the second, unfinished volume of the *Old Regime and the Revolution*). But now the important *caveat*. All of this does not mean that anyone who emphasizes the foreign relations of the Revolution is necessarily a better or more profound historian than someone else who concentrates on its social history. The hierarchy of importance of these relative factors is activated by the quality of the historian and of his work: one may prefer Albert Sorel's approach to Jaurès's, or Tocqueville's to Mathiez's: still Jaurès and Mathiez are to be preferred over hundreds of second-rate writers who may have indeed placed the French Revolution within the great general historical movements of its times but whose vision and whose historianship are superficial.

There is a last point which I wish to make. In this book I have often tried to draw attention to the condition of the often inescapable involvement of what happens with what people think happens; and in this chapter I tried to illustrate that this is true of such things as economic events as well as of ideas of national interest. There are, however, different levels of our awareness of this condition—perhaps corresponding, conversely, to the relative hierarchy of levels suggested in this chapter. By this I mean that while the axiom that what happens is involved with what we think happens is not immediately apparent in economic or in social matters, it is much easier to demonstrate it to people in instances referring to what they, with an unconsciously revealing phrase, often call the "higher things of the mind." When we speak of a telepathic event or what nowadays is called an "extrasensory" occurrence (when, for example, we are suddenly conscious of something happening to someone whom we cannot see or hear), when we speak of a religious experience (an inner vision or a sudden sense of a close understanding of a God), when we speak of art (the effects of a poetic phrase or of a painting), it is obvious that what we are speaking of deals with our thinking, that our consciousness is intimately involved, nay, inseparable from the experience itself. But as we move lower along this relative hierarchy of events, this involvement of consciousness becomes less and less obvious. While it is relatively easy to suggest how the factor of national characteristics involves not so much physical conditions as it does mentalities (that, for example, Dr. Johnson was a prototypically English while Voltaire was a prototypically French eighteenth-century thinker), this becomes more and more difficult to demonstrate in politics and in society and finally in economics, since we are accustomed to regard the latter as if it were involved with but the complexities of material circumstances. Thus the economic historian is tempted to deal with what happened to people (a good harvest, or bad laws) or what they did to things (how they coined their monies, or how they invested them), without considering how the consciousness of people was modifying, and indeed on occasion creating, their very experiences. I am, on the other hand, tempted to think that some of the greatest contributions to historical thinking might be made in the future by historians of economics who would understand the historical, and therefore inevitably anthropomorphic, conditions of economic life, including the historical complexities of its causalities, and the essential and intrusive factor of human consciousness. I said "greatest," because such a radically new demonstration of the realities of economic life will be admittedly very difficult, if it is seriously pursued at all. I believe, however, that sooner or later more and more thinking people will have to recognize in every field this condition of the inevitable involvement of mind in matter, historically and not only philosophically speaking: the progress of this recognition in itself being part and parcel of the evolution of our consciousness, in the Western world at least.

Appendix to Chapter V. The problem of religious history

There is a field of history, the history of religion, which, because of its very nature, does not belong in the hierarchy suggested above. Its problems are complex and, to a great extent, unique. It is difficult enough to find out what people thought; it is even more difficult to find out what they believed—and this may be especially true in our democratic times when what people think and what they believe are often different matters. I said earlier that what people think is not pre-empted by the history of ideas; surely what people believe is not pre-empted by the history of religions. Yet religion (especially in the original, binding sense of the word—re-ligio) still plays an important part in the beliefs of people, in all kinds of beliefs of all kinds of people: it is still one of the sources of certain deep-seated assumptions about life and death that somehow, no matter how loosely, bind the woolliest bundles of personal beliefs together. But the religious sources of some of these beliefs may lie deeply buried; they are not always conscious, and thus they often do not properly belong to the realm of historical investigation.

Moreover: why bother? The Western world, we are told, has entered the post-Christian age. Three hundred years ago the majority of the peoples of the white race believed, or they professed to believe, in the divinity of Christ: this is no longer so. During the last one hundred years a very large erosion of religious belief and of religious practice took place in Europe, and to a lesser extent in the United States. Early in the twentieth century the "Christian" designation of certain institutions and philosophies, of intellectuals and political parties, began to refer to a certain minority, separate and distinct from the rest: and now the majority of our professional intellectuals think of themselves as being post-Christian thinkers. Yet perhaps the "post-Christian" adjective is an intellectually presumptuous, and even an inaccurate one. During the nineteenth century the expansion of Christianity went on at the same time when religious belief declined: numerically speaking, it was then that the greatest expansion of Christianity occurred, in Asia, Africa, Oceania. In another sense the wide application of Western humanitarianism—the abolition of slavery, for example—sprang from the conscience of certain Western nations, reflecting, in turn, certain fundamentally Christian ideas. Note that the decline of Christianity and the decline in the respectability of Christian religions may be two different things. It may be even possible (though not perhaps probable) that the loss of certain forms of faith may be a symptom of eventual religious and spiritual progress, since the latter may involve a deepening of spiritual consciousness. Let us not, however, overestimate the present import of "ecumenicism" and of all kinds of fashionable "dialogues." On many fundamentally spiritual matters true communication between "post-Christian" intellectuals and believing Christians (particularly Catholics) is very difficult.

The principal problem that concerns us here is not post-Christianity but the problem of the history of religion in democratic ages. For one thing, the history of the United States demonstrates amply the respectability of religion in a democratic society, all of the legalisms of the separation of "church" and "state" notwithstanding. Tocqueville was one of the earliest foreign observers who noted this development, which went counter to the intellectual categories and expectations of the nineteenth century: he thought that religion, and perhaps particularly the Roman Catholic religion, would prosper in a democratic society such as the

United States. The complex problem is that of ascertaining how much of this prosperity and respectability of religion was the result of religious rather than of social factors. This, of course, is always the principal difficulty facing the historian of religious beliefs, but it is especially difficult during democratic times. In any event, we must keep in mind the tendency of a democratic society toward respectability as well as toward a certain fideism. The cult of Reason, after all, was less of a democratic phenomenon than something peculiar to the sometimes aristocratic intellectualism of the eighteenth century. I, for one, am often tempted to see in our times many symptoms suggesting the eventual probability of a rapid, and sometimes brutal, transition from an age of reason to an age of faith—by which I mean not at all a return to traditional Christian religiosities but an increasing willingness, by masses of people, to believe, if necessary, at the expense of thinking: perhaps the inescapable ultimate consequence of our interregnal condition of moral and cultural chaos.*

But let us return to history. "In fact," Burckhardt wrote nearly one hundred years ago, "we have not yet experienced the full impact of the masses, of sheer numbers, on religion, but it may yet come." Let us not speculate about the influence of religion in an age of the masses: we have enough of a problem with its history: how to describe it? In any event religious history is no longer merely ecclesiastical history, the history of a Church, or of churches. But beliefs cannot be measured. Statistical information about religious behavior tells us little that is solid. A Gallup poll in the mid-1950's informed us that 96 percent of all Americans believed in God—or, rather, they *said* they believed in God: for one of the complexities of democratic ages is not only the inevitable inconsistency between what people believe and what they do; there is another difficulty, on a deeper level, the discrepancy between what people say they believe and what they really believe. In 1938 more Catholics went regularly to Mass in Koblenz than in Cherbourg. We also know from a chit left among the papers of the Gauleiter that in the Nazi plebiscite of Easter Week of 1938, 87 percent, though not the officially announced 99 percent, of the people of that traditionally Catholic Rhenish city voted in Hitler's favor. Were, then, the people of Koblenz or of Cherbourg the better Catholics? The question is not a rhetorical one: I cannot tell. Again, the historian should not attribute motives: he must only point out discrepancies between avowed beliefs and actual practices when these are evident.

He must consider the historicity of religious events. There is such a thing as the Catholicism of Spain: there is such a thing as Spanish Catholicism, too. As E. I. Watkin wrote in his excellent Postscript to his *Roman Catholicism in England.* "History cannot pierce the walls which enclose personal experience of God, His hidden action in souls." On the other hand, the Church is not a "purely spiritual community"; she is "composed by members, clerical and lay alike, of every degree of holiness or the lack of it"; she is part of history, a fact which is "at once her strength and her weakness, but in either case inevitable."[1] To some extent this, too, is an essential portion of the evolution of our historical consciousness. There was a time when the Church, even in the West, was hostile to historical thinking: the damning sense still inherent in *heresy* indicates this, this word having derived from *choosing* in Greek. (Consider, then, its antithesis, *orthodoxy*, when applied to history, about which Maitland wrote: "An orthodox history is a contradiction in terms.") Acton recognized this, as he wrote Newman in 1861 that one must strive for the reconciliation of Science with Religion, that what was needed was "the encouragement of the true *scientific* spirit and *disinterested* love of truth." At that time "scientific" meant something broader than what it suggests now. Still, we ought perhaps to rephrase Acton's statement: what we need is the encouragement of the true *historical* spirit, together with the *interested* love of truth: it is not so much science or philosophy but the study of history which must be reconciled with religion.

Thus religious history, especially in our democratic age, must be broader than church history, it must be a constituent of cultural history, and not merely a separate branch of history, it must concern itself with reciprocal influences, with the historical behavior of religious people and of religious institutions, with the influence of historical conditions, and perhaps especially with national cultural tendencies, with religious behavior of *all* sorts.° The few following examples are taken at random: like most of this chapter, they involve the history of Roman Catholicism, but only because it is with the history of this religion that I am relatively best acquainted. The greater the distance from Rome, the more radical and rapid was the break with the old religion during the sixteenth century. Why did this happen? How did the exceptions to it occur? Was it or was it not significant that, apart from a small core of French Gallican bishops, it was the hierarchs from the farthest edges of Roman Christendom, that is, American and Croatian and Ukrainian bishops, who were most reluctant to accept the dogma of papal infallibility during the Vatican I Council of 1869-1870? Popes have condemned national wars; but bishops and national Catholic leaders have not always followed them. Why did Pius X

---

[1] "It is the strength of a visible tangible institution able to act as a powerful force within and upon its historical environment, even in unfavourable circumstances, to create a religion-culture in which the activities and expressions of the human spirit are influenced and to a large extent determined by its creed. It is the weakness of the limitations and compromises imposed by the historical situation. Alloy depreciates the purity of gold. But, as von Hügel pointed out, gold without alloy is unusable."

say in July, 1914, that "the war Austria-Hungary is fighting is a just war"? How and why did the jealousies between Spanish Jesuits and Portuguese Franciscans during the early seventeenth century in Japan play into the hands of their Dutch and English Protestant opponents who, in turn, helped to deliver them to the dreadful persecution by the Japanese government that destroyed Christian life in Japan for more than two hundred years? What was the role of national ambitions in the controversies between French Jesuits and Italian Franciscans in Shantung during the 1880's and 1890's? We have only lately begun to examine the complex record of German Catholics during the Hitler era; and we must not gloss over such things as the mass murders and the forced conversions effected in 1941-1942 during the brief and bloody history of the Croatian state, actively supported (and defended sometimes even in retrospect) by certain Croatian Franciscans.* The study of religious history is *par excellence* the study of problems not of periods. Professor Lavisse said that the Falloux Law had been "one of the decisive events of the nineteenth century," not only because of its cultural consequences but because the struggles around its enactment had been full of significance, reflecting deep divisions between two groups of French Catholics—controversies which were paradigmatic, just as, say, the history of Bavarian Catholics in the 1920's and 1930's may be paradigmatic. Gregory XVI condemned the "Leftist" Lamennais in 1832; Pius XI condemned the "Rightist" Action Française in 1926: but these decrees did not issue from purely theological considerations: as Rémond put it, a pontifical decision such as the condemnation of the Action Française in 1926 had been "solicited, wished for, prepared; it came to consecrate a tendency that had been already crystallizing for some time." It is fortunate that portions of the Vatican archives, relevant to more recent times, have become accessible to historians lately: they must not be monopolized by specialists in church history.

The divergence between theological affinities on the one hand, and historical relationships on the other, is a difficult problem. I referred to it in passing in Chapter I, as I suggested the existence of certain deep-seated historical differences between Western and Eastern Christians, Catholics and Orthodox, all of the liturgical similarities of their rites notwithstanding. Even now when the ecumenical aspirations toward one Christian church have become so important, it may be still dangerously misleading to strive for unity by deliberately ignoring those differences between East and West, including Eastern and Western Christians, that have manifested themselves throughout history through different national mentalities.* In any event, the principal characteristic of the Western Christian attitude is the belief in the historic, as well as in the divine, Christ. "As St Paul clearly saw," Professor R. C. Zaehner wrote, Christianity is also "the scandal and the foolishness of the Cross," the historical and not only the miraculous and supernatural story of His life. Oriental religions, while they "have held certain doctrines which are not unlike the Christian doctrines," as Christopher Hollis put it, have not been historical; "they have asserted, 'This is the sort of thing that must have happened. Otherwise things do not make sense.' They have not asserted, 'This is what did happen in Palestine two thousand years ago on certain dates when the Emperors Augustine and Tiberius were on the Roman throne.'" For the Western mind the claims of Christianity are not only supernatural, they are historical—whence the partial fusion of the Jewish and the Greek (and later of the Protestant and the Catholic) traditions which are manifest in certain practices of the Western ethics of rhetoric. And the very recognition of this is an achievement of our historical consciousness. "The nineteenth-century ideal," as the Protestant theologian Ethelbert Stauffer recently wrote in his Introduction to *Jesus and His Story*, "was a *biography* of Jesus—that is to say, a representation of the psychological development of Jesus, of his mind and his activities, rendered with narrative vividness, analytic insight, and plausibility. Whether this was a legitimate ideal is a moot question. At any rate, we know today that it was unattainable. What, then, may our ideal be . . . I reply: a *history* of Jesus. . . ."* There is a desideratum as well as an admonition implicit in these statements.

The fact that Jesus, unlike other mythical founders of religions, was generally reluctant to perform miracles is evident from His own words. The fact that He was tempted by the devil suggests, too, that His historical life was not automatically predestined, that He had free will, that He had choices, that He was responsible for his acts: He was a potential saviour who became then an actual one (Matt. 4:1-11). John 20 adds that He did miracles only "that you may believe that Jesus is the Christ, the Son of God, and that believing you may have life in His name." This condition is emphasized by many responsible Christian theologians.

The Christian heritage of Western civilization derives, therefore, not only from our recognition of the virtues of His teachings but from our capacity to emulate His human acts. This belief in His historical existence is a higher task than the belief in Him in his capacity of a miracle-maker, credulity being almost always easier than a personal striving for the realization of certain ideals. Let me repeat: to many people it is easier to believe in the Christ-God at the expense of the historical Christ: we have yet to face new varieties of superficial credulity. Having taught American Catholic students for nearly twenty years, I have been struck on occasion by the reluctance of some of the weaker minds among them to see in the coming of Christ a historical event.

The deepest problem for the historian of religion may lie in the double hierarchy of events. It is the only field of history where we may speak of two kinds of events: temporal and transcendental ones. And the historian, just as he cannot exclude the consideration of temporal influences on religious institutions and actions, cannot altogether exclude religious experiences because of their supernatural claims. An event such as Lourdes belongs to history in more than one way: it happened, after all, to a human person on this earth; it also had an evident effect on temporal events in this world—including, for example, the development of the tourist industry in the western Pyrenees. On the other hand, the general historian, at least from evidence up to now, cannot really assert that the apparition at Lourdes was a more important event *in 1858* than the secret conference at Plombières of Napoleon III and Cavour in that year because, at least for contemporaries, it wasn't: yet he cannot altogether deny the place of the Lourdes event within the history of France. Recently D. B. Wyndham Lewis wrote about "La Salette, Lourdes, Pontmain, in chronological order: the trilogy of momentous nineteenth-century happenings on French soil. . . ." The transcendental meaning of these happenings is not for historians to ascertain, but it is their legitimate task to ascertain at least the extent of the temporal influence of these events in history. And this may change in the long run. Perhaps Jean de la Mennais, the humble brother of the flamboyant "Féli" Lamennais, who founded a teaching order, the Frères de l'Instruction Chrétienne de Ploërmel, which is still flourishing, may have done work that proved more enduring than that of his famous brother; perhaps, in the long run, the work of St. John Baptist de La Salle has been more enduring than that of his contemporary Mazarin. From the theological viewpoint every human event is important: for God an event that seems to have little impact or importance or significance may be more decisive than the largest evident milestone in a man's career.[2] *We* do not know. Still sometimes history suggests to us amazing reevaluations of the respective importance of certain events, in retrospect.

The earthly consequences as well as the very existence of Christ have been historical events. The earthly consequences of His life turned out to be more important than those of his contemporary Augustus Caesar. On this point historians and Christians are in accord. There is, moreover,

---

[2] Here is an example. A makes a slighting remark about B. The slight is unrecognized, unheard by B. The event still happened, since C may recognize it (and eventually regard it as significant in the light of earlier or later developments of A's relationship to B). But if neither B nor C nor anyone else has heard or recognized the slight, and if A does not follow it up later, then for all *historical* purposes the event did not happen—except *internally* for A. It did not actually involve others. Still, it remains an event within his own relationship with God—something which transcends the hierarchy of historical events (and the categories of human evidence).

another potential point of accord between them. For both the universe is geocentric as well as anthropocentric, the earth being the center of the historical as well as of the Christian universe—for the historian because man, the subject of his study, lives on this earth, and also because all of the different views of the universe have been the products of the mind of man, formulated from this earth; for the Christian because the Son of God appeared in no other but human form, and on no other planet but this. A non-Christian historian is of course not compelled to believe this. Yet it is not only because of the accepted convenience of the Christian calendar but because of the historicity of Christianity that the appearance of Jesus Christ within history marks, at least for most of us in the West, the most important division of historical time.

VI

THE REMEMBERED PAST

or the functions of recognition

(1) I am, therefore I think, therefore I am

Very reluctantly I am about to fill the next few pages with a certain description of myself: for I see no clearer way to introduce this chapter, in which I am passing from a description of certain historical factors to the description of certain functions of historical consciousness. I am falling back on this personal illustration for no other reason than that even though there are many things about myself that I do not know, it is still myself that I know best among all human beings who lived, who live, and who shall live on this earth. Yet to begin with a personal illustration does not, fortunately, mean to end with it.

With this in mind, then, here is a primitive illustration of my argument. As I look at the history of my life I, too, can distinguish a certain hierarchy of conditions. The condition that I was born and brought up in Hungary is, for example, a more important characteristic of my person than that I am an American citizen. The condition that I am a Catholic is more important than the condition that I teach in Catholic colleges; on the other hand, the condition that these are American colleges in the middle of the twentieth century are important characteristics beyond the mere category of their being "Catholic" institutions. The "fact" that I am now forty-three and the other "fact" that I was born in 1924 are equivalent, mathematically speaking: but historically speaking they aren't: the second has a certain significance which is different

from that of the first. And it is this historicity of our existence that
Descartes did not consider. So let me reverse his famous phrase.
Sum, ergo cogito. I am, therefore I think.

But this is not enough. Who am I? I have a diary that my father
kept during the first year of my life. Many things in it, including
photographs, reflect the atmosphere of central European family life
that was recorded in the massive bourgeois novels of its time. But
there is more to it. Unlike his father, my father was a physician, a
radical, an agnostic. His personality was complex. Supremely ego-
tistic but also surprisingly sentimental, an amateur classical scholar
but also a freethinker, he believed in Progress and in Science. He
was a captain in World War I where he earned high decorations,
including a military knighthood; at the same time he was anti-
monarchist, anticlerical, a radical liberal with socialist leanings. The
family record in the diary is interspersed with his political ruminations. On February 17, 1924, for example, he writes (I am translating this from the Hungarian) of the then present: "stormy times,
great times," and of "the thunder of tremendous events now happening," of "a strange kind of new dawn in the East. *Ex oriente lux.*
It may be a sign for the salvation of mankind." "In the West, too,
humanity advances. The Labor government of Ramsay Macdonald
ruled England. Germany, Austria are republics. Italy a monarchy
only in name. In our country, alas, darkest reaction still rages: but
perhaps here, too, things may be slowly improving. The finances of
the victorious French are corrupt to the bottom; there the bloody
demagogues of militarism are still in the saddle," but sanity and
reason may be at work there, too. He ends this entry with a sentimental expression of hope. "Sleep, my son, sleep: by the time your
consciousness awakes you may see a lovelier, a better, a
nobler world." As I turn the pages of this diary I experience sentiments of veneration, of gratitude. Still I know that my father's history was wrong. He held certain illusions and beliefs that I do not
possess. He wrote "stormy times," "terrible chaos," when 1924 was
one of the more peaceable years between the wars. "The strange
kind of dawn in the East" was to be Stalin's peasant darkness.
Ramsay Macdonald, that supreme nonentity, no more "ruled England" than had Edward VI. "Germany, Austria republics; Italy a
monarchy only in name"—this, among other things, led to Hitler's
and Mussolini's dictatorships. "Darkest reaction still raging" in

Hungary: in none of the remaining thirty-two years of his life would my father see more freedom in Hungary than what prevailed during the conservative regimes of Bethlen and Horthy in 1924. And, had "militarism" in France had its way, my father, one of the million foreign lovers of Paris, might not have had to live through that bitter dazzling day sixteen years later when Hitler's army marched down the Champs-Elysées. As I grew up, as my consciousness awoke, I was not to see "a lovelier, a better, a nobler world."

I was born in 1924, the year Lenin and Wilson died. My father was born in 1883, in the year Marx and Wagner died. He died in 1956, in the year of the Hungarian Revolution, the year my son was born.

I believe with Newman that the sum total of good and evil in this world probably remains constant, that our world in 1967 is neither better nor worse than the world in 1924. But I see certain things better than my father saw them—not because I am a better man than he was, not because I am a historian while he was a physician, and not even because history is the teacher of life: rather the reverse: because *vita magistra historiae* rather than *historia magistra vitae*, because I was born in 1924 and not in 1883, because I have lived through other historical experiences, because children, in a sense, are older than their fathers.

But only in a sense. *Vita magistra historiae* is not enough either. We have become conscious not only of the historicity of our existence but of the historicity of our cognition, too. Let me therefore round out this phrase. Not only does life govern history: life governs history which, in another sense, governs life: *vita magistra historiae magistra vitae*—life the master of history the teacher of life—a phrase in which the same truth exists on two levels, and the logic of which is not circular but spiral.

Let me, thus, round out the reverse Cartesian phrase too. *Sum ergo cogito ergo sum.* Again, the logic in this seemingly—but only seemingly—circular statement is not mathematical but historical. I was born as a human being. I exist. I think. And my recognition of the historicity of my thinking lends another dimension to my existence: the two *sums*, the two "I am's," reflect two levels; and the causalities implied by the two connecting *ergos* are slightly different, too. I am, therefore I think, therefore I am.

It should be rather evident that anyone who holds, as I do, such a post-Cartesian view, can no longer feel attracted by that scientific ideal of objectivity which has been the principal result of the Cartesian method in the intellectual history of Western civilization. I said "feel," since I remember how very early in my life the word "objective" (unlike "detached" or "impartial") sounded dull and only faintly approbatory to me; certainly my budding interest in historical knowledge was motivated by something else than an interest in objectivity; for some time, including my university years, I did not mind the intellectual opprobrium often associated with subjectivism. It took me some time, however, to understand how subjectivism was neither the true counterpart nor a necessary corrective of objectivism; to recognize the necessity to transcend not only these categories but to understand the inadequacy of their antithesis. But I need not employ illustrations from my personal history to pursue this argument onward from this point.

(2) Objectivity and subjectivity, or personal knowledge

One of the curious symptoms of the cultural chaos and of the intellectual schizophrenia which is so prevalent in our times is the persistence of public belief in the ideal of objectivity in historical science at the same time when subjectivism is running rampant in letters and in arts. As I am writing the final draft of this chapter (January, 1967), the Kennedy-Manchester controversy is in the news. The public reaction to this affair, a tempest in the celebrity teapot, is relevant to what I am writing about:* for practically all the people who have made various comments about this controversy seem to agree on one point or, rather, on one shibboleth: they have one misconception in common. It would have been better, they say, if the account of President Kennedy's last days had been left for an objective historian to write in the more distant future. Now, there are all kinds of things wrong with this way of thinking —which is, we must admit, historical thinking of sorts. It is not true that the distance of time will necessarily produce a better perspective for the eventual historian (especially not when the subject—four days of a routine political trip by a President—depends on many small details). It is not true that a professional historian is necessarily more competent than a magazine writer in his ability to reconstruct such an episode. All of Manchester's shortcomings notwithstanding (and there are many of them), there is something ludicrously naïve in the image (conjured, among others, by Governor Connally) of a young talented Ph.D., working amid his archives, say, thirty years hence, an American Scholar wearing rimless glasses, perhaps of the University of Texas, writing *the* Definitive History, in order to present the nation with the Objective Historical Truth. There is no such thing as a definitive history, because there is no such thing as an objective history. All there is is the last word on the subject. But in history, unlike in other human conventions, including law, *the last word on the subject* means something very different from *the case is now closed.* "The last word on the subject" means, rather, that the case has been reopened, as indeed it will be reopened, again and again, in the minds of human beings, in our minds.

In our minds. What disturbed me in the Kennedy-Manchester controversy was the peculiar persistence of the illusion of "objectivity" when applied to history: that the safe and unquestionable truth about something that happened exists somewhere, extraneous as it is to our minds, and that it would be dug up one day by a reputable scientific student of the reputable social science called history, in order to appropriately present it, in the form of a neat package, to be deposited in the libraries of the nation and of the world. But this is a nineteenth-century article of belief. The Oxford English Dictionary defines "objectivism" (1872): "The tendency to lay stress upon what is objective and external to the mind; the philosophical doctrine that knowledge of the non-ego is prior in sequence and in importance to that of the ego; the character (in a work of art, etc.) of being objective." This assumption that the antiseptic separation of the observer from what is observed (or, in other words, the separation of "subject" from "object," of "present" from "past") is the absolute precondition of truthful observation does not make sense, historically speaking. What is inherent in this assumption is the belief that for different persons the same conditions of observing the human past must necessarily lead to the same results: a consequence of the categorical application of the method of the natural sciences to history.

The insufficiency of these objectivist assumptions was, then, recognized by certain European thinkers in a variety of fields during the second half of the nineteenth century, a reactive development that was to influence a number of historians, especially after 1895. I have mentioned this development earlier, in passing:[1] for it was symptomatic of our deepening historical consciousness: in many ways the recognitions of the "subjectivists" represented an advance over the nineteenth-century illusions of scientific objectivism. But this reaction was not, and is not, enough. On one very important point the basic assumptions of the subjectivists have been wrong. I have touched on this point, too, earlier in this book, but I must repeat it for the sake of the argument of this chapter. This point is that, according to the subjectivists, the historian is inevitably the product of history. The clearest expression, in English, of this philosophy, exists in the words of the neo-idealist Collingwood.[2] Having recognized that, say, a German historian who was born in 1900 would see the past differently from a French historian who was born in 1800, Collingwood concluded that "there is no point in asking which was the right point of view. Each was the only one possible for the man who adopted it."

The only one possible? It is on this point that the subjectivists, from the early Croce to the later Becker and Beard, slid into error. They could not really liberate themselves from the scientific world-view, from Descartes's world divided into subjects and objects, and from Newton's world where causes always and necessarily precede effects, and where the present is always the product of the past.* They went wrong not because they were attacking the illusion of objectivity: they went wrong because, like the objectivists, they were thinking in terms of direct causes, of products. The chastened (but, still, pseudo-Marxist) Carr, in his more sophisticated version, pronounced in 1961, falls into the same error: "Before you study the historian, study his historical and social environment." There is much truth in this but it is far from the entire truth. I was born in 1924, in Hungary, of bourgeois parentage; there may be

[1] See above, Chapter I, p. 20. Marrou on Renan: ". . . one ought to re-read *L'avenir de la science* in order to realize the tragedy of the convictions of the generation of 1848: they convinced themselves, and they convinced the civilization of the West, to follow a road which has then revealed itself to have been an impasse. Yet these men had been our masters! I am asking my young readers to realize how enormous has been, then, our task, this effort to redress the balance."

[2] Greatly admired by the now fashionable German theologian Rudolf Bultmann; see his *History and Eschatology* (New York, 1957); on the fallacy of "the only one possible" see above, p. 166.

other historians who were born in 1924, in Hungary, of bourgeois parentage; I doubt very much that they share some of my fundamental historical views. It is all very true to say that, having been born and brought up in Hungary in the twenties and thirties, I am a different kind of person from, say, a Soviet or an American historian born in the twenties and brought up in the thirties; but to let it go at that is really not enough, not at all. It is a twentieth-century, an automobile-age version of Tolstoy's nineteenth-century nonsense of History as a Locomotive. The important thing is where the driver is going and not, as Tolstoy thought, the mechanism of the locomotive; the important question is "what is Carr driving at?" and not "what make is this Carr?"

The recognition that different persons see the past (and also the present) differently and that thus every historian is different does not mean that because he is the product of his past he cannot do otherwise. I said something about the insufficiency of our present notion of causes (as well as about the consequent tendency to regard human beings as products) in Chapter IV, and I shall still have something to say about the now necessary reconsideration of causalities later. At this point I wish to say that my perception of the world is neither objective nor subjective: it is personal. And by "personal" I do not mean "individual"; for the unique unit of history, the human being, is neither a subject nor an individual— he is a person which, unlike "individual," is not an abstraction. His life is never entirely separated from that of other human beings; indeed, the historicity of his personality exists precisely, as we have seen, in his relationships with them. And in this respect the inadequacy of the objective:subjective antithesis corresponds to the inadequacy of the—largely nineteenth-century—social antithesis of individualism:collectivism.

Historical knowledge is personal knowledge—including personal self-knowledge. For us Descartes's division of the world into objects and subjects no longer makes sense.[3] I said "no longer," because this

[3] Bultmann, op. cit.: ". . . the relation of subject and object which is characteristic for natural science [but even there it is no longer completely valid: see below, Chapter VII, pp. 286 ff.] has no value for historical science. Historical science is objective precisely in its subjectivity, because the subject and object of historical science do not exist independently from each other." It is precisely this "precisely" which tends toward abstraction in this otherwise common-sense statement.

is a historical recognition. Not only am I speaking as a historian and not as a scientist or as a logician; what is far more important, these categories of "object," "subject," "objective," "subjective" cannot and and should not be discussed in the abstract, because they are historical words and not merely philosophical categories. They are words whose present meaning began to emerge about three hundred years ago, consequent to the then intellectual revolution in western European minds; and I say "revolution" not only because of the consequences of the new scientific cosmology of the seventeenth century but also because the very meaning of these modern scientific keywords changed at that time.[4]

I think, then, that now, three centuries later, we may be moving toward another intellectual revolution, having discovered the illusory nature of categorical objectivity (and, as we shall see later, not only in the humanities), as the very words "subject" and "object" have become somehow dull and blurred in our minds, and as "objective" (somehow like "progressive") is no longer as shining and approbatory as it was only a few decades ago. At this point we must understand how the evolution of historical consciousness enters into these matters. It is, namely, through such an evolution that we are capable of transcending certain categorical antitheses as they become corroded by historical experience, as we are "outgrowing" them rather than "solving" them.

Having, then, comprehended the inherent limitations of the ideal of objectivity, we cannot return to a prescientific and pre-Cartesian view of the world. This may be obvious to the point of a platitude: but I am mentioning it here, too, in order to draw attention to that portion of Descartes's achievement which even now remains largely unaffected by the otherwise collapse of his world-system. For we must recognize not only the enormous effects and many benefits of the scientific method but also the condition of how Descartes, at the threshold of the Modern Age, arrived at the threshold of the kind of human introspection which, perhaps even more than the scientific method, has become a principal inheritance of our civiliza-

---

[4] The *O.E.D.* about *objective:* "Of or pertaining to the object or end as the cause of action . . ." before 1768. *Subject:* "The substance in which accidents or attributes inhere, late ME. The substance of which a thing consists or from which it is made—before 1775. The mind, as the 'subject' in which ideas inhere —after 1796." *Subjective:* "correl. to Objective 1707."

tion. And yet this most famous of all Cartesian phrases, *cogito ergo sum*, represented an important but also stunted recognition of that great scientist-philosopher. Descartes's recognition, through his rigorous exercise of introspective logic, that the mind is an inexpugnable category of reality, marked a very great step forward in the evolution of our consciousness. This should appear especially when we consider that before Descartes's time things that we call objects had been generally regarded as possessing inherent qualities emanating from themselves, and completely irrelevant to the human mind.[5] *Cogito ergo sum* represents, therefore, that achievement of self-knowledge (in other words, of internalization) which, together with historical consciousness and the scientific method, was the most important intellectual development in the seventeenth century. And yet this was a stunted recognition, in Descartes's case. For it may be said that the meaning of this achievement escaped him almost entirely. Having realized the distinctness of internal knowledge from external reality, he did not really relate them to each other. Like his attempts to introduce the then minimal requirements of theology into his system (which some of his critics regarded as mere lip service), his attempts to establish the connections between the internal functions of mind and the operations of the external world must strike us as extraordinarily feeble. And the reason for this is that Descartes, unlike Pascal, was not really very much interested in the internal functions of mind: having recognized its existence, he rather let it go at that: he was a mathematician, geometrician, scientist: he was principally interested in the external order of the world. It is therefore that, all of the merits and all of the reputation of *cogito ergo sum* notwithstanding, the principal results of the Cartesian philosophy and of the Newtonian system of the seventeenth century were and still are to be found in their effects on the natural sciences, that is, not on man's knowledge of man but on his knowledge of his environment.

It indeed seems that Western civilization, during the last one thousand years, may have shifted its intellectual emphasis twice:

---

[5] Barfield: It was thus that the Romans spoke of events as "auspicious" or "sinister," and that medieval people spoke of an herb possessing such and such a virtue, or of the bones of a saint being holy, whereas "when we speak of an object or an event as *amusing*, on the contrary, we know that the process indicated by the word *amuse* takes place within ourselves."

from theology to humanism, and then to scientism—or, in other words, it seems that while in the Middle Ages the principal business of man's intellect was considered to be man's knowledge of God, thereafter the emphasis may have changed to man's knowledge of man, until lately it became man's knowledge of his environment. These are enormously broad generalizations, of course. But I am mentioning them here only in order to emphasize, once more, that we cannot return to a prescientific humanism for many reasons, one of them being that prescientific humanism was not sufficiently historical. I think that we may be capable of shifting our attention once more—that is, if civilization does not collapse, something that is no longer merely a remote possibility—in the direction of man's knowledge of man: but this will be different both from the literary humanities as well as from social science, in the sense that it will have to be introspective as well as historical. The twentieth-century phenomenon of history as the remembered (rather than merely the recorded, or narrated) past reflects the (often disorderly) deepening of our historical consciousness, and this is something which is inseparable from conscious introspection, from the necessity of self-knowledge. "Know then thyself, presume not God to scan": this is a Socratic statement in the first line of the famous couplet, to which Pope then added: "The proper study of mankind is man." But my argument is that Socrates' *know thyself* was different from Pope's which, in turn, is different from ours. From the Hellenic *philosophia* through enlightened humanism to historical personalism our historical consciousness has become broader and our self-consciousness deeper. Not only can we draw upon historical experiences and examples that Pope did not, and could not, know; but we can argue, as Pope could not, that "the philosophical doctrine that knowledge of the non-ego is prior in sequence and in importance to that of the ego" has not fulfilled our expectations and that, indeed, it cannot fulfill them—and this in itself is a recognition resting not on philosophical categories but grown out of historical experience during the last one hundred years. What Pope said was that the study of mankind should be our main object: to this we add that the study of mankind is necessarily personal, beginning with ourselves.[6]

[6] *Beginning with ourselves.* I beg my readers' leave to introduce a personal note once more, for the sake of illustration. One day in May, 1963, driving down

From now on "know thyself" should mean: know your historical circumstances, in order to be aware of yourself and of your tendencies as fully as possible; in order to be able to transcend them. *In order to be able to transcend them;* because there is another thing; beyond knowing your historical circumstances, "know thyself" also means, know your likes and dislikes. I know that I tend to dislike Bolsheviks, Nazis, Ukrainians, Californians, Cossacks, Japanese, Puritans, Byzantines, Presbyterians, Marxists, Russian choristers, English intellectuals, German musicians with a Rudolf Serkin face, Bavarian businessmen with a BMW face, Midwestern waitresses with the faces of old trolley cars, academic liberals with small salt-and-pepper mustaches, pipe-smoking chairmen of departments who have a gap between their front teeth, ex-Communist Communion Breakfast speakers, Jewish high-pressure salesmen, magazine editors, television producers, Grand Marshals of St. Patrick's Day Parades, intellectuals whose heads resemble the form of an electric light bulb, Argentinian diplomatists who wear sunglasses . . . My potential list may be interminable (gentle reader, so is yours). But at least I did not state, categorically, that these are *all* people whom I dislike: I said that these are types (and a human "type" is always, to some extent, an abstraction) that I *tend* to dislike. And in many instances I have learned (with what is perhaps one of the most nourishing kinds of intellectual satisfaction) that my prejudices had been wrong, that I could correct, supersede, overcome my initial tendency because the impressions and the expressions of a particular person convinced me to do so. Convinced: and why? "What really happened," Professor Oakeshott once wrote, "is only what the evidence obliges us to believe." But this kind of "evidence," composed of my impressions and of another person's

---

the country road not far from our house I experienced a moment of great happiness. It was a glittering cool morning, full of green and gold, dappled with sunlight and the shimmering richness of fresh, wet, leafy trees. A moment later it occurred to me that while in another century someone touched by such a sense of happiness may have felt the need to exclaim his utter thankfulness to God for having created these leaves, these trees, this sun, I felt a deep gratitude to Him for having created *me,* that is, *my capacity* for perceiving and appreciating these trees, this sun; of allowing me to participate in this world, in this universe, in this way.

Not "I am a camera" (Isherwood, 1932: an affectation of modern objectivity); I am a dark-room.

expressions, is at least as much internally and morally, as it is externally and technically, convincing. In any event, it is better (and, in the long run, safer) to know one's prejudices from the beginning, rather than to cultivate them subconsciously, either by suppressing them, or refusing to know them by clothing them through all kinds of rationalizations. The understanding of the illusory qualities of objectivity may be the beginning not only of wisdom but, paradoxically, of charity, too: for it may be a step toward a higher level at the same time when objectivity may be a cloak for weakness or indifference (which is probably why the "safe," impersonal rhetoric of science appeals so much to the cautious, sallow academician in the twentieth century). But life is only worth living if we know what we like and what we don't: and this kind of knowledge lends another dimension—sensual as well as intellectual—to our experience. Moreover, liking and disliking are not altogether the same. We must *cultivate* what we like, and *recognize* what we dislike:* for the recognition of a prejudice, like the diagnosis of a disease, may—I'm not saying that it will—be halfway to its corrective cure.

It is perhaps significant that the limits of objectivity were recognized by Tocqueville and Burckhardt better than by Ranke: unlike the latter, the aristocrat Tocqueville and the patrician Burckhardt admitted and knew many of their personal inclinations and their existing prejudices: and it is perhaps precisely for this reason that they succeeded in overcoming them on occasion. "I began my study of the old régime full of prejudices against the clergy," Tocqueville wrote, "I ended it full of respect." (How few of our professional intellectuals would dare to admit such a thing nowadays, let alone put it in a book!) Burckhardt in one of his lectures made a beautiful distinction between *Vorliebe* and *Parteilichkeit*, a personal tendency of being attracted to, and affected by, certain places, peoples, cultures, as distinct from mere partisanship; the former was good and proper, the latter wrong.[7] The person of the historian is to determine his work, Burckhardt said. "We are not objective." "Personal participation is unavoidable."*

[7] Burckhardt to Nietzsche: "I never dreamt of training scholars and disciples in the narrower sense, but only wanted to make every member of my audience feel and know that everyone may and must appropriate those aspects of the past which appeal to him personally, and that there might be happiness in so doing. I know perfectly well that such an aim may be criticized as fostering amateurism, but that does not trouble me overmuch."

The recognition of the objectivist illusion does not reduce, it rather enhances, the general validity of personal knowledge. For this is the wonderful mystery: knowledge is personal; and at the same time it is universal. We are not atomized individuals but persons: we are unique and yet an integral element of the *entire* human race, of *all* history. When I say "this is true" or "this is interesting" or "this is what really happened," I am expressing only a personal view; at first sight, it seems presumptuous to say such things, when by "this is interesting" I really mean that it interests *me*. But I am capable, under certain conditions, to transmit some of this personal sense of interest to others to whom I am addressing myself. And there is more to this: what is *actually* interesting to me is at least *potentially* interesting to every human being. When I say "this is true," this is an expression of my personal feeling of truth: but somehow this corresponds with something general, or perhaps even universal, which is more than merely "subjective" or "individual." The now fashionable kind of environmental subjectivism cannot go beyond a certain level of honesty, since it says, at best, something like the following: "I am writing or saying this because, at this time, this is my subjective impression; and since it is a subjective impression, it cannot be absolutely certain." But the purpose of human knowledge is understanding rather than certainty; and, moreover, the issue involves too, as we have seen, the purposes of the expression, which are perhaps even more personal* than are the motives of the impression. What the historian should say, instead, is something like this: "I am writing or saying this because this is at this time my personal way of seeing and saying something that I believe to be true."

We all work with ideas and standards that are, to some extent, peculiar to ourselves, but somehow these correspond to ideas and standards that each of our readers has been personally developing in some form or another. We are usually more conscious of our purposes than of our motives; on the other hand, we are especially responsible for our expressions. If, then, by historical "relativity" we mean not only the historicity of every form of human cognition but also of every form of human expression, it should be obvious that this idea of relativity is neither a feeble nor a senseless one; for this "relativity" of *truths* means not the absence but the potential richness, not the nullity but the multiplicity of *truth*.*

(3) About imagination

As I recall instances of my early interest in history I think that I am safe in assuming that my experiences were similar (though not of course identical) to the experiences of many other adolescents. Imagination was the vitalizing element in those first flashes of historical interest. Those early crystallizations of a specific curiosity, the desire to know more about particular matters in the past—what certain people "really" did, and how things "really" looked—were activated, if not altogether created, by imagination. Thus this kind of interest, and the knowledge it would produce, was something different from a Cartesian category: for Descartes, as Professor Ogg put it in his *Europe in the Seventeenth Century*, "insisted on eliminating the mental processes which can be linked with bodily functions, such as imagination and memory. Childhood he regarded merely as a period of error. . . ." Yet imagination and interest, as well as imagination and memory, are hardly separable. Their inseparability does not, moreover, change essentially from childhood to adulthood, save that increasing maturity means the increasing recognition of how interests must be cultivated, and of how imagination and interest may nourish each other. "For," as Veronica Wedgwood wrote, "ultimately the understanding of the past, in so far as it is achieved at all, has to be independently achieved, by a sustained effort of the imagination working on a personal accumulation of knowledge and experience." "Sustained effort" is good: because not only are men often governed by their imagination; they are governed perhaps even more often, as Bagehot said, "by the weakness of their imagination"—which then includes a certain incapacity for that kind of self-knowledge that, as we have seen, is an essential component of our historical consciousness.

Self-knowledge, and the existing potentiality of past-knowledge are involved intimately with imagination—a word which suggests a colorful mental construction on the one hand, and an inward tendency on the other. *Imagination,* somewhat like *insight, inspiration, intuition, interest,* has not only a romantic but an introspective connotation. Many of the illustrations of this chapter must, therefore, unavoidably deal with human phenomena that do not, strictly speaking, belong to historical research. The part played by the imagination, as Collingwood rightly put it, "is properly not ornamental but structural"; and the meaning of this truth goes beyond our interest in history. If, for example, imagination is more than a superstructure of perception, the term "Extrasensory perception" is, strictly speaking, misleading, for *all* human perception is, to some extent, extrasensory. Since this is not a treatise of phenomenology or of perception, the philosophical profundities of which I am ignorant (though I am happy to know that "perception," before the seventeenth century, meant the collection of rents), I cannot develop this theme further, except to say that it involves the fundamental difference which I dared to mention a few pages earlier in a footnote, in the form of intellectual shorthand, when I said "I am a dark-room" instead of "I am a camera"—suggesting the difference between considering human organs as passive recipents of impressions on the one hand, and the human being as the active developers of impressions on the other.*

It is because of our imagination that we may see movement in a sculptured block of stone, or that a sketch of a few lines may strike us as more "real" than a color photograph. Yet I am concerned here not with the function of imagination in art but, rather, with the potential evocative power of certain remnants from the past. I said "potential," because their evocative power is not an inherent property of themselves; the most perfectly preserved building or document becomes evocative, indeed, "historical," only through our imagination. On the other hand, the more complete and the more authentic that remnant of the past, the more it will appeal to our historical imagination, because of the peculiarly realistic tendency of the latter. Jaurès the positivist expressed this feeling in a fine simile: having pored over hundreds of old pamphlets, prints, caricatures, he thanked the staff of the Musée Carnavalet for their help in "gathering these living pictures, these rustling and stirring leaves, still full of the warm and colorful sap of the Revolution. And," he added, "I also take pleasure in throwing them again to the wind of life." All of us are aware of the evocative power of certain photographs:[8] it is not mere antiquarianism that stimulates, or indeed

---

[8] André Malraux said that the existence of photography added a new dimension to our knowledge of art. It may give a new dimension to our knowledge of history, too. But the understanding and the practice thereof is only in its infancy: consider only the ridiculously haphazard manner with which our history textbooks include certain photographs for the sake of illustrating . . . God only knows what.

excites, our interest as we encounter a daguerreotype, say, of a boulevard during the siege of Paris in 1870; it is a kind of interest which is inseparable from our imagination which, in turn, is an ineradicable component of our perception of the past. We cannot eliminate it from our minds, we cannot suppress it, if we cannot bury it—and this is a condition which we need not at all regret; indeed, we should rather rejoice in knowing it, no matter what the categorical desiderata of certain objectivists may be.

But let me now turn to the converse function: from what imagination does to history to what history does to our imagination. What I mean is that the imagination, and therefore the perception, and therefore possibly even some of the visual faculties, of our ancestors in the Middle Ages were different from ours: they saw certain things in certain ways because they thought of them in certain ways. This is a very difficult matter to illustrate (certain art historians have nonetheless attempted it with more or less success). In most parts of Europe and America the sight of women's ankles excited men's interest in 1900 but no longer in 1920. Of course between these two dates fashions—not only fashions in clothes but cultural fashions—had changed: or, in other words, a certain aspect of the forbidden fruit was no longer forbidden. On the other hand the cult of nakedness on the beaches and elsewhere, too, in the name of modern "sexual freedom," does not seem to have eased or lessened the mental preoccupations of people with sexual imagery: rather the contrary. The changing direction of erotic interests cannot be entirely the product either of environmental changes or of the hereditary subconscious; neither the explanations of cultural anthropologists, nor those of orthodox Freudians, will do.

"Poets," said Pascal, "have no right to picture love as blind; its bandage must be pulled off and it must be given the use of its eyes." Being capable of love at almost any time is one of the major capacities in which men differ from animals, one of the reasons for this being that the development of this capacity is involved with imagination (whence the circumstance that certain men with high intellectual powers have been highly successful lovers.)* Ortega y Gasset as well as his *bête noire* Stendhal recognized, in their different ways how, contrary to modern Freudianism, lust is not, as Ortega put it, "an instinct but a specifically human creation —like literature. In both, the most important factor is imagination. . . . The sexual instinct . . . in man . . . is almost always found to be indissolubly united, at least, with fantasy." To this I should add that sexual perversion may be often not the result of a hormonal or physical imbalance but of existential and historical conditions, involving a disease of imagination. "The notorious disproportion between the sexuality of man and woman," Ortega wrote, "which makes the normally spontaneous woman so conservative in 'love,' probably coincides with the fact that the human female usually enjoys less imaginative power than the male"—which, let me add, may explain why male homosexuality is almost everywhere more frequent than is Lesbianism, lust being a product of imagination, and men being more imaginative than women.*

"L'amour," said Talleyrand, "est une réalité dans le domain de l'imagination." Let me return to the nowadays underestimated relationship between sexual and social aspirations that I mentioned in a previous portion of this book: for it is through a certain kind of existential and historical imagination that their entanglements exist. In one of his extremely rare comments upon the sensual intercourse of the sexes Dr. Johnson ascribed their delight "chiefly to imagination. Were it not for imagination, Sir, a man would be as happy in the arms of a chambermaid as of a Duchess. But such is the adventitious charm of fancy, that we find men who have violated the best principles of society, and ruined their fame and their fortune, that they might possess a woman of rank." "The Duchesse de Chaulnes," wrote Stendhal, "used to say that a duchess is never more than thirty years old to a snob." Yes: the element of vanity is often a principal factor in sexual ambitions. (Not only did Stendhal, in *De l'amour*, make brilliant comparisons between vanity-love and sympathy-love and passion-love; he wrote that even "in sympathy-love and also perhaps during the first five minutes of passion-love, a woman in taking a lover takes more account of the opinion that other women have of him than the opinion she has of him herself.")

But here we arrive at a very important issue. There must be *some* kind of a proportionate relationship between our imagination and reality; and I find it very significant that this must happen in our sexual aspirations which, after all, spring from deep recesses of ourselves and which, as we have seen, are always to some extent involved with fantasy. Those who claim that realism is nothing more than an aesthetic or philosophical convention miss this point altogether.[9] A duchess may never be more than thirty years old to a snob: but, as Stendhal also wrote, "whoever dreams of making love to a queen? . . . at any rate," he added, "until she gives him some encouragement?" There must be some proportion between circumstances and aspirations, between image and reality: generally speaking, men do not fall in love with distant queens. Our imagination is not separate from our existential reality; it is personal and historical; it does not exist in a void.

My readers must excuse me for having roamed this far in order to illustrate my argument—which, after all, involves fundamental things concerning human nature. It may be perhaps understandable why a historian's mind gravitates in that direction. This is what happened, for instance, with the great Dutch historian Huizinga who devoted a book to the exposition of his argument concerning human nature: according to him man was *homo ludens*, "man who plays." Profoundly aware as he was of the factor of imagination, Huizinga concluded that what we often see as the "functional" or "practical" part of human behavior is, in reality, inseparably connected with—indeed, that it is often subordinated to—"nonfunctional," "impractical," "irrational" elements, which Huizinga saw as elements of *play*. He recognized that there is an irrevocable element of play in most human activity: not only in games and sports but in art and politics and war, since each of them has a certain kind of ritual, unwritten rules, parades, etc. Moreover "the play-concept, as such," Huizinga wrote, "is of a higher order than seriousness. For seriousness seeks to exclude play, whereas play can very well include seriousness." Note the relevance of this to the above-mentioned problematic relationship between image and reality. For we may have to go a step further: there may be an implicit contradiction within Huizinga's original thesis. On the one hand, he said that "we play and know that we play, so we must be more than merely rational beings, for play is irrational." On the other hand, he stated that "human civilization has added no essen-

---

[9] Hence the intellectual shortcoming of those (and any excessive Freudian interpretation tends in that direction) who say that sexual ambitions are symbolic categories. A picture book of abstract nudes will not sell, and a person who is habitually aroused by the sight or touch of a sexual object (including a "fetish" of any kind) will want this to be as realistic (or "lifelike") as possible.

tial feature to the general idea of play." This implies that in this respect we do not differ from animals, since animals play, too; and when Huizinga later says that "play only becomes possible, thinkable and understandable when an influx of *mind* (his italics) breaks down the absolute determinism of the cosmos," this suggests that animals possess rational qualities. But there is more to this. The recognition of the relationship between what is imaginary and what is real is a uniquely human characteristic, which usually does not appear until a certain stage of the evolution of consciousness. This means that all human play derives not only from imagination but also from a *recognition* of imagination—a condition which is observable among children as well as among adults. We must round out Huizinga's phrase: we play really when we know that we play while we play. The "inside" knowledge that the play is fashioning reality but that it is not really reality furnishes some of the delicious daydreaming sense of play: which corresponds, I think, to our recognition of the intimate connection between imagination and reality. (We call a painting "realistic": in it the two edges of the highway converge in the distance, even though we *know* that "in reality" they do not converge.)

And here we find, as indeed in many other instances of human experience, that if you push one element to the extreme, you may arrive at its very opposite. The worst spoilsport of the play is the boy who keeps shouting that it is only play, and nothing but play, whereby he destroys the play: conversely, at the other extreme, the play may be destroyed as it is being pushed toward "100 percent realism"; once it is cut off from the knowledge that it is play, it degenerates into deadly seriousness. Huizinga recognized the danger, in our times, of "the fatal shift toward overseriousness;" he was particularly concerned with its characteristics in our professionalized sports and other mass "entertainments." In the arts we have now moved from the exaggerated "naturalism" of the nineteenth century to the no less exaggerated "abstraction," pushed, too, to overseriousness (the very word "abstract" suggests overseriousness, inorganic, antiseptic, lifeless as it is): to the overseriousness of nonrepresentation which, in the strict sense of the word, is a contradiction in terms, since the artist must represent *some* kind of reality.* And this is the supremely important qualification of our historical condition: our historical consciousness inevitably binds us to some kind of reality: historical representation cannot be abstract: our past-knowledge is at the same time imaginary and real. (In this sense, therefore, unreal=unhistorical.) Thus re-presentation is neither mere substitution, nor is it purely symbolic abstraction. The symbol must be representative of something real. In the Western world our historical consciousness activates this recognition of the intimate involvement of "play" with "seriousness," and of image with reality—which is why historical consciousness may be one of our most vital intellectual assets. Our modern spoilsport is the "practical" advocate of computer civilization, our destroyer of play is the "bohemian" advocate of abstract art: both err in the direction of overseriousness. Dogmatism may degenerate into scientism and vice versa; the first happened during the waning of the Middle Ages, the latter now with the passing of the Modern Age; both go against the grain of our tradition of reason. When play becomes a serious business, when symbols as well as scientific concepts are no longer representative of anything besides themselves, when objects and categories of abstractions are accepted as if they were living realities, we face tendencies which may be typical of other civilizations but not of our own where, as I wrote before, "idealism" and "realism" are not at all antithetical, and the principal rational tradition as well as the rational capacity of which reflects a unique sense of proportionate realism in many of its manifestations.

A sense of proportion is a mark of human maturity: and the quality of maturity involves the deepening of the range of imagination. Precisely this capacity is endangered by the now fashionable drug- and other sense-hallucinatory practices, reflecting, as these do, tendencies toward barbarism and primitiveness. In the first place hallucination is something entirely different from memory: it is oriented toward an illusory, incoherent and discontinuous future, away from the reality of a continuous, and continuing, past: it desires the blotting out of reality, unlike memory which is attracted by the deepening of it. In the second place (in order, not in importance) hallucination, far from representing a deepening of consciousness itself, represents a return to a more primitive form thereof: dependent on external stimulants it moves, all of its psychological claims notwithstanding, in the very opposite direction from that of "internalization": like "inspiration" it is fundamentally passive. Imagination, on the other hand, is fundamentally active. Its conscious recognition and its cultivation began only about 170 years ago in the Western World, coming out of the Romantic revival, where it developed together with historical consciousness, with "internalization," and with the recognition of the potentially mature and fruitful connection of idealism with realism.

The recognition of the connection between image and reality, then, furnishes the acuity of our consciousness. Whatever tends to be uninteresting is either something with which we are excessively familiar or something which is utterly alien to us: and this is not a Philistine concept but a vital tendency of mind. Perhaps this is why, historically speaking, we are usually attracted to places and periods about which we already know something. It is the barbarian who, on the one hand, equates routine with tradition while, on the other hand, he may be attracted by things that are radically, completely "exotic" and "new," that is, unreal beyond the range of his imagination, of his personal knowledge. ("Strangeness," wrote Owen Barfield in *Poetic Diction*, "in fact, arouses wonder when we do not understand; aesthetic imagination when we do.") Mental growth, then, involves not only the conscious cultivation of imaginative knowledge but also of a certain introspective realism. I wrote about an instance of this earlier as I mentioned evidence to the effect that interest in contemporary history arises at a later stage in adolescence than does interest in more remote and fantastic scenes and periods. Before that I wrote, too, that our interest in the past is different from that evinced by other civilizations precisely in the sense that our interest is more historical, directed as it is in most cases to the age closely preceding ours, to places and people with whom we can enter into existential and imaginative contact with relative ease. Our historical curiosity, therefore, is neither "idle" nor "exotic." Probably this is why for so many of us scenes on this earth are more interesting than those on the moon; I would rather see Constantinople before I see Timbuktu; the story of Napoleon interests most of us more than does the story of King Tut. . . .

But not necessarily so: we may find King Tut very interesting indeed—when we recognize in his story some things that we *already* know.

(4) About memory and time

If, then, imagination is an inescapable element of human cognition, so is memory—which, in turn, may be a perhaps inevitable element of imagination itself. In trying to exclude imagination and memory, Descartes ignored really two of the most important components of knowledge, perhaps as he overlooked the condition that most of our knowledge is past-knowledge. At first sight it may seem that whereas memory is directed to the past, imagination is directed mostly to the future; but even when imagination is directed to the future it can hardly envisage it except in terms of the past, for imagination as well as memory *come* from the past, no matter where they may be going. Imagination does not create images that are completely new. What memory and imagination together help create are always, to some extent, recognitions, including, of course, new varieties of recognitions. The common sense of the English language intimates this truth, since we employ the word "recognition" more often and more broadly than the word "cognition." Perhaps this usage in itself suggests how every cognition is, to a great extent, a recognition, involving some kind of association relative to something that we already know—the reverse of this truth being that remembering is something more than a mental reaction; it is, rather, a kind of construction; as the young Ortega y Gasset wrote in 1914 about the act of seeing: it "consists of applying a previous image which we have to a present sensation."[10]

Now the functions of this kind of "historicity" within our knowledge again transcend, of course, the fields of professional historians; but they should at least consider them in passing, the reason for this being that the nature of knowledge and of past-knowledge are not different at all. Just as perspective is a component of reality, and imagination of perception, memory is not a super-

---

[10] Julián Marias on Ortega's *Meditations on Quixote*: "The point is that we do not consider real *what actually happens,* but a certain manner of happening *that is familiar to us.*" (Ortega: "And if a series of events takes an *unforeseen* turn, we say it seems *incredible.*") Paul Valéry: ". . . any prediction we are able to make can only be, by the very nature of all prediction, more or less historical; it excludes, consequently, everything that is so new that our vocabulary must lack even the words to conjecture about it. Our vocabulary is, in effect, only a form of history reduced to assimilable, usable, and living elements."

structure but an inevitable component of cognition.[11] I am not dealing here with scientific theories of cognition, and not even with
many of the functions of memory,* I am concerned with the historicity of our knowledge and of our memory. And here I am pleased to
report that historians and psychologists are not far apart. Long after I
finished the first complete draft of this chapter I chanced to look at
two basic works on memory written by psychologists, Sir Frederic
Bartlett's *Remembering* and Professor Ian M. L. Hunter's *Memory*,
and I was struck by the correspondence of our observations—or, I
should rather say, recognitions. When, for example, Dr. Hunter
states that all "learning" is inseparable from its "motivation"; when
"forgetting," according to the studies of the American psychologists
Jenkins and Dallenbach, "is not so much a matter of the decay of
old impressions as it is a matter of the interference, inhibition, or
obliteration of the old by the new"; when Sir Frederic says that
both learning and remembering are profoundly influenced by the
process of interpreting, it should be evident that the conclusions of
these eminent psychological scientists correspond with many of
the assertions in this book about historical thinking. "Exactly
how the reconstructing of the past is achieved is the chief mystery
of memory," Professor Hunter writes. "It is a mystery which psychology has failed to dispel. Perhaps it is a mystery which will
never yield up its secrets to the methods of empirical scientific investigation. But the fact that it is a reconstructing rather than a
literal reproducing points up a principle which seems to have universal application (a principle which is eloquently elaborated in Sir
Frederic Bartlett in his book *Remembering*)."

Historical consciousness depends on the cultivation not only of a
certain imagination, but of a certain kind of memory. I write "certain" because this kind of remembering-memory is something
different—it is certainly more purposeful—from the recall-memory
which some people may develop and which is, somewhat inaccurately, called "photographic" memory in popular parlance. It should
be evident that the kind of memory nourishing historical conscious-

---

[11] Certain experiments in the psychological mechanics of perception indicate
this clearly: our perception of a material thing (a playing-card in the so-called
Ames experiment) unconsciously depends on our already existing concept of
playing-cards—whence an illusion results that is, properly speaking, not optical
but historical.

ness involves something more than mechanism: we can recognize its existence without fully understanding its causes: as we saw earlier, we do not enter into the past through causality alone but through sudden mental "jumps" of recognitions, activating a kind of sympathetic or interested participation. The functions of remembering, therefore, transcend space and time and mechanical causality. The child is father of the man in the sense, too, that his experiences acquire another dimension of value through the development of his consciousness; in other words, as the child's experiences are remembered (which means: re-recognized, and newly reconstructed) by the grown-up man, a new dimension occurs. And this is what the evolution of historical consciousness is all about. Historical knowledge is potential, not only actual; historical recognition is the actual perception of something about which we already know something; it is the development of potential knowledge at the conscious level.[12] The remembered past is, of course, minuscule when compared to the entire past. There should be, logically, an enormous problem inherent in the immense discrepancy between the size of these two categories, between the tininess of the fragments from the past that we "actually" know and the enormous amount of things that we "potentially" understand. But in reality there is no such enormous problem. In the first place, as Pascal said, we often understand more than what we know, to which I shall add that this happens almost always through some kind of remembering. In the second place, history is a form of thought resting on common sense and on everyday language—something which facilitates (though probably it does not create) the really amazing condition that not only is there no essential difference between present-knowledge and past-knowledge but that there is not very much difference between the nature of our knowledge of those fragments

---

[12] Pascal, Pensée 14: "When a natural discourse paints a passion or an effect, one feels *in oneself* the truth of what one reads; it was there all the time but one did not know it. Hence one is inclined to love him who makes us recognize it; he has opened up to our sight not his own riches but ours." (Also Pensée 64: "It is not in Montaigne but in myself that I find all that I see in him.") In her *Joan of Arc* Victoria Sackville-West cites a statement by F. W. H. Myers with admiration: "For genius is best defined—not as an unlimited capacity for taking pains, but rather as a mental constitution which allows a man to draw readily into conscious life the products of unconscious thought"—"a pregnant phrase," she adds, "which grows the richer in suggestion the more one ponders over it."

of the past that we personally "witnessed" and of our understanding
of those that we had not. A modern woman may understand many
things about Cleopatra simply through "secondhand" or "third-hand"
knowledge, that is, reading about her at a distance of two thousand
years, for many reasons: because human nature does not change,
because she may understand some of Cleopatra's personal characteristics, her femininity, her problems, because she belongs to the
same genus and species as her sister. I wrote "sister" for a number
of reasons, one of them being that I cherish the poetic truth about
the unity of mankind, living and dead; the other, that literally speaking, too, it is not unpleasant to think that after two thousand
years each of us may have at least one drop of Cleopatra's blood
in his veins. But this has little to do with race, and not even with
the more fashionable thing called the collective unconscious. It has
to do with the fact that our personal knowledge of the past is part of
the universal history of mankind, that we are human repositories
of *all* mankind's historical experiences in the past, which is why
we potentially understand everything that is historical while, conversely, everything that is historical is potentially understandable.
It is thus that our tiny actual, and our enormous potential, knowledge of the past are two components of the same condition. They
are, more than often, charged with meaning through the functioning
of our imagination and of our memory. They are, in any event,
intimately involved; indeed, they overlap in many ways, some of
which strike us at times as fantastic and perhaps even mysterious.

Their overlapping has something to do with the *human* phenomenon of time,* which means, with the overlapping of past and
future through our minds. I touched upon this once before, in passing, as I wrote about the "pull of the future" involving a specifically human causality, whereby certain "effects" may even "precede" certain "causes." Historians should consider some of the epistemological implications of this human phenomenon of the relativity
of time. This does not mean that they must devote themselves to
Einsteinian studies with the zeal with which some of them have
turned to Freudianism. What historians ought to keep in mind about
time may be summed up briefly. First, they ought to understand its
relativity in the sense of Tennyson's simple line: "Today is yesterday's tomorrow and tomorrow's yesterday." Second, they must understand the illusory nature of the "present," the abstract nature of

its category as well as the condition of how the essence of the "present" is obscured, at closer sight, by the unceasing overlapping of "past" and future." Third, they must understand the fundamental distinction between abstract time and living time. Bergson's philosophical recognition (1892) of this important distinction between "time" and "duration" preceded Einstein's relativity theory by thirteen years: but it is not only that historians may read Bergson with more profit that what they may get from reading their Einstein; it is, as we shall see in Chapter VII, that much of modern physics has bypassed Einstein, whose relativity theory still maintains a sharp boundary between past, present, and future, whereas quantum theory led physicists to perceive that even in the world of matter these boundaries are not concrete, that "past" and "future" overlap.*

History, in other words, has an effect on our notions of time, as it has on our imaginations. The notion of "absolute" time was, in its way, typical of the Bourgeois Age. In the thought of the Middle Ages time and eternity, as Christopher Dawson wrote, were "far more closely bound up with one another than they were in classical antiquity or to the modern mind. The world of history was only a fraction of the real world and it was surrounded on every side by the eternal world like an island of the ocean." After that, the medieval world went to seed because of a certain primitive overintellectualization: for, just as certain theologians in the fifteenth century attempted to measure the physical weight of the soul, others tried to define the geographical positions of Christendom and world in the concrete forms of an island, forcing certain metaphysical truths into the Procrustean beds of primitive scientific categories. Then, about four hundred years ago, we were beginning to learn something about the relativity of this concept of our position in space; and now we have to learn something about the relativity of our notion of time, that what we had been thinking of as absolute "time," too, is but a concept of the human mind, a *fictio,* that mathematical time and living duration are two different things.

We may have glimpsed something about this condition as we considered such phenomena as "time lag" or "momentum," the implications of which may include certain simple historical illustrations of the relativity of time. For there is such a thing as the acceleration or the slowing down of history: it is not only a poetic metaphor that there are times when human hearts are beating faster, and when human minds leap and bound. Historical thinking, like energy and perhaps even life, moves in "bundles," "quanta," "energy packets" on occasion; there are critical times when suddenly many things are happening at about the same time, just as much of human creative activity may occur in crystallizations and conglomerations of energy, activated as they are through intuitions and imaginations and the rush of memories: sudden fusions, jumps of the mind. (Harold Nicolson's felicitous phrasing of intuitive inspiration: "a sudden flash or fusion between sense and fantasy, between reason and imagination.") Our spirit, Huizinga wrote, is "continually sparking between matter and mind"—which is something quite different from the Majestic and Irreversible and Slow and Gradual (that is, elephantine) March of Evolution. *Natura nil facit per saltum:* nature proceeds not by leaps. Perhaps; but man does. "Great wits," said Sterne, "jump." And all human understanding (including our understanding of the fragmentary record of the past, Dilthey's "hermeneutical" knowledge) flashes through holes and gaps in the evidence, "jumps" in the development of thought, leaping across inconsequences in the document or argument before us, gaps which are at times instructive to us precisely because of their inconsistencies. There is no human being who has not experienced the relativity of time (though he may not have recognized its meaning); that there is a sense of time which resides within ourselves, whose dimensions may on occasion stretch to impossible lengths or contract within an instant to the standing stillness of death,[13] and that this personal sense of time does not always correspond to the mechanical and mathematically progressing—and therefore man-made—categories of clock and calendar. (The modern cliché addressed to "enemies of progress" who "want to turn the clock back" is, therefore, quite wrong. When they are out of kilter with time—or what is more important, *with our needs*—clocks are supposed to be turned back. That is what they are for.) *

---

[13] The hypothesis about the human tendency of seeing the history of one's life flashing backward with lightning speed in the moment before death may be suggested, too, by two recent medical observations: first, that the last phase of human life shows remarkable similarities to the biological functions and conditions of infant life; second, that unconscious patients in extreme agony or pain, and *irrespective of their sex* (Freud!), tend to cry out for their mothers and only very rarely for their fathers.

Let me return, for the last time, to the phenomenon of recognition. What happens when we travel to new places, new scenes? Our mind flickers between the old-new and the new-old, rather than between *the* new and *the* old. Our pleasures spring not from wholly new cognitions but, rather, from our recognitions: for we recognize things that we had expected to see, things that we had seen somewhere (and, with is more important, *somehow*) before; things that we had imagined and anticipated more or less consciously. The wholly unexpected plays a relatively small part in these experiences. Now I believe that, were we able to travel not only through space but also through time, we would experience similar sensations: *if, instead of visiting Portugal or Greece, we could visit the 1750's or the 1880's,* the functions of our recognitions would be substantially the same. We would be fascinated and surprised by some things, repelled and disillusioned by others; we would encounter certain unexpected features of life that we would nonetheless immediately recognize; we would get used gradually to others; and the most interesting and vivifying experiences would probably involve the crystallizations, in our consciousness, of suddenly developing recognitions of things and ideas that, in some way or another, we may have already known (or that we would think we have known). But, of course, we do travel through time as well as through space: 1966 in California is not 1966 in Portugal. Certain nations are cultural prototypes and, therefore, historical ones: Amsterdam in 1966 is not only a Dutch city but it represents fragments and portions of the Bourgeois Age; the Spain of the 1840's fascinated Gautier and Borrow not only because it was "exotic" but because it was "backward," Mozarabian and also medieval.

In our minds,[14] past, present, future sweep and swirl dust and magic into each other all the time.* As T. S. Eliot said, "If one can really penetrate the life of another age, one is penetrating the life of one's own"; and the past remains latent in the present, as Owen Barfield wrote, "perhaps in something the same way as it does in the meaning of a word." Thus history, the remembered past, may

---

[14] God says to Abraham: "I am He, fear not, for I am before the days were." "Before ever I say I was, I am" (Isaiah 48:6). Jesus: "Truly, truly, I say to you, before Abraham was made, I am" (John 8:58). "And Daniel recalled/Years that were not yet born," wrote Manzoni. "The soul is born old in the body," said Wilde to Gide, "it is to rejuvenate it that the latter grows old. Plato is the youth of Socrates. . . ."

be, as Berdyaev put it, "the triumph of memory over the spirit of corruption."

(5) About free will and the acquisition of characteristics

I must be frank. The historical philosophy which I am attempting to present (and re-present) in this book is reactionary—reactionary rather than conservative—by which I mean, among other things, that this emphasis on historical consciousness *reacts* against the misconceptions, shibboleths, evil theories, and primitive nonsense about human nature which are now widely prevalent and propagated among many people. ("Reacting," too, means something living, whereas decomposition is progressive. The dead can't react.) This meaning of "reactionary" may be, therefore, considered in a positive rather than in a negative sense: or, in other words, in the sense of its "forward-looking" *purpose* rather than in the sense of a "nostalgic" *motivation*. I felt it necessary to write this down in order to explain what I mean by the kind of historical philosophy which, as we have now seen, is post-Marxian as well as post-Cartesian and post-Freudian and post-Einsteinian, to which I must now add the designation post-Darwinian and post-Mendelian. For, again, I find that I cannot avoid devoting a few pages to the discussion of a condition which, strictly speaking—but perhaps only very strictly speaking—ranges beyond the accustomed circle of professional historical interests: I am compelled to return, for the last time, to the phenomenon and to the conception of human free will.

I have written about it earlier, on a number of occasions. That men are free and responsible moral agents is the fundamental principle of historical thinking: no free will, no history—no history in *our* sense of history. There exists on this point a salutary harmony between the Western historical and the Western Christian concept of human nature: for even historians who may not accept the religious doctrine of free will proceed still from the recognition of its functions, whence the circumstance that the good historian is often an *anima naturaliter christiana*, and surely an *anima naturaliter occidentalis*. Now, of all the tenets of our Western heritage of thought it is free will which is most endangered nowadays by the scientific and pseudoscientific philosophies prevalent among us, widely disseminated in education—with the evident results of a sense of helplessness and of a weakening of the will to live, of a super-modern kind of fatalism especially widespread, alas, among the outwardly so active and dynamic people of the United States.

On the other hand, a reaction against classic determinism had begun earlier in this century—though intellectual leadership has neither been very courageous, nor very consistent in drawing attention to this reaction. Still, it is no longer only through abstract philosophical arguments and moral syllogisms that arguments for free will may be made; physicists have discovered, too, how Kant, for example, did not take sufficient account of will (and of purpose) in his philosophy. In 1927, around the same time that certain physicists had arrived at corresponding conclusions, a cogent argument about the limitations of determinism was proposed by the German historian Meinecke, who warned his colleagues against the "overestimation of causalities"; not unlike Huizinga or Ortega or Madariaga or Bergson, Meinecke spoke of the breakthrough of powers of human spirit and of human will, transcending on occasion mechanical or biological causality. Meinecke's propositions were not widely known in the English-speaking world; but even there the trend among historians for some time now has been to accept criticisms of historical inevitability (even when these are not very cogently made). Still, it would be a fatal error to underestimate the recurrent attractions which determinism, in one form or another, has for professional intellectuality in the twentieth century —a tendency which, as we have seen, had been predicted by Tocqueville more than 130 years ago.

It is important, at this point, to correct certain notions about free will. One of the interregnal tendencies of the modern mind is the habit of acknowledging the existence of something like free will but considering it at the same time as something extraneous, an additional superstructure over the basic biological mechanism. This is an error similar to the sophistic but, in reality, primitive attempt which wishes to "correct" determinism by simply adding the factor of Pure Chance (this is how Bury, toward the end of his life, tried to qualify his own theory of historical determinism). Already Bagehot, who otherwise recognized the function, as he had put it, of certain "moral causes," slipped into this error in *Physics and Politics:* "The Free-Willist," he wrote, "holds the will to be an extraordinary incoming something." But it is neither extraordinary nor incoming: it is, rather, ordinary and outgoing. There are scientists who will admit nowadays that there is "something" beside the physiological functions of human nature: but, whatever the "something" might be, it is this "beside" which is misleading, implying as it does a sharp separation between physical and nonphysical characteristics, whereas free will may actually involve physiological functions, and not only vice versa.

There is yet another danger of unrealistic sophistry. Certain scientists have mentioned "free will" as they spoke of the uncertainty factor of the atomic particles. But this is nonsense: atomic particles are not free moral agents, they have no souls. There seems to be a superficial analogy in the behavior of electrons and of people: the behavior of small numbers of electrons, like the behavior of individuals, is often unpredictable, whereas the behavior of large quantities of electrons averages out so that it is reasonably and even accurately predictable. But, in the first place, as de Broglie has already suggested, it is questionable whether there is such a thing as an "individual" electron at all; and, in the second place, men are unpredictable not only individually but sometimes collectively too. Unpredictability, moreover, does not necessarily mean inconsistency: the predictability of reactions and the consistency of human actions are not the same. The falseness of the logic of determinism (and of "purely" mechanical causality), when applied to human affairs, lies inherent in its premise to the effect that every human action is a mechanically determinable reaction. Of course it would be foolish to deny that every human action is a mere reaction *to some extent,* just as every instance of human cognition is *to some extent* a mere recognition; but we have seen how every kind of cognition involves a certain kind of purposeful construction, and the personal consciousness and the consequent responsibility of every human action consist precisely in the extent in which it is more than an "automatic" reaction.

It is important not only what we are but what we want to be: because to some extent we become what we want to be (and also because, at least to some extent, we are already what we intend to become). It is thus that certain functions of free will may suggest that human characteristics may be acquired and transmitted to succeeding generations. Few statements will strike the modern scientific mind as more heretical than this one: it runs against the accepted fundamental principles of genetics and of biological science of the the last one hundred years.

And yet consider the inconsistency of the latter principles when they are applied to human affairs. Consider our schizophrenia regarding race. On the one hand, the contemporary intellectual practice is to deny simply that race, and racial tendencies, exist. On the other hand, the belief in biological acids and genes and hormones is unchallenged, meaning that the characteristics of human beings are mechanically predetermined by the hereditary biological process alone. On the one hand, all is the product of Environment: all, including the innermost spiritual life of a person. On the other hand, all is Heredity—all, including his capacities of intelligence and memory. But this is maddeningly inconsistent. And these inconsistencies are either slurred over or they are "solved" through a crude distinction: all of the physical and biological characteristics of human beings are supposed to be inherited and immutable, while all of their psychological and cultural characteristics are supposed to be acquired and mutable. (This nonsense is, then, compounded further by a recent shift in the scientific vocabulary, as the word "culture" is increasingly appropriated by sociology as if it were but another term for "environment," while "biology" is used as if it were synonymous with life. But life has preceded biology, and it is more than biology, just as culture is more than environment, and race than heredity.) All is Society, all is "Culture," say the environmentalists: take a Russian baby and bring him up in France and he will be a typical Frenchman—to which the answer should be: keep that Russian baby in Russia and he will be an even more typical Russian. On the other hand consider a "typical" Russian baby who was brought to France, brought up in France, who acquires French habits, tastes, expressions, marries a Frenchwoman at thirty and returns to Russia at the age of forty: has he not become something different not only from other "typical" Russians but from the kind of person he would have become had he stayed in Russia all his life? I came to the United States in 1946, I married my wife in 1953, our son was born in 1956. I believe that, had I remained in Hungary and met and married my American wife there, our son would have had certain characteristics different from his present ones—by which I mean *physical* as well as nonphysical ones—not only because of another environment, but also because his father would have been a different person at the time when the mother was fertilized by his seed. The Corsican Bonaparte was brought up in France: the significant condition is not whether he was a "typical" Corsican or a "typical" Frenchman: it is, rather, the condition that he wanted to live in France and not, say, in Italy, and that his becoming a Frenchman obviously affected the *history* of his life together with his *personal characteristics*.

Historically speaking—or, rather, historically thinking—personal characteristics are not merely biological ones. Darwin may have been "the Newton of biology" (the word "biology" was invented by Lamarck in 1802); still we must consider that for history, the *par excellence* human knowledge, Darwin or Mendel do not necessarily signify an advance of knowledge over Lamarck. For the usual argument has been off-center. It tried to ascertain what is and what is not *inherited*, rather than what are human *characteristics*. It concentrated on the mechanical *causes* of these characteristics rather than on the myriad *functions* of the characteristics themselves. It treated these characteristics as if they were ultimately scientific categories, as if human beings were composed only of physical characteristics of varying complexity. Darwin found that the law of natural selection was inexorable, Mendel found that heredity can be calculated and ascertained: yet what Darwin found out about natural selection and what Mendel found out about the pea is not very relevant to human beings—who may indeed acquire characteristics, all kinds of characteristics, and eventually transmit them to their heirs. I suggested this condition earlier in these pages when I wrote about the functions of certain human aspirations, of the ways in which the human mind and human consciousness disrupts routine causalities. "No duchess is more than thirty years old to a snob," said Stendhal; Balzac said that after a while "one becomes responsible for one's face." Sometimes husbands and wives grow alike.[15] The social climber finds a dish that otherwise may have been distasteful to him, delicious as it is being served at an elegant dinner party. A man acquires tastes, aesthetic and sensual, intellectual and material, during his lifetime: he transmits some of these to his son: isn't that an acquired characteristic? Isn't even race

---

[15] Raymond Radiguet: "It often happens that a mental likeness may have its effects upon the physical as well. Glance and carriage may alter: several times strangers took Marthe and me for sister and brother. . . ."

—I repeat, a cultural as well as a biological factor—an acquired characteristic, after all?* The children of immigrants to America, England, Israel, Germany often look startlingly different from their parents, and these changes are racial and physical, not only mental ones. Nearly sixty years ago Professor Boas, during his anthropological investigations for an American commission investigating immigration, found that, curiously enough, the so-called "primary" racial characteristics, including cranial indices, underwent mutations among second-generation immigrants of the same race, and in some cases even within one generation in America.[16] Other anthropologists found that the children of Oriental immigrants in America have grown taller than the children of the same parents who have been brought up in China or Japan; but they have, of course, drawn the wrong conclusions, attributing all of these changes to different material conditions—food, climate, environment. But the acquisition of characteristics does not happen merely through environment. It is not merely an unconscious, mechanical, chemical, automatic process; the change involves personality, aspirations, the human spirit, with its component of will. The environmentalists as well as the materialists fail (or, rather, they do not wish) to comprehend this (including, of course, the Stalinist biologist, Lysenko, with his drastic theory of environmental determinism). But the basic human factor is personal, not environmental, since men may transcend all kinds of tendencies, the influences of environment as well as of heredity: as the Austrian neuropsychiatrist Viktor Frankl recently wrote, man is "no 'product' at all, except in the sense that his life is the result of his choices; he himself is formed by his own choices; and his education, really, means the education of his capacity to choose."

There is a small minority among biologists who have lately begun to recognize this condition: that there is a force controlling our physical development, a force which exists within our own organism. It is in this respect that Lamarck, who is dismissed by most modern scientists, may have been ahead of Darwin, since La-

[16] "The head form," wrote Boas, "which has always been considered one of the most stable and permanent characteristics of human races, undergoes far-reaching changes due to the transfer of people from European to American soil . . . not even those characteristics of a race which have proved to be most permanent in their old home remain the same under the new surroundings . . . the whole bodily and mental make-up of the immigrants may change. . . ."

marck spoke of "efforts of internal sentiment," even though he did not recognize the uniquely human function of free will. ("Lamarck," Professor H. Graham Cannon recently wrote, "makes it abundantly clear by continually referring to the 'inner feeling' of animals that he had a very shrewd idea of what we would nowadays call the subconscious activity of organisms. He considered that the inner feeling in lower animals took the place of the will in higher forms.") A return to some kind of neo-Lamarckianism will, however, not do. The issue supersedes the antinomian categories of Darwin vs. Lamarck or Mendel vs. Lysenko, of hereditary vs. environmental determinism. What we must recognize is that determinism, no matter in what form or no matter under what disguise, has been found wanting, even though the deadening effect of momentum in the history of ideas in our century continues to obscure this recognition.[17] Since, however, these matters belong to the history of ideas, historians have an especial responsibility to preach what they practice (or, rather, what the best among them have always practiced): to speak out and say that there exist much more complex, and more profound, connections between human minds and human bodies than what scientism has been telling us for more than a century now. I am not saying that personal intention can always overcome inherited or even acquired characteristics: but by suggesting that all kinds of persons may acquire all kinds of characteristics, and that acquired characteristics may be inherited by our descendants, I have attempted to assert, once again, the potential superiority of the human spirit over mechanical causalities, because life is stronger than theory, and history is not merely determined by material and psychological factors when it is formed by the free will of men.

(6) About a historical philosophy

Readers who have come with me this far will recognize that this book does not represent an attempt toward a philosophy of history but that, rather to the contrary, it attempts to draw attention to a historical kind of philosophy. Still it is not enough to state this by a verbal juxtaposition.

---

[17] Jacques Barzun already in 1940: "The misfortune was that when mechanism began to be questioned, for scientific reasons, the general public had become persuaded of its absolute truth; it could think in no other terms and it felt that all other views were simply 'prescientific.' "

Since philosophies of history seem to have been the particular by-products of a certain phase in the evolution of modern historical consciousness we cannot ignore them altogether. The literal translation of "philosophy of history," from the Greek, means the love of historical wisdom. But we mean something else by this term. We mean a systematic philosophical study of history, something that was first developing in the minds of such different people as Vico, Voltaire, Hegel in very different ways, and which then in the nineteenth century led to many erudite works attempting to construct new systems, categories, historical definitions out of their search for historical patterns through their comparative study of world civilizations. All of this, I repeat, was part and parcel of the growth of our historical consciousness. It was one of the consequences of the romanticism of the early nineteenth century which, as we have seen, was such a powerful stimulant of the rapid crystallization of the historical form of thought in Europe—a stimulant which could also lead to grave misuses of historical thinking, perhaps especially in Germany (and in those countries which were then strongly influenced by German intellectual tendencies and forms of erudition). One of these ambiguous developments which may not have received the attention it deserves, was the intellectual discovery of the mystical East by the romantic West. This "renaissance" of the Orient* contributed greatly to the widening of the European world-view: but it has also played a fatal role in the decline of Western self-confidence, the end of which is not yet.

The increasingly systematic study of comparative civilizations developed thus together with the intellectual tendency to construct philosophies of history accordingly: as early as one hundred years ago Burckhardt became sharply critical of this: the philosophy of history, he wrote, is "a centaur, a contradiction in terms: for history coordinates, and hence is unphilosophical, while philosophy subordinates, and hence is unhistorical. . . . The danger which lies in wait for all chronologically arranged philosophies of history is that they must, at best, degenerate into histories of civilizations . . . otherwise, though claiming to pursue a world-plan, they are colored by preconceived ideas. . . ." My own intellectual development may have reflected successive phases of this recognition. I, too, was first interested in history, then in the philosophy of history, then in historical thinking. In the central European intellectual tradition early in life I was attracted by Spenglerian analogies, metaphors, imperial declines, weighty terms; I even devised systems of my own; but around 1953, *aetatis* 30, I began to react against philosophies of history, *all* philosophies of history; I recognized that, as Nietzsche put it, "building systems is childishness," a very important phrase that Spengler should have pondered; I uneasily felt the presence of the crabbed tendency which Bergson saw as "the infirmity of genius" and about which Georges Sorel tellingly wrote that it is "the danger of becoming one's own disciple, as has happened to the greatest philosophers when they have endeavored to give a perfectly symmetrical form to the intuitions they brought into the world."

If, as Walter Schubart wrote, "he who studies history without being a philosopher is a mere chronicler," he who now studies philosophy without history is a mere sophist. It is relatively easy to construct a philosophy of history without knowing much history. The more history one knows the less one is—or, rather, should be—disposed to have a definite and sytematic philosophy of history, the main reason for this disinclination being one's recognition of the myriad uncategorizable varieties of past human experience. What the historian may now be inclined to develop, more or less consciously, is a kind of epistemology of history instead. I said "now" because this, too, is a response to a historical situation, to the conditions of our thinking in the Western world in the twentieth century when, in an important sense, *all* philosophy is epistemology now. Let me repeat: our recognition of historical thinking—which, as we have seen, involves the recognition of the historical dimension of our existence as well —suggests that we may have transcended the phase of our interest in philosophies of history. Instead of the more pretentious ambition of the eventual knowledgeability of all history we are about to recognize a more chastened but perhaps more profound aim: to understand something about the historicity of knowledge.

Still, we ought not dismiss all the philosophers of history out of hand. From Vico and Voltaire to Spengler and Toynbee they represented at times the highest intellectual aspirations of a certain period. In this sense their works were involved with the developing consciousness of historical thinking; for, while philosophy preceded the study of history among the Greeks, historical thinking precedes and underlies the study of philosophy from the seventeenth century onward. Perhaps this explains the shortcomings of some of the great modern philosophers of history, who still subordinated *historia* to some kind of *philosophia* at a time when the study of the latter had already become dependent on the conditions of the former. They were historical thinkers: but they were not yet adequately conscious of their own historical thinking. We cannot really blame most of them for that. They were still educated in the classical tradition. Moreover, some of their insights and recognitions have enriched our minds: we ought to respect them for this. We need not list their numerous mistakes; and whether their pattern was linear or cyclical, recurrent or progressive, need not concern us much. They devoted great efforts, often of a lifetime, to the charting of the outlines of the developing knowledgeability of universal history. We may now recognize that this was a chimera: but from this recognition new and fruitful truths may spring. The direction of our inquiries (remember that *historia* meant "inquiry," too, in Greek) is intensive rather than extensive, as we are interested not so much in what human records may tell us about the nature of history as in what history may tell us about human nature.

"General history," wrote the young Tocqueville at the age of twenty-four, "is useful only in respect of the light which it throws on human nature." And one of the things that history illuminates about human nature is that it is "normal" and "unique" at the same time, that its moral range is immense, that men are *both* beasts and angels. Now this is a different statement from the fundamentally nineteenth-century, liberal, gray statement that "men are neither beasts nor angels," as Arthur Schlesinger, Jr., put it at the end of his *The Age of Jackson* (1945).[18] The former represents a higher level of recognition, a recognition not *between* two antitheses but *above* them. For we have come around to this new-old recognition not so much because of Freud's New Science of Man but rather because of our own historical and existential experiences during this century. We know, or ought to know, that our problem—*"the trouble with us"*—is not that our nature, in spite of the surface of civilization, harbors primitive and fundamentally subhuman residues: our troubles exist because we are fundamentally human.

[18] This, at any rate, is shallower than the Pascalian formulation (*Pensée* 358): "Man is neither angel nor brute, but the pity of it is that in trying to behave like an angel he behaves like a brute."

The greatest Western historians have always understood that a sane understanding of human nature literally pre-empts the need for a philosophy of history. Therefore, they knew, too, that—save for certain specialized branches of research—there is, strictly speaking, no such thing as a historical *method*,[19] even though history has become a principal, perhaps the principal, Western *form* of thought. Now, this recognition, as I indeed suggested in the first pages of this book, is a good tiding: but we must be aware of its enormous handicaps during the present, interregnal condition of the modern intellect. First, while our interest in the past (together with our recognition of the functions of memory) may be more widespread and even more profound than heretofore, on the other hand that kind of veneration of the past which, no matter how uncritical it may have been, characterized and stimulated some of the highest achievements of the Renaissance, has been, at least for the time being, lost. Second, while traditional standards of judgment (which, however, were not always historical standards) are no longer strong, on the other hand the applications of historical thinking are still too weak. The most evident examples of this exist in the field of politics and statesmanship. The Russian intelligentsia fifty years ago knew more history than had the French philosophes two hundred years ago: yet the ideas of the Russian Revolution were very un-historical. Woodrow Wilson was a professor of political science and of history: yet his understanding of contemporary historical forces was shallow, and he consequently contributed to the catastrophic failures of the peacemaking after World War I. Theodore Roosevelt's political philosophy was more "backward" than Wilson's, and yet Roosevelt's historical judgment and world political estimates, in retrospect, stand up better than Wilson's. Franklin Roosevelt's mind, too, was rather unhistorical.* If we compare his estimates of the historical and political consequences of World War II with Churchill's, there can be no question that the latter's estimates were more reasonable and his predictions more accurate—precisely because, among the three principal world leaders at that time, Roosevelt's ideas were the most "progressive" and scientific, whereas Churchill's

---

[19] Mommsen: "History is one of those academic subjects which cannot be directly acquired through precept and learning. For that, history is in some measure too easy and in some measure too difficult. The elements of the historical discipline cannot be learned, for every man is endowed with them."

were the most "reactionary" and historical ones. Of course, history is not predictable, it does not repeat itself (though historians do, including this one); it does not, strictly speaking, teach us what to expect and what to do; but in another sense our historical understanding does suggest what is not likely to happen, what not to expect, what not to do. In this sense, and in this sense only, are the "lessons" of history practical ones: we *can* *learn* from the past, through the quality of our partial understanding of it.[20] In 1922 Lincoln Steffens, the American progressive writer, returning from Soviet Russia, announced that he saw The Future and it worked. No: the future does not work. The future may attract: but it is the past that has worked.*

And the past is still working. We keep working and reworking it in our minds. We are, all, prophets about the past. Historically and existentially speaking, we do not solve our problems: we, rather, outgrow them. Let me illustrate this with a somewhat primitive example. The reaction to pro-Communism is anti-Communism; and the reaction against certain extreme manifestations of anti-Communism may be anti-anti-Communism. Now this is obvious. But what is not so obvious is that we may speak of two kinds of anti-anti-Communism. There is the anti-anti-Communist who is the compulsive moderate: ideologically thinking, he tries to assume a position in the middle, between the two seemingly (but only seemingly) opposite poles. He may, therefore, often give the impression of a "pink"—which, unfairly alas, in popular parlance, does not mean an equal mixture of red and white but someone who is *tending* toward the red. And there is the anti-anti-Communist who, instead of remaining in-between, tries to rise above these categories: historically thinking, he may transcend the level of these opposites,

---

[20] Burckhardt: "To know the future is no more desirable in the life of mankind than in the life of the individual. And our astrological impatience for such knowledge is sheer folly . . . a confusion of all desire and endeavor." To this I shall add that great historians such as Burckhardt are prophets nonetheless: they are *prophets about the past,* and consequently they are such valuable guides for the present and the future. Nietzsche feared the effects of too much historical knowledge: he said that we must know how to forget as well as how to remember at the right time. This is very true; but, then, this is just what our historical thinking may achieve. Huizinga: the historical sense is a "high-level manifestation (*eine hohe Form*) of that sense of quality with which a true connoisseur is capable of distinguishing a true work of art from a false one, an original from its reproduction, one style from another."

in which event his anti-anti-Communism is, in reality, *post*-Communism and *post*-anti-Communism at the same time. For while mathematically, statically, ideologically, categorically speaking "anti-anti" *does* mean a middle position, historically speaking this is *not* so at all.[21]

Pre- and *post-* may be, therefore, more meaningful prefixes than *pro-* and *anti-*. The former are historical, the latter ideological. They may mark the difference between, say, the anti-Communism of a de Gaulle and of a Goldwater. But these are, as I said, rather primitive illustrations. The emphasis on *pre-* and *post-* over *pro-* and *anti-* is not a categorical rule, and it is neither mechanically nor automatically applicable. Historical thinking is incomplete and unsystematic. It must proceed from the assumption that not only the records of the past but their perception through human memory are necessarily imperfect. But then this knowledge of limitation is the gateway to knowledge. All communication is incomplete:[22] but this does not mean that human communication is meaningless. "The road," wrote Cervantes, "is better than the inn." This is not an exhortation for picaresque novelists alone; it is equally valid for Western historians.

I have said before that the principal task of historical thinking is the reduction of untruths—a task which is now inextricably involved with the degeneration of our languages. "Our intelligence," Huizinga wrote, "requires that that inevitable nominalism—which makes us continually split and dissolve every image, every idea,

---

[21]When the Russians occupied my native country in 1945 and I witnessed the stupidities and the brutalities of the Communist mind I became a convinced anti-Communist. Less than ten years later in the United States I did not hesitate to state on occasion that I was an anti-anti-Communist—not only because I reacted against the stupidities and brutalities of McCarthyism, and not only because I felt that the then general American tendency to see the struggle of the two great world powers principally in terms of ideologies was politically dangerous and historically nonsensical, but also because of my conviction that Communism was not much of a domestic danger in the United States and that even the Soviet empire was changing. This kind of "outgrowing" of the old antitheses is not, however, an automatic consequence of historical evolution or even of increasing maturity; it is merely the consequence of historical thinking, of historical recognitions of changing historical situations.

[22] What A says to B, no matter how clearly, no matter with how good an intention, is always something slightly (and always to some small extent profoundly) different from what B hears him say (and, of course, different also from what C and D subsequently read into their conversation).

even down to the atom, into its components—be supplemented by an equally inevitable realism."* "The error of the Middle Ages, on the whole," Dorothy Sayers wrote in 1946, "was to use analogical, metaphorical, poetical techniques for the investigation of scientific questions. But increasingly . . . we have tended to the opposite error—that of using the quantitative methods of science for the investigation of poetic truth. But to build poetic systems of truth, the similarities must be not quantitative but qualitative, and the new unity that will emerge will be a world of new values." That this world of new values depends on history is now admitted by some of our greatest scientists. They have arrived at this recognition through their understanding of the limitations of science: that, while life is a supreme reality, science deals with abstract models that do not *really* exist,[23] with formulas that refer to abstract situations, in an abstract language which is less real than our natural and historical languages. There is a deep wisdom latent in the expressions "it is a true story," *une histoire vraie, eine wahre Geschichte,* meaning in popular parlance that the events *really* happened, in *life,* in *real* life.[24] But meanwhile the realism of our Western languages is weakening; more than a century ago people called the first locomotive an iron horse; in the twentieth century Americans call a certain kind of person "the sparkplug of the organization." From the description of a mechanical contrivance in

[23] Jeans: All the concepts "which now prove to be fundamental to our understanding of nature . . . seem to my mind to be structures of pure thought, incapable of realization in any sense which would be properly described as material."

[24] Huizinga: "Anyone surveying the nomenclature of his intellectual domain realises at once that he is constantly using words and notions which forty years ago [around 1890] did not exist. [But] history constitutes an exception in this respect . . . because there the terms of everyday life must generally continue to be the only medium of expression." Heisenberg: "The concepts of natural language are formed by the immediate connection with reality; they represent reality. It is true that they are not very well defined and may therefore undergo changes in the course of centuries, just as reality itself did, but they never lose the immediate connection with reality. On the other hand, the scientific concepts are idealizations; they are derived from experience obtained by defined experimental tools, and are precisely defined through axioms and definitions. Only through these precise definitions is it possible to connect the concepts with a mathematical scheme and to derive mathematically the infinite variety of possible phenomena in this field. But through this process of idealization and precise definition the immediate connection with reality is lost."

terms of the organic world we have moved to the description of a human being in mechanical terms. And even more depressing than this philosophical deterioration is the suggestion of the deteriorating sense of reality: for the first black and gaunt and high-necked locomotives looked a bit like iron horses, whereas human beings do not look like spark plugs at all. . . .

This is not the place to expatiate once more on the unique relationships of history and language, except to say that the historian's duty to be artist as well as moralist involves something different from the older kind of humanism. "The truth is," said Dr. Johnson two hundred years ago,

that knowledge of external nature, and the science which that knowledge requires or includes, are not the great or the frequent business of the human soul. Whether we provide for action or conversation, whether we wish to be useful or pleasing, the first requisite is the religious and moral knowledge of right and wrong, the next is an acquaintance with the history of mankind and with those examples which may be said to embody truth, and prove by events the reasonableness of opinions. Prudence and Justice are virtues and excellences of all times and of all places; we are perpetually moralists, but we are geometricians only by chance.

We must now complement this Augustan statement. We have been geometricians not only through chance but through history; and we are now near the end of a phase of history when the *esprit de la géométrie* and the mathematical concept of reality seemed the best (and, increasingly, the only) approach to truth. But now as the antinomies of idealism and realism,[25] of objective and subjective knowledge prove to be inadequate, we may find anew the potential harmony of an idealistic and realistic view of life. Aware of the limitations of the human intellect but aware, too, of the superb imaginative powers of mind, knowing our smallness and yet our situation in the center of our historical universe, understanding our inevitable participation in this universe, we are becoming more and more conscious of the historical reality of our existence in the world.

[25] Coleridge: "Poetry is not the proper antithesis to prose but to science." Emmanuel Mounier: "The opposite of pessimism is not optimism—but an often indescribable personal radiance of clarity, simplicity, compassion, stability and charity."

It may be that the future of Western thought will be historical: but, I repeat, this does not mean a philosophy of history but a chastened historical philosophy, concentrating on the historicity of problems and of events, assuming the uniqueness of human nature anew, presenting no new definitions, no freshly jigsawed categories, emphasizing the existential—and not merely philosophical—primacy of truth: a more mature achievement of the human mind than even the mastering of certain forces of nature through the scientific method, and certainly more mature than the simplicist conception of causalities. Truth is an existential, a sensual as well as an intellectual experience. It exists within us. The truth is always richer than the lie. "The profoundest of all sensualities," D. H. Lawrence wrote, "is the sense of truth." "Mysteries," said the theologian Jouve, "are not truths which exceed us, but truths that include us." "The true artist," Camus said, "forces himself to understand instead of judging"; and the historian Marc Bloch wrote that "not to understand is to admit defeat." For the taste for truth must be, perhaps more than ever before, cultivated within ourselves. This task far transcends the historical profession. It involves all mankind, even though its recognition issues from a peculiarly Western concept of truth: from the primacy of man's knowledge of man, aware of its incompleteness but also aware of the condition, for the first time in centuries, that man's knowledge of nature is *inevitably* imperfect, too. Hence the possibility of the emergence of a new and historical philosophy: history as a form of chastened thought.

(7) About a historical cosmology

Until about a century ago it was taken for granted that the human person, in one way or another, was fundamentally different from other living beings. This was not only a religious affirmation. The whole moral and intellectual edifice of humanism and of the Enlightenment rested on it. The most progressive achievements and institutions of humanitarianism—liberal reforms or the abolition of slavery—flowed from this secular realization of human dignity. During the last one hundred years, then, we have been told that this uniqueness of man does not exist, that the difference between men and other living beings is one of mere degree and that, consequently, the previous distinctions between human sciences and natural sciences no longer hold, the study of man being an intrinsic part of the study of nature.

One could argue against this intellectual development on traditional grounds, drawing either on religious arguments or on the rich cultural heritage of the humanists of the past. But let me say again that our situation is *post*-scientific rather than *pre*-scientific. We must proceed from something else: from the recognizable limitations of nineteenth-century scientific philosophy, indeed, of Cartesian objectivity. During the last one hundred years man's consciousness of himself has grown to the extent that we can recognize how the observer and the observed cannot be entirely separate categories—not in the human sciences and, as we shall shortly see, not in the natural sciences either, since we are coming around to recognize that the latter are but products of the human mind. Nature preceded man but man preceded the science of nature; indeed, he created the science of nature. This, of course, is a historical recognition. The argument that human knowledge cannot be subordinated to natural science is no longer merely the humanistic application of a metaphysical proposition. It is a recognition that has developed, at least on one level, through historical thinking. And, on another level, this recognition has been an intrinsic part of the evolution of human consciousness. For the recent philosophical concern with the nature of history, and not merely with the human past as such, reflects a kind of evolving awareness which in itself is deeply significant.

There are two ways in which we can speak of progress in history. In the Christian sense history is a teleological process, moving toward the end of mankind, the Day of Judgment. This may or may not be complemented by another recognition, which is that there is such a thing as human evolution, but perhaps *only* in the sense of the evolution of our consciousness—an evolution which, if determined at all, is determined from the inside. Since history is a kind of philosophy made up by examples, and since every one of these examples has actually taken place, every generation is *potentially* richer in its consciousness; it has more examples to draw upon, it knows more varieties of human behavior, ever different incarnations of human problems, more evidences about the complexities of human acts and about the divagations of human hearts. I wrote *potentially* because, as I said earlier, the increase of the historical information available to us does not necessarily mean a corresponding increase of historical understanding.[26]

But that is another story. There is something more directly relevant to our argument. And this is that within the universe our situation is unique, that we can no longer disregard the central condition of our existential involvement in the universe.

The epistemological recognition of the centrality of human nature is complemented by two corresponding recognitions of great importance: by the restoration of our situation in the center of the universe (in space), and in the center of history (in time). There is nothing very high-flown about this: it is part of our efforts at the restoration of common sense. The earth may or may not[27] be at the mathematical center of some universe; but it is the center of *our* universe, and the most important part of the universe, at that. This, again, is no longer merely a poetic but a pragmatic statement. It springs, first and foremost, from the recognition that it is senseless to talk about a universe which exists apart from our minds.

In addition, a sensible argument about our centrality in the universe was made in 1942, during one of the darkest years of this century, by Teilhard de Chardin—again, as in Toynbee's case, not in his somewhat overrated *magna opera* but in a small essay, "La Place de l'Homme dans l'Univers." What is man's place in the universe? Until the sixteenth century no one would doubt that

[26] Indeed, the character of the latter may depend on our quality of love. In this sense a Christian and a historical understanding of human nature may very well complement each other—especially now when our world is suffering from a decay of love, a condition which is obscured by the grim preoccupation with sex, and obfuscated by an increase of bureaucratic welfare and of legalistic tolerance, with the corresponding decline in human sensitivities. In this sense we are already living in a world where unassuming love, again, becomes, curiously and existentially, practical.

[27] It may, in a sense, after all. About this "after all" see below, p. 288. Also Camus in *The Myth of Sisyphus:* "Galileo, who held a scientific truth of great importance, abjured it with the greatest ease as soon as it endangered his life. In a certain sense, he did right. (From the point of view of the relative value of truth. On the other hand, from the point of view of manly behavior, [Galileo's] weakness may well make us smile.) *That* truth was not with the stake. Whether the earth or the sun revolves around the other is a matter of profound indifference. To tell the truth, it is a futile question. On the other hand, I see many people die because they judge that life is not worth living. . . ."

man was in the center. Then, from Galileo to Darwin, "this some-what naïve anthropocentrism of our ancestors" rapidly dissolved; indeed, during the nineteenth century "excessively so." In a few generations man has been reduced to near-nothing in a universe where his earth is but an insignificant grain of sand, and where Homo sapiens seems but "a poor little leaf, among millions of other leaves on the great tree of life." Yet, after having reached this extreme point of man's "de-centration," the pendulum now seems to return toward a new concept of man's "centrality."[28]

If we look at a scale marking the size of bodies in the universe, man occupies a position in the middle, just about exactly between two extremes (the size of the galaxy, 10^{22} cm, or 100,000 light years; the size of molecules, 10^{-20} cm, or billions of these within the space of a dot).[29] What is more important (and this, too, Pascal had sensed) is that these two extremes of size are not only quantitative but qualitative, meaning that, as we approach these extremes, the essential properties of matter become transformed. In our central, terrestrial, moderate, reasonable, human zone of life the rules of Euclidean geometry hold, simultaneity prevails, light and heat are definable, inanimate objects are generally immobile: this is not so at the far extremes, in the dimensions of the very large and of the very small.

But man is not only in the "middle": he is also the *most* complex of all organisms. And this "complexity" is a dimension too. In a universe of the two near-infinities of the very large and the very small, man is "in the middle": but in the sense of the dimension of "complexity" man is not merely in the middle but he represents a third extremity. To put this in other words: there is no such thing as *totally* inert matter: every element in the universe contains, to some small degree, an element of "inferiority," or call it "spon-tainety" or "con-science." In the most primitive of bodies this fac-tor remains imperceptible, even though there, too, it exists to a minimal extent: but at the most complex extremity of man this factor, through man's thinking capability, becomes dominant.

[28] "L'Homme, non plus centre d'un monde statique (ceci est bien fini)—mais l'Homme, cependant, element extrasignificatif, ou même principal, d'un Monde en mouvement: telle est le perspective que la Science commence à entrevoir—force de sincérité dans son effort à dépasser elle-même."

[29] "Pris entre l'Immense et l'Infime, l'Homme flotte vraiment, comme le pressentait Pascal, entre deux abîmes."

It is thus that the older anthropocentric view of the universe contains much that is still true; but we must conceive and understand it on a higher level. And it is thus that the Baconian and the Newtonian view of human nature and of the universe is no longer as relevant to our situation as it was for a long time. Bacon's famous statement that "knowledge is power" must seem to us to be not much more than a platitude, and a relatively shallow platitude at that, the main reason for this being that we can no longer proceed from the assumption that man's principal business is the knowledge of his environment; to the contrary, our historical *and* scientific experiences in the twentieth century militate for the thesis that man's principal business is his knowledge of man. But let me repeat for the last time that this is now something more than a moralistic or traditionalist reiteration of Socrates' "Know thyself," or of Pope's "The proper study of mankind is man." It is a rediscovery on a deeper level. Of all living beings in the universe man is the most complex one; therefore the study of man by man is not only higher in the hierarchy of knowledge than his study of less complex organisms, but his understanding of the human conditions of knowledge is inseparable from his study of nature, of matter, of thought, indeed, of everything. This existential condition is no longer the exhortation of antiscientific aesthetes or of religious philosophers alone; it is inherent in the discoveries of the greatest scientists themselves. Pascal has proved truer than Descartes; we are, again, back in the center of the universe; and we must, anew, confront ourselves alone.

And as we find ourselves, again, in the "center" of "space," we may find ourselves in the "center" of "time," too.

Perhaps the Darwinian notion of human life on this earth has been wrong on both ends. At the one end Darwin and his scientific followers fantastically elongated the history of man on this earth, pushing its beginnings back from the Biblical version of a few thousand to hundreds of thousands of years, as they point at the bones of what they call Java or Peking man. On the other end their presumption also involved the future, reflecting their basically nineteenth-century scientific optimism, since according to their time scale Homo sapiens would have a long history of progress ahead of him. Yet, in our present historical situation, the question arises whether this still makes much sense. When these words are written, in the 1960's, we certainly have a different view (*and a different feeling*) about the end of history than even a generation ago. Because of many events (and especially because of the "progress" of science and of technology) the end of the world, through *our own* capacity of destroying all human life, has become, for the first time in history, a reasonable possibility. It is therefore, no longer unreasonable to assume that the span of human history of this earth may be far shorter than what Darwinism and scientism have been implying, and that it may indeed come to an end a few thousand years after Christ.

I have already said that the historian ought to believe that the earth is the center of the universe, and that the Christian historian ought to believe that the central event of all history was the coming of Christ to earth*: but this is not my point here, and whether we call the end of history the Last Judgment or the Second Coming is not my point either. My point is that there may be, after all, no such thing as "pre-historic" and "post-historic" man, but only historic man, whose story may have begun sooner than we have been accustomed to think, and which may end, too, sooner than we have been accustomed to think.

But this is not really "a point": it is a question: *our own* question, about ourselves: and fortunately (for the Christian minority among my readers I shall say, by the grace of God) it is at least in part answerable by ourselves, by our future actions, influenced as these inevitably are by our conceptions of our past.

VII

⚜

HISTORY AND PHYSICS

or the end of the Modern Age

(1) The historical development of modern physics

I began this book with the proposition that the outlines of the passing of a great phase of history are by now recognizable, and that people in all walks of life have begun to sense the collapse of hitherto generally accepted ideas—whence the extraordinary intellectual confusion of our times, the widespread feeling of mental seasickness, and the loss of appetite that many people have for life itself. And it might seem as if with this book I may have contributed to this confusion. My attacks on the scientific world-view and my admittedly "reactionary" emphasis on the historical view of the world may seem to some as if it were a burning of bridges, or else the erection of yet another wall in the already badly divided and rent house of the Western mind: a haughty and quixotic Immodest Proposal. For what I have argued was, mainly, that of the two great achievements of the modern European mind since the seventeenth century, of the scientific and of the historical form of thought the latter is the more profound one; but, then, my argument was taken from the historical point of view; and I have merely suggested in passing, here and there, that certain scientists have themselves become skeptical of the scientific world-view, without explaining this in any way or detail.

My remaining task is, therefore, to explain, beyond humanistic assertions and generalizations, what the adjective *post-scientific* might really mean. And I cannot but reveal in advance one of the themes of this last chapter, which is the hope that lies on the other side of despair. For I must begin by exclaiming a Good Tiding, which lies hidden in the increasing correspondences of certain recognitions: for, while the recognition of a disease does not amount to its cure, it does represent the potentiality of the cure. At the time when the still popular concepts of mechanical science and the general ideas of progress have sprung leaks, the depth and the meaning of these leaks have been recognized by certain great scientists, too; and this in itself is a testimony to the enduring vitality, to the honesty, to the *con-science* of Western thought.

The elements of a potential harmony between historical and scientific thought are already here. It is only because of the extraordinary intellectual confusion of our times that the existence of this harmony has gone either unrecognized or that it has been rather wilfully obscured by certain vested interests of the mind. And the recognition of this harmony, too, depends on the recognition of a certain development in the hierarchy of thought. As I am writing this a full one hundred years have passed since Bagehot wrote his *Physics and Politics*: but note that the title of this chapter is "History and Physics." This movement of the emphasis from the physics of historical force to the history of physics, marks, in itself, the developing historicity of our consciousness. Let me repeat that history cannot be explained scientifically, whereas science can, and indeed it must, be explained historically; and let me add that this is especially true of modern physics during our interregnum.

For this is not merely the audacious approach of a historian who professes his wide ignorance of the natural sciences. It is significant —and it suggests the present validity of the historical form of thought —that twentieth-century physics may be best understood through the history of its development. The most important books on the meaning of quantum physics, written by physicists themselves, have attempted to explain quantum theory through the intellectual history of its discoveries. And since the meaning of some of these discoveries (or perhaps we should say: of these new recognitions) is revolutionary, as they mark the collapse of the absoluteness of certain accepted categories of thoughts, I, an outsider, must also attempt to sketch the historical development, and the historical correspondences, of some of these recognitions. They at least suggest the direction in which Western thought may (though I cannot say it will) be beginning to move. They, in any event, suggest what we have already left behind.

Physics is the fundamental science of matter. (Indeed, it may be said that physics *is* natural science: that chemistry, for example, is but a subdivision of physics.) What, then, did the fundamental scientists of matter discover early in the twentieth century, at the apogee of the age of materialism? Around 1900 "science could well feel complacent." There are many testimonies to this complacency at a time when it seemed that the scientific explanation of the universe was becoming completed. In the words of Banesh Hoffmann, an American physicist, had not science, by 1900, "reduced the workings of the universe to precise mathematical law?"

Had it not shown that the universe must pursue its appointed course through all eternity, the motions of its parts strictly determined according to immutable patterns of exquisite mathematical elegance?[1] Had it not shown that each individual particle of matter, every tiny ripple of radiation, and every tremor of ethereal tension must fulfill to the last jot and tittle the sublime law which man and his mathematics had at last made plain? Here indeed was reason to be proud. The mighty universe was controlled by known equations, its every motion theoretically predictable, its every action proceeding majestically by known laws from cause to effect. . . . The pioneering had been done and it was now only a matter of extending the details of what was already known. A few men with almost prophetic powers were able to discern the stealthy approach of distant storms, but their warnings did little to disturb. . . . Physics was essentially solved. . . .

It is symbolic that it was in 1900, at the opening of this century, at a time which in the history of the Western world is a kind of watershed (and not only because of the roundness of the figure), that the ideas of the great German physicist Planck had crystallized, as he himself told us. During a summer walk in the woods outside Berlin Planck suddenly turned to his son and told him for the first

[1] This word "elegance" is my only quibble with this excellent and eloquent passage (Banesh Hoffmann, *The Strange Story of the Quantum; an Account for the General Reader of the Growth of the Ideas Underlying Our Present Atomic Knowledge.* New York, 1947). *Elegance* derives from *discrimination; choice.* It is the *esprit de géometrie* that mistakes symmetry for elegance (not to speak of the condition that assymetry, suggesting movement, is more dynamic than is symmetry).

time that he may have made a discovery comparable perhaps only to Newton's.

What was that discovery? What were its implications and its consequences? Since I am not a physicist I can but describe them in a necessarily imprecise manner.

Here is a rough sketch of their sequence. Since physics deals with all matter, sooner or later its systematic investigations will bounce against the most difficult and elusive of physical questions: what are the properties of light? Pythagoras solved this simply. He did not bother to define whether light consisted of waves or of particles. He stated that light flows out from luminous bodies in every possible direction (a statement which, incidentally, corresponds to some of the present rediscoveries of modern physics). Two thousand years later Newton defined light as formed by luminous particles. This theory began to be questioned during the nineteenth century until Maxwell's theories in the 1870's "established" that light consisted not of particles but of waves. In 1887 the experiments of Hertz found that Maxwell's electromagnetic waves had the same properties as waves of light.

But then, in 1900, Planck found that the pulsations of these waves did not flow regularly. They came in irregular jerks, representing bundles of energy. These he named *quanta*.

In 1905 Einstein found that, instead of being a wave, a quantum of energy was a particle—but that such a quantum of energy changes in time, and that thus matter and energy, in certain circumstances, are dependent on the dimension of time. This is the basis of his relativity theory (one of the implications of which, stated *vulgo*, is that two by two do not *always* make four).

By about 1920 confusion set in among physicists. Light was at once a wave and a particle: but, if so, how could one possibly imagine its size and shape? This was the central question. By 1923 de Broglie found that particles turn into waves as they move; he said that light was *both* particle and wave.

Between 1925 and 1927 Heisenberg confirmed that, indeed, *both* statements were true. The result was his principle of uncertainty or indeterminacy (amounting to the recognition, among other things, that we may never be able to see the atomic particle "as it is," since we cannot determine precisely either its position or its speed).

At this point the propositions of the German Heisenberg, of the French de Broglie, of the Danish Bohr, of the English Dirac, of the Swiss Pauli, of the Austrian Schrödinger, divergent and often opposed to each other but a few years before, converge: by 1928 the quantum mechanical revolution was accomplished and accepted among physicists.[2]

Since that time certain physicists and philosophers of science were trying to draw the broader implications and the epistemological conclusions of these new principles of physics. These philosophical inquiries were retarded by the Second World War when the contacts between some of the most eminent physicists of the world were interrupted in more than one sense (and when many physicists were occupying themselves with the technological task of translating some of the discoveries of modern physics into atomic weapons). In 1955 Heisenberg proposed a wide-ranging philosophical synthesis in his Gifford Lectures at the University of St. Andrews; these were published in the United States in 1958 under the title *Physics and Philosophy*.

Twenty-five or thirty years, therefore, had passed from the first discoveries of the inadequacy of the Newtonian system of "classical" physics until the systematic realization of the meaning of these discoveries; and another twenty-five or thirty years passed until the broader philosophical meaning of these matters was to be presented. It is perhaps not wholly surprising that historians have devoted little attention to these matters during the time of Hitler, Stalin, the Second World War, the atom bomb, the cold war. We shall see, moreover, how the deadening hand of time lag in the movement of ideas lay heavy upon many physicists and, indeed, upon the minds of most of the contemporary scientists as they could not quite bring themselves to admit the radical philosophical implications of these new ideas. On the other hand *we* can no longer excuse our minds from this task. For we shall now see that many of the things that I have suggested in this book about the structure of events have been confirmed, at first sight perhaps unexpectedly, from an entirely different prospect, coming from an entirely different direction. Save for isolated instances, a few pages in a posthumous Ortega article, in a few apocalyptic passages by Guardini, and in

[2] But about Einstein's reluctance to accept it see below, p. 304.

very scattered philosophical references by certain historians,[3] this has not yet been recognized or applied to the humanities, indeed not to most of our Western corpus of thought. Yet it has become, by and large, possible to say that "modern man has moved on beyond the classical, medieval and the modern world to a new physics and philosophy which combines consistently some of the basic causal and ontological assumptions of each," as F. S. C. Northrop put it in his attempt to introduce Heisenberg's Gifford Lectures to American readers in 1957. He added that this "coming together of this new philosophy of physics with the respective philosophies of the culture of mankind . . . is the major event in today's and tomorrow's world." He asked the question: "How is the philosophy of physics expounded by Heisenberg to be reconciled with moral, political and legal science and philosophy?" Let me attempt to answer: through historical consciousness; through historical thinking.

(2) Heisenberg's recognitions. The end of the scientific world-view

Let me, therefore, insist that what follows is not the breathless attempt of an enthusiastic historian to hitch his wagon to Heisenberg's star, or to jump on Heisenberg's bandwagon, to use a more pedestrian metaphor. Rather, the contrary: my wagon is self-propelled, and a Heisenberg bandwagon does not exist (at least in the United States, among one hundred people who know the name of Einstein, not more than one may know of Heisenberg). It is the philosophical, rather than the experimental, part of Heisenberg's physics that I am qualified to discuss; my principal interest in this chapter springs from the condition that among the physicists of this century who have made excursions into philosophy I have found Heisenberg's philosophical exposition especially clear, meaningful and relevant to the general theme of this book; and I have drawn upon some of his writings in this chapter because I want

---

[3] For example, by the maverick old American historian James C. Malin (whose writings must, however, be read with great caution, even if with great sympathy); by the thoughtful paper of the Austrian Hugo Hantsch ("Zur Methodik der neueren Geschichte," 1952), by Diana Spearman, *Democracy in England* (1957); Reinhold Schneider, *Wesen und Verwaltung der Macht* (1954).

to present some of his courageous epistemological recognitions in a form which every English-speaking historian may read and understand easily. I have arranged these matters in order to sum them up in the form of ten propositions, the phrasing, the selection, and the organization of which is entirely my own: it is but their illustrations which come from the sphere of physics, described as some of them were by Heisenberg, mostly in his Gifford Lectures. They are illustrations in the literal sense: they are intended to illustrate, to illuminate new recognitions, certain truths, in the assertion of which this writer, as indeed any historian in the twentieth century, is no longer alone.

First: there is no scientific certitude. Atomic physics found that the behavior of particles is considerably unpredictable: but, what is more important, this uncertainty is not "the outcome of defects in precision or measurement but a principle that could be demonstrated by experiment." Physicists have now found that while they can reasonably predict the average reactions of great numbers of electrons in an experiment, they cannot predict what a single electron will do, and not even when it will do it.[4] The implications of this are, of course, the limitations of measurement; of accuracy; of scientific predictability—all fundamental shortcomings of "classical," or Newtonian, physics—they suggest the collapse of absolute determinism even in the world of matter.

Second: the illusory nature of the ideal of objectivity. In quantum mechanics the very act of observing alters the nature of the object, "especially when its quantum numbers are small." Quantum physics, Heisenberg says, "do not allow a completely objective description of nature."[5] "As it really happened," (or "as it is really happening")

[4] Heisenberg: "One can never simultaneously know with perfect accuracy both of those two important factors which determine the movement of one of these smallest [atomic] particles—its position and its velocity." Also: "It is impossible to determine accurately *both* the position and the direction and the speed of a particle *at the same instant.* If we determine experimentally its exact position at any given moment, its movement is disturbed to such a degree by that very experiment that we shall then be unable to find it at all. And, conversely, if we are able to measure exactly the velocity of a particle, the picture of its position becomes totally blurred."

[5] Not only in quantum but in relativity concepts, too, "simultaneity" is, for example, inadequate: if two persons saw two things far apart happen at the same time, they might not find that the things happened at the same time. It is true that in relativity situations this happens only in extreme circumstances. But the significance of this physically demonstrable discovery is decisive: as de Broglie said, too, it is philosophical as well as scientific.

is, therefore, an incomplete statement in the world of matter, too. We are ahead of Ranke. "In our century," Heisenberg wrote in *The Physicist's Conception of Nature*, "it has become clear that the desired objective reality of the elementary particle is too crude an oversimplification of what really happens. . . ." "We can no longer speak of the behaviour of the particle independently of the process of observation. As a final consequence, the natural laws formulated mathematically in quantum theory no longer deal with the elementary particles themselves but with our knowledge of them." In *Physics and Philosophy* he explained this further:

> We cannot completely objectify the result of an observation, we cannot describe what "happens" between [one] observation and the next . . . any statement about what has "actually happened" is a statement in terms of the [Newtonian] classical concepts and—because of the thermodynamics and of the uncertainty relations—by its very nature incomplete with respect of the details of the atomic events involved. The demand "to describe what happens" in the quantum-theoretical process between two successive observations is a contradiction *in adjecto*, since the word "describe" refers to the use of classical concepts, while these concepts cannot be applied in the space between the observations; they can only be applied at the points of observation.

In biology, too, "it may be important for a complete understanding that the questions are asked by the species man which itself belongs to the genus of living organisms, in other words, that we already know what life is even before we have defined it scientifically."[6] The recognition of personal participation is inescapable.

Third: the illusory nature of definitions. It seems that the minds of most physicists during the present interregnum still clung to the old, "logical" order of things: they were always giving names to newly discovered atomic particles, to such elements of the atomic kernel that did not "fit." Yet the introduction of the name "wavicle" does preciously little to solve the problem of whether light consists of waves or of particles; and it may be that the continuing nominalistic habit of proposing new terms (sometimes rather silly-sounding ones, such as "neutrino") suggests that illusion of the modern mind which tends to substitute vocabulary

---

[6] Niels Bohr: In biology we are concerned with "manifestations of possibilities in that nature to which we belong rather than with outcomes of experiments which we can ourselves perform."

for thought, tending to believe that once we name or define something we've "got it." Sometimes things may get darker through definitions, Dr. Johnson said; and Heisenberg seems to confirm the limited value of definitions even in the world of matter:

Any concepts or words which have been formed in the past through the interplay between the world and ourselves are not really sharply defined with respect to their meaning; that is to say, we do not know exactly how far they will help us in finding our way in the world. We often know that they can be applied to a wide range of inner or outer experience but we practically never know precisely the limits of their applicability. This is true even of the simplest and most general concepts like "existence" and "space and time" . . . . The words "position" and "velocity" of an electron, for instance, seemed perfectly well defined as to both their meaning and their possible connections, and in fact they were clearly defined concepts within the mathematical framework of Newtonian mechanics. But actually they were not well defined, as is seen from the relations of uncertainty. One may say that regarding their position in Newtonian mechanics they were well defined, but in their relation to nature they were not.

Fourth: the illusory nature of the absolute truthfulness of mathematics. The absoluteness of mathematical "truth" was disproven by Gödel's famous theorem in 1931;[7] but even before that, in the 1920's, physicists were beginning to ask themselves this uneasy question; as Heisenberg put it:

Is it true that only such experimental situations can arise in nature as can be expressed in the mathematical formalism? The assumption that this was actually true led to limitations in the use of those concepts that had been the basis of physics since Newton. One could speak of the position and of the velocity of an electron as in Newtonian mechanics and one could observe and measure these quantities. But one could not fix both these quantities simultaneously with an arbitrarily high accurracy. . . . One had learned that the old concepts fit nature only inaccurately.

Mathematical truth is neither complete nor infinite (the velocity of light added to the velocity of light may amount to the velocity of light; on the other end of the physical scale there can be no action smaller than the quantum of action; and under certain physical

---

[7] But already Goethe in his *Theory of Colours:* "What is there exact in mathematics except its own exactitude?"

conditions two by two do not always amount to four).[8] Quantum theory found, too, that certain mathematical statements depend on the time element: Heisenberg realized that p times q is not always the equivalent of q times p in physics (when, for example, p means momentum and q position). What this suggests is that certain basic mathematical operations are not independent of human concepts of time and perhaps not even of purpose. That certain quantities do not always obey arithmetical rules[9] was suggested already in the 1830's by the Irish mathematical genius Hamilton; and the Englishman Dirac, still to some extent influenced by nominalism, tried in the 1920's to solve this problem by asserting the necessity to deal with a set of so-called "Q numbers" which do not always respond to the rules of multiplication. But perhaps the "problem" may be stated more simply: the order in which certain mathematical (and physical) operations are performed affects their results.

Fifth: the illusory nature of "factual" truth. Change is an essential component of all nature: this ancient principle reappears within quantum physics. We have seen that the physicist must reconcile himself to the condition that he cannot exactly determine both the position and the speed of the atomic particle. He must reconcile himself, too, to the consequent condition that in the static, or factual, sense a basic unit of matter does not exist. It is not measurable; it is not even ascertainable; it is, in a way, a less substantial concept than such "idealistic" concepts as "beauty" or "mind." We can never expect to see a static atom or electron, since they do not exist as "immutable facts"; at best, we may see the trace of their motions. Einstein's relativity theory stated that matter is transmutable, and that it is affected by time; but the full implications of this condition were not immediately recognized, since they mean, among other things, that the earlier watertight distinctions between "organic" and "inorganic" substances no longer hold. "A sharp

[8] Heisenberg: "It would not be fundamentally unimaginable that, for example, a future extension of mathematical logic might give a certain meaning to the statement that in exceptional cases $2 \times 2 = 5$, and it might even be possible that this extended mathematics would be of use in calculations in the field of economics."

[9] For example the so-called irrational numbers, which are both odd and even numbers at the same time; or the square root of 2, which cannot be fixed or measured.

distinction between animate and inanimate matter," writes Heisenberg, "cannot be made." "There is only one kind of matter, but it can exist in different discrete stationary conditions." Heisenberg doubts "whether physics and chemistry will, together with the concept of evolution, some day offer a complete description of the living organism."

Sixth: the breakdown of the mechanical concept of causality. We have seen how, for the historian, *causa* must be more than the *causa efficiens*, and that the necessarily narrow logic of mechanical causality led to deterministic systems that have harmed our understanding of history, since in reality, through life and in history this kind of causation almost always "leaks." But now not even in physics is this kind of causation universally applicable: it is inadequate, and moreover, "fundamentally and intrinsically undemonstrable."[10] There is simply no satisfactory way of picturing the fundamental atomic processes of nature in categories of space and time and causality. The multiplicity and the complexity of causes reappears in the world of physical relationships, in the world of matter.[11]

Seventh: the principal importance of potentialities and tendencies. Quantum physics brought the concept of potentiality back into physical science—a rediscovery, springing from new evidence, of

[10] Heisenberg: "The use of the concept of causality for describing the law of cause and effect is of relatively recent origin. In previous philosophies the word *causa* had a very much more general [meaning]. . . . [Already] Kant used the word 'causality' in a nineteenth-century sense. . . ." Kant was convinced that his concept of causality would be "the basis of any future metaphysics called Science," but he has been proven wrong; and, as Heisenberg says, "it is interesting to see where his arguments have been wrong. . . . We know the foregoing event. But not quite accurately. We know the forces in the atomic nucleus that are responsible for the emission of the alpha particle. But this knowledge contains the uncertainty which is brought about by the interaction between the nucleus and the rest of the world. If we wanted to know why the alpha particle was emitted at that particular time, we would have to know the microscopic structure of the whole world including ourselves, and that is impossible. Therefore, Kant's arguments for the *a priori* character of the law of causality no longer apply."

[11] De Broglie (1939): "Even the notions of causality and of individuality have had to undergo a fresh scrutiny, and it seems certain that this major crisis, affecting the guiding principles of our physical concepts, will be the source of philosophical consequences which cannot yet be clearly perceived." Banesh Hoffmann (1947): These are "hard, uncompromising, and at present inescapable facts of experiment and bitter experience . . . directly opposed" to the Newtonian way of scientific thinking.

some of the earliest Greek physical and philosophical theories. Heraclitus was the first to emphasize this in the reality of the world: *panta rei*, his motto, "Everything Moves," "imperishable change that renovates the world"; he did not, in the Cartesian and Newtonian manner, distinguish between being and becoming; to him fire was *both* matter and force. Modern quantum theory comes close to this when it describes energy, according to Heisenberg, anything that moves: "it may be called the primary cause of all change, and energy can be transformed into matter or heat or light." To Aristotle, too, matter was not by itself a reality but a *potentia*, which existed by means of form: through the processes of nature the Aristotelian "essence" passed from mere possibility through form into actuality. When we speak of the temperature of the atom, says Heisenberg, we can only mean an expectation, "an objective tendency or possibility, a *potentia* in the sense of Aristotelian philosophy." An accurate description of the elementary particle is impossible: "the only thing which can be written down as description is a probability function"; the particle "exists" only as a possibility, "a possibility for being or a tendency for being." But this probability is not merely the addition of the element of "chance," and it is something quite different from mathematical formulas of probabilities:

> Probability in mathematics or in statistical mechanics [writes Heisenberg] means a statement about our degree of knowledge of the actual situation. In throwing dice we do not know the fine details of the motion of our hands which determine the fall of the dice and therefore we say the probability for throwing a special number is just one in six. The probability wave of Bohr, Kramers, Slater, however, meant more than that; it meant a tendency for something. It was a quantitative version of the old concept of *potentia* in Aristotelian philosophy.

We have already met Heisenberg's question: "What happens 'really' in an atomic event?" The mechanism of the results of the observation can always be stated in the terms of the Newtonian concepts: "but what one deduces from an observation is a probability function . . . [which] does not itself represent a course of events in the course of time.* It represents a tendency for events and our knowledge of events."

Eighth: not the essence of "factors" but their relationship counts. Modern physics now admits, as we have seen, that important factors may not have clear definitions: but, on the other hand, these factors *may* be clearly defined, as Heisenberg puts it, "with regard to their connections." These relationships are of primary importance: just as no "fact" can stand alone, apart from its associations with other "facts" and other matters, modern physics now tends to divide its world not into "different groups of objects but into different groups of connections."[12] In the concepts of modern mathematics, too, it is being increasingly recognized how the functions of dynamic connections may be more important than the static definitions of "factors." Euclid had said that a point is something which has no parts and which occupies no space. At the height of positivism, around 1890, it was generally believed that an even more perfect statement would consist in exact definitions of "parts" and of "space." But certain mathematicians have since learned that this tinkering with definitions tends to degenerate into the useless nominalism of semantics, and consequently they do not bother with definitions of "points" or "lines" or "connection"; their interest is directed, instead, to the axiom that two points can be always connected by a line, to the relationships of lines and points and connections.

Ninth: the principles of "classical" logic are no longer unconditional: new concepts of truths are recognized. "Men fail to imagine any relation between two opposing truths and so they assume that to state one is to deny the other," Pascal wrote. Three centuries later Heisenberg wrote about some of C. F. von Weizsaecker's propositions:

It is especially one fundamental principle of classical logic which seems to require a modification. In classical logic it is assumed that, if a statement has any meaning at all, either the statement or the negation of the

---

[12] This recognition corresponds, significantly, with certain philosophical principles first proposed by Dilthey. H. A. Hodges, *Wilhem Dilthey—An Introduction:* "Philosophers have devoted endless trouble to discussing how we come to be aware of physical objects and how far subjective elements enter into our experience of them. They have talked as if our world consisted entirely of such objects, and as if the knowledge of them were our chief intellectual concern. Yet the most significant of our experiences lies in our relations with other people"—that is, when two microcosms meet—"and the nature and the extent of the knowledge which we have of other people is a question of equal importance with"—I would say that it is a question of *superior* importance to— "the first. Dilthey is the first philosopher in any country to tackle the question seriously and systematically, and his work has started a new movement in German thought. . . ."

statement must be correct. Of "here is a table" or "here is not a table" either the first or the second statement must be correct. "Tertium non datur," a third possibility does not exist. It may be that we do not know whether the statement or its negation is correct; but in "reality" one of the two is correct.

In quantum theory this law "tertium non datur" is to be modified . . . Weizsaecker points out that one may distinguish various levels of language. . . . In order to cope with [certain quantum situations] Weizsaecker introduced the concept "degree of truth". . . . [By this] the term "not decided" is by no means equivalent to the term "not known". . . . There is still complete equivalence between the two levels of language with respect to the correctness of a statement, but not with respect to the incorrectness. . . .

Knowledge means not certainty, and a half-truth is not 50 percent truth; everyday language cannot be eliminated from any meaningful human statement of truth, including propositions dealing with matter; after all is said, logic is human logic, our own creation,

Tenth: at the end of the Modern Age the Cartesian partition falls away. Descartes's framework, his partition of the world into objects and subjects, no longer holds:

The mechanics of Newton [Heisenberg writes] and all the other parts of classical physics constructed after its model started out from the assumption that one can describe the world without speaking about God or ourselves. This possibility seemed almost a necessary condition for natural science in general.

But at this point the situation changed to some extent through quantum theory . . . we cannot disregard the fact [I would say: the condition] that science is formed by men. Natural science does not simply describe and explain nature; it is a part of the interplay between nature and ourselves; it describes nature as exposed to our method of questioning. This was a possibility of which Descartes could not have thought [?] but it makes the sharp separation between the world and the I impossible.

If one follows the great difficulty which even eminent scientists like Einstein had in understanding and accepting the Copenhagen interpretation of quantum theory, one can trace the roots of this difficulty to the Cartesian partition. This partition has penetrated deeply into the human mind during the three centuries following Descartes and it will take a long time for it to be replaced by a really different attitude toward the problem of reality.

We cannot avoid the condition of our participation. Throughout this book I tried to draw attention to the personal and moral and historical implications of this recognition, that instead of the cold and falsely aseptic remoteness of observation we need the warmth and the penetration of personal interest: but this is no longer the solitary longing of a humanist, a poetic exhortation. For "even in science," as Heisenberg says in *The Physicist's Conception of Nature*, "the object of research is no longer nature itself, but man's investigation of nature. Here, again, man confronts himself alone."[13] And the recognition of this marks the beginning of a revolution not only in physical and philosophical but also in biological (and, ultimately, medical) concepts, springing from the empirical realization that there is a closer connection between mind and matter than what we have been taught to believe. Still, because of our interregnum, decades and disasters may have to pass until this revolution will bring its widely recognizable results. Yet we may at least look back at what we have already begun to leave behind.

After three hundred years the principal tendency in our century is still to believe that life is a scientific proposition, and to demonstrate how all of our concepts are but the products of complex mechanical causes that may be ultimately determinable through scientific methods. Thus Science, in Heisenberg's words, produced "its own, inherently uncritical"—and, let me add, inherently unhistorical—philosophy.[14] But now "the scientific method of analysing, [defining] and classifying has become conscious"—though, let me add, far from sufficiently conscious—"of its limitations, which rise out of the [condition] that by its intervention science alters and refashions the object of investigation. In other words, methods and object can no longer be separated. *The scientific worldview has ceased to be a scientific view in the true sense of the word.*"

These are Heisenberg's italics. They correspond with the arguments of this book, in which I have tried to propose the historicity of

[13] Heisenberg in *Planck's Discovery and the Philosophical Problems of Atomic Physics:* "There are large areas of phenomena that cannot even be approximately described by the concepts of classical physics. . . . The science of nature does not deal with nature itself but in fact with the *science* of nature as man thinks and describes it. This does not introduce an element of subjectivity into natural science. We do not by any means pretend that occurrences in the universe depend on our observations, but we point out that natural science stands between nature and man and that we cannot renounce the use of man's intuition or innate conceptions."

[14] Cassirer: "There is in the Cartesian mind a kind of natural distrust, almost an antipathy, for history."

reality as something which is prior to its mathematicability.[15] They represent a reversal of thinking after three hundred years: but, in any event, such recognitions involve not merely philosophical problems or problems of human perception but the entirety of human involvement in nature, a condition from which we, carriers of life in its highest complexity, cannot separate ourselves. The condition of this participation is the recognition of our limitations which is, as I wrote earlier, our gateway to knowledge. "There is no use in discussing," Heisenberg writes, "what could be done if we were other beings than what we are."[16] We must even keep in mind that the introduction of the "Cartesian" instruments such as telescopes and microscopes, which were first developed in the seventeenth century, do not, in spite of their many practical applications, brings us *always and necessarily* closer to reality*—since they are interpositions, *our* interpositions, between our senses and the "object." We may even ask ourselves whether *our* task is still to "see" more rather than to see better, since not only does our internal deepening of human understanding now lag behind our accumulation of external information, but too, this external information is becoming increasingly abstract and unreal. Hence the increasing breakdown of internal communications: for, in order to see better, we must understand our own limitations better and also trust ourselves better. At the very moment of history when enormous governments are getting ready to shoot selected men hermetically encased in plastic bubbles out of the earth onto the moon, the importance of certain aspects of the "expanding universe" has begun to decline, and not only for humanitarian reasons alone; we are, again, in the center of the universe—inescapably as well as hopefully so.

[15] Galileo (like Descartes): "The book of nature is written in the language of mathematics." This statement would have seemed revolutionary (and perhaps even nonsensical) to, say, Machiavelli, a century before Galileo; it became dogma a century or so after Galileo; and now, three centuries later, it is becoming nonsense again. The absolutist Hobbes on mathematical geometry: "the only science that it hath pleased God hitherto to bestow upon mankind." Spinoza: "If mathematics did not exist, man would not know what truth is." No: if man did not exist, there would be no mathematics (and if truth did not exist, there would be no man).

[16] Novalis: "Man is the Messiah of Nature," a forerunner to Weizsaecker's ". . . man is earlier than natural science." Heisenberg: Man must resign himself to the condition "that his Science is but a link in the infinite chain of man's argument with nature, and that it cannot singly speak of nature 'in itself.' "

Our problems—all of our problems—concern primarily human nature. The human factor is the basic factor. These are humanistic platitudes. But they have now gained added meaning, through the unexpected support from physics. It is thus that the recognitions of the human condition of science, and of the historicity of science—let me repeat that Heisenberg's approach is also historical[17]—may mark the way toward the next phase in the evolution of human consciousness, in the Western world at least.

(3) The correspondences

Need I still insist that many of Heisenberg's propositions about physics—indeed, that sometimes the very language of his recognitions—correspond with many of the propositions by this writer in this book dealing with history? Of course these are correspondences, not analogies; they are not interchangeable; they do not form a system. Still, their portents go beyond the two fields of historical philosophy and philosophical physics. They suggest that in our times new ideas about the relationships of human life and of the universe, of mind and matter, may be emerging, often independently from each other, coming from the oddest sources, different places, through different routes. It would already be possible to string together a list of striking statements by certain scientists, historians, poets, writers, philosophers in the middle of the twentieth century, in order to illustrate certain profound convergences of the human spirit, indicating the evolution of what may be called post-modern thought in the Western world.* Yet such a presentation, no matter how impressive, would be insufficient. It is almost always possible to find some people who tend to agree with you, no matter how unpopular or unrecognized your ideas may be; a mere listing of corresponding statements may give a disproportionate impression of their influence and importance or even of their significance. We must recognize

[17] See, for example, his summary in *The Physicist's Conception of Nature:* "1. Modern science, in its beginnings, was characterized by a conscious modesty, it made statements about strictly limited relations that *are only valid within the framework of these limitations.* 2. *This modesty was largely lost during the nineteenth century.* [His italics.] Physical knowledge was considered to make assertions about nature as a whole. Physics wished to turn philosopher, and the demand was voiced from many quarters that all true philosophers must be scientific. 3. Today physics is undergoing a basic change, the most characteristic trait of which is a return to its original self-limitation. 4. The philosophic content of a science is only preserved if science is conscious of its limits. . . ."

the existence of certain correspondences: but it is through a historical approach that their significance may properly appear.

Once more I must insist how this eminent reasonableness of the historical approach has been recognized, in one way or another, by certain scientists. Nearly forty years ago E. A. Burtt wrote in *The Metaphysical Foundations of Modern Science* that "whatever may turn out to be the solution" of the modern problem of cosmology (and of physics) "an indispensable part of its foundation will be clear insight into the antecedents of our present thought-world."

Possibly the world of external facts is much more fertile and plastic than we have ventured to suppose; it may be that all these cosmologies and many more analyses and classifications are genuine ways of arranging what nature offers to our understanding, and that the main condition determining our selection between them is something in us rather than something in the external world. *This possibility might be enormously clarified by historical studies* [my italics] aiming to ferret out the fundamental motives and other human factors involved in each of these characteristic analyses as it appeared and to make what headway seemed feasible at evaluating them, discovering which are of more enduring significance and why.

"To ferret out the *fundamental* motives" (again my italics) in the minds of scientists long dead may be too much to ask; but when we use the historical approach we are on the right track, even though we must be more modest. Our task is to sketch not the conditions of individual intellectual creation but the historical correspondences of certain intellectual recognitions.

Some of these correspondences are relatively simple. Around the middle of the seventeenth century, for example, as Ernest Mortimer observed in his excellent study of Pascal, "only a few months separated . . . Galileo's death, Newton's birth and the appearance of Descartes' *Principia Philosophica* with its preface, the *Discours sur la méthode*." Darwin and Marx died within a few months of each other, at the very time when Ortega was born. But there is, of course, more to this historical problem of corresponding thinkers than correspondences in the life span of certain generations. In the physical sciences, and particularly in their technical applications, there is often an expectable convergence of certain achievements that are about to be reached toward the end of certain phases of evolving research. Thus, for example, the mutation theory in biology (something roughly corresponding to the form, but by no means to the essence, of the quantum theory in physics, involving the discovery that genetic evolution may occur in "jumps") was reached in 1902, at the same time by De Vries in Leyden, Tschermak in Vienna, Correns in Berlin. This is the kind of achievement which consists of the discovery of answers to questions that have been outstanding and precisely formulated for some time before: it involves the "filling of gaps" whose existence and place has been recognized. (With all the respect due to the before-mentioned eminent scientists these are, therefore, coincidences that are different in degree but perhaps not in kind from the inventions of such things as electric light or the automobile engine: for there are reasons to believe that, had Edison's experiments failed in 1879 or Benz's in 1885, someone else would have produced the first electric bulb and the first automobile engine around the same time or, in any event, not much later.)

Outside applied science the historical development of ideas is, of course, less predictable—though, as I wrote before, in our democratic times much of the earlier independence and unpredictability of the humanities also has been eroding. Still, what happens when really significant correspondences occur? They involve not so much the "filling of gaps" as coinciding recognitions of the inadequate level of "research," of the insufficient depths, or heights, of the prevailing "dialogue" (Bernanos: "the worst, the most corrupting lies are problems poorly stated"); and this calls forth, of course, not so much new answers as new questions (or, perhaps, new recognitions of old questions) by solitary thinkers whose main fields of study may be quite different but who possess similar qualities of personal interest. It is thus that they are literally *dissatisfied* with the inadequacy of the prevailing categories of thought. It is thus that their different paths converge: for, let me repeat, the way to certain truths leads through a graveyard of untruths.

And this graveyard lives within the minds of living human beings. The graves, the tombstones, the thinning line of mourners, the gravediggers, the lonely walkers through the nocturnal yard do not exist in the abstract. The history of science is the history of scientists, and the history of thought is the history of thinking men. This is why the historical conditions of new recognitions are so important; but at the same time the very conditions of our historical knowledge set limits to our pursuit of the historicity of their correspondences.

These are the natural limitations of intellectual history, the inevitable circumscriptions of the otherwise so significant and meaningful pursuit of the pedigrees of certain ideas. I touched upon these limits earlier. In the deepest sense what we must keep in mind is the paradox that no human idea is entirely original and wholly independent —while, on the other hand, the personal perception and the expression of even the most obvious and most ephemeral platitude lends (*lends* rather than *gives*) the latter an inevitable minimum of originality.[18] In the narrower and more precise sense we must consider the inscrutable complexities of the distance from the "first" (the quotation marks are intentional) appearance of an idea within the consciousness of a person through its first rational formulation in his mind to its first public expression (which is really the farthest point back where the historian's tracing may start) and to the, in our times increasingly complicated, process of its dissemination among other people, its fertilization of their minds, its recognition by them. It is perhaps because of this necessity of a right "climate" that "dissemination" is a good word. On the other hand, the sprouting of seeds in men's minds is miraculous in its causal complexities; the physics of nature do not apply.[19]

Let me, therefore, attempt for the last time a quick survey of certain "climates of opinion:" for this historical approach may explain something about the complex and confusing and difficult evolution of the Western mind toward the end of the Modern Age and during the present phase of an interregnum.

Much has been written about that climate of opinion of a little more than a century ago which helped to insure and, indeed, to create the conditions of receptivity for Darwin's propositions. Not

[18] For example, Ortega in 1923: "In the introduction to my first *Espectador,* which appeared in January, 1916, when nothing had yet been published on the general theory of relativity [Einstein's first publication on his recent discovery, *Die Grundlagen der allgemeinen Relativitaetstheorie* was published in that year] I put forward a brief exposition of the doctrine of perspective, giving it a range of reference ample enough to transcend physics and include all reality. I mention this fact to show the extent to which a similar cast of thought is a sign of the times."

[19] Valéry: "A drop of wine falling into water barely colors it, and tends to disappear after showing as a pink cloud. That is the physical fact. But suppose now that some time after it has vanished, we should see, here and there in our glass—which seemed once more to hold *pure* water—drops of wine forming, dark and *pure*—what a surprise! . . . This phenomenon of Cana is not impossible in intellectual and social physics. . . ."

only progressive scientists but Marx and Engels, too, hailed Darwin (the former said about the *Origin* that it was "a basis in natural science for the class struggle in history" and considered dedicating *Das Kapital* to Darwin; the latter that "just as Darwin discovered the law of evolution in organic nature, so Marx discovered the law of evolution in human history"). This does not, of course, mean that Darwin was a Marxist (though it does mean that Marx was a Darwinist). Darwin and Comte, the atheist Marx and Mendel the Moravian abbot, Buckle the liberal historian and Zola the dogmatic realist, Maxwell the physical and Spencer the social scientist, they were very different men. But there were broad correspondences in their principal ideas: as Gertrude Himmelfarb put it in retrospect about Darwin and Marx, "as their philosophical intent was similar, so was their practical effect": they all believed in the progress concept of history and in the mechanical-mathematical order of the universe, and this was to be typical of the thinking of an era. Of course these are imprecise generalizations. No period of history is of one piece. Anyone with more than a superficial knowledge of history can point out contrary currents of thought (and what is perhaps more important, of sentiment) within the so-called Victorian Age. But, no matter how deep, these contrary currents were of rivulet width, eventually washed under by the swelling stream of accepted ideas the power of which is still far from being spent, and the influence of which has spread far beyond Europe. In 1856, shortly before the *Origin* was completed (and a few months before Comte died) Buckle put down an archetypal statement of these ideas as he wrote: "In regard to nature, events apparently the most irregular and capricious have been explained, and have been shown to be in accordance with certain fixed and universal laws. This has been done because men of ability and, above all, men of patient, untiring thought, have studied natural events with the view of discovering their regularity: and if human events were subjected to a similar treatment, we have every right to expect similar results." These are the ideas that have become—thoughtlessly perhaps—accepted by large masses of people who for the first time received the benefits of modern education. Save for the sonorous Latinities of its prose, this 1856 statement is hardly different from what in 1966, 110 years later, a computer technologist at, say, General Electric's Space Center—or, indeed, an Official Advanced

American Thinker such as Buckminster Fuller—was saying and presumably, thinking. Darwin, who died in 1882, was justified in his optimistic assumption as he said that he would trust the definition of the human species to be settled by the opinion "of a majority of naturalists," as he knew that these were about to take their stand on his side. As Samuel Butler wrote around that time: "I attacked the foundation of morality in *Erewhon*, and nobody cared two straws. I tore open the wounds of my Redeemer as he hung upon the Cross in *The Fair Haven*, and people rather liked it. But when I attacked Mr. Darwin they were up in arms in a moment." Of course; for, as E. I. Watkin put it once in a pithy sentence, the liberal world at the end of the nineteenth century "went forward with triumphant assurance, confident in its own enlightenment in reason, freedom and progress, and failed to notice that its heart was a void."

Yet shortly before the twentieth century began, a European intellectual reaction against nineteenth-century categories of thought started to crystallize. Let me repeat that there had been many individual manifestations of such a reaction earlier, Nietzsche for example: but it was not until about 1894 that we may see a coagulation of recognitions. Around that time an antimaterialist reaction, particularly in the Latin nations of Europe, corresponds with the emergence of a new kind of philosophy, involving the phenomenology of consciousness, in Germany. Menéndez y Pelayo, Unamuno, Croce, Sighele, Pareto, Sorel, Bergson, Proust, Le Bon, Péguy, Dilthey, Rickert, Simmel, Einstein, Freud . . . but, again, a catalogue of names will tell us little. In the broader sense there is a kind of antimaterialist "vitalism" corresponding in the recognitions of such different workers in such different vineyards as, say, Bergson or Planck or Wilde, many of whom may have been entirely unaware of each other's existence. At any rate, between 1894 and 1905 Planck discovers a hole within the closed mechanical concept of the universe; various Latin European thinkers propose, independently of each other, the existence of principles of intuitive cognition; Bergson and Einstein and, in his way, Proust start to think and talk about the relativity in time in different ways.* In the narrower, and more precise, sense, too, some of these correspondences are remarkable, since they are reflected by the very language of their different proponents. In 1899, for example, the German historian Alfred Dove wrote Rickert: "We do not enter into contact with the past through causality alone, but leap across the entire intervening causal space by the force of simple sympathy," a statement not only completely contrary to the assertion of the popular philosopher Haeckel, written in the same year, that "the great abstract law of mechanical causality now rules the entire universe, as it does the mind of man," but which corresponds amazingly with the terminology which was to be employed by Planck within a year.[20]

The second, and no less remarkable, wave of crystallizing correspondences occurred twenty-five years later, in the twenties, mostly in the intellectually supercharged atmosphere of Weimar Germany, at the time of the second great "jump" in the historical evolution of modern physics. Around 1926 the inadequacy of mechanical causality and of categorical objectivity, together with "indeterminacy" were recognized not only by the agitated physicists such as Heisenberg, Bohr, Pauli, Schrödinger, Bridgman, already in some contact with each other: corresponding statements were made at the same time by many different thinkers, including historians such as Huizinga and Meinecke. What is remarkable about the significance of these recognitions is that they go beyond the assertions of the 1894–1905 period, as they represent a striving for a higher kind of harmony. "Physics and history," Huizinga wrote in 1926, "are natural subjects for comparison . . . it appears that attempts of a new rapprochement are coming rather from the side of the natural sciences, whose theory of exactitude has not remained unmodified. . . ." In an important essay, published in 1928, Meinecke proposed new and fundamental limitations of causality as he suggested the existence of "supra-causal" influences. Perhaps the most incisive expression of the themes then developing may be found in an essay by the philosopher Karl Joel, entitled "Superseding the Nineteenth Century in the Thinking of the Present"*—an exquisite summation of a trend of thought that had been developing among the finest minds of Europe in the twenties. In what were once "exact sciences" this trend may have reached its culmination in 1930–1931 with the Bruxelles-Solvay Congress of physicists (to which I shall briefly return) and in Gödel's revolutionary theorem about the inevitability of human preconceptions in mathematics.*

Yet, for many reasons and, as we shall shortly see, perhaps princi-

[20] It would be interesting to know whether Planck's choice of the word *quantum* may not have had something to do with the high intellectual currency of this word at that time in Germany. (Nietzsche in *The Will to Power:* "Quanta of power alone determine rank and distinguish rank. . . .")

pally because of political ones, these converging and crystallizing aspirations for a post-modern philosophical harmony were soon washed under. Within his above-cited essay Meinecke in 1928 wrote that "the aspiration toward harmony must continue as an impulse, and could only die out if our culture were completely to decay or to collapse"; yet he already warned not only against "ossified academicism" but also against "subjectivism running riot." He may have sensed something like the coming of Nazism, of a hurricane of an anti-bourgeois and antirationalist reaction against what seemed to have been the hypocrisies of bourgeois civilization; something ultimately destructive. And, of course, this is what happened through Nazism, whose antirational and often primitive and brutal intellectual practices drove many of the best Western minds back to the "Left"—a movement particularly evident in the English-speaking world.* By the end of the thirties Heisenberg and some of his German physicist colleagues were suspected to have been working for Hitler; Unamuno, neglected by the masses and by the publicists of Left and Right alike, died tragically alone; Ortega was regarded as not much more than an unusually intelligent reactionary gadfly by those leading intellectuals of the West who, except for a few scattered conservative anti-Nazis on the Continent, pinned their remaining hopes and illusions again on the "Left."

At this point I must say something about the inevitable relationships of the history of ideas and of the history of world powers. I made a passing reference to the world historical importance of the 1875–1941 period in the first chapter of this book, and now I cannot avoid saying something about this, though necessarily in a kind of intellectual shorthand. The history of ideas in this period of European history still remains to be written—precisely because the movement of ideas in this period amounts to much more than intellectual history. Let me sum it up with one generalization, surprising as this might seem at first sight. From about 1875 to 1941, all superficial impressions to the contrary notwithstanding, Europe moved toward the Right, not the Left. (The very categories of this generalization are, of course, not precise: the "Europe" in it does not apply to Russia; Britain is a partial exception, and "Right" and "Left" are not clear-cut categories nowadays. But for the sake of intellectual—or, rather, historical—shorthand this generalization must do.) From about 1875 to 1941 European thought was influenced increasingly by a reaction against, and in some cases by a transcendence of, the categories of the nineteenth century, by a reaction against liberalism as well as against positivism, against free-trade capitalism as well as against socialist internationalism, against democratic materialism as well as against the mechanical-scientific world-view.* From about 1875 to 1941 in the political and social and cultural life of Europe's peoples the most powerful and dynamic factor was that of nationality: and the roots of this historical factor (speech, for instance) were fed from a deeper kind of consciousness than the political thought which had characterized the earlier nineteenth-century dialogue between liberals and conservatives about the proper compounds of liberty with equality. From about 1875 to 1941, contrary to the Marxist (and to the later Leninist and Wilsonian) predictions, it was not the struggle of classes, and not the struggle of liberal vs. Communist internationalists, but the struggle of nations that formed the principal and world-shaking events. From about 1875 to 1941 the history of the world was marked by the decline of multinationality, of the old Russian, Austrian, Turkish, Spanish empires and by the rise of new national powers such as Germany or Japan. From about 1875 to 1941 the principal development within Europe was the rise in the power and prestige (only briefly interrupted after 1918) of Germany. And after 1941 it was not only the defeat of German power but the bankruptcy of German-type nationalism which marked a turning-point in the history of world politics as well as in the evolution of European ideas; for the very condition that Germany and Fascism represented some of the most extreme and primitive applications of this 1875–1941 reaction against the nineteenth-century world-view either alienated or disillusioned or literally drove underground some of the actual and potential intellectual advocates of this reaction.

Thus, while this antimaterialistic reaction of the European spirit —or, what may be more important, this *first* post-materialist and *first* post-modern movement in its history—did not have much to do with politics when it began to crystallize after 1875, it was destroyed by world political forces after 1941. In any event, it cannot be properly assayed without reference to the history of nations during the same period. It is true that, as Péguy said, the massive interference of politics and of its rhetoric leads to the degeneration of truth and of thought. But it is precisely because of this massive and pervasive interference of politics that the history of ideas cannot be treated in an isolated category. Not only were there correspondences between the late-nineteenth-century intellectual reactions against positivism and the political reactions against parliamentarism, or between the reactions against materialism and against capitalism, or later between philosophical neo-idealism and political Fascism. There exist, too, relationships between world political developments and the applications of the new ideas. There are some evident examples of these correspondences throughout the history of the new physics. Haven't we seen, for example, that 1900 marks the end of the indisputability of the Newtonian world order as well as of the confidence of the Bourgeois Age, that Planck's discovery of the hole in the mechanical-physical universe occurs at the very time when the cracks appear in what Mrs. Tuchman recently called *The Proud Tower?* The 1894–1905 period is, for example, not only an enormously important turning-point in the history of ideas; it is an enormously important turning-point in the political history of the world; it was then that the United States and Japan first arose as world powers, whereby the destinies of Britain and of Germany and of Russia changed radically (their statesmen took notice of this and altered the course of their respective ships of state, something that was to lead to the First World War). In the 1920's the indeterminacy revolution coincided with a defeat of the "Left" in Europe from which it has not yet recovered (the feebleness of the bourgeois parliamentary regimes and the depressing failure of capitalism led not to Leftist revolutions but of Rightist dictatorships enjoying widespread mass support).[21] And the "American" phase of the Second World War, after 1941, certainly cor-

[21] In 1930, at the Bruxelles-Solvay Congress of International Physics, Einstein, refusing to admit the Heisenberg uncertainty principle, suffered a humiliating defeat, which was administered by Bohr. I am not saying that this was a political event. I am saying that this event, and the time of its occurrence, has a significance in the general cultural history of Europe, involving politics to some extent. For there is a certain correspondence between Einstein's defeat in 1930 and the failure of German Marxism, with its interpretation of Economic Man, at that very historical moment. They were, both, failures of the deterministic thinking of the nineteenth century; and, in view of more universal historical developments of that time, it is at least significant that this happened in 1930. (On the more vulgar level of mass political beliefs it is true what Klaus Mehnert wrote in 1951: "The German people's journey from Liebknecht to Hitler, and the Russian people's journey from Lenin to Stalin, were parallel performances of the same process. In both cases . . . the journey was one from dialectic to magic. . . .")

responded with the construction of the first atomic bombs, by refugee scientists, in the United States. For it is history, not "science," which explains both how and why these atomic bombs were made. The "causes" of the atom bomb are historical (and, ultimately, personal); they are scientific and technical only on a secondary level of "causes." The principal causes of the making of the bomb include Hitler, the Second World War, and the persecution of the Jews in Germany. The bomb was made when it was made, in the way it was made, and for the purposes it was made, not merely because at a certain phase of scientific development a certain stage of technological know-how was reached but principally because in a certain phase of history in the consciousness of certain eminent scientists there had arisen the fear that other scientists might be building an atom bomb for Hitler. Technically speaking, the important stages in a history of the atom bomb are the splitting of the uranium nucleus by neutrons in 1938–1939, the functioning of the first nuclear reactor in Chicago in December, 1942, the exploding of the first bomb in New Mexico in July, 1945, and the bombs finally cast on Japan in August, 1945; but the technological character of these stages ought not obscure the principal motive factors in its creation which, as in every historical act, were formed by personal choices, through historical thinking and historical consciousness, and conditioned by the political, racial, national, religious, and ideological inclinations of responsible men.[22]

We may be too close to assay the meaning of the last twenty-five years with detachment. Yet certain things are hardly arguable about it. While the terrible record (and, what is more important, the defeat) of Hitler Germany discredited, at least for a time, much of the cause of neo-idealism, the world triumph of the Soviet Union

[22] Perhaps it is not fanciful to outline the following correspondences:

1894–1905 Beginning of the breakup of the Newtonian universe, of the Bourgeois Age, of the European political system in the world.

1926–1932 Indeterminacy in physics and in mathematics; neo-idealism and Fascism in Europe; even Russia moves away from internationalism, and the United States from nineteenth-century liberal capitalism.

1941–1945 Manufacture of the first atom bomb; end of the European Age; the United States and the Soviet Union rule Europe and most of the world.

1955– Scattered re-recognitions of a post-modern universe; the American-Soviet atomic monopoly nearing its end; Russian and American influence weakening in Europe.

and especially of the United States after 1945 revitalized the cause, among intellectuals, of neo-positivism. I wrote "especially" of the United States, because the intellectual and the cultural influence of Soviet Russia proved to have been extraordinarily feeble after 1945, even in those countries which now belonged within her political sphere of influence. During the last twenty-five years we have witnessed the widespread and wholesale development of the cultural "Americanization" of much of the world. And yet it is quite possible that this phenomenon of Americanization may have been, by and large, more superficial than it seems at first sight. In most places of the world in the twentieth century "Americanization" simply means "modernization," or, in other words, the adaptation and application of American techniques of mass production and of mass distribution. Still, there are certain reasons to believe that the influences of American forms of thought have not penetrated deeply enough to affect the ways and the preferences of thinking (something that is quite different from the preferences of professional intellectuals) of the nations of Europe at least. I have dealt with this subject in *Decline and Rise of Europe;* let me only add here that one of the reasons for this continuing and, indeed, developing divergence between the United States and Europe is that while the predominant tendency of American thinking is still progressive, on certain levels of European thought after 1945 a predominant tendency has been "neo-conservative.[23] "Marxism," said the physicist Max Born in 1957, "teaches that the communist economy is a historical necessity and derives its fanaticism from this belief. This idea comes from physical determinism, which itself arises from Newton's celestial mechanics. But, in fact, physics abandoned this theory about thirty years ago . . . in the light of which"—and, let me add, in the light, too, of historical experience—"the communist belief that Marxist predictions will necessarily be realized appears grotesque. American thought," Born continued, "for its part, is at the mercy of a superficial pragmatism which confuses truth and utility. I cannot

[23] The Swiss philosophical writer Peter Duerrenmatt (not to be confused with the dramatist) in 1960: "In the last resort, the European resistance was conservative. A kind of conservative attitude . . . has contributed to the fact that the politics of Europe after 1945 have been something more than merely successful experiments in economic and social life." "The question whether Europe will survive depends on the strength or on the weakness of its peoples' will to exist."

adhere to it. . . . Europe is not bound to one or the other of these extreme and absurd doctrines. . . ." This is a prototypical expression of a European attitude seeking increasingly for its independence from accepted Soviet and American patterns of thought (it is perhaps symbolic how the date of the Born statement nearly coincides with de Gaulle's assumption of power in France in 1958). Born's condemnation of the United States is perhaps unduly summary and primitive in its phrasing; I shall have something to say about the increasingly elusive essence of "utility" a few pages later, as I shall attempt to demonstrate how the utility of much of present-day technology has become more and more questionable; and I must insist, too, that more and more Americans are beginning, for the first time, to nurture doubts about their once unquestioned idea of technological progress, while it is by no means sure that Europeans, at least in the near future, will reject the bondage of that "Americanization" of life (and, to some extent, of thought) which irritates men of the stamp of Born.

But this is a question of the future with which we are not here concerned. What concerns us here is the necessary recognition that the development of the really significant intellectual currents of our times, and of their correspondences, are, at least for the time being, disturbingly obstructed and severely circumscribed by the interregnal conditions of our culture at present. I have said some things about this interregnum in Chapter I of this book. I shall not repeat them here. It is true, as Heisenberg said in his Gifford Lectures, that "the connections between the different branches of science have [recently] become much more obvious than they have at any previous time." Yet it is also true that the breakdown in internal communications, which is so characteristic of our interregnum, has led to the inability and the unwillingness of eminent scientists and intellectuals to act upon these connections, not to speak of their failure to recognize their inherent correspondences. Indeed, for the first time in many centuries, the basic assumptions of certain men of science and of certain professional intellectuals, otherwise members of the same culture and in some instances of the same country, are worlds apart. This general breakdown of communications has led, as we have seen earlier, to the condition that during our interregnum, ideas, all asseverations to the contrary, are moving with painful slowness indeed. And yet already in 1895 (again the date is significant) Gustave Le Bon could write that "the true historical upheavals are not those which astonish us by their grandeur and violence. The only important changes whence the renewal of civilizations results, affect ideas, conceptions, beliefs. The memorable events of history are the visible effects of the invisible changes of human thought. . . . The present epoch," he continued, "is one of these critical moments in which the thought of mankind is undergoing a process of transformation. . . . The ideas of the past, although half destroyed, being still very powerful, and the ideas which are to replace them being still in process of formation, [our] age represents a period of transition and anarchy. . . ." Indeed even now most people, including historians, and even including large numbers of applied scientists, have not recognized that the notion of scientific certitude was mortally wounded between 1895 and 1930. It was in 1941, for instance, that Jacques Barzun attempted to demonstrate to Americans, within the covers of one book, that the nineteenth-century idea of progress was full of holes, passé, even though Barzun recognized that the hold of old ideas was still very strong.[24] "To reverse such ingrained habits of thought and work," he wrote then, "cannot be done in an instant. It will take much work and a very different kind of thought in a fresh direction. But the difficulty of the task should only spur our efforts in the one realm which we have under some sort of immediate control: our minds. Failing this, the possibilities which Henry Adams foresaw seem likely to come true all at once: cynical pessimism among the leaders of mankind; a vast revival of semi-religious superstition; a brutish dictatorship by capital or labor." Those, then, who read Barzun's *The House of Intellect,* published nearly a quarter of a century later, will recognize that this author has even deepened his own humanistic pessimism about the reign of

---

[24] In *Darwin, Marx, Wagner: Critique of a Heritage.* "No greater mistake can be made than to consider Nietzsche's break with Wagner a personal quarrel resulting from a difference of opinion about music. It is much more. It is the first critical repudiation of the second half of the nineteenth century by a herald of the twentieth." But: ". . . the general public of our century has never departed from the Darwinian faith that the scientist is the man to do it." Also: ". . . what physicists have learned from the history of their science has not yet been learned by the biologists"—and let me add that this is as true today as when this was written more than a quarter-century ago—"which accounts for the curious fact that while some physicists are becoming a new sort of 'vitalists,' most biologists are still for the most part mechanists—like the ordinary man."

cynical pessimism among the intellectual technocrats now clambering into positions of leadership in our Western societies.

For it is not among the common people that the slowness in the development of new ideas is most apparent. As Arthur Koestler wrote in *The Sleepwalkers* (1958), "The inertia of the human mind and its resistance to innovation are most clearly demonstrated not, as one might expect, by the ignorant mass—which is easily swayed once its imagination is caught—but by the professionals with a vested interest in the monopoly of learning. . . . Innovation is a twofold threat to academic mediocrities: it endangers their oracular authority, and it evokes the deeper fear that their whole, laboriously constructed intellectual edifice might collapse." And not only to academic mediocrities. Perhaps it is not even so much the hold of old ideas as of certain habits and tendencies of thought which is so deadening. "In our mind and speech the world is still Darwinian, Marxian, Wagnerian, but beneath the thick crust are the fires of new thoughts which must modify or destroy the old," Barzun wrote in 1941. *But the crust is very thick.* "It has taken more than a quarter of a century to get from the first idea of the existence of energy quanta to a real understanding of the quantum theoretical laws," Heisenberg wrote. "This indicates the great change that had to take place in the fundamental concepts concerning reality before we could understand the new situation." And despite the very great importance of these recognitions, "very little has been gained for the general situation of our age . . . very little of this development has reached the public so far . . . [even though] it looks very much as if this development [would] have repercussions in the sphere of philosophy." This was written more than ten years ago: yet nothing much has happened. The new ideas are difficult to accept, wrote the American mathematical physicist Banesh Hoffmann more than twenty years ago, "because we still instinctively strive to picture them in terms of the old-fashioned particle, despite Heisenberg's indeterminacy principle. We still shrink from visualizing an electron as something which having motion may have no position, and having position may have no such thing as motion or rest." For this difficulty of seeing involves more than difficulties of visualization that are caused by old and ingrained habits of an optical nature. It involves the deeper difficulty, consequent to the condition that we see with our minds and, indeed, with our hearts: that, to a considerable extent, we see what we want to see. Perhaps this is why even Freud could not liberate himself from certain nineteenth-century concepts of science and of causality, and why Einstein stuck so blindly and obstinately to the contractual idea of the world, to the symmetrical and mathematical concept of order in an Old Testament manner ("God does not play dice," he said) as he would reject Heisenberg's recognitions. Like the majority of scientists, Einstein refused to think through some of the fundamental implications of the discoveries of the new physics, even though, in the long run, these implications might become more important than the discoveries themselves. And it is perhaps precisely because of their unwillingness to break with certain intellectual categories and mental circumscriptions, as well as because of certain historical and political conditions, that the reputations of Freud and Einstein,[25] especially among intellectuals in the English-speaking world, are still so high.

I said "intellectuals," because they are especially involved in the conditions of our interregnum. We have now entered a phase in history when the monopoly over learning and the publication of intelligence have fallen to professional intellectuals—an anomaly, especially in the history of the English-speaking peoples, going against the grain of the nonintellectual genius of their character, and against their traditions of nonspecialization and of common sense (the noun "intellectual," designating a specific kind of brain-person, became widespread in English only around 1890; like "intelligentsia," it was a term imported from Socialist and Russian usage). This emergence of a meritocracy whereby distinctions of formal education replace the older distinctions of wealth and of birth is, contrary to the once optimistic pipe dreams of nineteenth-century liberals and Socialists, a poisonous development. It is, at any rate, typical of our interregnum.

(4) End of the Modern Age

And now I must end this book by returning to the theme with which I began it: the growing disillusionment of people with what-

---

[25] "Future generations may well call our era the Age of Einstein. . . ." Jeremy Bernstein in a slick review-article on the history of quantum physics in *The New Yorker*, April 19, 1966.

ever is called "modern," and their increasing doubts about "Progress." We have seen that at the beginning of the Modern Age the idea of progress and the historical consciousness arose together in the minds of men. I have tried to show what has happened—or, rather, what has been happening—to our historical consciousness: how important, and how widespread it has become now, toward the end of the Modern Age. And what has happened to Progress? Something very serious has happened to Progress. Let me show this on a very basic and common-sense level, dealing with what, in everyday parlance, are called "the material facts of everyday life" in the Western world.

It is, simply, that we can no longer expect such radical improvements in our living standards as what had happened to our grandparents and to our great-grandparents in the half-century before the First World War. At any rate, the material conditions in *their* lives changed much more than have ours during the last fifty years. This may be surprising: and yet it is so. Let me illustrate this through a rapid retrospect, for which we are situated propitiously, since the period from the Civil War to World War I and the period from World War I to the present are approximately of the same length. The following comparisons are, moreover, generally valid not only for the United States but for the industrially advanced countries of western Europe. Starting with the most fundamental phenomenon, the average expectancy of life, for all classes, in this portion of the world was 42 to 44 years around 1865; by 1915 it jumped to 58, while by 1965 it climbed slowly to 67. The general average of infant mortality in Europe and North America was nearly 24 percent in the 1860's: this dropped to about 6 percent by 1915, reaching the present plateau of 3 percent two decades ago. Our ancestors were intimately acquainted with the terrors of pain: but by 1914, for the first time in the history of mankind, it was possible for a European or an American to live through long stretches of decades without ever experiencing acute pain in any form. It was not only the advance in anesthetics, it was the great general progress in medicine which had made giant strides during the fifty years before World War I, as indeed the above-mentioned figures indicate; it is true that medical research and certain techniques have achieved astonishing things during the last fifty years dealing with relatively rare diseases and operations: but the over-all portents of these cannot stand comparison with what had happened during the fifty years before World War I, and there is reason to believe, for example, that in 1914 the services of a good family doctor who had graduated from a reputable medical school were in many ways better than of what the average family can avail itself nowadays when general practitioners have become rare and when the once close contact between physician and family is almost non-existent. In 1865 the great majority of the white race was still illiterate; by 1915, for the first time in history, in North America as well as in Europe the great majority of people knew how to read and write. Compulsory public education, in North America and in western and central Europe, by 1914 reached the average age of eleven, and after four or five years of schooling its recipients had acquired a minimum facility of expression, something that can not be taken for granted today. So far as the standard comforts are concerned, very few of our ancestors enjoyed constant heat, running water, ample light one hundred years ago: but all of these amenities—house-wide heating, indoor plumbing, electricity, not to speak of hot water, fans, elevators—were invented during the nineteenth century and they were made available to something close to the majority of the people, at least in the United States, by 1914, the only post-1914 invention of this kind having been air conditioning. Let me repeat: living conditions, for large numbers of people, changed more radically during the fifty years before 1914 than at any time in recorded history before or after. The same thing is true about communications. Napoleon could progress from the Seine to the Tiber no faster, and no differently, than could Julius Caesar two thousand years before: yet a century later one could travel from Paris to Rome in less than twenty-four hours in a comfortable sleeping-car. The locomotive, the steamship, the motorcar, the submarine, the airplane; the radio, the telegraph, the telephone—they were all invented and put into practice before 1914, the only post-1914 invention of this kind having been television. Of course there is a difference between the supersonic jet plane and the Wright Brothers' contraption, but it is a difference in degree not in kind. Sixty-five years ago one could travel from New York to Philadelphia in one hour and forty minutes, on comfortable and well-appointed trains available at every hour of the day. Not only have comfortable and well-appointed trains, at least in the United States, nearly ceased to exist; but also, jet planes and superhighways and all the recent governmental double-talk about high-speed rail lines not-withstanding, I strongly doubt that we shall in our lifetime travel from city to city in such speed and comfort as could our ancestors more than fifty years ago.

It is, of course, true that much of the progress in the fifty years before 1914 affected only a small portion of mankind, certain nations and certain social classes; but, then, this survey of progress is neces-sarily restricted to what we, with some imprecision, call "the Western world" (not to speak of the condition that the very idea of progress was a specifically Western idea). Moreover, in the United States at least, these radical improvements in the conditions of life already before 1914 had begun to affect the majority of people: they were no longer restricted for the use of a minority. My purpose, in any event, was not to paint the picture of a golden age before 1914: those Good Years were as maggot-ridden as any others in the history of mankind: all I wished to suggest is that those who keep talking about our Revolutionary Age of Dizzying Change and of Unprece-dented Progress literally don't know what they are talking about.

What we have seen during the last fifty years are improvements and ever more widespread applications of earlier inventions as they have been made available to millions. Yet even in the routine spheres of life it may be arguable that the momentum of progress has slowed down to a mechanical crawl. With all the machines at our disposal, it is at least possible that many of the material standards of life for large numbers of people—especially in the most "ad-vanced" nations of the Western world—may have declined as much as they have advanced. I do not only mean the upper classes; more is involved here than the servant problem or inflation, which are consequences rather than causes. These matters have little to do with per capita money income or with other economic statistics: they are involved, instead, with such things as the declining quality and the deteriorating durability of materials and, what is more important, with the declining sense of the permanence of personal possessions (very much including the increasing impermanence of residence)—all matters that reflect the general feeling of insecurity and of rootlessness which is characteristic of our times, and perhaps of every interregnum in history.

If we, then, turn to the motivating (that is, accepted and accept-able) ideas toward the end of the Modern Age we will find not only that, as I have been insisting often in this book, they move remarkably slowly, but also that they are painfully old. International organization, world government, disarmament, the population explosion, the administrative society, the welfare state, mass production, automation, progressive education, psychoanalysis, abstract art, Greenwich Village, tubular furniture, emancipated women —they were current, accepted, in evidence, *idées reçues* in . . . 1913. After everything is said, Kennedy's (and Dulles', and Acheson's, and Hull's, and Hoover's) ideas were souped-up Wilsonian ideas, whereas Wilson's view of the world and of America's role in the world was very different from Lincoln's. . . . Our avantgarde have become a kind of rear-guard. Consider the recent (1963) exhibition on the fiftieth anniversary of the famous 1913 Armory Show. The great jump was that from Ingres to Cézanne, not from Picasso to Picasso; from the *Salon des refusés* in 1863 to Utrillo, Pissarro, Vuillard in 1913 not from Armory Show (1913) to Armory Show (1963). From Tennyson to Yeats, from Brahms to Ravel, from Renan to Valéry, from realists to surrealists—jumps, all kinds of jumps; from Stravinsky to Stravinsky, from Kandinsky to Jackson Pollock, from the Dadaists to Genêt, from Blok to Yevtushenko, from Robinson Jeffers to Allen Ginsburg, from Frank Lloyd Wright to Buckminster Fuller a hobbled skip, and I am mentioning what are nowadays called "the exciting people," the "forward-looking minds" of our times.

I, for one, wish that President Kennedy had read something like the following passage from Georges Bernanos before he, in 1961, exhorted the people of the United States to "get moving ahead." "This world believes it is moving ahead," Bernanos wrote in 1946,

because it holds a most materialistic idea of moving ahead. A world in motion is a world that clambers up slopes, not one that tumbles down. No matter how fast you fall down a hill, all you are doing is falling down. Between those who think that civilization is a victory for man in the struggle against the determinism of things . . . and those who want to make of man a thing among things, there is no possible scheme of reconciliation. . . .[26]

26 "The European Spirit and the World of Machines" in *Last Essays*. Also: "The democracies have been decomposing, too, but some decompose more quickly than others. They have been decomposing into bureaucracies, suffering from it as a diabetic does from sugar, at the expense of his own substance. In the most advanced cases, this bureaucracy itself decomposes into its most degraded form, police bureaucracy. At the end of this evolution, all that is left of the state is the police. . . ."

I often think that in the Western world—and perhaps particularly in the United States—a new great division among men may have already begun to form. On the political and ideological level this is obscured by the continuing deadweight of old categories of ideas and of their antiquated terminology. As we have seen earlier, the adjectives "liberal," "conservative" and even the designations "Right" and "Left" make less and less sense now. Indeed, it was as early as a century ago, around 1870, that the importance and the meaning of the classical nineteenth-century antithesis of "liberals" vs. "conservatives" was beginning to fade. During the eighty-odd years that followed, liberalism and conservatism were giving way to the confrontation—and, eventually, to the compounding—of two rather more deep-seated and more elementary forces, nationalism and socialism. Is it not possible that the principal division in the political thinking of the future may crystallize on yet another, more profound level: between partisans of reason and partisans of progress, between those who *still* see no sense in resisting the increasing mechanization of the world and those who *no longer* share this outdated idea of Progress? I certainly find it to be significant that in the United States the opposition to superhighways and the moon rockets and computers and large-scale construction programs and supermodern gadgetry and gimmickry is crystallizing, perhaps for the first time, in the minds of the very people—"liberals" and "progressives"—who in the past used to be among the enthusiastic propagators of a materialist optimism; and, what is more important, among all kinds of people whom the old political and ideological categories no longer fit. Yet much time will have to pass until this opposition to the still prevalent ideas of Progress becomes widespread enough to be effective: for this requires not only increasing efforts of propaganda but increasing consciousness in the minds of people of the reasons for their opposition—a difficult process, since, as we have seen, many decent people have not yet succeeded in thinking things through, in freeing their minds from many of the corroded shackles of ideas that were, after all, progenitors of certain monstrosities of which their minds have become only belatedly aware.

That epoch in the history of Western civilization that we call the Modern Age (it may be called, with more or less equal justice, the Political Age or the Atlantic Age or the Bourgeois Age, it matters hardly which), which opened about three or four hundred years ago, is now passing out of our lives, but, of course, not wholly: it is also changing into something new. As Ortega put it in 1914 (there is something symbolic in the coincidence that the printing of this first book of his, the *Meditations on Quixote,* was completed by a Madrid firm on July 21, 1914), each historical epoch is involved with a basic interpretation of man: but "the epoch does not bring the interpretation; it actually *is* such an interpretation." Consider, then, three stages in our view of human nature. The writers of the *Encyclopédie, circa* 1760: "Since all our direct knowledge comes by the senses, all our Ideas are consequently due to Sensations." Darwin, *circa* 1860: "I look upon all human feeling as traceable to some germ in the animals." *Circa* 1960, this no longer makes sense. On the occasion of the one-hundreth anniversary of Darwin's *Origin* (1859), Joseph Wood Krutch, an American humanist and naturalist, surprised the readers of *The American Scholar* by setting up Darwin's view of human nature as against Dr. Johnson's radically different view of human nature and of human knowledge in *Rasselas* (1759), and expressing clearly his preference for Johnson. "Between the two centenaries," Krutch mused, ". . . there yawns a gulf that we may or may not someday cross again." I hope that we may: but, then, this involves a mental bridge which we must cross before we get to it: we must recognize that the possibilities for crossings exist, though on a different level than heretofore. Or consider the prototypal "problem of modern man," as Aldous Huxley put it after the First World War. "God as truth, God as $2 \times 2 = 4$," that's not "so clearly all right," say Gumbril Jr. in *Antic Hay.* Is "there a chance of their being the same?" Are "there bridges to join the two worlds?" Well—has this 1922 problem retained its freshness? doesn't it have a curiously musty, old-suit touch, like the theatricality of an old Bloomsbury cape? and I mean, even to people who may not be aware that the "gap" between "relative" moral and "absolute" scientific truths no longer exists, since, to start with, $2 \times 2 = 4$ ceased to be an Absolute Truth? "Scripture says that the sun moves and the earth is stationary, and science says that the earth moves and the sun is comparatively at rest," Newman wrote in 1845. "How can we determine which of these opposite statements is the very truth till we know what motion is? If our idea of motion is but an accidental result of our present senses, neither proposition is true and both are true; neither true philosophically; both true for certain practical purposes in the system in which they are respectively found." Fifty years later, in 1895, Andrew Dickson White[27] in his A History of the Warfare of Science with Theology in Christendom attacked this statement with contempt. "A hopelessly skeptical utterance," White said. "For what were the youth of Oxford led into such bottomless depths of disbelief as to any real existence of truth or any real foundation for it? Simply to save an outworn system of interpretation into which the gifted preacher happened to be born." Yet at least in one important sense Newman's 1845 idea of the universe (or, rather, of our participation in the universe) has proved to be more enduring than White's 1895 positivism, just as some of us find Johnson's 1759 views of human nature more relevant to our lives than Darwin's 1859 propositions. In 1958 Professor Polykarp Kusch, an American physicist and Nobel prize winner, found it necessary to write in the Columbia University Forum: "I think that the modern scientific mind would be less outraged by Newman's statement than were his critics at the end of the nineteenth century; it would concede that Newman had some prevision of ideas that have become basic to much of contemporary scientific thought." (It is only that few "modern scientific minds" have either the convictions or the courage which would compel them to "concede" this as Professor Kusch has done.)

Between 1450 and 1690 there occurred a revolution in our concepts of the universe, at a time when most people in Western Christendom (the term "Europe" had only a geographical meaning in 1450) still believed in the divinity of Christ. By the end of this transition, great thinkers, such as Newton, practiced outwardly while they no longer believed.[28] After 1900 there began another revolution in our concepts of the universe, at a time when most

[27] It is perhaps significant that this social Darwinist and Teutonophile public figure was also the first president of the American Historical Association.

[28] Kepler: "The purpose of the world and of all creation is man. I believe that it is for this very reason that God chose the earth, designed as it is for bearing and nourishing the Creator's true image, for revolving among the planets. . . ." But Sir George Clark about Newton: "In 1698 the English parliament, of which Sir Isaac Newton had been and was again to be a member, passed an Act which made it a penal offense to deny the divinity of Christ. After Newton's death it was found from his unpublished papers that he himself did not believe in the doctrine of the Trinity as he understood it; but the fact was not clearly published until the twentieth century."

people (including many churchgoers) do not believe in God, though a minority may—again or anew.[29] Certainly now, a century after Pio Nono's Encyclical Letter and *Syllabus Errorum* (1864), which marked the maximum point of divergence between science and religion, the pendulum has swung back so that religion and science may be at hailing distance from each other. But this simile of a pendulum, with its circumscribed two-dimensional swinging back and forth, is not quite right.* Our recognitions are historical: our historical consciousness has been evolving, that is, deepening; there is progress, here, after all, progress of a kind: the new recognitions develop on a higher level. (New religious recognitions, too, do not signify a return to earlier believing: they signify the results of non-unbelieving.) Descartes's mathematical conception of the world was not only insufficiently religious, it was unhistorical —which is why Pascal has at least as much to tell us as Descartes (and Tocqueville at least as much as Voltaire[30] and surely more than Marx).

As the Modern Age emerged, there emerged with it the modern concept of "Europe"—a political concept of a system of states which was replacing the earlier concept of Western "Christendom." This modern political concept crystallized during the second half of the seventeenth century, at the same time when the new idea of the universe and of the physical world had become accepted among savants, and when a number of important turning-points occurred in the history of the Western world; among other things, it was then that the influence of Russia and of North America on the political history of Europe became discernible. Now, toward the end of the Modern Age, the *political* primacy of Europe is gone; yet it is now that the adjective "European" shows some signs of acquiring a *cultural* sense, beyond its geographical or political meaning. This de-

[29] Planck: "For religion, the idea of God is at the beginning; for science the idea of God is at the end." Ellen Juhnke during the discussion after Heisenberg's 1958 lecture on Planck: "Is it not an extraordinary thing to see such syntheses being outlined in our atomic and atomized era?"

[30] Voltaire thought that the most important person in modern history was Newton. So did Marx. Yet Marx's contemporary Tocqueville a century after Voltaire, a century before Heisenberg (1858): "A hypothesis which permits the prediction of certain effects that always reoccur under the same conditions does, *in its way* [my italics], amount to a demonstrable truth. Even the Newtonian system has no more than such a foundation."

velopment has, of course, little to do with economic associations and with international bureaucracies; but it may have something to do with the recent weakening of Russian and of American influences over Europe, influences which seemed to have been so dominant after 1945. It is by no means certain that we shall see an independent European confederation (note that I am not even speaking of a "United" Europe). Yet there is something symbolic in the condition that now, when "Western man" confronts himself alone, the notion of "Europe" may—but only may—assume a higher sense, too.[31]

Meanwhile ideas that had once come from Europe, the consequences of European genius, may destroy the world, a possibility which exists because of the fateful divergence between two forms of thought, between historical thinking and scientific method, these two supreme achievements of the passing Modern Age. I have tried to assert the hierarchy of their relationship throughout this book, that scientific method is inseparable from scientific thinking that is, really, historical thinking. This is now recognized by some of us, including certain scientists: but long perilous times may have to pass until these recognitions bear fruits for our childrens' children.

On the one hand our interregnum is more dangerous and it might last longer than we think. "We live at a time," Tocqueville wrote 130 years ago, "that has witnessed the most rapid changes of opinion

[31] Burckhardt *circa* 1875: "Is the tendency of Europe still a rising or a falling one? This can never be decided through calculations. Its peoples are, still, not exhausted in a physical sense, and in a spiritual and moral sense one must always reckon with the existence of still invisible forces. Even now."

Christopher Dawson *circa* 1955: "Neither Christianity nor humanism is dead. They still possess an infinite capacity of spiritual regeneration and cultural renaissance. What is passing away is the utopian idealism which was the original inspiration of all the revolutionary ideologies. Now that they have been brought down from the clouds to solid earth they have gained temporal power, but they have lost their old appeal. In so far as they continue to press their total claim to man's spiritual allegiance, they must inevitably drive civilization further and further toward nihilism and self-destruction.

"The vital task of Europe at the present time is to resist this tendency and to recover and fortify the two great spiritual traditions which are the roots of its culture. This is a difficult task, and one which cannot be achieved without great moral and intellectual efforts. But it is by no means an impossible task, and since Europe was the original creator of the ideologies, she has a special responsibility and a special opportunity for finding a solution to the problems which the ideologies have raised."

in the minds of men; nevertheless it may be that the leading opinions of society will before long be more settled than they have been for several centuries in our history; that time has not yet come, but it may perhaps be approaching." That time has certainly come. "It is believed by some that modern society will be always changing. . . ." he went on. "For myself, I fear that it will ultimately be too invariably fixed in the same institutions, the same prejudices, the same manners, so that mankind will be stopped and circumscribed; that the mind will swing backwards and forwards forever without begetting fresh ideas; that man will waste his strength in bootless and solitary trifling, and, though in continual motion, that humanity will cease to advance." This kind of enormous intellectual stagnation marks already the age in which we now live.

On the other hand the striving toward harmony has not ceased: and some of us may glimpse, here and there, that kind of hope which is on the other side of despair. "Our civilization," Ortega wrote in one of his last essays, a decade or so ago,[32] "knows that its principles are bankrupt—dematerialized—and that is why it has doubts about itself. But it does not seem that there ever was a civilization that died, and a full death, from an attack of doubt. I seem, on the contrary, to recall that civilizations have perished for the opposite reason—from petrification or arteriosclerosis of their beliefs."

On the one hand, not only may the Modern Age or the European Age be over. Something much more important has happened. We have created monstrous institutions of scientific technology that are governed by puny men; and it is precisely because science is part and parcel of human history that, for the first time, THE END OF THE WORLD IS IN SIGHT.

On the other hand, this now so suddenly closer Day of Doom can be adjourned, indeed it can be indefinitely postponed—by the sheer quality of our determination to live. And this quality—ultimately, and really, a quality of consciousness—has now become involved,

---

[32] 1951, 1957 ("The Past and Future of Modern Man"). But already in the 1930's in "History as a System": "Physical science can throw no clear light on the human element. Very well. This means simply that we must shake ourselves free, radically free, from the physical approach to the human element. Let us instead accept this in all its spontaneity, just as we see it and come upon it. In other words, the collapse of physical reason leaves the way clear for vital, historical reason." (I read this in 1959.)

irretrievably, with our historical way of thinking, with this new child which, out of the ancient marriage of realism and idealism, may yet become Europe's greatest gift to mankind.

POSTSCRIPT

Historical Consciousness is a reasonably precise title for this book in English, since all of us are historical thinkers now, while some of us are professional historians only by choice. This is, too, why I must say something about the history of this book, one of its principal arguments being that the history of anything may form a reasonable explanation thereof.

During my university years I first felt a vague dissatisfaction with the professional circumscriptions of academic historiography; I was impressed with those historians and teachers who suggested that historical materials are potentially limitless. Early during my career as an English-speaking historian I learned how the meaning of documentary evidence may be distorted or obscured by a management of words, that a historical account of certain events may be written in which all details would be "factually" correct and yet the over-all impression would be false. At the same time I was attracted by the relationships of certain factors in international history, involving such things as the endurance of national characteristics or the movements of popular sentiment. I wanted to explore and describe the functions of some of these relationships; and in August, 1955, I set out to write the first chapters of what was then to have been a large-scale historical study of them. In the first two chapters I was about to attempt a description of what I saw as the problems of historiography peculiar to our democratic age, a preoccupation which crystallized in my mind around the phrase, "the change in the texture of history." This crystallization was decisive; for soon thereafter I convinced myself that this should be the central theme of my book. I changed my scope and set out on a revised course. (In a neoclassical mood I gave the title *Prohistoriographica,* in the seventeenth-century manner, to this putative book with a high poop and full of sail.)

My course remained the same; but I changed the book again. I had grown sufficiently sensitive to the traditions of English prose to comprehend that if I wanted to write anything that would be worthwhile, it was not enough to write this kind of book in my capacity of a professional intellectual for other professional specialists. More important was the condition that I became more and more interested not only in the change in "the texture of history" but in what I would call "the structure of events." It was around this time that the title *Historical Thinking* crystallized in my mind.

This was a crucial time in the composition of this book. A freely offered and broad-minded grant from RELM Foundation, together with a sabbatical half-year, made it possible for me to complete large portions of the first draft. Then, in the fall of 1959, when the manuscript of that draft was nearly completed, I was exhausted, and plagued by certain doubts. In my chapter addressed to contemporary history I was exhorting historians to write history rather than write about history. But wasn't this precisely what I have been doing in this book? What was the use of all of these theses and theories and arguments? As Santayana said, "In the great ages of art nobody talked of aesthetics." Wouldn't it be a more reasonable thing to take a piece of recent history *and write it*—and demonstrate thereby the validity of my arguments about the hierarchy of certain historical forces? On a yellow pad I wrote out a table of contents for two books. One of these potential histories would deal with the world conflict of the United States and Russia. My editor at Doubleday Anchor Books took up my suggestion. I wrote *A History of the Cold War.* It is bad form for an author to refer to his other books but I cannot avoid mentioning this narrative essay in contemporary history, since it played a role in the writing of *Historical Consciousness.* First, this turned out to be a welcome interruption in more than one way; my mind was refreshed. Second, "the working model" worked. It is thus that the structure of *A History of the Cold War* manifested some of the ideas of *Historical Consciousness,* especially those set forth in the present Chapter V;[1] conversely, some of my illustrations in the text of that chapter have been taken from *A History of the Cold War.*

An eminent publishing house gave me now (1961) a contract for what was then still entitled *Historical Thinking.* Yet as I was preparing the manuscript for publication the prospects of this book darkened before me. Certain editorial suggestions revealed certain fundamental misunderstandings of the general purpose of this book and of the thinking of its author. More important, this was happening at a time when wholly unreadable books have been spewed out with automated ease, and when academic reputations were being established on the occult grounds of obscure vocabularies. (With the help of the Rockefeller Foundation this book would not have been written.) Yet I myself was not convinced completely of the merits of the style of the then manuscript; therefore, in 1962, I set myself to recast the book anew. I reduced the text; depressed as I had become with the cramming of junk that passes for furniture in most academic inns and houses of intellect, I threw out almost all of what is nowadays—often wrongly—called "scholarly equipment." I boiled away all of the connecting tissue, by which I mean that the ideas of the book now stood alone in separate passages, merely following each other in isolated chunks. The new form of this book now emerged, stark and rough on purpose, like a primitive stone cathedral of *idées mères.* I made another unorthodox change, as I chose to introduce each chapter by a summing-up of the personal history of the development of those among my ideas which were relevant to the theme of that chapter: but I tried to make it clear that this somewhat unusual practice was nothing like intellectual autobiography but that it flowed from my conviction that historical

---

[1] *A History of the Cold War* was divided in two parts, "The Main Events" and "The Main Movements." In introducing the latter I wrote: "I am attempting a comparative description of . . . the movements, developments, tendencies of the American and Russian societies, states, nations, concepts, and ideas . . . on successive levels. Thus the order of this second part is as follows: IX. The Two Peoples: the tendencies of their societies. X. The Two Societies: the tendencies of their political theories. XI. The Two States: the development of their national interests. XII. The Two Nations: the development of their national character. XIII. Conclusion: the great historical movements of our times. This successive order is not an arbitrary one. We shall proceed, by and large, from what is most obvious but least significant to what may be most significant and perhaps least obvious."

knowledge is inevitably personal. I gave this manuscript to my then publisher in October, 1963. We could not agree. I put the manuscript away.

Now I turned again to the writing of another book which sprung from my convictions about the shallowness of much of what passes for the study of "international relations" nowadays. But I could not, for long, keep away from my principal concern; and the last chapter of *Decline and Rise of Europe* (published in 1965) was a kind of summary of some of the arguments of the present work. After my return from a year's professorship in France I concluded that I must yet write a new, abbreviated and discursive version of this book, about which I was also preparing a series of short lectures to undergraduates. Through a chance encounter in the house of our neighbors and friends I met my present editor and publisher who gave me the encouragement I needed. I began this last, and if I may say so, succinct version in March, 1966, and finished it in May, 1967. Because of the publication of another book with the title of *Historical Thinking* I changed the title to *Historical Consciousness* which I now indeed prefer.

When I began this book I was a young man; by now I have lived longer than I shall live. When I began it I had lived in the United States for less than a decade; soon after its publication I shall have lived more of my life here than in my native country. During the twelve years of its composition the intellectual climate, perhaps especially in the English-speaking countries, has worsened. So far as the narrowly particular theme of *Historical Consciousness* is concerned, during the last twelve years there has been increasing interest among specialists in philosophical and methodological theorizings about history; but their speculations, with few noteworthy exceptions, have been ordinarily chaotic and extraordinarily feeble. (While in 1955 an afterglow of the neo-humanistic and Christian-democratic intellectual atmosphere that had followed World War II still illuminated the speculations of theorists of history in the Western world, by the early Sixties—especially in the English-speaking countries—this has given way to a confused vogue of neo-positivism and neo-Marxism, amounting to little more than to artificially sophisticated reformulations of the, in reality, antiquated and corroded categories of social scientism, a development confirming, alas, General de Gaulle's political assertions to the effect that the English Channel is still at least as wide as is the Atlantic Ocean.) The broader and more widespread aspects of intellectual endeavor, too, have been marked by alarming symptoms of dissolution, including that of the Anglo-Saxon traditions of common sense and of the English language, the preoccupation with its guardianship having been adandoned by most intellectuals for more advantageous occupations. ("It will never be known," wrote Péguy in *Notre Patrie,* "what acts of cowardice have been motivated by the fear of not looking sufficiently progressive.")[2] Yet these melancholy developments have not weakened my belief that among all kinds of people, in these very times, and even in the United States, appetite for all kinds of historical knowledge, and their historical consciousness in many different ways, were growing. Thus, again, my conviction has been the very opposite of Lincoln Steffens' celebrated dictum when he, returning from the Soviet Union to the United States about the time that I was born, said that "he saw the future and it worked." More than two decades later I fled my native country, as she had fallen into the clutches of the Soviet Union, because I saw that the Soviet system was not the future and that it did not work. I saw the future: and it was the past. Of course I was a historian, not a scientist or a social engineer. But there was more than that. I came to the United States twenty-one years ago precisely because in many ways it represented the past, because it was a country where after two world wars many of the liberal decencies of the nineteenth century were still working, where personal freedoms, academic liberties, certain rights to privacy still existed. And here I saw a people who were about to grow out of those cramped mental habits of late adolescence when sharp but undiscriminating eyes are narrowly fixed at an illusory future; I saw many among them beginning to be saddened and solidified by the sense of the past. I could not then, and I cannot still now believe that the future of the West is California. The future *is* the past: I have not departed from this belief: I have but recognized some of its implications.

[2] But I have been impressed, too, by what he wrote to Sorel: "You are right, but one has no right to be right unless one is willing personally to pay the price of demonstrating the rightness of the truth."

I have nothing to say about the method and the style and the organization of this book which must speak for itself. Still, I must anticipate criticism on two points. First, I omitted a bibliography because of the large scope of this book: for in this kind of work even the most extensive bibliography, no matter how impressive its equipment, would amount to padding. Second, I must defend myself against the possible charge that I may have relied heavily on certain "conservative" thinkers, such as Tocqueville, Burckhardt, Ortega, Huizinga, Valéry, etc. I am not A Conservative, and I have not relied on them. I included passages from their various writings only for the sake of illustrating my often necessarily short expositions of certain arguments. This illustrative, and not exegetical, character of my quotes should also appear from the condition that I have included them, for the most part, in a somewhat unorthodox fashion, in footnotes. The two exceptions to this practice are Tocqueville and Heisenberg, on certain writings of each of whom I have drawn considerably in a subchapter. Consequently I cannot avoid mentioning here two snippets of auto-history.

My interest in Tocqueville's writings preceded my speculations on the texture of history, while some of my Tocqueville studies, manifested, in part, by an article and a book, took place also during the composition of *Historical Consciousness*. Yet from my reading of Tocqueville, more than a dozen years ago, I gained conclusions that are somewhat different from those of my American friends. Whereas Tocqueville, perhaps for the first time, provided them with the example of a respectable modern thinker who was critical of democracy, it was Tocqueville who reconciled me to democracy. Whereas Tocqueville pushed them a little to the "Right," he moved me toward the "Left." Many modern scholars have failed to see that Tocqueville was a demophile as much as he was a demophobe, that he was something more than a liberal conservative or a conservative liberal, that he did not quite belong together with Mill, Bagehot, Acton, his Victorian English contemporaries, conservative liberals who, with all of their more-or-less generous espousal of political liberty, felt and on occasion expressed a deep-seated fear of democracy, a distrust of the people. It was Tocqueville (whose understanding of the sources of the French Revolution was very different from Burke's) who helped me understand the deeper meaning of what Burke meant when he said that the people must never be regarded as incurable.

When I began to write this book in 1955, I was aware of the unorthodoxy of some of my ideas; but I also knew that there is no such thing as a wholly original idea, and I knew something about the contemporary existence of at least similar, and sometimes corresponding, propositions scattered in a variety of expressions by a variety of people, tucked away in odd corners: historians, novelists, philosophers, poets. I was only vaguely aware of the philosophical condition of modern physics at that time. In the winter of 1957–1958 I came upon (and, since I do not believe in "pure chance," I shall not say "entirely by accident") certain writings on the development of quantum physics, including Heisenberg's Gifford Lectures. I was struck immediately by the correspondences of many of our arguments, and by the coincidence with which some of Heisenberg's statements—and sometimes their very phrasing—mirrored my own historical recognitions. Thus my propositions were unexpectedly confirmed from yet another direction. But I also saw that now my task was greater than what I had conceived it to be earlier, that I was face to face with the task of giving a reasonable form to the historical recognition of the existence of a profoundly important and relatively recent development in Western thought. Thus I chose to read more about the historical development of modern physics, all of which meant more work and, as I well knew, more risk, eventually leading to what is now the last chapter of this book. But I shall insist very emphatically that I did not succumb to the temptation of forcing Heisenberg's physics into the Procrustean bed of a "system" of my own; and, while the inclusion of these materials lengthened the argument of this book, it did not change its direction. Let me indeed add that on a certain level of my thinking I may not have been unprepared for this unexpected encounter with Heisenberg in 1958; while I was startled at the sometimes uncanny extent in which some of our key statements happened to coincide, I was not altogether surprised by the correspondence of our recognitions.

So much about the history of my labors. When I exclude all of its interruptions I still find that of the last twelve years I have devoted more than eight to the writing of *Historical Consciousness*. I was set aback when I learned that *Labor ipse voluptas* —"Work Is Joy"—was the motto that the great Ranke had chosen when he was about to be ennobled by the King of Prussia; I rather agree with Pieper, Eliot, Ortega that leisure is the basis of culture. I also believe that while much of this world is absurd, it is still the best of all possible worlds, and that it is not a world of increasing injustice. History is often the story of the crimes and of the follies of mankind, but it is an instructive story: good men and good causes seldom triumph in this world but evil men and evil causes come to ruin in this world in the long run, and sometimes in the short run, too. Coming from a religion which certainly does not promise the triumph of justice and of truth in this world, I have often claimed to see in this condition of the historical corruptibility of evil an *extraordinary* gift by God Who reminded (note the implicit meaning of the historicity of our consciousnesses within this verb to *re-mind*) us of the Word through the Incarnation; Who still conceived this world, otherwise a vale of tears, to be the best of all possible worlds for us; Who does not tempt us beyond our strength; Who made us capable of overcoming despair. Thus it is perhaps not maudlin to admit, in conclusion, that during the composition of this work I have experienced much suffering, and more than a little joy.

1955–1967
"Old Pickering School House"
Williams' Corner, near Phoenixville,
Pennsylvania

CERTAIN NOTES

4   *Unhistorical education*
Orwell about London slums, 1933: "History was the hardest thing to teach them. Dorothy had not realized how hard it is for children who came from poor homes to have even a conception of what history means. Every upper-class person, however ill-informed, grows up with some notion of history; he can visualize a Roman centurion, a mediaeval knight, an eighteenth-century nobleman; the terms Antiquity, Middles Ages, Renaissance, Industrial Revolution evoke some meaning, even if a confused one, in his mind. But these children came from bookless homes and from parents who would have laughed at the notion that the past has any meaning for the present." The difference between 1933 and 1967 is that this attitude is no longer the mark of the untaught and of the bookless: there are millions of university graduates in Europe, America, Russia whose knowledge of history is abysmally low and who think that to laugh at the notion that the past has any meaning for the present is the mark of the progressive intellectual.

5   *Historical consciousness . . . even in California*
I am not referring to the high prices antiques bring in Beverly Hills or in San Francisco, and not to the high prices which bring professional historians to Californian universities and rest-centers. Nor am I referring to American political "conservatism" which is fanatical, ideological, and technological, characterized as it is by a profound ignorance of history together with a vast belief in the efficacy of airplanes. I am referring to evidences of a deepening American desire less for a more meaningful future than for a more meaningful past. I found a startling piece of evidence for this strong (but confused) yearning in the article by the wild young leader of the Berkeley riots in 1964, Mario Savio, significantly entitled "An End to History": ". . . impersonal bureaucracy is the efficient enemy in a 'Brave New World.' . . . The bureaucrat, [the] administrator . . . occupies an a-historical point of view . . . the bureaucrats hold history as ended. As a result significant parts of the population both on campus and off are dispossessed, and these dispossessed are not about to accept this a-historical point of view. . . . [There] is part of a growing understanding among many people in America that history has not ended, that a better society is possible, and that it is worth

dying for . . . an important minority of men and women coming to
the front today have shown that they will die rather than be standardized, replaceable and irrelevant."

6   *Man earlier than natural science*
This fundamentally important epistemological recognition was also
expressed by Goethe, in his *Theory of Colours,* in the Preface of
which he wrote that "strictly speaking, it is useless to attempt to express the nature of a thing abstractedly. Effects we can perceive, and
a complete history of those effects would, in fact, sufficiently define
the nature of the thing itself. We should try in vain to describe a
man's character, but let his acts be collected and an idea of the character will present itself to us . . . [as] the history of an individual
displays his character, so it may here be well affirmed that the history
of science is science itself. We cannot clearly be aware of what we
possess till we have the means of knowing what others possessed
before us. . . ."

8   *Huizinga's definition*
In the Cassirer Festschrift (*Philosophy and History: Essays Presented
to Ernst Cassirer,* Oxford, 1936) Professor D. R. Cousin's translation
is somewhat different: "History is the intellectual form in which a
civilization renders account to itself of its past." Since I do not know
Dutch I am reproducing the German translation (by Professor Werner
Kaegi) of the original which appeared with Huizinga's approval:
"Geschichte ist die geistige Form, in der sich eine Kultur ueber ihre
Vergangenheit Rechenschaft gibt."

11   *Richardson:* Historein
"The verb *historein* occurs only once in the New Testament (Gal.
1:18)—significantly, it relates to St. Paul's having gone to Jerusalem
to 'get to know' Cephas, presumably with a view to acquainting himself with the historical facts of the Christian story from the best available source." Alan Richardson, *History—Sacred and Profane* (The
Bampton Lectures delivered in Oxford in 1962), Philadelphia, 1964.
(One of the few really valuable modest books in English during the
present boom of historists' theoretics: perhaps significantly, the
author is not a professional historian.)

13   *Progress and historical consciousness*
Owen Barfield: "Where we speak of *progress* and *evolution,* the
Middle Ages could speak only of *regeneration* and *amendment.* . . .
When we try combing the dictionaries—Greek, Latin, English, and
others—for words expressing a sense of the 'march of history,' or
indeed of a past or future differing at all essentially from the present,
we are forced to the conclusion that this kind of outlook on time is a
surprisingly recent growth. . . . Perhaps the [medieval] lack of historical imagination is brought home to us most forcibly by the prevalent
belief that—apart from the Chosen People—all the inhabitants of the
pre-Christian world were doomed to eternal exclusion from paradise.
When we recollect that for some time the doctors of medieval universities were obliged to swear upon oath that they would teach nothing

contrary to the doctrines of a Greek philosopher who must already have been in this situation for three hundred years at the birth of the Redeemer, and when we further reflect that it was the acute brains of these very doctors which were engaged in building up our present thinking apparatus, we may well feel inclined to give up as hopeless the task of sympathetically recreating the medieval cosmos in our imaginations—unless we realize, as indeed the history of meanings clearly shows, that it is not merely ideas and theories and feelings which have changed, but the very method of forming ideas and of combining them. . . . Possibly the Middle Ages would have been equally bewildered at the facility with which twentieth-century minds are brought to believe that, intellectually, humanity languished for countless generations in the most childish errors on all sorts of crucial subjects, until it was redeemed by some simple scientific dictum of the last century." *History in English Words*, London, 1926.

14   *Historical awareness; self-awareness*
About historical awareness, Logan Pearsall Smith in *The English Language:* Even more interesting than words as historical documents "is the evidence of language about the growth of the sense of history itself, the change that the modern conceptions of order and progress have produced in our way of regarding past ages." A good example of this is *anachronism*, "used in the seventeenth century for an error in computing time; its modern meaning, first found in Coleridge, is very significant, and conveying as it does the idea of a thing which is appropriate to one age, but out of harmony with another, it expresses a thought, a way of feeling, which is very modern, and which would not have needed expression at an earlier period." About self-awareness: "Probably to each of us the sense of his own personality, the knowledge that he exists and thinks and feels, is the ultimate and fundamental fact of life. But this sense of personality, of the existence of men as separate individuals, is one of the later developments of human thought . . . these changes of language, thought, and feeling were not confined to England, but belonged to a general movement in which the whole of civilized Europe took part—one nation borrowing from the other as new developments arose."

22   *Goethe, Hegel, America, Europe*
Goethe, *Amerika du hast es besser:* "America, you're better off than we are/Than our aged land, the continent/You have no dilapidated castles/No ancient monumental stones./Your soul, your inner life/Unhampered, undisturbed by/Useless memory/And senseless strife." Hegel (the same Hegel who said: "The idea is the absolute"): Amerika, "Land der Sehnsucht für alle die, welche die historische Rüstkammer des alten Europa langweilt": the desired place for all of those who are weary of the historical armory of old Europe.

24   *Asian history*
During the 1957 conference on Asian history in London this was confirmed by earnest and serious Asian historians themselves. Professor Pillay, of Madras University, confessed that "Indians of the past,

despite their high intellectual attainments, lacked the historical spirit."
Dr. C. Hoykaas: "One would be completely at a loss for a picture of
the past if one had to confine one's self to Indonesian 'historiography.'"
Dr. Bambang Utomo: modern Indonesian history has been determined
by propaganda; it is certainly "not solely directed by the search for
truth. . . . Up to this day our historiography has not produced contributions to the science of history. No Indonesian has yet reported discoveries or new facts or unknown documents or new interrelationships
between already known facts or events. All the knowledge of the
[main] authors is based on Dutch literature, or on traditional literature that has been made accessible by Dutch scholars."

24   *Differences in mentality*
The famous letter of the Khadi to Layard: "The thing you ask of me
is both difficult and useless. . . . As to the previous history of this city,
God only knows the amount of dirt and confusion that the infidels
may have eaten before the coming of the sword of Islam. It were un-
profitable for us to inquire into it. O my soul! O my Lamb! Seek not
after the things which concern thee not!"

25   *Physical and spiritual feelings . . .*
To speak of physical *and* spiritual feelings sounds curious nowadays.
But even two hundred years ago people spoke of animal spirits and
of vital spirits and of natural spirits: "animal spirits," before the
seventeenth century, meant spirits spiritual, not zoological, coming
from *anima*=soul. A curious paradox: during our increasing consciousness of ourselves during the last three hundred years we, in the West,
at the same time shallowed our concept of the "mind." Since Descartes we have thought less and less of "spirit." (Despite Descartes
the French escaped some of the debilitating consequences of this
development: at least on occasion their word *esprit* applies to mind
and spirit and soul alike.) No doubt this was an understandable and
sometimes creditable intellectual reaction against sanctimonious
double-talk in the name of "spirituality" and "soulfulness." Still it
meant not a deepening but a shallowing of the terms with which we
had once described the internal processes of our thinking. Then,
around 1890, "spiritual" factors began to reappear again under the
name of "consciousness" (and, of course, of "subconsciousness");
and in the twentieth century we have been ready, again, to acknowledge the existence of such factors—even though we still shy away
from words such as "spirit" and "soul."

25   *Japanese language*
Fosco Maraini: The Japanese language is very abstract: but, still, "it
fails as an instrument of abstract thought; when it comes to the world
of ideas and their logical exposition all the defects of its qualities are
brought harshly to light. Its allusive vagueness . . . makes it incapable
of constructing sentences of unequivocal meaning." (And this illustrates a very important point, to me, which is that the overintellectualization of life—and the oversymbolization of reality—is an Oriental
rather than a typically Western phenomenon.) It confirms, too, what
I noticed during the Second World War: the Japanese regime was less

totalitarian than Stalin's Russia and than Hitler's Germany: yet the most fantastic exaggerations and untruths were to be found not in the Russian or German but in the Japanese war communiqués. Perhaps they reflected the kind of tradition according to which it was a serious crime to bring bad news to the emperor. Again, Maraini: " 'Beauty is truth, truth beauty' illustrates another aspect of our western attitude. Not only must beauty shine out in the world, but it is linked by subtle, ancient and deep subterranean veins with truth." And not only with *truth*; also with *right*, a word which, for example, is relatively recent in the Japanese language, originating with the modernizing revolution of 1868. Maraini: "The concept of 'right' in the East is entirely different from that with which we are familiar; a right is not a right in our sense, something to which you are inherently entitled by virtue of your existence, but a concession granted from outside and above, and therefore liable at any time to be revoked."

26   *Soviet "sources"*
It is perhaps not a coincidence that the finest Russian historians were the most thoroughly "Westernized" ones (Vinogradoff, Rostovtzeff, Karpovich, Florinsky). During my studies in diplomatic history I found a corresponding tendency: during certain phases of Russian history the observations of foreign diplomatists are first-rate sources, and not only for the history of foreign relations—while the reverse is not so: the observations of Russian diplomatists in the West are important sources only when these diplomatists are themselves very much "Westernized" personalities. In 1959 I wrote: "Despite the interplay of Great Russian diplomacy and Communist machinations I think it is safe to say that even if we were to see some day the dispatches of the relatively more intelligent kind of Soviet Ambassador such as Maisky or a Dekanozov, dealing with the dramatic first period of the Second World War, their importance would exist only because of their rarity value: they would not compare to the dispatches of a Schulenburg, of a Gafencu, of a Kennan, of a Coulondre, of a Rosso, of Western diplomatists in Moscow whose dispatches are historical sources of primary interest, since the observations of their authors transcend the routine record of diplomatic matters on occasion." I suppose that this was confirmed by the publications of the memoirs of certain Soviet diplomatists (Maisky, Berezhkov, etc.) in the sixties.

27   *The Tolstoy locomotive on the Berlin track*
In a celebrated book, *The Hedgehog and the Fox* (1954), Sir Isaiah Berlin, of Oxford fame, developed the thesis that Tolstoy had a split personality, half realistic writer, half religious mystic, and that this explains the astonishing appendix on historical philosophy with which Tolstoy felt he had to burden the last volume of *War and Peace*. Apart from the fact that Tolstoy's—extremely unhistorical—historical philosophizing intrudes in the very text of the great book itself, Berlin completely misses the point, which is not only the Oriental tendency of Tolstoy's mysticism but also of his scientism. The Marquis de Voguë (1883) knew better: he said that Tolstoy was a mixture of "chemist and Buddhist," a phrase that Chesterton borrowed: "the mixture of

an inhuman Puritan and a presumptuous savage"; see also Orwell's pithy essay, "Lear, Tolstoy and the Fool" in *Shooting an Elephant and Other Essays* (London, 1953).

27   *Dostoevsky, Tolstoy*
W. Schubart, *Russia and Western Mind* (1950): "According to a remark of Berdiayev's, Dostoevsky is the greatest Russian philosopher" (pp. 103–104). But (p. 181): "Dostoevsky has no feeling for tradition." J. N. Figgis, *Political Thought from Gerson to Grotius* (1916): "From the point of view of Christian ethics self-sacrifice, which means the spirit of giving, is not at all identical with the self-annihilation which is the last word of the pessimism of modern times, and of some systems of Oriental ethics. Love does not destroy; it enhances individuality. The gulf between the Christian ideal of Love, and the ideals of Buddha, Schopenhauer and Tolstoi, which mean the destruction of the individual, is at bottom irreconcilable. Yet both by adversaries and believers, the mistake of confounding the one with the other is often made."

27   *Historicity of Christianity: Western and Eastern traditions*
Historically, rather than *theologically*. By this I mean that while in liturgy or in theology Russian Christians have more in common with Roman Catholics than with liberal Western Protestants, historically this is not so; there is a common past and a common fund of understanding, funneling into a common (or, at least, similar) cultural conception of human nature which most Christian believers (and many Jews) in the West by and large share, and which is different from the religiosity of many Eastern Christians. For example, while *liturgically* (at least for certain Catholics) Easter is at least the equivalent of Christmas in importance, in reality (with the partial exception of the Irish and of the Spanish) for centuries Catholics in the West have celebrated Christmas with greater personal interest than Easter, whereas the opposite has been true in Russia, where the feast of Easter (the miracle of Christ manifesting Himself as God) has appealed to the believers more strongly than Christmas (the historical coming of Christ to earth as Man).

29   *Magical know-how*
Consider, for example, the ludicrous implications of the telegram that the Japanese government was to have sent to Professor Charles A. Beard after the Tokyo earthquake in 1923. The telegram read: BRING YOUR KNOWLEDGE OF DISASTER. (Yet Fact has become stranger than Fiction: instead of recognizing the ridiculous character of such an appeal, such an eminent American historian as Richard Hofstadter cited it as an example of what historians could do; at the same time (1958) the *American Historical Review* revealed the existence of a "Disaster Research Group," staffed by historians, of the National Academy of Sciences under the National Research Council—an American intellectual disaster, indeed.)

30   *Europe and historical thinking*
Burckhardt: "The development of the West shows the truest marks of [historical] life. From the struggles of opposites something quite new

always emerges; new oppositions replace the old ones; it is not a mere, senseless, almost identical and automatic repetition of military and palace revolutions, as happened during seven hundred years in Byzantium and even longer in Islam. Here in Europe men change through every one of these struggles and manifest this change: we can look into a thousand different manifestations of the human soul and we may even date the style of the prevailing spirit in different decades, while at the same time the national, religious, local elements and other innumerable spiritual nuances make their influence felt. Yet at the same time these things have not always been pleasing or fruitful; they were struggles of life and death."

"Only one thing always deadly for Europe: an oppressive mechanical force, either the force of conquering barbarian peoples or the accumulating instruments of power exercised by one state or by one tendency (masses today)."

Otto Brunner: "The origins of historical thinking are European; it is a Western achievement. A very great achievement: but it has its own dangers, too. Yet the great spiritual movements of Europe were never without their dangers. They have been challenges. . . ."

36 Story *and* History

The gap between the popular employment of "a story" and "a history" is often small in English. The Italian *storia* and the German *Geschichte* mean story as well as history. Certain French historians (Corbin, Dardel) tried to establish a distinction between *l'Histoire* (upper case: objective) and *l'histoire* (lower case: subjective). It wasn't worth the fuss. *Historiographer* did not take in English, *historiographe* fared not much better in France. There are shades of distinctions between *storiografo* and *storico* in Italian; *Historiker*, *Geschichtsschreiber*, *Geschichtswissentschaftler* all exist in German, but, still, the terms overlap very much: in my English-German dictionary "historian" is *Geschichtsforscher* and "historiographer," *Geschichtsschreiber*, which makes little sense. I understand that there are more definite distinctions further to the East, in Russia and in China. But, then, that is my very point: the retention of the broad meaning of "history" in our Western languages suggests that our historical instinct is unique, traditional, enduring.

46 *Bourgeois*

Bourgeois was a particular historical phenomenon, western European rather than eastern European, hardly Russian and not even American —unlike *middle-class*. (The sharp separation of city from country did not exist in Russia; there is no Russian equivalent for *bourgeois*, *burgher*, *borghese*, the Russian word is merely *city-dweller*, devoid of the implications of civic or political rights. The bourgeoisie in Europe preceded European capitalism (H. Pirenne: "The first known mention of this word occurs in France in 1007"); and the surviving bourgeois now are not identical with the more universal phenomenon of a middle class. This is a point which Charles A. Beard missed, when he wrote "that, in theory, America has one class—the petty bourgeoisie —despite proletarian and plutocratic elements which cannot come under that classification, and that the American social ideal most

widely expressed is the *embourgeoisement* of the whole society—a
universality of comfort, convenience, security, leisure, standard possessions of food, clothing and shelter." All of these are middle-class,
and not bourgeois, aspirations. The latter often sprang from a conscious emulation of the habits and standards of aristocracies: and it
was the achievement of patrician standards of culture and of responsibility which marked the finest things of bourgeois culture—which is
why we ought to shake off the pejorative sense attached to the still-
present employment of *bourgeois* (and transfer it, on occasion, to
middle-class). We should no longer abide by the distorted Marxist
usage of the term: we should, instead, recall its more spacious older
sense, with its pre-capitalist suggestion of a free citizenry. *Bourgeois*
is an old word; in English, too, it was used centuries before *middle-
class* (O.E.D.: 1812). The former is a historical, the latter a sociological, adjective. In retrospect, bourgeois culture appears as a historical reality; there is such a thing as the Bourgeois epoch.

54   *Xextra*
One of the now present cultural heroes in the United States, an elder
statesman and adviser of Presidents, is Mr. Sol Linowitz, the Chair-
man of Xerox Corporation, who made his fortune in the mass manufacture of copying machines, and his reputation in having thereby
engineered what is nowadays called a Cultural Explosion. (He was
made Ambassador to the Organization of American States in October,
1966.) The xerophagous nature of the American public has not been
lost on investors, since Xerox has had a spectacular surge of fortune
on the New York Stock Exchange. What has been lost is the original
meaning of xerophagy: "the eating of dry food, esp. as a form of
fasting practised in the early church" (O.E.D.).

69   *More written, less read*
And yet just because more is being written does not mean that more
is being read—a condition which is ascertainable among many of the
writers themselves. Reading is usually less of an intense activity than
is writing: it requires less concentration. The modern historian must,
however, consider the mental consequences of the mechanized and
schizophrenic ways of our modern lives: the alarming and, in some
cases, fatal dispersion of mind which results in the weakening and in
the reduction of attention during reading. No sane person will nowadays read a newspaper or even a magazine in its entirety, from the
first to the last paragraph. There is no harm in this; the harm lies
in the condition that millions of literate people are no longer accustomed to read anything through, including books, from cover to
cover. This disease of inattention has affected the very people who
should be struggling against it: publishers, editors, professional intellectuals, reviewers.

70   *Who are "the people"?*
Paul Valéry (1931): "The word *people*, for example, had a precise
meaning when it was possible to assemble *all* the citizens of a city
about a mound, or in the Champ de Mars. But the increase in numbers, the passage from thousands to millions, has made of this word

a monstrous term whose meaning depends on the sentence in which it occurs."

70   *Who were "the people"?*
Giannotti, the Florentine historian, tended to equate the people with the poor: "even when they may desire liberty," he wrote, "being poor and living in abject and vile conditions, they are capable but of service, not of rule." The liberal Scipione Ammirato in 1599 called the "volgo una bestia senza pensieri e nelle cose sue non fa niuna distinzione dal falso al vero," full of vices but without any *virtù*. A little later, *populus* and *popularis* gained some respect, especially among certain Neapolitan writers. (In 1621 Ludovico Zuccolo accused Ammirato for his blanket condemnation: the people are not always beasts, and one must distinguish between *populus* and *vulgus*.)

72   *"People" and "populace"*
De Coux, one of the forgotten early Christian Socialists who preceded Marx, wrote in the *Avenir* in 1831: the politicians and the historians debate questions which are "of no importance by comparison with the leprosy of *pauperism* which is ravaging Europe. But like the astrologer who is so busy looking at the stars that he did not see the abyss that was open before him, we fix our attention on the lofty regions of the political world, as if the interests that are canvassed there must have a permanent influence on the fate of our country. If we really want to know about that, we must look much lower down—in the midst of these multitudes who are called 'the people' when they are needed but who are otherwise referred to as 'the populace.' . . ."

72   *"People" of different nations*
I must say something at this point about the national variations of "the people." *Volk, peuple, populo,* "folk," *pueblo,* "people": they sound different: they *are* different. The Russian *narod* and the German *Volk* have an unusually broad meaning, since they include nation as well as people—which differs from the general western European tradition of the distinct "nation." (In many Oriental languages, including Arab tongues, distinctions of "nation" and "people" do not exist.) Thus *Volk* is broader than "people": it is almost "nation"—which, for example, is not the case of the Spanish *pueblo*. Conversely, *populacho* (e.g. the English pejorative "populace") is less pejorative in Spanish than is the German pejorative *Pöbel* (e.g. mob, a snarl at the French *peuple*). *Le populo* is French slang for populace.

76   *"Opinion" of different nations*
Again the distinct meanings vary according to national traditions. The German *Meinung* is broader than the English "opinion": it suggests inclination, tendency rather than intellectual conclusion (*nach meiner Meinung*: "after" my opinion, the Germans say). *L'opinion publique,* in French, too, is broader than the English meaning: it includes *moeurs*, "mores, habits," etc. *Öffentliche Meinung* in German means opinion that is not only public but "open."

77   *Public opinion in England in the 1840's*
See Bagehot's famous essay on Peel; also Gilbert A. Cahill. "The Protestant Association and the Anti-Maynooth Agitation of 1845" in

the *Catholic Historical Review*, October, 1957: "By 1845 the Protestant wing of the Conservative Party was advocating the acceptance of public opinion as the guide of legislation. Threatened by a crystallizing opinion on the Corn Law issue, it sought to maintain its position by getting the support of the public on the Maynooth issue. . . ." The Leicester *Journal* on August 16, 1845, called for plain and forceful action by "every conservative director of public opinion."

78   *Early histories of public opinion*
The first general history of public opinion, W. Bauer, *Die oeffentliche Meinung und ihre geschichtlichen Grundlagen* (Vienna, 1922), is not much more than a history of the press. Hezekiah Niles, one of the first popular American historians, said in the Preface of his *Principles and Acts of the Revolution in America* that he intended to put forth evidence "to show the *Feelings* that prevailed in the Revolution, not to give a *History of Events*." He did nothing of the sort. Nor did Bancroft. Walter Lippmann's famous *Public Opinion*, written after World War I, did not speak of popular sentiment, which the author regarded evidently as identical with public opinion. About the shortcomings of the great French historians of the nineteenth century in this respect see Paul Ourliac's brilliant essay in Gaston Berger, ed. *L'opinion publique* (Paris, 1956), together with Rémond, *op. cit.* The literature of public opinion and of its history has greatly increased during the last fifteen years; this is not the place for its bibliography; let me only mention the few valuable works with which I am acquainted: F. Tönnies, *Kritik der öffentlichen Meinung* (Berlin, 1922), and "Zur Theorie der öffentlichen Meinung" in *Schmollers Jahrbuch*, 40 (Berlin, 1923); E. Stoetzel, *Theorie des opinions* (Paris, 1943); and the excellent Wilhelm Hennis, *Meinungsforschung und representative Demokratie* (Tübingen, 1957).

80   *Evocation of the majority*
This evocation of a majority (Maitland: "a shout is the test") for the sake of maintaining the impression of public unity, survived for long in such peculiar institutions as the Polish *liberum veto*. And there are echoes of that medieval sentiment in the United States even now. Consider the modern, and at the same time curiously medieval, the mechanized and at the same time Breughel-like, sound of the great American political conventions, ending up with the image of an overwhelming majority, of the impression of irresistible unanimity.

81   *Who are the "majority"?*
"When all is said," wrote E. I. Watkin recently about the English Reformation, the majority of not only the people but of the clergy, too, "were vicars of Bray for the most part." John Adams' estimate is well known: in 1774 one-third of Americans were supposed to be Loyalists, one-third Patriots, one-third undecided and uncommitted. "While nearly every prominent man took sides," wrote G. P. Gooch of the beginnings of the English Civil War, "a certain number found this either difficult or impossible or unnecessary. A few demanded time to think the matter over. . . . In one case, the inhabitants of an entire country pledged themselves to remain neutral. Many quietly changed

with the times . . . this sentiment of neutrality was common to the greater mass of the working classes." In the history of foreign affairs such divisions of opinion have been often exaggerated. Was "British opinion" seething with sympathy for Greece in the 1820's? There was a Whig and Radical minority arguing for the Greeks; there was a Tory minority standing pat and stolid, an attitude which favored the Turkish cause; and, as Harold Nicolson wrote in *Byron: the Last Phase*, "in the third place there was a vast majority who knew nothing whatsoever about the question."

82   *Questionnaires of opinion*
Some time ago I was honored by having been chosen among "a select minority of educators" in order to furnish an opinion-profile of attitudes relating to a certain American industry. Two representatives visited me to elicit my choices in more than two hundred questions. I am leaving aside the condition that many of these questions were rather indifferent to me: whereby the meanings of the choice-answers which I gave to them were essentially different from my answers to other questions which may have existed in my mind, in one form or another, before I had been faced with this particular poll. My point is the feeling of irritated inadequacy that I experienced after having completed this most detailed questionnaire. (I believe that I share this feeling with every thinking person who fills out questionnaires, especially those involving beliefs and opinions: the very categories of the preformulated choices, no matter how well they may have been composed, are almost always cramped, artificial, unreal.) Had I been asked to write three sentences about my opinions about that particular industry, I believe that my attitudes would have appeared in a much clearer and truer form, since the very choice of my phrases could have been revealing.

83   *Conditions of electoral studies*
These conditions are historical analysis and historical comparison. Electoral history is meaningful only in more or less traditionally democratic, or politically experienced, societies. (It is very well to remind ourselves that Lenin and his party were a minority in the first—and last—elected Russian parliament in 1918: but, let us face it, the maddeningly contradictory Russian electoral results of 1917–1918 are not very meaningful.) The electoral results must be compared with the records of past elections. Also, its minute scrutinies must involve a small, stable, and relatively compact electoral region with its population. Finally, the historian must be fully aware of the condition that political parties in modern democracies are interested, above all, in the paramount task of electing their nominee: that their efforts in eliciting popular sentiments are often subordinated to the electoral calendar. Thus certain "issues" may be automatically inflated before the elections—especially in the United States, where the biennial and quadrennial regularity of elections often mechanically accelerates the political, but not the deeper historical, rhythm of events before every second or fourth November.

88   *Newspapers: information and opinion*
It is instructive to observe that whereas in the past the value of the
"class" newspaper lay often in the quality of its editorial opinions
that were perused daily by thousands of intelligent readers, in our
times the intelligent reader prefers the better papers *not* because of
their editorial opinions but because of their still distinctive sources of
information, since in these newspapers at least some attempts are
made to maintain the older separation of information from opinion,
that is, the dispatches of their recognized correspondents from col-
umnists and editorials.

89   *Newspapers: publicity and advertising*
The modern practices of publicity affected advertising more profoundly than the reverse. In the nineteenth century the principal
function of advertisement was to convey commercial information; in
the twentieth century its principal function is the suggestion of
popular preferences—through practices which range from subtle
rhetoric to primitive appeals to mechanical and sub-mental reflexes.
This should be of interest to the historian and not only to the sociologist, for at least two reasons: first, because a study of advertisements
in the twentieth century is instructive not so much as it gives us information about economic, social, commercial conditions but as it
suggests prevalent fads in rhetoric and popularity; second, because of
the excessive dependence of the press on advertising. (It was because
of the growing demand on commercial information three hundred
years ago that newspapers began to flourish; but at the zenith of their
influence, during the nineteenth century, the press depended less on
advertising than either before or afterward; during its decline, in this
century, the press has become desperately dependent on advertising
again.)

90   *American "materialism"*
The usual critique of the "materialist" democracies—notably of the
United States—is shallow. Few people attribute as much importance
to certain ideas as do Americans, whose very "materialism" is idealist
rather than pragmatic or sensual: it springs not at all from an attachment to material goods but from an attachment to an idea of what
these goods represent in the world order. Hence, too, the peculiar
nature of American social conformism, which is different from the conformism of England, another Protestant democracy; the English will
tolerate all kinds of eccentrics because of their relative indifference to
private ideas, but when Americans regard eccentric behavior as dangerous, this happens because they suspect that behind this kind of
behavior dangerous and destructive ideas may lurk.

96   *Interregnum*
There is, namely, yet another reason for the importance of contemporary history nowadays: and this is the interregnal character of
our age. Napoleon: "My usual reading fare when I go to bed is the
old chronicles of the third, fourth, and fifth centuries. I read them or
have them translated for me. Nothing is more curious, or less known,
than the change from old ways of life to new ones, than the transition

from the ancient political bodies to the new ones that were founded on their ruins." Voltaire: "I would recommend that the study of history begin with the century just before Charles V, Leo X, and Francis I. That is the time when there occurred in the human mind, as in the world itself, a revolution which changed everything." Burckhardt: "As you see, I like times that are *à cheval*, on the frontier between the Middle Ages and modern times. It is truly exhilarating to depict the variety of life in those times, for the sake of its many different forms and its vitality. And long before the dustmen have got their refuse-carts moving, and shout disagreeable things after us, we are already over the hills and far away." Elsewhere he said that the confusion of interregnal times is a potential store of riches for us ("in besonderm und hoechstem Grade lehrreich") because of its contrast with the passing age, involving its rich variety of mutations, changes, the manifold forms of new life, the new pulse, "finally because of the great notoriety of everything."

103   *Becker's paper*
With some exaggeration Harry Elmer Barnes wrote that if this paper of Becker's were ever published it would "probably come to have the same place in historical science that the theory of indeterminacy occupies in contemporary physical science." (*A History of Historical Writing*, Oklahoma, 1937.) The paper was published posthumously in the *Western Political Quarterly*, September, 1955, and reprinted thereafter, among others, in Meyerhoff, ed. *The Philosophy of History in Our Time* (New York, Doubleday Anchor Books, 1959). The contemporaneity of Becker's lecture and of indeterminacy theory (1925–1927, see above, Chapter VII, pp. 276–277) should not obscure the condition that Becker's lucid contribution was less original than, say, Heisenberg's: but Barnes's simile is worth noting, if only because a parallel does exist between the inadequate recognitions of the philosophical consequences of indeterminacy in the wider world of the sciences and the inadequate considerations given to this kind of epistemology in the smaller world of American historians, among whom, as I wrote earlier, few still accept the definition of history as a "science" and yet the overwhelming majority still teach and write as if history were largely determined.

104   *Facts meaningless by themselves*
There is a passage in the autobiography of an iconoclastic journalist, Claud Cockburn's *A Discord of Trumpets*, which may be read with profit by historians: "To hear people talking about facts you would think that they lay about like pieces of gold ore in the Yukon days, waiting to be picked up . . . by strenuous prospectors whose subsequent problem was only how to get them to market. Such a view is evidently and dangerously naive. There are no such facts. Or if there are, they are meaningless and entirely ineffective; might in fact just as well not be lying about at all until the prospector—the journalist—puts them into relation with other facts, presents them, in fact, and then they become as much a part of the pattern created by him as if he were writing a novel. In that sense, all stories are written back-

ward—they are supposed to begin with the facts and develop from there, but in reality they begin with a journalist's point of view, a conception, and it is the point of view from which the facts are subsequently organized. . . ."

110   *Language and history; language and science*
Logan Pearsall Smith in *The English Language:* "For it is not too much to say that a contradiction between language and history rarely or never occurs. When a new product, a new conception, a new way of feeling, comes into the thought of a people, it inevitably finds a name in their language—a name that very generally bears on it the mark of the source from which it has been derived." There can be no doubt, he wrote a few pages earlier, "that science is in many ways the natural enemy of language. Language, either literary or colloquial, demands a rich store of living and vivid words—words that are 'thought-pictures,' and appeal to the senses, and also embody our feelings about the objects they described. But science cares nothing about emotion or vivid presentation; her ideal is a kind of algebraic notation, to be used simply as an instrument of analysis; and for this she rightly prefers dry and abstract terms, taken from some dead language, and deprived of all life and personality."

110   *The associations of words*
Their associations are even more real than are the associations of "facts" in our mind. I suggested earlier the onomatopoeic quality of "water." Logan Pearsall Smith on the suggestive power of words like "bump," "dump," "slump," "thump," etc.: this is "due partly to the direct imitation of natural sounds, but more to the movements of the vocal organs, and their analogy with the movements we wish to describe; an explosive sound describes an explosive movement, as in *blast* or *blow,* while a sound suddenly stopped suggests a stopped movement, and a prolonged sound a movement that is prolonged also. But probably these analogies are mainly formed by association; a common word established in the language describes a sound or action, and its sound comes to be connected with the thing that it describes. Other words are formed on its model, and finally the expressive power of the sound, suggesting as it does so many other words of similar meaning, becomes a part of the unconscious inheritance of those who use the same form of speech." This is an important argument, suggesting the historicity inherent even in onomatopoeia: or, in other words, that the history of expression may encompass the history of thought, since it is not only that the latter leads to the former but also the reverse.

111   *The debasement of Language*
Owen Barfield (1952): ". . . we should recognize, I think, that those —and their number is increasing—who are driven by an impulse to reduce the specifically human to a mechanical and animal regularity, will continue to be increasingly irritated by the nature of the mother tongue and make it their point of attack. The strategy is well advised. Language is the storehouse of imagination; it cannot continue to be

itself without performing its function. But its function is, to mediate transition from the unindividualized, dreaming spirit that carried the infancy of the world to the individualized human spirit, which has the future in its charge. If therefore they succeed in expunging from language all the substance of its past, in which it is so naturally rich, and finally converting it into the species of algebra that is best adapted to the uses of indoctrination and empirical science, a long and important step forward will have been taken in the selfless cause of the liquidation of the human spirit."

Yves Congar (1954): ". . . language is not merely the symbol of ideas which would exist of themselves: language also shapes ideas. It contributes, before the thought is expressed, to the very formation of the mechanics of thought, and to the formation of that kind of inner mirror wherein our perceptions are 'refracted'; it really constitutes the climate which is called 'the mind.' "

Reinhard Wittram (1958): "Je aermer der sprachliche Ausdruck wird, desto geringer ist seine Nuancierungsfaehigkeit, desto weniger kann auch vom Vergangenen heraufgeholt und wiedererweckt werden. Historische Anschauungskraft und sprachliche Ausdrucksfaehigkeit korrespondieren miteinander. Ob das eine mit dem anderen zum Untergang bestimmt ist, wissen wir nicht." (The poorer the ability of expression, the poorer the ability to discriminate, and consequently the poorer the ability to reconstruct or evoke the past. Historical perceptiveness and the facility of expression correspond with each other. Whether the decay of the one inevitably means the decay of the other we do not yet know.)

Dwight Macdonald (1962): "The language of a people . . . is a record of its past that has much to say to the present. If this connection is broken, then a people gets into the condition of a psychotic who has lost contact with his past. . . ."

112   *Honor≠honneur: "same" words in different languages*
This is what every intelligent translator knows: his task is not the replacement of a word with its equivalent in another language but to express the meaning and the purpose of the original author as closely as it is possible. The preference for a meaningful over a literal translation does not mean, of course, that these two kinds mutually exclude each other: simply, a good translation will be meaningful not because it is literal; it will be literal when it is really meaningful—the *factum-fictio* relationship again.

116   New Grub Street: *certain late Victorian sensibilities*
Examples: not only how these people talked but that they may have been more frank in their letters than in their conversation. On another level *New Grub Street*, being in part a *roman à clef*, at least in one instance furnishes interesting information about the origins of *Tit-Bits*, of the first English mass newspaper, the harbinger of what G. C. K. Ensor was to call the Press Revolution in his Oxford history of *England 1870–1914*. Or consider this phrase by Jasper Milvain: "Well, at all events, she's intellectual, and very rich"—an indication that as late as 1888 the new usage of "*an* intellectual," the noun, had not yet taken root among literary people in England.

121   *Classless society=end of the novel?*
Few novelists, however, have tried to grapple with the theme of another kind of relationship which, in my opinion, remains a very meaningful one. This is the relationship of persons not of different social aspirations but of different national consciousnesses—which, as I suggested earlier involves not only different attitudes but, through different ways of expressions, different nuances in forms of thought. (I believe, for instance, that one of the sources of the success of Nabokov's *Lolita* resides in the portrayal of the relationship between the middle-aged *European* man and the *American* adolescent girl, and that this gives not merely spice but substance to our interest in their carnal commerce.) Such a novel could be, however, undertaken successfully only by an author who is deeply conversant with the different cultures, habits of expressions, forms of thought of different nations.

124   *Background and foreground*
This development may correspond with a development in modern painting. That a great painter establishes a high kind of harmony between foreground and background is obvious. (Macaulay in 1828: "History has its foreground and its background, and it is principally in the management of its perspective that one artist differs from another. . . .") That in painting, as in writing, selectivity is important is obvious, too: this is inseparable from the understanding of the voids, of what to omit (and not merely for the sake of "effect"). In the great Renaissance, baroque, Augustan paintings, no matter what their themes, the foreground tended to be personal while the background was historical: a recognizable scene or landscape, full of contemporary reality (even in religious paintings whose setting could be expected to be timeless). After the impressionists, then, the background in the paintings of modern masters is thinning out—indeed, so much so after a while that the paintings of many modern masters suggest the feeling that our historical societies are becoming empty of real and meaningful content. Well before the event of Hiroshima the surrealistic backgrounds, from di Chirico to Dali, show more and more of a dead landscape, empty, cold, abandoned by people, at most pointing toward some kind of burning lonely eternity: whatever historicity may still exist in them, it has moved into the foreground.

134   *Difficulties about the "evidence"*
Chapter II, pp. 59–62. Any intelligent person living in an authoritarian or totalitarian state soon learns how to read between the lines —or, rather, how to read *into* the phrases—of newspaper articles and official speeches and statements; he may detect a change in the course of the government by the slightest turn of a phrase, by a toned-down adjective, by the tiniest historical allusion. In this respect Stendhal's *Charterhouse of Parma*, which was rediscovered by American intellectuals after 1945 as if it were the classic precursor of the politico-intellectual *romans policiers* by Koestler, dealing with totalitarianism, has been long outdated: for in Parma the people were intricate but their expressions were clear, which is not true of the twentieth century, with their democratized masses of people, with their mumblings

and rumblings. Anyone who had anything to do with the slightest kind of opposition in a modern police state will know the importance of his estimate of the tendencies of popular sentiment, of the inclinations and ideas of great numbers of anonymous people on whose potential cooperation—or, rather, on whose lack of hostility—his life may depend. Such considerations of potentiality involve the intentions and also the expressions of all kinds of people. Thus, for instance, in this century of police states and standardized opinions, documents lose their older historiographical meaning: their interpretation is, as we have seen (pp. 58–63) more difficult; their tendency and their purpose must be taken into consideration. For example, people may use the official jargon in order to conceal their opposition; while, on the other hand, even intelligent people may thoughtlessly repeat official phrases and slogans for a long time after these have become senseless and unnecessary even from a personal and politic point of view. Indeed, I think that Dostoevsky was quite wrong when he drew such great stark dramatic portraits of the conflicts of personal conscience: the testimonies of an Ehrenburg in the East (or of an Oppenheimer in the West) reveal personal motives that are petty rather than enormous, resulting in sordid entanglements of truths with lies which come out dull, boring, verbose. It is a truism that the historian should not study documents in a legalistic manner, concentrating on their single literal meaning at the cost of their spirit: certain events of the Second World War ought to have made this clear: the enormity of the Nazi crimes, for example, was such that many of the acts of their accomplices are simply not susceptible to judicial, while they *are* susceptible to historical, investigation.

137 *"How it happened . . ."*
Let me correct in this respect the usual criticism of Ranke's famous phrase, *wie es eigentlich gewesen.* This criticism has concentrated on the adverb *eigentlich* ("really," "truly," "uniquely"—G. P. Gooch, Ranke's principal English exegete, translated it as "actually") as this adverb suggests the historian's scientific ability to fix the meaning of past events once and for all. Yet it is in a different sense that Ranke's somewhat platitudinous phrase may be slightly askew: not in the sense of the meaning of the adverb *eigentlich* but in the very definiteness of the verb *gewesen* (an abbreviation of *gewesen war*), with its suggestion of something definitely closed, a static account of the past—which history is not.

148 *Men doing things to ideas*
Thus the principal shortcoming of German categorical idealism may be summed up by pointing at the primitive, one-way causality which marks its concept of a *Zeitgeist*—when, in reality, it is the person (*every* human person) who is more important than *any* idea, since it is not the person who is part of the idea, but the idea which is part of the person.

149 *History of ideas and intellectual history*
Intellectual history, and even the history of "intellectuals," may, of course, form a legitimate object of research on occasion: but its circumscription is difficult, depending on the historian's sense of propor-

tion. It is a legitimate object because ideas still percolate "downward," even though this movement is cumbrous, difficult, slow; and because intellectuals tend to isolate themselves from the people, whereby especially in the English-speaking countries, they are to some extent a distinguishable group. The number of Communists and Socialists in the United States in the 1930's was insignificant: but it was significant that in 1932 many reputable American intellectuals and artists subscribed to a Communist proclamation, and that some of them entered the bureaucracies of the New Deal: though few of them remained dedicated Communists, they did contribute to the formation of a certain climate of opinion whose effects were indirect but widespread. It is, then, because of the historical existence of climates of opinion that in certain times and on certain occasions intellectual history is important, because it marks great cultural turning-points (examples of such turning-points are 1748–1750 in France, 1835–1847 in Continental Europe and in Russia, 1845–1850 in Britain. Gertrude Himmelfarb sketched very well one of the latter's aspects in her chapter "Climate of Opinion on the Eve of the *Origin*" in her *Darwin and the Darwinian Revolution*).

149   *Conservatism and American anti-Communism*
Thus, for instance, T. S. Eliot's aphorism about the character of conservative political thinking—that radicals proceed from propositions to policies, and conservatives from the contemplation of events to propositions—refers to a specifically historical conservatism, certainly not shared by American "new conservatives."

152   *Idealism and realism*
Let me, at this point, mention my personal feeling, which is that when I say "I am an idealist," nowadays this communicates a realistic rather than an abstract way of looking at things and, curiously enough, perhaps even a certain kind of "tough-mindedness" rather than sentimentalism. All this is very different from what these things had suggested in the nineteenth century: it is the materialists among us who are abstract and often sentimental: and I feel that I am not alone in sensing this.

155   *Scientific and historical causalities*
The term "reductionism" has recently been introduced by Professor Michael Polanyi to denote the kind of ideal knowledge which, proceeding from mathematical physics, conceives "all things whatsoever to be intelligible ultimately in terms of the laws of inanimate nature." But this somewhat hobbling term "reductionism" suggests a brutal, direct, primitive, common-sense approach, as it pulls subtle and complex ideas down to earth: and this is not telling enough, since the principal proponents of scientism in the twentieth century ought to be criticized for exactly the contrary approach, for refusing common sense as they substitute vocabulary for thought. "Reductionism" is a useful word perhaps in one sense only: in referring to the singularly primitive and narrow concept of scientific causality.

155   *Comte and causality*
It is interesting to note that, with all of his positivism, the founder
of modern sociology was more historically minded than were most
of his followers: yet Comte could not liberate himself from the
notion of a simplistic causality, since he believed that the exact
knowledge of our future will issue from our eventually exact knowledge of our past—a classic example of naïve historicism.

156   *Marrou*
In this important passage (*De la connaissance historique*, pp. 273–
274) he draws a certain parallel between psychoanalysis and historical
knowledge: in spite of certain extreme and unreasonable claims and
pretentions of the former, there exists a certain similarity in their
functions, whereby a man may free himself from certain burdens of
the past that weighed upon him when he can find them, face them,
and integrate them in his consciousness. (I have slightly paraphrased
Marrou's French for the sake of clarity in English. The original versions read "La connaissance de la cause passée modifie l'effet présent";
"La connaissance historique libère l'homme du poids de son passé.")

162   *Attribution of motives*
Marx and Engels indulged in it as much as the racial determinists.
The former in *The German Ideology*, 1846: historians are wrong when
they write about the factor of politics or religion; these are "*the illusions of that epoch*" (their italics); "religion and politics are only
forms of true motives." Hitler in his *Table Conversations*, 1942: "I
knew of a Jewish journalist in Munich who seemed to write decent
patriotic stuff. But she was even more dangerous than the others. She
wrote that way in order to mislead us, because she was a Jewess." G.
Schoepflin, a Hungarian ex-Communist, about the Rajk trial, 1949:
"To talk about Rajk's conspiracy is ridiculous. The leaders saw in
Rajk not an actual opponent of the Party, but a *potential* leader of
eventual opposition in the future. Therefore he had to be annihilated."
In 1954 Senator Joseph McCarthy was "investigating" the American
journalist James Wechsler, who had been a juvenile Communist but
broke with the Party at the age of nineteen, in 1937; and since
Wechsler had expected certain questions about this one-time association, he produced confidently a sheaf of clippings and documents
registering the Communists' bitter attacks on him. McCarthy was not
impressed. "How do we know," he asked, "that you didn't quit them
on Moscow's orders?"

164   *Unexpressed motives: a historian's discernment*
A good example of this kind of discernment appears in a passage by
Professor Herbert Butterfield. "It is essential to discover where lay
[Machiavelli's] peculiar genius, and to find out what in real life was
his dominating passion," he wrote; "in particular to keep in mind the
declared intention . . . of his political thought." (My italics.)
By coincidence it was Butterfield who later dealt with what may
be a classic case of suggesting the existence of motives on the basis of
a very small fragment of historical evidence. He described how Beth-

mann-Hollweg's famous expression, "a scrap of paper," uttered on August 4, 1914, to the British Ambassador, may not have been accurately translated by the latter. For the Ambassador made "the phrase more picturesque by a translation which might well have come most naturally to his mind . . . there is possibly a reason why the term which he used was one that would come readily to the mind of the Ambassador at the moment. At his house there had recently been a private production of a play by Sardou, translated into English under the title *A Scrap of Paper;* and he himself had had a part in the production. Here is the kind of point which, if contemporaries do not settle it, may be too elusive for future historians to establish. But it is difficult to produce a watertight demonstration. . . ."

165   *Motives alone count not*
Cardinal Feltin at the Institut Français in South Kensington, 1955: "What is the religious situation in France? What is the situation of the Catholic Church in France? It is extremely difficult to give a true picture of the underlying state of religion in France. Nothing is more dangerous than to make a judgment from the outside; yet my survey must be from the outside, *as I cannot pretend to penetrate the souls of my fellow-countrymen. On the other hand, by their behaviour people to some extent reveal their disposition.*" My italics.

165   *Doing the right thing for the wrong reason . . .*
That is: the Good Pagan is better than the Bad Christian—historically speaking, as far as we know, in this world. This is not Pelagianism: by it I mean that the pagan who has acted like a Christian is preferable to the Christian who has not acted like a Christian.

165   *The character of the historian*
It is true that a good man can write bad history. It is not true that a bad man can be a good historian. (Perhaps this is the real reason behind Macaulay's statement: "A history in which every particular incident may be true, may, on the whole, be false.") In this respect, too, his personal character is reflected in the history he writes (through his choice of words), and by writing history, he deals with free moral agents in his own capacity as a free moral agent. On the other hand, it is as true of him as of the artist that, as Jean Dutourd put it in a lovely phrase, "La place et la valeur qu'il faut attribuer à une couleur ou à un adjectif sont des connaissances indispensables pour rendre l'âme vraiment forte."

182   *Historical sociography*
It is, of course, possible to describe past societies and their habits without much reference to their historical conditions. Hence the occasionally defective historicity not only of sociology but also of many things that pass for social history. It is, of course, true that the description of certain societies must be less historical than of others, which is why the sociology of certain ahistorical societies is more interesting to us than their general history; their social habits are more instructive than their politics. They involve their routine life, at best a kind of *histoire intime.* As Gilberto Freyre wrote: "For the sociological interpretation of the Brazilian social past it means little, almost nothing,

that in 1822 Brazil ceased to be a colony in the purely political sense. Other political changes, so prominent in chronological history, are insignificant from the same point of view. Hence the greater importance given to a sort of psychological-sociological time. For the Brazilian past here sought for has been almost exclusively the past that the French call *histoire intime,* and the Spaniards sometimes describe as *intra-historia.* When the Goncourts wrote of an histoire intime that it was a *roman vrai* and would eventually become *la vraie histoire humaine,* they had a vision of a modern development in both history and literature."

188   *Stalin and National Socialism*
It was, I think, in 1932 that the Soviet press, on Stalin's orders, ceased to call the German Nazis by their name. Ever since that time they referred to the latter as Fascists or Hitlerites. (Lib-lab journalism in the West quickly followed this practice.) I find it quite possible that Stalin ordered this since he understood how the National Socialist term would fit his Russian regime rather well: the growing currency of the National Socialist adjective might have had certain intellectual consequences which could have been uncomfortable to Stalin. (And later Stalin was indeed influenced by some of the successful practices of German nationalist totalitarianism, though he would not admit this.)

200   *Folk, people, nation*
Among Germans the vague and strong *das Volk* often supersedes *die Nation.* The English, on the other hand, have never been a *Volk* or a race: as Dorothy Sayers wrote in *Unpopular Essays* (1941): "The comparative absence of folk-music and folk-customs from England is remarkable . . . and the English have never had a folk costume at all. The thing that ties them together is not a consciousness of common blood as much as a common law, a common culture, and a very long memory of national consciousness. The law, generally speaking, is Saxon; the culture, generally speaking, continental." No less a profound Russian thinker than Wladimir Weidlé wrote (*Russia Absent and Present*) that the Russians were, perhaps until recently, "a people not a nation." ("A nation is simply the spiritual body that a people acquires in the course of its history: it is a changing form that even while changing remains faithful to itself. Though it never lacked genius, though it was still less lacking in enduring patience, the Russian people, in the whole seven centuries of its ancient history, never once achieved this form of embodiment.") The avowed Christian and agricultural romantic Tolstoy, in his famous essay "Patriotism and Christianity," revealed his fundamental misconception of patriotism, incapable as he was of distinguishing it from nationalism; yet this distinction was wholly understood by the avowed non-Christian and Socialist Englishman, George Orwell.

200   *Relationship to land rather than blood*
This is not the place to expatiate upon this tremendous subject, except to suggest that historians must recognize that there is more to the influence of land on history than mere romantic rhetoric, and that this

kind of argument has not been the monopoly of reactionaries or of conservatives. (Victor Hugo: "The configuration of the soil decides many of man's actions and the earth is more his accomplice than people believe. . . ." Madariaga: "Men cannot take possession of a land without that land taking possession of them.")

201 *The word* nationalism
In France *nationalisme* appears in a dictionary in 1823; it is a romantic word, unlike the earlier *patriotisme* with its classical tinge. It may have come to France from Germany. Soon the two terms are confused, until later in the nineteenth century they become monopolized by the Right (in 1793, even in 1830, and on occasion as late as in 1871, patriotism and Jacobinism went often hand in hand; by 1900 the opposite is largely true). At this point I cannot refrain from speculating whether French "integral nationalism" would have developed quite as it did, had not Germany risen above France during the nineteenth century; for it is possible that Maurras (as indeed was the case with Renan) may have been somehow influenced by the German practice of the identity of *Staat* and *Volk,* in spite of his shrill insistence on anti-Teutonism and on Latinity; Maurras's famous distinction of *le pays réel* from the *pays légal* was, after all, not much more than the expression of the *völkisch* idea with Gallic clarity (*Volk* has no French equivalent).

203 *Nationality becoming a cultural phenomenon*
This is an enormous and complicated subject. I have tried to suggest some of its manifestations, in *Decline and Rise of Europe,* especially chapters V and VII. Let me add that I find it possible that a reaction against the now developing global mass culture may be developing on a deeper level—whereby what is best in poetry and in letters may remain the particular patrimony of each nation, translatable only with difficulty; while translatable and interchangeable with ease will be the more-or-less ephemeral and superficial writings, journalism, and technical works by intellectuals.

218 *Flight from reason*
As Chesterton put it in a somewhat primitive manner: when people no longer believe in a Deity it is not that they will believe nothing: they will, on the contrary, believe anything. Consider, too, Belloc's ruminations (1924) in *The Cruise of the "Nona"*: "Well, what will come out of that welter, that corruption into which the decomposition of the Christian culture is now dissolving? What I think will spring out of the filth is a new religion. I think there will arise in whatever parts of Christendom remain, say, 200 years hence . . . some simplified, odd, strong code of new habit, comparable to the sudden code of habit which Arabia constructed on the ruins of Christian doctrine in the East . . . a new religion, because human society cannot live on air. . . . This conception of a new religion (and, therefore, an evil one) arising out of the rottenness of the grave of truth, seems today at once fantastic and unpleasant. Unpleasant I admit it is; fantastic I do not believe it to be."

219 *Cultural atmospheres and churches*
In 1772 the Pope felt compelled, because of political and cultural pressures, to dissolve the Jesuits. Less than two centuries later John Foster Dulles, this descendant of Dutch Presbyterians, felt he had to sport a tremendous green tie on St. Patrick's Day. For by the 1950's identification with Catholicism had become a political advantage on the American national level. Of course this relatively recent blossoming of St. Patrick's Day into an American *national* fiesta has little to do with the history of religion: but little is not nothing. No matter how trivial its symptoms may be, they mark the rise in the respectability and in the influence of an important religious group within the population of the United States, and consequently they may be significant, even though they signify a development which is at least as much sociological as it is religious.

220 *Mass conversions*
In the Western Church the episodes of forced conversions have become relatively rare. ("I believe with Theodor Haecker," François Mauriac wrote, "that only individuals are capable of being converted. Churches are not converted. Conversion is an individual drama, not a collective one.") We might add: lately. There are distinct differences between the Western and the Eastern Christian mentality in this respect, too, reaching back to the past. After all is said, Constantine, the greatest political benefactor of Roman Christianity, was not canonized. His Russian "equivalent," St. Vladimir, was canonized by the Eastern Church, because of his national merits, even though he was a barbarian tyrant (the German canonical historian Thietmar of Merseburg called him *"fornicator immensus et crudelis"*) who had ordered the population to the banks of the Dnieper in 998 to be baptized under pain of death.
Consider, on the other hand, the history of the Uniates, of those Orthodox Christians in the Western Ukraine (called "Ruthenians" at the time) who were "reunited" with Rome in 1594–1596. The history of the Union of Brest was reconstructed in admirable detail by Professor Oscar Halecki. Yet was that Roman victory sufficiently solid? Was it not too dearly bought? I am asking the question only as a historian; I cannot ascertain, or doubt, the spiritual benefices that may have accrued to many thousands of Ruthenian souls. But the history of the Ruthenian population in Poland and in the Ukraine for 350 years thereafter often showed how the religious allegiances of many would only follow the fluctuations of national power over their lands.

220 *Russia: folkish nationality and religiosity*
About differences in mentalities see above (p. 27). To this I wish to add that the ahistoricity of the Russian religious mentality was coupled with its nationalism of a peculiar kind. Beginning about 1900 this was recognized by some of the best Russian religious thinkers. Thus D. Stremoukhoff, *Vladimir Soloviev et son oeuvre messianique*, cited by Fr. Yves Congar: "Soloviev could therefore say that in the system of the Slavophiles, religion has no place, that their stylized

Orthodoxy, their 'Orthodoxism' (*pravoslavnicanie*) is much more faith in the Russian people than in the Orthodox and Christian faith of that people. He was even to go further and declare that Orthodoxy is for the Slavophiles the true religion because the Russian people confess it, since it is 'an attribute of the Russian nationality.'"

221   *A history of Jesus*
In this book Stauffer marshaled much of the available evidence, including the painful fragments of records of Jesus' trial before the Great Sanhedrin, including the Sanhedrin's acknowledgment of His miracles; Stauffer emphasizes (as does Zaehner) that the evidence of the Qumran scrolls does not diminish Jesus' uniqueness, since the Qumran Essenes would have condemned him as swiftly and mercilessly as had Caiaphas: on the other hand "Jesus himself . . . was far less the child of his times and of his people than has hitherto been thought."

227   *Tempest in the celebrity teapot*
Let me confess at this point that the public reactions of principal figures associated with this controversy, including leading members of the American political and intellectual elite, cast a certain shadow on the thesis of this book about the potentially beneficial evidences of the now widespread interest in history on all levels, for this seems to go hand in hand with widespread misconceptions about what history is, and this is indeed a disturbing thing (as Professor Page Smith wrote in his good *The Historian and History*: ". . . many of the ills which maim and distort the modern psyche have their source, in large part, in a faulty sense of history or of the historic.") Nearly everybody has been wrong. The Kennedys were wrong for having commissioned an "authorized" account by an ambitious enthusiast in the name of "history" (and, of course, by refusing to read the stuff themselves). Manchester was wrong for having accepted such a circumscribed commission (and, of course, for having tried to wiggle out of his commitment to submit his manuscript to his patrons. He tried to keep up his sycophancy, however: recently he wrote in a letter to the *New York Times* that it was of course "unthinkable" for Mrs. Kennedy to have read the manuscript: presumably the inability to think involves the inability to read). Manchester's critics are wrong when they insist on Mrs. Kennedy's right to privacy, as it is rather evident that what she consistently wished for was not privacy but a very special kind of custom-made publicity for her own. And the Kennedys' critics are wrong in saying that the family has "a duty to history," for the sake of "the historical record," which "the public has the right to know", for not only does the public domain already include a depressingly enormous quantity of material on these four days in November, 1963, a kind of historical record of elephantine dimensions typical of a democracy, to which Manchester's human-interest trivia represent, at best, a puny little contribution; but, also, no one has any duty to history except to live honestly and decently.

229   *The shortcoming of subjectivism*
There is, in this respect, a correspondence between the fundamental assumptions of the subjectivists and of Nazidom: and, even though

many of the former may not have been conscious of this, it probably flows from the German origins of their philosophy, and from the specifically German character of its idealism. (See also above, pp. 20, 296–7, on the historical significance of the 1895–1941 period in European intellectual history.) For example, the most evil factor in Nazi thinking was not the assumption that Jews were different from Germans (this, after all, would have been but a new version of the older assumption that Jews were different from Christians): it was their modern scientific assumption that Jews were different biological products and that therefore their motives and purposes were inevitably different and harmful.

235 *Knowing and liking*
Knowing why we like someone heightens and sharpens that experience, sensually as well as intellectually; but knowing why we dislike someone does not necessarily sharpen that experience. (Furthermore: when we like someone, we want to like him *more;* when we dislike someone we do not, normally, want to dislike him more. There are, of course, neurotic exceptions to the latter rule.)

235 *Objective and subjective statements*
The inadequacy of the objective-subjective antithesis may appear as we consider certain forms of expression. At first sight it seems that writing or speaking in the first person singular ("I think that Dulles had a bad influence on Eisenhower in 1955") is "subjective" compared to the more "objective" form of the third person singular ("Dulles had a bad influence on Eisenhower in 1955"). Of course both statements must be illustrated, and their historical validity depends on the plausibility of their evidence. But it is not necessarily true that the first version is "subjective" and the second "objective"; in both cases it is *I* who am writing, telling, *expressing* certain things outward, to an audience. (It is therefore that I have felt compelled, for some time, to either append or introduce in my books brief statements about my personal purposes; the source of this compulsion was not exhibitionism but my conviction that all historical writing is a personal construction, and that there is at least a modicum of "auto-history" in every kind of history.)

236 *Ex-pression*
According to St. Augustine, the Christian is the interpreter of the Word: the gift of his existence comes from God, but somehow this gift does not mean much until he shares it out. As Klibansky put it in his essay ("Platonism in Augustine"), "through being passed on it is increased." Thus the Christian is not one of a Chosen People, not a mystical and passive recipient of a precious Truth: he is something active.

236 *Historical "relativity" and the richness of truth*
R. Wittram: "Daraus, das eine Philosophie auf ein Zeitalter relativ ist, folge noch nicht, dass sie nicht wahr sein koenne. . . ." ("Just because a certain philosophy is 'relative' to its time does not mean that it cannot be true.") Jacques Barzun: "The old problem of the casuists all arose from the rigidity with which rules are commonly stated and en-

forced. . . . There has been no way yet discovered of preventing either absolute or relative rules from being disobeyed or from cloaking hypocrisies. The only safeguard is in the conscience of the free agents we call men . . . the right understanding of relativism must lead not to greater laxity everywhere, but to greater firmness in moral intention, greater precision in intellectual, greater subtlety in esthetic." Marrou: The problem is not, as even Raymond Aron puts it (in his *Introduction à la philosophie de l'histoire*), where the limits of historical objectivity may be. "The real problem is . . . what are the conditions of historical knowledge; or, in other words, it is that of truthfulness in history, and the supreme criterion of this is not objectivity." ("Le vrai problème est le problème 'kantien': A quelles conditions la connaissance historique est-elle possible? ou pour mieux dire celui de la vérité de l'histoire, dont l'objectivité n'est pas le critère suprême.")

238   *Seeing and thinking*
This is the profound issue at stake between Newton's *Optics* and Goethe's *Theory of Colours*. I cannot refrain from mentioning a personal illustration at this point. It is a common human experience that we are able to see certain colors and vague patterns when our eyes are closed. Are these patterns sense impressions? To some extent they are (increasing pressure on the closed eyelid will produce changes in the colors and patterns), but not wholly. This may appear through the following experiment. In a dim or dark room sit or lie with your eyes closed, next to another person: keep telling each other what you see. While some of your "impressions" may be similar, after a while it will be more and more difficult to separate them from what you are imagining, largely because of what your partner is telling you. In other words, the products of your imagination keep floating into your mind *and eye*: you cannot stop them. Still, on occasion you can discover that some of these impressions are more illusory than are others. In such a situation the following statement would, thus, make sense:
            I thought that I saw a castle.
            No, I saw that I only thought a castle.

239   *Intellect and erotic capacities*
While it is true that an excess of intellectual occupations, together with an excessively sedentary existence, may diminish the force of sexual appetites, the potentiality of sexual capacities is not necessarily diminished thereby. In this respect the inferiority feelings of modern intellectuals and of many modern people in regard to darker and more "earthy"—not to say "savage"—peoples may be unwarranted. The barbarian may be capable of all kinds of rape: the less imaginative he is, the more indifferent he is to the purpose of his sexual ambitions (including the qualities of his partner); but the reverse side of this is that, being deficient in imagination, his erotic capacities are dependent on the recurrences of his hormonal appetites. It is even possible that, contrary to common belief, the sexual potentialities of the white race, at least for a long time, have been exceptional. But this was a cultural not a biological factor of race, the result of certain capacities for imagination; Gilberto Freyre writes that the Negro and

Indian women in Brazil were amazed at the spontaneous capacity of the Portuguese to pounce upon them so often and so unpredictably.

240 *Participation in lust and shame*
A nude dead is normally less exciting than a nude alive, and a sleeping nude is less exciting than the same woman consciously displaying her charms. There is of course no rule of how large an exposure of her body would produce how much sensual excitement. Yet tendency and purpose enter: it is more interesting to see half-nudity in the process of undressing than in the process of dressing; and it is usually more interesting to see (even at an unattainable distance, or in a photograph) a woman undress for our tantalizing edification than to see her as a Peeping Tom—or, in other words, as a nonparticipant. Now this point of *participation* is of cardinal importance. We are stimulated by the mere sight of female pudenda because of our imagination (sight is the most intellectual of all of our senses: the erotic stimuli of animals are different)—and also because of our ultimately moral (and not merely acquired) sense of *shame* (a now forgotten word, like *vanity*). For lust is not only generated through imagination; it is generated, too, by a common human sense of shame. If, as I believe, love is an expression of the human desire of forming a community of two, lust involves the desire for a community in shame, or at least for a partnership in shame.

242 *Absurdity*
I am no longer impressed with the argument of many modern artists to the effect that the absurdity of their art reflects the absurdity of our world. It is not so much the present condition of the world but the accepted image of its development which is absurd. The modern artist is plagued not by the absurdity of his condition but by the increasing meaninglessness of his purposes. This means that while the faker-artist can get by in spite of the inadequacy of his craftsmanship, the true artist is still capable of recognizing his craft, which is to infuse meaning into this world.

246 *Memory and dreams*
And yet I have been interested in the function of memory within dreams. I tend to agree with the general belief that we may be dreaming all the time while we remember our dreams only sometimes: but I think, too, that the dream is not only inseparable from the recognition of the dream: the recognition of the dream *is* the dream itself. We always transform things through our perception and imagination of them to some extent: but in dreams I am inclined to think that we transform them wholly. The tree outside my window exists apart from my memory of it: but my dream does not exist apart from my memory at all.

Thus, when we remember dreams, not only does our consciousness receive impressions of our subconsciousness; rather, our consciousness acts upon our subconscious as much as the reverse—indeed, as when we are awake. But here is the difference: I think that dreaming may not so much mean a subliminal functioning of our minds as a subliminal functioning of our memories. We do not really *think* as differently when we are asleep as we *remember* differently. (And consider, too, that of all of our physical conditions in our dreams it is the condition of time—duration-time—which is most disrupted and affected.)

248   *Time and creation*
See pp. 284, above; p. 355, below. Heisenberg: "It is impossible to define in rational terms what could be meant by the phrase 'time has been created.'" Reinhold Niebuhr on St. Augustine: he established "the significance of memory as part of the image of God." Emil Brunner: "Augustine certainly made a great discovery when he first dared to propose, in the *Confessions,* that the world is neither atemporal and eternal, nor created at a certain moment in the sequence of time, but that the world and time have been created together, they have the same beginning in creation; from then on it became a senseless question to ask what God had been able to do before the creation of the world. The whole scheme of before and after (i.e. the framework of time) can be posited only with creation, and it is thus presented as a temporal creation. The depth and boldness of this idea cannot be adequately admired by us, but if we consider the most recent results of astrophysics we can only be astounded at the genius of the thinker who recognized intuitively, as a truth of faith, without any scientific basis, an idea which—paradoxical as it may appear—imposes itself today to scientific thought as truth: the result, partly, of Einstein's theory of relativity and of Planck's quantum physics."

249   *Time going backward?*
At the same time we must remain realistic: for the recognition of the relativity of Time, like that of the relativity of Facts, is in itself no cause for rejoicing. I said that the medieval world went to seed when people tried to force transcendental realities into nominalistic definitions, scientific categories. This is what may be happening now in reverse: people forcing new "discoveries" into all kinds of philosophical and scientific categories where these do not belong, and the result is not increasing harmony but surrealistic nonsense. This is the case of the nonsense that has been bandied about "time going backward." It *is* now possible to imagine not only mental but physical situations where our concept of time would no longer prove to be absolute. But this refers to the mathematical concept, not to the human experience of duration: clock time may go backward but our life won't: we will not get younger but older in Einstein's hypothetical spaceship. Very much older.

251   *Time within ourselves*
Let me now add a different illustration from a common experience. We took an important competitive examination on Monday. We are told that the board of examiners make their decision on Wednesday, that the results are mailed out on Thursday, that we shall get them in the mail by Saturday. Now, being what we are—human beings—we keep praying (or, for the sake of nonbelievers, let me say hoping) *beyond* Wednesday, that is *after* the time that our reason knows the decision to have been taken. I believe that this all-too-common

human tendency is not altogether attributable to superstition and not even to the momentum of a psychic routine. What works within us is a residual trust in some kind of causality (which believers may call "the workings of a benevolent Providence") that may transcend the limits of space and of time: a wishful belief which suggests, too, how deeply ingrained within us is the sense that what happens is inseparable from what we think happens.

257 *Race a cultural factor*
I find it significant that the following passage appeared in the autobiography of Richard Coudenhove-Kalergi, the founder of *Paneuropa*, that is, of the first important movement for European union in the twentieth century. His father was Austrian, his mother Japanese. "I often wonder," Coudenhove-Kalergi wrote in *Crusade for Pan-Europe* (New York, 1943), "what would have become of me if my father had not . . . decided [to bring me up in Europe]. Then I might have grown up a Japanese child, educated in Japanese schools to be a Japanese patriot; and not only my mind and soul would have evolved differently, but my features as well. For every living being adapts itself unconsciously to its surroundings, and many Europeans who spend their lives in the Far East acquire Oriental features. . . . So not nature but destiny made a European of me—a fact which, I feel, prevented me from becoming a European isolationist, for it makes me ever conscious that even Europe is but a branch of the wider brotherhood of man which I have always considered my true nation and fatherland."

259 *The* renaissance orientale
This original development, coming from Germany after 1800, has had but one important historian, Raymond Schwab, who recorded some of its phases in *La renaissance orientale* (Paris, 1950). While recognizing the many scholarly results of this movement, Schwab was sufficiently perceptive to recognize within it the curious mixture of romanticism and anti-Christianity, of mysticism and racism. One of its forerunners (Leibniz) said already that the Teutonic was the purest language, the one "closest to God," *because* it had come from Asia. By 1800 Schlegel would equate romanticism with the East ("Im Orient müssen wir das höchste Romantische suchen"). The teaching infected the romantic and nationalist Catholics (Görres translated Firdousi and wrote a curious "History of Asia"; Quinet on Görres's nationalism: "un patriotisme asiatique"). Thereafter a generation of scholars (as Schwab shows, many priests among them) publicly deplored the Greek victory at Marathon. Orientalism now appeared as a field of study in the academies and the universities (in 1840 its practitioner Jules Mohl was among the first naturalized Germans who became a professor at the Collège de France). "The great thing in philosophy nowadays," Quinet wrote in 1841, "is Oriental pantheism, transformed and re-represented by Germany." "Voilà la grande affaire qui se passe aujourd'hui dans la philosophie. Le panthéisme de l'Orient, transformé par l'Allemagne, correspond à la renaissance orientale, de même que l'idéalisme de Platon, corrigé par Descartes,

a couronné, au XVIIe siècle, la renaissance grecque et latine.") The Oriental renaissance became a Germanic reaction against the Latin- and French characteristics of the first Renaissance. (Schwab: "une Renaissance du véhément.") The result was Gobineau ("Everything came from Asia," 1865), Wagner's Buddhist Aryanism (cf. Schwab's excellent chapter on "le bouddhisme de Wagner" ("W. fait du Bouddhisme une annexe à un cycle mystique du Moyen Age chré- tien"), and that peculiar form of German cultural pessimism in which asseverations of racial superiority were inextricably mixed with the Götterdämmerung sentiment prophesying the collapse of the West. Thus William II, Spengler, Hitler: while bewailing the Yellow Peril, the Decline of the West, and professing admiration for British racial qualities, they sought an alliance with Japan, declared Christianity outmoded, and nearly destroyed Europe. (Luis Diez del Corral: "[La] idea de humanidad europea . . . recibirá golpes mortales en el curso del siglo XIX. Schopenhauer y sus seguidores introducirán peligrosos elementos orientales en el pensamiento europeo, el dar- winismo, el moderno maquiavelismo, el capitalismo desmedido, los movimientos nacionalistas, acabarán por quebrar el sentido de la idea de Occidente." (The idea of European humanism receives a mortal blow during the 19th century. Schopenhauer and his successors intro- duce dangerous Oriental elements into European thinking . . . they undermine the ideas of the West.)

262   *A Roosevelt story*
A curious example of this appears during an episode in the link of events leading to the making of the atomic bomb. According to Jungk it was Alexander Sachs, a New York banker and an intimate friend of the President, who in October, 1939, convinced Roosevelt of the validity of this project; and he convinced him with a historical story. It was the story of how Napoleon lost his bid for world domination because he had been unimpressed by Robert Fulton's proposal when Fulton had offered to build him a fleet of steamships with which he could have invaded England. Now this Fulton story is a pretty story, except that it is largely untrue, and quite unreasonable. It is unreason- able and unhistorical (even though such a serious historian as Acton seems to have believed in it for a while). No serious naval historian will believe that Fulton's rickety untried steamships could have brought ninety thousand French soldiers (for that was the minimum Napoleon thought would be needed) across the rough English seas in 1803. Churchill would have been unimpressed by that story; Roosevelt was impressed by it.

263   *Utopian ideas*
Are utopias really important milestones in the history of ideas? In studying the history of the idea of Europe I was not unimpressed with the European conceptions of such statesmen as Napoleon, Talley- rand, Metternich, Churchill, de Gaulle, while I grew less and less im- pressed by the works of the early prophets of a united Europe— Leibniz, Kant, Penn, Hugo, even Briand. They were unrealistic be-

cause they were unhistorical. And the reverse. Were their plans the plans of people who lived, as the popular saying goes, "three hundred years too soon"? I do not think so. When an idea is born three hundred years too soon this means that it is premature: instead of being a sign of the future it is, paradoxically, an expression of its time and not much more, just as a stillborn baby is, for once, a mere product, a product of its parents, deprived of its potentialities of inherent growth. While historical insights are prophecies about the past, prophecies about the future are projections of the present.

265 *About European realism*
Walter Schubart: In *Oblomov* "Goncharov describes a servant who used to recite poetry in secret. When his master, who surprised him doing so, asked him whether he understood the verses that he was declaiming he replied: 'Master, if I understood the verses, they would not be poetry' . . . Incomprehensibility contributes to reverence and awe . . . the theory of Indian poetry, too. . . ." Christopher Hollis: ". . . all European thought is infused with a spirit that is notably absent from other literature—what might in some contexts be called the spirit of realism and perhaps more accurately the belief in the reality and value of history. . . ." Even non-Christian individualism could find "an intellectual justification in some such maxim as that of St. Thomas Aquinas that there were as many separate types of excellence as there were separate individual souls, and which would obviously be unintelligible to a Buddhist, to whom the purpose of existence is to escape from individuality into Nirvana."

272 *The central event in history*
With this in view, however, it behooves the Christian historian to meditate upon the relative closeness of this central event to our times; and, of course, to consider whether the history of mankind does not divide in two great phases, and that we now live in the second phase that stretches from Christ's first to His second coming. For, if so, we are the Jews of the Second Age; and we must be, then, keenly aware of the painful chance that the Second Coming will offer us, as we know from Christ's own words as well as from the history of the First Coming that the majority of the chosen people may miss their supreme opportunity, that we will be called but that few among us will deserve to be chosen.

284 *Sequence in time*
Thus the collapse of absolute determinism and the inadequacy of our mechanical concepts of causality involve the relativity of time together with the more profound and metaphysical distinctions between time and duration, mathematical and physiological time. Heisenberg in *The Physicist's Conception of Nature*: "Since Einstein's discovery in 1905, we know that between [the] 'future' and 'past' there exists an interval whose extension in time depends on the distance in space between an event and its observer. Thus, the present is not limited to an infinitely short moment in time. . . ." Also: "Atomic physics has moved ever further from the concept of determinism. At first, from

the very beginnings of atomic theory, the laws governing large-scale processes were looked upon as statistical laws. Although determinism was in this way preserved in principle, in practice it means that we took account of our incomplete knowledge of physical systems. Then, in the first half of our century, incomplete knowledge of atomic systems was recognized as being a part of theory in principle. Finally, in very recent years we have come to realize that on a small space-time scale the concept of a sequence in time has become problematical, and we cannot even tell how this riddle will ever be solved."

288   *The penchant for a certain realism*
Let me draw attention to Heisenberg's realism. At the age of sixteen he read in his Gymnasium physics' textbook that atoms were the smallest indivisible building stones of matter. But the illustration of this in the text showed atoms connected with hooks and eyes which were supposed to represent their chemical bonds. "I was greatly put off by this illustration. I was enraged that such idiotic things should be presented in a textbook of physics. I thought that if atoms were indeed such structures as this book made out—if their structure was complicated enough for them to have hooks and eyes—then they could not possibly be the smallest indivisible building stones of matter." From this angry recognition of unrealistic representation (he was unwilling to accept the complete divorce of symbol from representation, of image from reality) the courageous quest of a great European physicist grew out.

289   *Certain correspondences*
Example: In the early 1950's Boris Pasternak was writing *Dr. Zhivago*, in the icy and terror-ridden Russian backlands of Europe at the same time when José Ortega y Gasset wrote one of his last essays in Madrid about the possible dawning of a new European form of thought and when Heisenberg was preparing his Gifford Lectures. Now Ortega was aware throughout his life of what was going on in the high reaches of German philosophy; and he had met Heisenberg. I doubt whether Pasternak ever read Heisenberg; and yet throughout *Dr. Zhivago* there are scattered philosophical recognitions which are not only curiously post-modern and post-mechanistic but the very phrasing of which corresponds very much with some of Heisenberg's phrases in his Gifford Lectures. ("Direct causes operate only within certain limits; beyond them they produce the opposite effect." "The logic of her speech was not rational but emotional." "To make philosophy one's speciality seems to me unnatural and strange." There are many more such phrases in that great book.)

293   *100 years ago: a French reaction*
The first forerunners, beginning about 100 years ago, may have been the impressionists. For in painting and poetry and music the impressionist form of expression may have been the first revolutionary innovation of human perception and expression since the Renaissance. The impressionists saw that the human eye is, at best, an imperfect and unscientific "instrument," incapable of seeing "total" reality: but, while the human eye sees something *less*, it also sees something *more* than

"reality." Thus, for example, Monet is not only more of a realist than Picasso but also than Ingres; and Debussy and Ravel may have represented the most revolutionary innovation made in European music since Bach.

294 *1894–1905*
It was after I had set down the approximate markers 1894–1905 in the first draft of this book that I found that Huizinga had marked out this very period, thirty years ago: "In the controversy over the essence of historical knowledge such philosophers as Wilhelm Windelband, Heinrich Rickert and Georg Simmel, following Wilhelm Dilthey's lead, in the years between 1894 and 1905 for the first time provided the modern history of knowledge of the humanities with a basis of its own, thus liberating it from having its norms dictated by the natural sciences. . . ."

295 *Karl Joel*
"Die Ueberwindung des 19. Jahrhunderts im Denken der Gegenwart," published in *Kant-Studien* (Berlin, 1927). The best thinkers of the eighteenth century were anti-systematists (Maupertuis: *point de système*). The nineteenth century was full of inherent contradictions; yet most of its thinkers strove for systems. It wished to express the world in a mathematical formula. Not only Comte ("Mathematics is the basis of all science") but also the relatively conservative liberal Mill saw in causality the basic law of life. And this led to the mechanization of the modern world. But—and this is important—Joel argues that the struggle against nineteenth-century positivism must *not* lead back to the earlier, romantic or sentimental, idealism. The issue is greater (and the divisions profounder). "The early idealists and the late positivists" of that century belong together in a way: for both looked for absolute laws, genetic connections: the idealists within organisms, the naturalists in the external world of mechanics. But the organic and the inorganic world are inseparable. In any event, we know by now that physical events and not mathematical time are principal factors: "Newton's World-Clock is broken, in the new physics nature emerges from the iron hoops of classic mechanics and frees herself from the absolute constants of time, space and mass." We now know certain truths that the nineteenth century could not bear to know: for example, that Copernicus was not absolutely right and Ptolemy not absolutely wrong.

295 *Reaction in the twenties*
Lest some of my readers think that I am wildly extrapolating the significance of erratic reactionary intellectual developments among central Europeans let me quickly cite Orwell's summary of intellectual trends even in England during the twenties. In 1943 (in *Talking to India*, a relatively unknown essay) he wrote: "But now look at the writers who begin to attract notice . . . immediately after the last war: Joyce, Eliot, Pound, Huxley, Lawrence, Wyndham Lewis. Your first impression of them, compared with the others—this is true even of Lawrence—is that something has been punctured. To begin with, the notion of progress has gone by the board. They don't any longer

believe that progress happens or that it ought to happen, they don't any longer believe that men are getting better and better by having lower mortality rates, more effective birth control, better plumbing, more aeroplanes and faster motor-cars. Nearly all of them are homesick for the remote past, or some period of the past, from D. H. Lawrence's ancient Etruscans onwards. All of them are politically reactionary, or at best are uninterested in politics. None of them cares twopence about the various hole-and-corner reforms which had seemed important to their predecessors, such as female suffrage, temperance reform, birth control or prevention of cruelty to animals. All of them are more friendly, or at least less hostile, towards the Christian churches than the previous generation had been. And nearly all of them seem to be aesthetically alive in a way that hardly any English writer since the Romantic Revival had been."

296   *Back to the Left in the thirties*
By 1932 except for Wyndham Lewis and, perhaps, Yeats (and Nock, Pound, Beard in America) the movement was again to the Left; and even those who did not necessarily sympathize with the Left (such as Eliot) saw the future of the world in a "Leftist" direction. This is the trend of Huxley's *Brave New World* (1931) and of a satirical novel, *Public Faces* (1932) by the otherwise perceptive Harold Nicolson (who broke off his relations with Oswald Mosley's New Party that year).

297   *America different*
Things were, of course, different in America. This is why it was (and still is) a profound mistake to see in the 1925 Tennessee monkey trial the manifestation of the struggle between the twentieth and the nineteenth centuries: for those courtroom histrionics had little to do with that: in reality, Bryan's Puritanism was a strange survival from the seventeenth century, whereas Darrow's Zolaesque oratory for Progress was a prototypal attitude of the nineteenth. (And it is significant that this famous rhetorical confrontation, marking the Victory of Science and the Rout of Religion, occurred in the United States in 1925, at the same time when the discoveries of Europe's leading physicists were knocking the bottom out from that very concept of "Science" which Darrow, supported by a phalanx drawn from the rank of America's scientists, represented in that now legendary courtroom.)

312   *The idiocy of the universe as a clock*
Bernanos in *Last Essays* (1947): "Voltaire said, roughly, the more I see the universe, the less am I able to think that this watch keeps going without there being a watchmaker—a foolish line which has nevertheless filled untold numbers of priests with joy, all proud to think that the dear Lord would henceforth exist by the authorization of M. de Voltaire, gleeful, elated at the brilliant feat the dear Lord had performed at the expense of His personal enemy of *Ecrasons l'infâme!*—taking advantage of a moment of inattention on M. de Voltaire's part to make him sign a little paper of surrender. . . . Alas, in writing this cheap doggerel, M. de Voltaire wasn't at all concerned about saints, and the canons who honored him by quoting him at

prize-giving ceremonies perhaps were no more concerned than he was. . . . What the devil—this is the time to say it—could a watch-maker make of saints, I wonder. There is nothing less free than a watch, since all of its gears are in the strictest sense dependent upon each other. You will probably reply that the physical universe offers enough examples of precision machinery. But are you sure you haven't taken appearance for reality, as a being of an intelligence completely different from ours, thoroughly ignorant of language and writing, and totally illiterate, might go into ecstasies over the rhythm of voices and the symmetry of a page of printing and try to deduce from these things the principles by which they operate, without really knowing any-thing about their essentials, about what alone is important in all this, the thought, the thought always alive and free under the apparent constraint of the characters or the sounds which express it? What if life really were the free thought of this world, this world which ap-pears to be controlled and determined? Life, that is to say that mysterious and immaterial energy to which modern physics reduces matter itself."

IDEARIUM

Abstraction, abstractness, 25, 69, 73, 109, 146, 151, 241 *passim*
Absurdity, 351
Academic historianship, 17
Accuracy (of facts), 104
Acquisition of characteristics, 255 *passim*
Amateurs of history, 37, 98, 104
"Ancient," 13
Anticipation (of events), 137, 157
Anti-Communism, 149 *passim*, 263-4
Antiquated, 1, 17, 238
Archeology, 23
Association (of facts), 104 *passim*, 377-8
Authenticity (of documents), 58 *passim;* (of events), 128

Bourgeois, 12, 29, 32, 45-47, 82, 87, 118, 182-3, 203, 205, 331-2

Cartesianism, 224 *passim*, 268 *passim*, 286 *passim*
Causes, causalities, 7, 53, 89, 127, 139 *passim*, 153 *passim*, 205, 283 *passim*, 342, 343
Certainty, 157, 279
Change, 135 *passim*
Charity, 165
Christianity, 27 *passim*, 220 *passim*
Classification (of events), 131
Coincidences, 167 *passim*
Communications and meaning, 113, 121, 142, 264
Communism, 149 *passim*, 192 *passim*, 211 *passim*, 263-4, 297
Communities, 173
Complexity, 61, 269-70
Consciousness, 133, 155-6, 203, 215-6, 249 *passim*

Consequences (of events), 128 *passim*, 136 *passim*, 236
Correspondences, 169, 289 *passim*, 356
Cosmology, 267 *passim*
Cultural preferences, 68

Darwinism, 19, 140, 210, 258, 271-2, 303
Death (and the past), 35
Definitions, 8, 110, 280-1, 326
Democratic historianship, 50 *passim*
Democratization (of history), 32, 64 *passim*, 72 *passim*, 97, 132-3, 140-1, 144, 146, 186 *passim*, 203, 218 *passim*
Demography, 176
Determinism, 19, 28, 51-2, 206, 242, 253, 276 *passim*
"Documentary" reconstructions, 4, 32, 53 *passim*, 63 *passim*, 111, 123 *passim*
Dogmatism, 48, 242
Doubletalk, doublethink, 47-8
Dreams (and memory), 351

Eastern civilizations, 23 *passim*
Econometrics, 176
Economics, 105, 172 *passim*
Education (unhistorical), 324
Electoral choice, 83 *passim*, 334
Epic past, 118-9
Eroticism, *see* Sexuality
Ethnography, 23
Europe, European, 2, 12, 22, 172, 271, 300 *passim*, 312 *passim*, 327, 330, 355
"Event," 103
Evolution, 47, 250
"Exotic," 244

361

INDEX OF NAMES